D1528980

Asia Inside Out: Connected Places

ASIA INSIDE OUT

CONNECTED PLACES

Edited by

ERIC TAGLIACOZZO

HELEN F. SIU

PETER C. PERDUE

WITHDRAWN

Harvard University Press

Cambridge, Massachusetts
London, England

2015

Library of Congress Cataloging-in-Publication Data.

Asia inside out : connected places / edited by Eric Tagliacozzo, Helen F. Siu, Peter
C. Perdue.

   pages cm
  Includes bibliographical references and index.
  ISBN 978-0-674-96768-7 (printed book)
  1. Asia—Historical geography. 2. Asia—Geography. 3. Regionalism—
Asia—History. 4. Human geography—Asia—History. 5. Social networks—
Asia—History. 6. Geopolitics—Asia—History. 7. Asia—Economic
conditions. 8. Asia—Social conditions. I. Tagliacozzo, Eric. II. Siu, Helen F.
III. Perdue, Peter C., 1949–   IV. Title: Connected places.
  DS5.9.A74 2015
  950—dc23   2014043196

Contents

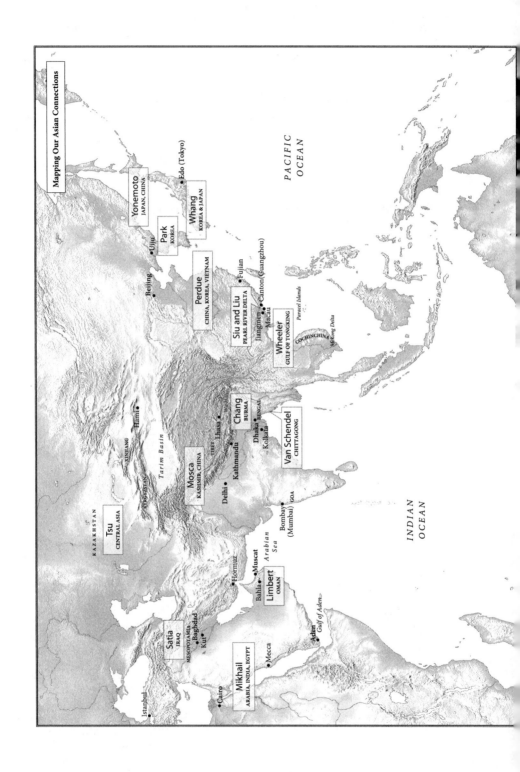

Mapping Our Asian Connections

PACIFIC OCEAN

INDIAN OCEAN

Yonemoto
JAPAN, CHINA

Edo (Tokyo)

Park
KOREA

Uiju

Whang
KOREA & JAPAN

Perdue
CHINA, KOREA, VIETNAM

Beijing

Fujian

Siu and Liu
PEARL RIVER DELTA

Canton (Guangzhou)

Jiangmen

Macau

Wheeler
GULF OF TONGKING

Paracel Islands

COCHINCHINA

Mekong Delta

Hami

XINJIANG

Tarim Basin

QINGHAI

Chang
BURMA

Wellin

Lhasa

TIBET

JINGKAI

Dhaka

Kolkata

Van Schendel
CHITTAGONG

Mosca
KASHMIR, CHINA

Kathmandu

Delhi

KAZAKHSTAN

Tsu
CENTRAL ASIA

Bombay (Mumbai)

GOA

Arabian Sea

Muscat

Hormuz

Bahla

Limbert
OMAN

Satia
IRAQ

Baghdad

MESOPOTAMIA

Kut

Istanbul

Cairo

Mecca

Mikhail
ARABIA, INDIA, EGYPT

Aden

Gulf of Aden

Introduction

Spatial Assemblages

HELEN F. SIU, ERIC TAGLIACOZZO, PETER C. PERDUE

Many scholars have described the twenty-first century as the era of the "Asian renaissance" (Godement 1993). After more than half a century of decolonization and socialist experimentation, a broadly interconnected Asia sees the rise of China and India as strong states and even stronger markets. Not only East Asia, but also the oil-rich Gulf region and Muslim and Buddhist Southeast Asia have joined this evolving paradigm. These intense flows of capital, people, goods, and cultural images across the landscape stretch our spatial imagination from Northeast Asia to reach as far as the Indian Ocean and the east coast of Africa. At the same time, the linkages over land and sea, which many call the New Silk Road, often map onto historical routes where trading emporiums served as multi-ethnic arenas for social exchange, cultural fusion and political conflict (Abu Lughod 1989; Brook 2008; Chaudhuri 1985; Curtin 1984; Goody 2006; Simpfendorfer 2009).

At crucial junctures, the likes of Marco Polo, Ibn Battuta, and Zheng He churned a cultural kaleidoscope that spanned continents. The terrain they traversed had not been contained within empires or emerging nation-states (Dunn 2005; Hansen 2000; Ho 2006; Waley-Cohen 1999). Places linked by these travelers' routes developed unique institutions for trade and settlement, and for pursuits of wealth, piety and power. What the historical global and the Asian post-modern share, in conceptual and empirical terms, are "spaces of flows" (Castells 1996). They range from maritime zones and mountain routes to port cities and oasis towns, crucial meeting points along diverse circulation paths (Hansen 2012; Subrahmanyam 1996; Tagliacozzo and Chang 2011). From the late twentieth century on, they have been hubs of global finance, migration, consumption, and services. Digital technologies now transmit the audacity of mega-city planning, the associated inter-referencing of urban designs and development aspirations, and reconfigured citizenship and national security instantaneously to a world audience (Harvey 1989; Holston and Appadurai 1998; Roy and Ong 2011; Sassen 1991). These spaces, physically compressed but structurally expansive, form arenas for intimate social encounters and deep cultural divisions; they also shape geopolitical conflicts and transnational contractual negotiations. Rather than being bounded units with static configurations, they are fluid assemblages made significant and meaningful by conscious human actions at crucial junctures (Bender 2010; Ong and Collier 2005).

As in *Asia Inside Out: Changing Times,* this volume aims to redefine conventional analytical components of "Asia." We highlight spatial connectedness in multi-scalar terms constructed at critical historical moments. The land and sea regions under scrutiny extend from Korea and Japan, along the coast of South China and Vietnam, onto the hills and deltas of South and Southeast Asia, and sometimes include mobile populations as far away as the Middle East and Africa. We share the belief that the making of localities and identities, in historical and modern times, has always activated translocal resources. As the introduction to the first volume states, these geographical identities "transcend simple divisions of land and sea, continental divides, political regimes, or religious and cultural boundaries." These interactive processes have created spatially significant moments. They have affected intensely charged discursive strategies as well as everyday praxis. By highlighting these processes, we see our analytical categories as conscious constructs and life worlds "in motion."

Our analysis is grounded in diverse scholarly traditions. New cultural geography, as seen for example in Lewis and Wigen's book *The Myth of Continents* (1997) has inspired us to rethink continental divides and the associated conceptual dichotomies between land and ocean systems, Asia and the West. Lewis and Wigen assert that "to the extent that geographers become interested not just in specific oceanic connections but more fundamentally in reimagining the globe by entertaining novel spatial configurations and regional schemes, both area studies and geography may find new sources of revitalization" (1999: 168). Indeed, critical human geography and social theories have transformed scholarly conceptions of space and place-making (Brenner 1997; Creswell 2004; Hayden 1997; Lefebvre 1991). Instead of taking places as natural, pre-existing receptacles of social content, these scholars highlight the power relationships and multiple meanings used to define space, place, place-based identities, and even wildernesses, or "non-places" (Augé 1995).

Adding historical specificity to processes of delineating space, Gupta and Ferguson (1997) turn to crucial junctures when political spaces are carved, boundaries made, and differences among populations defined and reconfigured. At a micro level of delineating spaces, Sudipta Kaviraj (1997) unveils the cultural/ mental mapping of Brahmin residents to explain their seemingly contradictory behavior inside and outside their homes, and to illuminate the clash of indigenous and colonial categories expressed in public and private spheres. Instead of beginning with fixed conceptions of spaces and places, this kind of analysis examines the historical and social conditions that created them.

Our place-making concerns are intertwined with the theoretical concept of human agency and "structuring" (Abrams 1982; Bourdieu 1977; Giddens 1979). We treat "place" as porous and encompassing, interactive with human agents who are embedded in structural positions, but who negotiate with malleable cultural meanings and historical experiences. In a volume on the conceptualization of the South China region as a conscious construct in the late imperial period, Faure and Siu (1995) elucidate the "civilizing process" whereby local inhabitants, be they elites or commoners, used symbolic and instrumental means to gain respective positions in an expanding polity. They contributed unity as well as diversity to an encompassing cultural repertoire by reworking kinship and descent, deploying deities for communal alliances, and imposing ethnic labels as discursive terms for societal membership. Michael Herzfeld's classic ethnography, *A Place in History: Social and Monumental Time in a Cretan Town,* eloquently unveils the meaning of the built environment, by showing how local residents pose their spatially embedded social practice against formal impositions by a national state intent on commercializing historical preservation.

Land-ocean interfaces exhibit special features of connectedness. In treating dynamic, interconnected littoral societies on their own terms rather than as margins to territorial civilizations, Fernand Braudel's study of the early modern Mediterranean blazed an important trail which others have extended to different regions and times, including the classical and medieval worlds, the Indian Ocean, Africa, and maritime Asia (Chaudhuri 1985; Curtin 1984; Hamashita 2008; Horden and Purcell 2000). Even more adventurous world historians try to connect the processes of the Mediterranean, Indian Ocean,

Historic mosque, Guangzhou. (Photo by Helen F. Siu)

Temple for the God of South Seas, Guangzhou. (Photo by Helen F. Siu)

Sikh guard at Chinese clan temple, Penang. (Photo by Helen F. Siu)

and East and South China seas to highlight historically global processes that have shaped our understanding of civilizations (Wong 1999). Using these theoretical constructs as analytical tools to examine spatial connections that cut across continental divides at various historical moments allows us to rethink the conventional geography of Asia.

Although the chapters in this volume generally move from east to west in a broadly defined "Asian" region, we have grouped them by analytical themes—maritime connections, mobile landscapes, and spatial moments dominated by colonialism, nationalism, and post-modernity. The volume starts with historical studies of trade networks, political transformation, and religious and cultural exchange among regions often identified as East and Southeast Asia. It ends with exploration of contemporary regional connections delineated as West Asia and the Middle East.

Maritime Connections

Stressing connections over vast oceans is not new. Economic historians have devoted sustained attention to trade on the Maritime Silk Road and the multi-ethnic cities along the China coast such as Quanzhou and Guangzhou (Chaffee 2008; Kauz and Ptak 2001; Macauley 2009; UNESCO Quanzhou International Seminar Committee 1991, 1994; Van Dyke 2005, 2011). However, some of these authors take an intact national space as a starting point from which diasporic impulses move outward to engage overseas or "foreign" trading networks. A recent edited volume on the maritime Silk Road (Kauz 2010) moves in a less Sinocentric direction by following the scholarly traditions of Braudel and Chaudhuri, treating the Indian Ocean as a coherent structure of land-sea trade, political relations, and cultural exchange. The authors' textual expertise is rich and diverse. However, even these chapters analytically remain within a political frame, with Iranian dynasties on the West-Asia side and the Chinese empire on the other.

We need to stress, however, that commerce in early modern empires, and nation states during colonial expansion, stimulated the circulation of material goods and migratory populations *beyond* regional or national boundaries. The institutions that profited from this commerce amassed great wealth, power, and ideological force but also provided unusual space for maneuver (Pearson 1996; Subrahmanyam 1996; Tagliacozzo 2005, Tagliacozzo and Chang

2011; Wills 2002; Zheng 2012, Sinn 2013, Siu 2010). The subsequent cultural fusion in regional arenas has been well documented in material objects (Crossman 1991; Sargent 2012), moral geographies (Bose 2006), language and cognitive maps (Sood 2011), cultural intimacies (Faure 2007), and in legal dilemmas (Blussé 2002; Stoler 1992). But the political ambiguities of these commercialized regions and the fluid cultural and political identities of those engaged with these places deserve more analysis. Continuing the momentum of these scholars, our volume explores land-sea and local-translocal dynamics on the regions' own terms, rather than framing their development from the perspective of administrative boundaries and national histories.

The first four chapters focus on maritime connections. Charles Wheeler uses the life and subsequent capture and harsh execution of a certain Chinese/ Vietnamese "pirate" to map out unbounded zones of land-maritime activities (zones of extroversion) in the Tongking Gulf during the nineteenth century. He treats the region not as rims to an ocean or land mass, but as a land-sea ecology supporting, in Braudelian terms, "simply a way of making a living." A sea-based population, including Nguyen lords, Tay Son rebels, and Minh Huong merchant elites, although branded by states as no more than "Chinese pirates," strategically shifted cultural orientations, social networks and loyalties to engage with land-based political entities. They built their regional coherence on recognition of difference. Collusion, intrigue and conflict drew in characters with ambiguous ethnicities whose livelihoods were anything but grounded. Rather than characterizing this zone that spread from the Fujian coast to Bangkok and beyond as "narrow seas" in a Mediterranean sense, Wheeler suggests "a world whose geography may make more sense as a space of flows . . . Networks of all kinds plugged into this great oceanic river, and from the river, extended far, wide and deep, into land as well as sea space." Such ecologies could be found in the Greater China seas (Antony 2010), inland seas of medieval Japan (Shapinsky 2009), the Pearl River delta of late imperial South China (Siu and Liu 2006), and the southwest coast of modern India (Subramanian 2009). As Wheeler points out, the metamorphoses of these populations were also "reminiscent of the Swahili of East Africa (Middleton 1994) or Huguenots of the Atlantic." It is important to go beyond the land-ocean dichotomy to highlight an analytical framework that treats these complex regional assemblages and the agency of their populations on their own terms.

Fishing boats in Zanzibar waters. (Photo by Helen F. Siu)

Spices in Indian Ocean trade, Muscat. (Photo by Helen F. Siu)

Nineteenth-century silver trade dollars. (Photo by Helen F. Siu)

The chapter by Siu and Liu echoes such thinking. It dissects a land-based ideology embedded in a local township gazetteer, the *Chaolian Xiangzhi*. The document, written in 1946 by one of the last Chinese literati figures in the twentieth century, is a detailed historical account of an island community in the Pearl River delta. A close reading of the gazetteer reveals that the author has privileged the cultural priorities of an agrarian empire. However, between the lines of lineage genealogies, official edicts, religious rituals, and literary writings, Siu and Liu uncover what has been left unsaid or marginalized. Supplementing such critical reading with ethnographic fieldwork and oral histories, they show how maritime networks and mobile livelihoods constructed the delta community. At a macro level, they highlight dynastic fortunes that intertwined with the ebbs and flows of inter-regional trade along the South China coast. They use the macro trends to frame local agency, exploring how populations drew on regional resources and cultural imaginations to fuel diverse mobility tracks. Siu and Liu argue that during the Ming and Qing dynasties, "indigenous settlers in Chaolian maneuvered between land and sea, agrarian economy and regional markets, frontier ventures and imperial institutions. They made community, secured their respective places in it and acquired distinctive identities. As fishermen, farmers, merchants, minor officials, smugglers, bandits and pirates, some rose beyond such discriminatory labels to become "landed" at various junctures of late imperial history. In the emerging sands of the Pearl River delta, state institutions hardly existed, but local populations were able to give the language of an agrarian-based orthodoxy a creative and complicit reading. Over the centuries, they made an economically viable community that straddled multiple translocal networks, and cultivated politically respectable and culturally significant selves. In these structuring processes, they contributed to the expansion and consolidation of an imperial order on their own terms."

Following a similar line of thinking, Willem van Schendel turns to another delta region, around the city of Chittagong, the surrounding coastal district and its uplands. He explores how various generations have turned a location into a succession of meaningful places, a process he terms "spatial moments" with varying "thickness" and "thinness" in experiential terms. Good fishing, fertile soil, and flood-free hillocks supported settlements and livelihoods. Furthermore, the physical attributes encompassed memories, moral imaginations and power-plays as people used them to inform their everyday practices and aspirations. Van Schendel argues that place-making is socially meaningful and continuous, and hence, history matters. Relying on the framework of Jessop et al. (2003), he studies dimensions of socio-spatial relations—places, territories, scales and networks. To tackle these intertwined dimensions requires "a grasp of detail" in the locality and "a width of scope" in the wider world. Van Schendel tests this approach by observing Chittagong at four points in time—1600, 1900, 1950, and 2010 CE. In 1600, it was an Asian trade hub, a principal swivel between a seaborne Indian Ocean network and the river-borne Brahmaputra-and-mountains network. In 1900, the maritime networks had collapsed, and Chittagong was surrounded by British-held territories. A new imperial ensemble made it a springboard for military expeditions and an Assam tea trade. The colonial town became increasingly Bengalized. With the political partition after British rule ended, Chittagong in 1950 became a lifeline for Pakistan. Place-making by new Muslim immigrants and state-led development experts produced a landscape of modernization. By 2010, it was a Bangladeshi metropolis, caught up in another twist of state formation and global intensification of networks. Van Schendel is well aware of the limitations of the four snapshots from Chittagong's long past, but he hopes to use these spatial moments to examine the "clashes, negotiations, compromises, and adjustments as people construct places out of a range of resources, human as well as non-human, and material as well as discursive."

Alan Mikhail examines Indian Ocean trade far beyond spices and textiles. He focuses on live animals in motion—horses and elephants—on ships between South Asia and the Middle East. Arabian and Persian horses, renowned for their strength, size and speed, were exported from the port cities of Aden and Hormuz and funneled through Goa and other ports in today's state of Kerala to independent kingdoms in India (and on to China) who used the horses for military ventures. This maritime animal traffic was the heart of a war economy spanning continents. Mikhail maintains that "for over a millennium, from antiquity well into the early modern period, the power provided by the strong muscles of horses found in the markets of Aden and Kish connected Middle Eastern pastoral economies to South Asian military ones."

Mikhail also explores another Indian Ocean animal economy—that involving elephants transported in the opposite direction. In the late medieval and early modern worlds, these animals were used in ritual displays by rival Ottoman leaders to show off "their abilities to command, control and display nature's bounty." In Istanbul and Cairo, these elephants "played an active role as instigators of imagination, projections of imperial authority, and symbols of Ottoman attempts to manage and come to terms with nature." The "war economy" of horses and the "charismatic economy" of elephants structured the trading of weaponry and wonder across the Indian Ocean. They also created intricate administrative infrastructures of upkeep, care, maintenance and knowledge circulation that molded human-animal relationships over continental divides.

Mobile Landscapes

In Asia's interior, as on the coast, scholars have also found rich materials for studying connections across borders. Many have studied military conquests, trade, religious and ethnic transformations across Eurasia. (Boulnois 2004; Crossley 2006; Hansen 2012; Lewis 2009; Lipman 2006; Mosca 2013; Perdue 2005; Harper and Amrith 2012, Wong and Heldt 2014). An exhibition at the Metropolitan Museum of Art in 2004, "China: Dawn of a Golden Age 200–750 AD," showed remarkable cultural creativity and fusion in some three hundred excavated objects ranging from Central Asian metal works, glass, textiles, Buddhist images, and Roman style pillars. The vast amount of "foreign" ideas, architectural forms, religion and art motifs brought by Central Eurasian nomads to an empire that was undergoing political fragmentation and social upheaval, makes us wonder what were the essential elements that formed traditional Chinese civilization during the first millennium CE. Similarly, an exhibition of Buddhist objects—sculptures, gold and silver ritual utensils, architectural relief excavated from the ancient region of Gandhara—displays the cosmopolitan orientations of multi-ethnic populations, religious beliefs and their representation.

The region's elites, patrons of Buddhism, derived wealth from trade routes linking the Arabian Sea, the Himalayan passes, Central Asia and China (Gandhara 2008; Watt/Metropolitan Museum of Art 2004). If this remote kingdom at the foothills of the Himalaya could be a node and crossroads for intense synthesis of continental scale religious traditions, one might need to rethink the concept of "Zomia" as simply a non-state spatial zone. Were these mountainous regions only zones of refuge from states and their civilizing processes (van Schendel 2002; Scott 2009), or were they also hubs for crucial "transient" activities? As the chapters by Chang, Mosca, Perdue and Yonemoto in this volume argue, areas officially marked as geographical, social or political "borders" were vibrant, venturesome places for those engaged with them on the ground. Highlighting the translocal representational significance of material objects, we explore the historical processes by which the discursive and the material constituted each other, forming fluid social and political landscapes. We stress the multiple translations and mediations of agents at their respective locations. In the discursive realm of place-based identity formation, ethnic labeling, and the ambiguities of borders, several chapters in the volume highlight the rhythms of openness and closure, fluidity and intensification over a vast land area similar to the chapters on maritime connections.

Chapters 5 through 8 show the extensive shifting of social and political landscapes often defined as bounded and stable. Yonemoto examines the crafting of diverse meanings of family (Japanese *ie,* Chinese *jia*) in early modern East Asia. Using diaries and family letters of literate elite women in Japan and China, she describes dynamic home-making processes, their multiple implications (social, institutional, spatial), and their gendered nature. Rather than treating home as grounded, Yonemoto turns to women who managed families and made homes as they relocated with their spouses. The intimate details of family management and social mobility in these texts reveal a world of social networks and political alliances far beyond a cloistered home environment. As daughters and wives of samurai, professional and official classes, these women had to adapt to their spouses' frequent change of work assignments and travel. They strategized to provide material security for their families, to maintain lineages' continuity through elaborate adoption and marriages, to promote social advancement within seemingly rigid cultural norms, and to reinforce the sense of a home base even when the reality of one grew uncertain and distant. The lives of Kuroda Tosako (1682–1753), Itō Maki (early nineteenth century), and Tang Yaoqing (1763–1831)—the wife of Zhang Qi, who raised five most accomplished daughters—illustrate the energies of these women (Mann 2007). They exhibited how literate women carried on a shared East Asian Confucian tradition. Yonemoto's critical reading provides rare glimpses of women's agency to maintain family and home in diverse historical moments. In discursive terms, their actions were inspired by patriarchal priorities of the times, but in practice, they were anything but conventional. Yonemoto argues that the Kuroda, Itō and Zhang family lines, in Susan Mann's words, "endured, in the end, through the will of its women."

The chapter by Peter C. Perdue also follows mobile people. It uses the movements of four male travelers (merchants, tributary envoys, an exiled

SHIFTING LANDSCAPES

Wahiba Sands in Oman. (Photo by Helen F. Siu)

Rice terraces near Dong village, Guizhou. (Photo by Helen F. Siu)

Backwaters of Kerala, India. (Photo by Helen F. Siu)

official and a scholar) to explore border-crossing during eighteenth-century Qing China. Chinese borderlands were by nature porous and ambiguous cultural zones spanning states with divergent cultures. Perdue argues that these borders, as social spaces, aroused feelings of alienation among residents and travelers. As sites of encounter for those who crossed them with diverse expectations, they generated unpredictable outcomes. The encounters revealed observations and reflections "filtered through historical knowledge and cultural biases," delineating the political landscape of a vast, land-bound Qing empire and beyond. Perdue begins with the travel diary of Pak Chi-wŏn (1737–1805), a reformist Korean scholar who used his on-the-ground observations to reach beyond standard categorizations of Han/Manchu culture and politics. He adds the experiences of a Central Asian trader Elianhuli and his companions who approached the northwestern border of the Qing empire (with 50,000 sheep!) on a tribute mission. While their experiences displayed "analogous processes of investigation, resistance, negotiation, and eventual acquiescence by border officials," these crossings embodied the mid-Qing's relations with its neighboring peoples. The third traveler, the Hanlin scholar Ji Yun (1724–1805), found himself embroiled in a case of corruption and banished to the frontier in Xinjiang. After being pardoned and returning home, he wrote a series of poems on his exile. They reflected "a wide-eyed awareness of the wonders of the landscape, recognition of the deep historical roots of the region and its radical difference from the core of China, and an activist attitude of what we might call "developmentalism," aiming to transform the region into a productive, integral part of the empire." His close ethnographic encounter with the natural marvels of the frontier contrasted sharply with his literati assumptions of a "progressive taming of sublime vistas by the empire's civilizing project."

The last traveler in Perdue's chapter came from the opposite corner of the Qing Empire. Lê Quý Dôn (1726–1784) was a high-ranking Vietnamese scholar on a trade mission to Beijing. He shared his contemporary Ji Yun's experience of the vast empire and its military and cultural prowess. He likewise had complex emotions about this empire's ideology. While endorsing the new Nguyen dynasty's submission to the Qing, he applied similar imperial ambitions for extending Vietnam's kingdom to the south. Perdue argues that the frontier expanded the horizons of both men, although Lê recognized more deeply the contingency of border relations and local agency in shaping political fortunes. For all four travelers, "border crossing meant a personal journey into alien territory and return to familiar lands with new perspectives. Like their later Western visitors, these Asian travelers reflected upon the position of China in the wider world, and used what they learned of China to carry on dynamic interactions that shaped the relations of China and its neighbors."

Matthew Mosca's chapter complements Perdue's study of the frontier and border crossing by examining Kashmir and Kashmiris through the perspective of Qing intelligence networks in the mid-nineteenth century. Mosca uses the arrest of a Kashmiri merchant (Ahmed Ali) on charges of spying, and his urgent petition to the East India Company in 1830, to unveil the ambiguous status of Kashmir as a place and its residents as a trading group in the eyes of the Qing court. He observes that Kashmiri merchants as a community were geographically dispersed within the Qing Empire, active throughout Tibet, Qinghai, and Xinjiang since the seventeenth century. Although faithful to Islam and their Kashmiri identity, some permanently resided in Lhasa and took local wives. Their trade networks reached westward through Afghanistan into Central Asia, and southward to the Coromandel Coast. At a historical moment when the Kashmir region seemed to be sliding towards British political influence in South and Central Asia, the Qing state activated its elaborate counter-espionage operations to assert some degree of centralized oversight over the flow of people and intelligence. However, there is tantalizing evidence that it may have tried to avoid explicitly elucidating Kashmiri ties to British India so as not to undermine the complex web of relationships facilitating cross-border trade in the larger Tibetan region. Mosca applies meticulous reading of multi-lingual documents and vivid details of the personalities involved to reconstruct zones of encounter with social networks and flows of information across the Himalayas. He directly addresses the theme of connected spaces by arguing that "between the pinnacles of power in Calcutta and Lhasa lay a chain of men linked variously by ties of kinship, community solidarity, and commerce—but also divided by nuanced calculations of their self-interest vis-à-vis two imperial structures. In this sense, they reflect the fine shadings of identity that emerge, as Charles Wheeler has shown in the case of the Minh Huong, when mutable group identities encounter the complex political and commercial terrain between competing polities."

Fast forward into the late twentieth century, in the northern Shan state of Burma, to an area as geographically and politically treacherous as that across the Himalayas. There stood a valley town named Tangyan. Its social history from the 1950s to the 1980s is the focus of Wen-Chin Chang's study. Despite its distance from political centers, flanked by mountains and un-navigable rivers, the area could hardly qualify for a "Zomian" status, in the sense of a place isolated from state power. Despite its location, Tangyan was a "lively, animated town." During various macropolitical changes, the town received waves of mobile populations—Han and Muslim traders, Yunnanese refugees, KMT guerrillas, opium growers in the Wa hills, dealers, intelligence gatherers, ethnic insurgents and even Burmese communists. Human traffic came with the flow of monies and commodities for long and short distant trade. They ranged from popped rice and peanut candies for the hill people, to opium and intelligence for wider markets beyond Burma. Chang engages in "process geographies" (Appadurai 2000) and circulation theory (Markovits, Pouche-padass and Subrahmanyam 2003) and argues that through nexuses of largely Yunnanese itinerant traders, the town of Tangyan has maintained ties with other hubs in relationships of mutual dependence. Together, they have contin-ued to grow and transform. The resultant landscape, physical, social, and po-litical, has been anything but fixed or bounded. It was a "circulatory regime" crisscrossed by multiple political entities, alliances and shifting affiliations.

Pushing West

As scholars use historical and ethnographic details to connect spaces, cultures, societies and economies across this broadly defined Asia, they have debated the emergence and changing nature of "modern world systems" (Abu-Lughod 1989; Goody 1996, 2006; Pomeranz 1998; Wallerstein 1974; Wong 1997). Like Eric Wolf, who wrote the classic book on global capitalism's transfor-mation of local communities, *Europe and the People without History,* Michel Rolph-Trouillot, who has discussed how multi-sited anthropological research can contribute to analysis of global transformations (2003), and Tim Mitch-ell's (2000) call to reexamine what we mean by "modernity," they challenge linear, Euro-centric conceptual schemas, and Asia's place in them. We can apply a similar mode of thinking to capture place-making processes in the colonial, national and post-modern eras.

Many theories of the contemporary world stress the determining role of new digital technologies. We certainly recognize that digital technology has promoted the compression of global time and place. It has reconfigured na-tion-states, hubs of commerce and the movements of populations and goods. But these post-modern global fluidities have not necessarily reduced the struc-tural and discursive powers of modern nation-states, nor have they eliminated the historical legacies that created enduring political and geographical structures (Brenner 2004; Ferguson 2006; Bender 2010). Our general concern for identifying significant spatial moments and their connectivity in the twenty-first century prompts us to ask how to conceptualize the intertwining of new and old state spaces with neo-liberal and post-socialist priorities.

The final group of chapters brings us to spatial moments in the age of modern nation-states. Pushing west from regions identified as East, Southeast and South Asia, our attention moves to their connections with Central Asia and the Gulf. Parallel to Willem van Schendel's efforts to see how space is turned into place over time, with diverse material resources, meanings and emotions, Priya Satia focuses on a pivotal moment in the early twentieth century, "the translocal, British and Indian invention of a place called Iraq, in the course of which the British articulated a new kind of developmentalist colonialism." Satia is interested in seeing how the colonial story unfolds more centrally than the lived experience of the region's inhabitants. Her critical reading of literary and textual sources in their construction of place echoes Siu and Liu's reading of *Chaolian Xiangzhi* on a delta community becoming "landed," and of Mosca's sleuthing of Qing court documents on espionage in Kashmir. Satia meticulously chronicles British understanding of West Asia initially as a "non-place," a barren, un-markable frontier zone, "a mere thoroughfare to the Indian jewel in the crown." It took a humiliating defeat at Kut in 1916 to cause old-fashioned imperial adventurers to rethink Mesopotamia's geo-political positioning between Europe and Asia. Subsequently, a new colonial development agenda armed with aerial technology and discipline not only made a place named Iraq worthy of redemption for a post-war Europe, it also remade India and highlighted its place in the overarching structure of the British Empire. Satia's chapter also asks if history is repeating itself, painfully, in the twenty-first century. "Certainly, our imagination about Iraq has evolved," she muses. "We have, for instance, broken the old habit of blurring it into India . . . and oil figures more prominently than grain in images of Iraq's share of global wealth. But the image of an autarkic, hermetic desert that forbids modern ideas and goods continues to tempt those dreaming of a regenerated Babylonia, and the years of sanctions and occupation in pursuit of that imperial folly have helped make the image of autarky something of a reality. With drones overhead, Iraq is once again the site of a first in the history of aerial technology, as we continue to speak a development language constituting itself as a neutral form of knowledge despite its role in producing the country's current devastation."

Flaming Mountains, Gaochang, Xinjiang. (Photo by Helen F. Siu)

Indian and Chinese goods in Muscat market. (Photo by Helen F. Siu)

African traders in Guangzhou. (Photo by Helen F. Siu)

Mandana Limbert's chapter on Oman also demonstrates the importance of accumulated translocal histories in place-making. Limbert centers her research question on a report in a United Arab Emirates newspaper on the frustrations of a 'Pakistani-Omani' with current marriage laws. The man complained that he had to wait five years for approval to marry a cousin from Pakistan, because a decree of 1986 had banned marriages between Omanis and foreigners. As Limbert asserts, "the statement of frustration that appeared in *The Gulf News* nearly twenty years later underscores broad and continuing tensions around the processes of citizenship, statehood, marriage, and place-making in Oman at the end of the twentieth and beginning of the twenty-first centuries." As we saw in Satia's chapter, boundaries of belonging in the Arabian Peninsula have been redrawn many times with geo-political agendas. Previous decades have seen the rise of the Gulf economies and massive migrations to the region due to labor demands. Institutional structures have stepped in to demarcate statehood and sovereignty and to determine the rights of nationals. These structures, backed up by exclusive and restrictive nationality and marriage laws, have posed unexpected personal dilemmas for large, mobile populations from Africa or Asia. Many non-Arab residents had long settled in the region with stateless identities defined by various moments of making Oman. Limbert's chapter calls our attention to "choke-points" in the management of place beyond immigration control, and argues that marriage, sexual relations, children and family formation are equally important policy matters for the new Gulf state. Oman's unique positioning between Africa, the Arab World, and South Asia, in geographic, demographic, economic and political terms, highlights the tensions generated by the juxtaposition of connected places, mobile populations, blurring borders, and the attempts by new nation-states to create a "homogeneous" citizenry.

The next chapter continues the discussion of thorny questions of nationality and space involving diasporic communities "out of place" in mainstream policy thinking. Jing Tsu uses the literacy and literary projects of the Dungans, Sinitic Muslim communities living in Kyrgyzstan, Kazakhstan and Uzbekistan, to underscore how languages survive beyond geographic and political spaces that are presumed to contain them. The Dungans were descendants of Chinese Muslim rebels who fled to Russia via Xinjiang in the nineteenth century. There is a strong emotional link to experiences of exile, and the absence of Chinese cultural influence has allowed the Dungans to lean toward Muslim customs and moral conduct. They survived various waves of modern Chinese nationalistic projects that intended to limit linguistic multiplicity and regional diversity and to reinforce political loyalties in the twentieth century. She challenges the basic assumptions of Area studies, which have privileged "nativity" and cultural coherence tied to clearly demarcated geographic/political spaces. Tsu argues that "amidst the current, enthusiastic turn away from established language heartlands to neglected outliers, the Dungans offer a unique specimen of Sinophone writing that developed outside of the influences of standard Mandarin." It is "Chinese" in its phonic form, with its own invented Cyrillic script for writing under heavy Soviet influence. Mixing words of Russian, Arabic and Persian into its vocabulary, the language remains rooted in oral peasant speech of Shaanxi and Gansu in northwestern China. Tsu looks for new critical venues as linguistic practices and spatial lines move apart. She asks a series of theoretically poignant questions for relating space, language, and polity. "What happens, for example, when languages grow and survive in between designated national spaces? Do claims of cultural belonging become more justifiable, precarious, or inflexible when language and script no longer reflect any single set of national stakes but persist in unexpected, anachronistic forms? If these fundamental attachments need to be rethought, what might this mean for the recent explosion of Sinophone studies—a move away from cultural and geographical Sinocentrism—and the simultaneous retreat from Area Studies—a paradigm perpetuated by the former geopolitical assumptions of the Cold War—that are moving us toward new geographies of inter-place and inter-area analysis?"

Park Bun-Soon turns our attention back to East Asia, specifically South Korea's multiple connections with an Asian renaissance of the twenty-first century. South Korea, small in area and population compared to its neighbors, lying at the margins of the continental-sized polities of Russia and China, rose from the ashes of colonization and war to exert economic and cultural influence in an increasingly affluent and dynamic Asia. As political leaders respond to South Korea's strategic positioning between Japan and China, economists examine Korea's impressive GDP growth and entrepreneurial prowess, finding Korean investments in agribusinesses and digital technology stretching as far as the Middle East and Africa. Consumers know Korea through its products—Hyundai automobiles, Samsung electronics, and the like. With new media technologies, is Korea's powerful impact turning increasingly "soft"?

In the final chapter, Whang Soon-Hee picks up the issue of Korea's soft power raised by Park and examines its cultural industry. From the perspective of cultural sociology, she focuses on the social impact of waves of Korean popular culture that have swept across Asia. Based on ten years of ethnographic research in a suburb of Tokyo where Korean popular culture has flourished, she has produced a pioneering study on cross-cultural translations. In the "modern" phase of the early 2000s, the South Korean television series "Winter Sonata" (Gyeoul Yeonga), and its Korean star Bae Yong-joon, became wildly popular in Japan. The Shin-Okubo district of Tokyo, or Korea Town, flourished as cafes, shops, restaurants, and tourist agencies promoted products related to the series. The Korea boom intersected with the rise of anime culture and its associated crazes to generate dedicated groups of young Japanese fans. They fixed their gaze on these stars as tall, slim men with an elegant style and "naughty" personalities. In Korea, the same stars played multiple roles in different dramas, but felt compelled to stick to these established images.

The "postmodern" phase began around 2009. The audiences broadened to a wider age-range, and spilled beyond Korea and Japan to include Malaysia, Taiwan, Singapore, Hong Kong, and China. New social media has allowed fans to network and improvise. The stars also gained greater flexibility to play their roles. This process has allowed young Asian consumers to create their own cultural worlds beyond national ideologies or Western cultural models. It remains to be seen if the Korean nation-state could exploit such "soft power" to become a lead player in an inter-Asian cultural sphere. With the latest popularity of Psy's music video "Gangnam style," Korea seems to be extending its impact on global popular culture as well.

Locally, this cultural transformation has remade specific urban landscapes. Shin-Okubo in Tokyo, once a lower class district filled with Korean migrants, is now thriving with a cosmopolitan touch. Last year, the plaza in front of City Hall in Seoul where citizens had demonstrated against former military regimes attracted eighty thousand fans to Psy's open-air concert. Like the other chapters in this volume, Whang's study shows how digital media thrusts popular culture across regional and national borders, and transforms the social meanings and uses of city spaces.

From the sensational Korean television dramas to the popularity of K-Pop, Korea has moved beyond sharing Confucian values with its East Asian neighbors to exert its own cultural identity and "soft power." With Psy receiving record hits on the Internet (the first singer to achieve one billion, and counting), Chinese teenagers flocking to Korean pop concerts, and Vietnamese brides dressing themselves up in Korean dress for their wedding photograph collections, one wonders if the Korean wave (*Hallyu*) is creating a new, connected Asia.

This volume thus highlights the conjuncture of historical circumstances in the making of connected places—the (macro) political forces, the (micro) strategies of personalities, the translocal institutional resources deployed, the meanings negotiated, and the structuring consequences of all of the above. We use the concept "spatial moments" in a broadly defined Asia to capture the dynamics of time-space analysis in both material and discursive forms. The following chapters present a wide variety of empirical sources, from early modern to post-modern periods, from oceans to land masses, stretching across continental divides from Northeast Asia to West Asia. Place-making in Asia, in our view, has involved multi-scalar processes. They are malleable structural assemblages, created by human agency and accumulated over the centuries.

References

Abrams, Philips. 1982. *Historical Sociology.* Ithaca: Cornell University Press.

Abu-Lughod, Janet L. 1989. *Before European Hegemony: the World System A.D. 1250–1350.* New York: Oxford University Press.

Antony, Robert, ed. 2010. *Elusive Pirates, Pervasive Smugglers: Violence and Clandestine Trade in the Greater China Seas.* Hong Kong: Hong Kong University Press.

Appadurai, Arjun. 2000. "Grassroots Globalization and the Research Imagination." *Public Culture* 12 (1): 1–19.

Art and Exhibition Hall of the Federal Republic of Germany. 2008. *Gandhara-The Buddhist Heritage of Pakistan: Legends, Monasteries, and Paradise.* Mainz: Verlag Philipp von Zabern.

Augé, Marc. 1995. *Non-Places: Introduction to an Anthropology of Super Modernity.* London: Verso.

Bender, Thomas. 2010. "Postscript. Reassembling the City: Networks and the Urban Imaginaries." In *Urban Assemblages: How Actor-Network Theory Changes Urban Studies,* ed. Farias, Ignacio and Thomas Bender, 303–323. New York: Routledge.

Blussé, Leonard. 2002. *Bitter Bonds: A Colonial Divorce Drama of the Seventeenth Century.* Princeton, NJ: Markus Wiener Publishers.

Bose, Sugata. 2006. *A Hundred Horizons: The Indian Ocean in the Age of Global Empire.* Cambridge, MA: Harvard University Press.

Boulnois, Luce. 2004. *Silk Road: Monks, Warriors & Merchants on the Silk Road.* Hong Kong: Odyssey.

Bourdieu, Pierre. 1972. *Outline of a Theory of Practice.* Cambridge: Cambridge University Press.

Braudel, Fernand. 1975. *Capitalism and Material Life, 1400–1800.* New York: Harper and Row.

Brenner, Neil. 1997. "Global, Fragmented, Hierarchical: Henri Lefebvre's Geographies of Globalization." *Public Culture,* 10 (1): 137–169.

———. 2004. "The Globalization Debates: Opening Up to New Spaces?" In *New State Spaces: Urban Governance and the Rescaling of Statehood.* Oxford: Oxford University Press. 28–67.

Brook, Timothy. 2008. *Vermeer's Hat: The Seventeenth Century and the Dawn of the Global World.* New York: Bloomsbury Press.

Castells, Manuel. 1996. *The Rise of the Network Society.* Cambridge, MA: Blackwell Publishers.

Chaffee, John. 2008. "At the Intersection of Empire and World Trade: The Chinese Port City of Quanzhou (Zaitun), Eleventh-Fifteenth Centuries." In *Secondary Cities and Urban Networking in the Indian Ocean Realm c. 1400–1800,* ed. Kenneth Hall, 99–122. Lanham, MD: Lexington Books.

Chaudhuri, K. N. 1985. *Trade and Civilisation in the Indian Ocean: An Economic History From the Rise of Islam to 1750.* Cambridge: Cambridge University Press.

Cresswell, Tim. 2004. *Place: A Short Introduction.* Malden, MA: Blackwell Publishing.

Crossley, Pamela Kyle, Helen F. Siu, and Donald S. Sutton, eds. 2006. *Empire at the Margins: Culture, Ethnicity, and Frontier in Early Modern China.* Berkeley: University of California Press.

Crossman, Carl. 1991. *The Decorative Arts of the China Trade: Paintings, Furnishings and Exotic Curiosities.* Woodbridge, Suffolk: Antique Collectors' Club.

Curtin, Philip D. 1984. *Cross-Cultural Trade in World History.* Cambridge: Cambridge University Press.

Dunn, Ross E. 2005. *The Adventures of Ibn Battuta, a Muslim Traveler of the Fourteenth Century.* 2nd ed. Berkeley: University of California Press.

Faure, David. 2007. *Emperor and Ancestor: State and Lineage in South China.* Stanford: Stanford University Press.

Faure, David, and Helen Siu, eds. 1995. *Down to Earth: The Territorial Bond in South China.* Stanford: Stanford University Press.

Ferguson, James. 2006. *Global Shadows: Africa in the Neoliberal World Order.* Durham, NC: Duke University Press.

Giddens, Anthony. 1979. *Central Problems in Social Theory: Action, Structure and Contradiction in Social Analysis.* Berkeley: University of California Press.

Godement, Francois. 1997. *New Asian Renaissance.* New York: Routledge.

Goody, Jack. 1996. *The East in the West.* Cambridge: Cambridge University Press.

———. 2006. *The Theft of History.* Cambridge; New York: Cambridge University Press.

Gupta, Akhil, and James Ferguson. 1997. *Culture, Power, Place: Explorations in Critical Anthropology.* Durham, NC: Duke University Press.

Hamashita, Takeshi. 2008. *China, East Asia and the Global Economy: Regional and Historical Perspectives.* Edited by Linda Grove and Mark Selden. London: Routledge.

Hansen, Randall. 2000. *Citizenship and Immigration in Post-War Britain: The Institutional Origins of a Multicultural Nation.* Oxford: Oxford University Press.

Hansen, Valerie. 2012. *The Silk Road: A New History.* Oxford: Oxford University Press.

Harper, Tim, and Sunil Amrith. 2012. "Sites of Asian Interaction: An Introduction," *Modern Asian Studies,* 46 (2/Special Issue): 249–257.

Harvey, David. 1989. *The Condition Of Postmodernity: An Enquiry into the Origins of Cultural Change.* Oxford: Blackwell.

Hayden, Delores 1997. *The Power of Place: Urban Landscapes as Public History.* Cambridge, MA: MIT Press.

Herzfeld, Michael. 1991. *A Place in History: Social and Monumental Time in a Cretan Town.* Princeton, NJ: Princeton University Press

Ho, Engseng. 2006. *The Graves of Tarim: Genealogy and Mobility across the Indian Ocean.* Berkeley: University of California Press.

Holston, James, and Arjun Appadurai. 1998. "Introduction: Cities and Citizenship," in *Cities and Citizenship*, ed. James Holston, 1–20. Durham, NC: Duke University Press.

Horden, Peregrine, and Nicholas Purcell. 2000. *The Corrupting Sea: A Study of Mediterranean History.* Malden, MA: Blackwell Publishers.

Jessop, Bob, Neil Brenner, and Gordon Macleod, eds. 2003. *State/Space: A Reader.* Malden, MA: Wiley-Blackwell.

Kauz, Ralph, ed. 2010. *Aspects of the Maritime Silk Road: From the Persian Gulf to the East China Sea.* Wiesbaden: Harrassowitz Verlag.

Kauz, Ralph, and Roderich Ptak. 2001. "Hormuz in Yuan and Ming Sources." *Bulletin de l'Ecole française d'Extrême-Orient* 88: 27–75.

Kaviraj, Sudipta. 1997. "Filth and the Public Sphere: Concepts and Practices about Space in Calcutta." *Public Culture* Fall 10 (1): 83–113.

Lefebvre, Henri. 1991. *The Production of Space.* Oxford: Blackwell.

Lewis, Mark Edward. 2009. *China's Cosmopolitan Empire: The Tang Dynasty.* Cambridge, MA: Belknap Press of the Harvard University Press.

Lewis, Martin W., and Kären E. Wigen. 1997. *The Myth of Continents: A Critique of Metageography.* Berkeley: University of California Press.

———. 1999. "A Maritime Response to the Crisis in Area Studies," *Geographical Review* 89 (2/Oceans Connect/April): 161–168.

Lipman, Jonathan. 2006. "'A Fierce and Brutal People': On Islam and Muslims in Qing Law." In *Empire at the Margins: Culture, Ethnicity, and Frontier in Early Modern China,* ed. Pamela Kyle Crossley, Helen F. Siu, and Donald S. Sutton, 83–110. Berkeley: University of California Press.

Macauley, Melissa. 2009. "Small Time Crooks: Opium, Migrants, and the War on Drugs in China, 1819–1860." *Late Imperial China* 30 (1/June): 1–47.

Mann, Susan. 2007. *The Talented Women of the Zhang Family.* Berkeley: University of California Press.

Markovits, Claude, Jacques Pouchepadass, and Sanjay Subrahmanyam. 2003. *Society and Circulation (Mobile People and Itinerant Cultures in South Asia, 1750–1950).* Delhi: Anthem Press.

Metcalf, Thomas R. 2007. *Imperial Connections: India in the Indian Ocean Arena, 1860–1920.* Berkeley: University of California Press.

Middleton, John. 1994. *The World of the Swahili: An African Mercantile Civilization.* New Haven: Yale University Press.

Mitchell, Timothy, ed. 2000. *Questions of Modernity.* Minneapolis: University of Minnesota Press.

Mosca, Matthew W. 2013. *From Frontier Policy to Foreign Policy: The Question of India and the Transformation of Geopolitics in Qing China.* Stanford: Stanford University Press.

Pearson, M. N., ed. 1996. *Spices in the Indian Ocean World.* London: Variorum.

Perdue, Peter C. 2005. *China Marches West: The Qing Conquest of Central Eurasia.* Cambridge, MA: Belknap Press of Harvard University Press.

Pomeranz, Kenneth. 2000. *The Great Divergence: China, Europe, and the Making of the Modern World Economy.* Princeton, NJ: Princeton University Press.

Ong, Aihwa, and Stephen J. Collier 2005. *Global Assemblages: Technology, Politics, and Ethics as Anthropological Problems.* Malden, MA: Blackwell Publishing.

Roy, Ananya, and Aihwa Ong, eds. 2011. *Worlding Cities: Asian Experiments and the Art of Being Global.* Malden, MA: Wiley-Blackwell.

Sargent, William R. 2012. *Treasures of Chinese Export Ceramics: From the Peabody Essex Museum.* New Haven: Yale University Press.

Sassen, Saskia. 1991. *The Global City: New York, London, Tokyo.* Princeton, NJ: Princeton University Press.

Scott, James. 2009. *The Art of NOT Being Governed: An Anarchist History of Upland Southeast Asia.* New Haven: Yale University Press.

Shapinsky, Peter. 2009. "Predators, Protectors, and Purveyors: Pirates and Commerce in Late Medieval Japan." *Monumenta Nipponica* 64 (2/Autumn): 273–313.

Simpfendorfer, Ben. 2009. *The New Silk Road: How a Rising Arab World Is Turning Away from the West and Rediscovering China.* New York: Palgrave Macmillan.

Sinn, Elizabeth. 2012. *Pacific Crossing: California Gold, Chinese Migration, and the Making of Hong Kong.* Hong Kong: Hong Kong University Press.

Siu, Helen F. 2010. *Merchants' Daughters: Women, Commerce, and Regional Culture in South China.* Hong Kong: Hong Kong University Press.

Siu, Helen F., and Liu Zhiwei. 2006. "Lineage, Market, Pirate, and Dan: Ethnicity in the Pearl River Delta of South China." In *Empire at the Margins: Culture, Ethnicity, and Frontier in Early Modern China,* eds. Pamela Kyle Crossley, Helen F. Siu, and Donald S. Sutton, 285–310. Berkeley: University of California Press.

Sood, Gagan. 2011. "Circulation and Exchange in Islamicate Eurasia: A Regional Approach to the Early Modern World." *Past and Present* 212 (1): 113–162.

Stoler, Ann. "Sexual Affronts and Racial Frontiers: European Identities and the Cultural Politics of Exclusions in Colonial Southeast Asia." *Comparative Studies in Society and History* 34 (3): 514–551.

Subramanian, Ajantha. 2009. *Shorelines: Space and Rights in South India.* Stanford: Stanford University Press.

Subrahmanyam, Sanjay. 1996. *Merchant Networks in the Early Modern World.* Brookfield, VT: Variorum.

Tagliacozzo, Eric. 2005. *Secret Trades, Porous Borders: Smuggling and States Along A Southeast Asian Frontier, 1865–1915.* New Haven: Yale University Press.

Tagliacozzo, Eric, and Wen-Chin Chang, eds. 2011. *Chinese Circulations: Capital, Commodities, and Networks in Southeast Asia.* Durham, NC: Duke University Press.

Trouillot, Michel-Rolph. 2003. *Global Transformations: Anthropology and the Modern World.* New York: Palgrave/Macmillan.

UNESCO "Integral Study of the Silk Roads: Roads of Dialogue" Project. "Newsletter." 3, 1993(April): 1. http://unesdoc.unesco.org/images/0015/001593/159314eo.pdf (accessed December 20, 2014).

Van Dyke, Paul A. 2005. *The Canton Trade: Life and Enterprise on the China Coast, 1700–1845.* Hong Kong: Hong Kong University Press.

———. 2011. *Merchants of Canton and Macao: Politics and Strategies in Eighteenth-Century Chinese Trade.* Hong Kong: Hong Kong University Press.

van Schendel, Willem. 2002. "Geographies of Knowing, Geographies of Ignorance: Jumping Scale in Southeast Asia." *Development and Planning D: Society and Space* 20: 647–668.

Waley-Cohen, Joanna. 1999. *The Sextants of Beijing: Global Currents in Chinese History.* New York: W.W. Norton.

Wallerstein, Immanuel. 1974. "The Rise and Future Demise of the World Capitalist System: Concepts for Comparative Analysis." *Comparative Studies in Society and History* 16 (4): 387–415.

Watt, James, et al. 2004. *China: Dawn of a Golden Age 200–750 AD.* New York: Metropolitan Museum of Art.

Wigen, Kären. "Culture, Power, and Place. The New Landscapes of East Asian Regionalism." *The American Historical Review* October: 1183–1201.

Wills, John E. 2002. *1688 A Global History.* New York: W.W. Norton.

Wolf, Eric. 1982. *Europe and the People without History.* Berkeley: California University Press.

Wong, Dorothy, and Gustav Heldt. 2014. *China and Beyond in the Medieval Period: Cultural Crossings and Inter-Regional Connections.* New York: Cambria Press.

Wong, R. Bin. 1997. *China Transformed: Historical Change and the Limits of European Experience.* Ithaca: Cornell University Press.

———. 1999. "Entre Monde et Nation: Les Régions Braudéliennes En Asie (Between Nation and World: Braudelian Regions in Asia)." *Annales* 56, no. 1 (1999): 5–41.

Zheng, Yangwen. 2012. *China on the Sea: How the Maritime World Shaped Modern China.* Leiden: Brill.

Placing the "Chinese Pirates" of the Gulf of Tongking at the End of the Eighteenth Century

CHARLES WHEELER

When is one more Mediterranean comparison one too many? This question occurred to me as I recently read a new book about the Tongking (or Tonkin) Gulf, a part of the South China Sea nestled between southern China and Vietnam. The book's creators declared that the gulf fit the Mediterranean model, just as many other books claim many other bodies of water do. But then, perhaps the answer had been a foregone conclusion: editors evidently chose the volume's articles based on their ability to serve an overarching Braudelian narrative that emphasized a basin-defined social continuity across space and time. Such tactics are common to the Mediterranean model enterprise: authors contributed evidence of long-term connection in the Tongking Gulf and subsequently declared unity. Indeed, signs of connection or exchange appear to be the only criteria for declaring a new Mediterranean. Is it any wonder, then, that they now appear everywhere on the planet? Yet signs of exchange are not enough to verify the unified field that the word "Mediterranean" now implies, at least from Braudel's view, because, at the very least, they are universal—"to live is to exchange" (Braudel 1972, 44; quoted in Sutherland 2003). So what, then, does simple connection distinguish? Puzzling over our current bundle of Mediterraneans, I wondered whether perhaps Michael Herzfeld was right: that all these Mediterraneans we perceive in world history are nothing more than the product of a circular argument bent on creating "excuses for everything" that the Mediterranean analogy enables (Herzfeld 2005). Indeed, this Mediterranean feels uncomfortably like one too many.

Whether people exchanged, therefore, is unremarkable to the world historian, or at least should be. *How* they connected—that is everything. Distinguishing features that mattered to Braudel—like the long-term patterns of interactions between nature and society, the resulting political economy and social geography, the map and rhythms of transhumance, the "networks of routine and round-trip exchange" (Wigen 2006) as well as institutions, types of carriers, processes of organization, the tempo of itineraries, and the processing of commodities, or the limits of this alleged region (which for Braudel never lay on the sea's rim)—these often fall to the wayside in our scramble to claim new territories of connection that suggest automatic unity. The evidence of messy contradictions, organic processes, the insidious entrapments that dialectic and the complicated overlapping of social ecologies reveal, and the agent's "creative battle against all odds" to transcend nature (Braudel 1972)—all this appears to fall to the wayside in favor of a unity that appears frictionless. Our new Mediterraneans, unbound from nature, become unified fields of fantasy as a result.

As a consequence, the Mediterranean acts less as an analogy and more like a fetish for an idealized cosmopolitanism, much as we have done with other over-used (and historically groundless) metaphors, like the Silk Road. This has become most apparent with the global application of the trope. The characteristics that began with the Middle Sea now apply to the Indian Ocean, the Atlantic (made up of many "Mediterraneans," including the Caribbean), the Bay of Bengal, the North Sea, the Baltic Sea, and the Black Sea. Moving on, even the hemispheric Pacific is said to have developed into a Mediterranean-like basin (or set of basins) in modern times (Blank 1999); some find this difficult to accept (Gulliver 2011), but not everyone. And now, thanks to the spreading belief in global warming, the Arctic Ocean has recently joined the list of Mediterraneans, after policy analysts and politicians in Nordic countries began to seriously consider the possibility that the warming "Arctic Ocean could become a new Mediterranean Sea at the top of the world," according to Iceland's Minister of Environment Svandís Svavarsdóttir (Braun 2011; Dodds 2010; Spinks 2011). Everywhere we look, we see Mediterraneans.

Where will the impulse to Mediterranean-ize stop? Karen Wigen and Martin Lewis (2009) once proposed to look at the world from the South Pole. From there, all the world looks like land fragments afloat on a single, global body of water. Is this not another Mediterranean? If so, the metaphor has somehow led us, like one of Bruno Latour's fetishes, to something akin to antiquity's Great Ocean Sea, dressed like a global cosmopolitan.

To be fair, our Mediterranean mythmaking isn't anything new. Braudel saw his share of Mediterraneans, too. He even saw it in the South China Sea, of which the Tongking Gulf is a part. Asia specialists have tended to credit this declaration of Mediterraneanness to the historian Denys Lombard, who made the claim in a grand study of Javanese sailing and trade in the 1970s, and who advanced this thesis until his death in the 1990s (Lombard 1990, 1994, 1995). Actually, Braudel had used the Mediterranean label himself many years before. Recalling an interview with the great *Annaliste* in 1979, Leonard Blussé recalled that the mention of the South China Sea "fired Braudel up":

> He immediately embarked on a lengthy and enthusiastic discourse explaining that the South China Sea was yet another "Mediterranean *Seeraum*" surrounded by cultures in which people were living with and breathing the same rhythms of time and sharing a common destiny. (Blussé 1999, 108)

Indeed, one can see the beginnings of this vision in his magisterial three volumes on capitalism and civilization, when he said that "Malay sailors . . . had always been fishermen, coastal traders and above all pirates" (Braudel 1984, 526). Even before Braudel, Southeast Asianists of an earlier generation invoked the Mediterranean analogy, as Heather Sutherland pointed out somewhat recently (Sutherland 2003). Of course, this Mediterranean suggested forms of cosmopolitanism and connection that Southeast Asianists could embrace more easily than Lombard's idea of a *Chinese* Mediterranean. Here, a resilient form of sinocentrism prevails. Leonard Blussé, for example, observed that it is "not altogether by chance" that we "happen to call [it] the *China Sea*," because the "*économie monde* dominating this maritime space was, *of course,* the Chinese one" (latter italics added; Blussé 1979, 129, 108). The idea has its shortcomings, to be sure. The monocultural adjective "Chinese" seems to contradict the essential idea of the Mediterranean as a cosmopolitan place. The "Chinese Mediterranean" view erroneously projects the idea that Chinese ships—and by inference Chinese people—were the primary vehicles of integration in the South China Sea. Southeast Asianist scholarship alone soundly refutes such a notion. Be that as it may, the label has stuck.

It seems that the bias of academic specialization is at play here. Indian Ocean specialists, (e.g., Braudel, Chaudhuri, and Pearson) after all, tend to insist on the sea as an extension of the Indian Ocean, as if to channel early twentieth century visions of a "Greater India" below the winds. Southeast Asianists have claimed the region as their own "human unit" since Anthony Reid's *Age of Commerce* (1993). Still, one can't help but think that Herzfeld is right: The Mediterranean has become our "excuse for everything" (2005), a means of projecting our world views on a wider map.

The challenge this problem raises is simple: Scholars must avoid Herzfeld's "Mediterraneanism," just as many of us have worked to steer clear of Orientalism. "What we should be doing instead," Peregrine Horden says, paraphrasing Herzfeld, "is looking at local particularities and placing them in potentially global comparative frameworks" (Horden 2005, 26). One point of comparison might be the Mediterranean—or not. Alternative approaches to constructing region may help us resist the temptation to replace longstanding nation-state and area studies with ocean rims, one of Mediterraneanism's strongest attractions.

With this in mind, I hope to use this chapter to resist the temptation to infer social unity from the Tongking Gulf's Mediterranean-looking shorelines and instead try to explain historical phenomenon peculiar to the region by reconstructing society, as Braudel did, from the water up. It derives its geographical structure from the society that produced it, by analyzing long-term patterns of mobility developed from a historical ecology driven, in part, by coastal, boat-centered societies. This analysis produces a geography that looks very different from the Mediterranean in form, but proves just as integrative and fluid all the same. Mobility contextualized, patterns appear that improve our ability to explain phenomena that have dogged past scholars, not just economic activities, but cultural expressions and political conflicts, too. The overall effect is a maritime model that possesses much improved ability to demonstrate the qualities in the Mediterranean that we may seek to identify: "a space that conjures up the history of coexistence—commercial, cultural, religious, political, as well as that of confrontation between neighbors aware of their . . . differences" (Abulafia 2005, 92–3).

Some degree of spatial context will have to be offered at the outset, and to this end, Hamashita Takeshi's model of Asian maritime zones works well. A "Tongking Gulf Region" fits well as a sub-region of his South China Sea zone. The study that follows will test whether history justifies the addition of such a model, in particular whether this Tongking Gulf sub-region helps to substantiate the existence and importance of the Sino-Vietnamese littoral that lines the South China Sea's western rim, where one of the world's most important sea lanes connected South and East Asia in the most direct way.

In hopes of trying to grasp the importance of difference, contradiction, and conflict to the process of creating regional unity, and to tease out signs of the tension that Braudel saw between the long-term rhythms of ecology and human agency, this chapter will examine the biographies of a group with a confusing identity: "Chinese Pirates." Pirates make a good choice, because of what they do. As David Abulafia points out: "Pirates interfered," but also constituted "a profitable and even well-controlled part of the Mediterranean economy" (Abulafia 2005, 69), a point to which David Starkey and other students of the economics of piracy would concur. Pirates were not only "intrinsic to the functioning of the state" (Anderson 1995, 189)—they often were intrinsic to their creation as well (Thomson 1994). Sometimes they developed as a response to immediate socio-economic or political circumstances (e.g., Antony 2003), but their responses to macro-economic shifts or outside political interventions were enveloped within a Braudelian kind of "destiny" shaped very much by long-term habitat, a well-documented phenomenon for the South China Sea region in which the Tongking Gulf sits (e.g., Junker 1999; Warren 1981, 1998, 2000; Wheeler 2006a, 2010). This is where "*Chinese* pirates" can be even more helpful. Within this ecology we can determine the long-term social streams, flows or patterns of mobility that suggest the social parameters or region within which these so-called Chinese pirates typically operated. This helps us to make social connections that in turn help us to transcend the limiting category of "Chinese pirate" with all its assumptions, so that we can understand their actual role in the "Chinese piracy" crisis of the late eighteenth century and the Vietnamese civil war with which it intertwined. From here, we can look beyond their misleading label to see the ways in which the identities, like the statuses, of the pirates profiled depended "above all [on] change in the political realm" in which they operated (Pérotin-Dumon 1991). In this way, replacing rims with social flows opens our eyes to social connections that we would otherwise be unable to perceive, which leads us to political, economic and cultural processes that collectively distinguish regions—in this case, a region at sea, where boundaries are never a good fit.

The following discussion divides into three sections. It aims to reinterpret one of the watershed moments in Vietnamese history, the Tây Sơn Uprising, and the central role that "Chinese pirates" played in supporting the Tây Sơn rebels who sought to unify the Vietnamese speaking world under their rule at the end of the eighteenth century. The first part introduces the problem of Chinese piracy in Vietnamese revolution, as well as a complicated group called the Minh Hương (roughly pronounced "ming hung"), through the story of a pirate leader captured in the Tongking Gulf Region. These Minh Hương turn out to have been important, and the second part of the article explains why, by showing that the Minh Hương community, its identity, its range of mobility, and its complex web of interregional relationships evolved within the context of the two major transoceanic social streams or flows whose complex political, economic and cultural networks produced the bonds and barriers that made the "Chinese" pirate identity possible. Last, it introduces two other Minh Hương figures that previous regional frameworks have over-looked, and whose biographies challenge standard narratives of both Viet-namese revolution and Chinese piracy at the end of the eighteenth century. All this derives from a regional perspective that seeks to deduce from patterns rather than infer from metaphors.

Capturing Lun Guili

In the spring of 1800, the governor of Zhejiang province petitioned the em-peror of China about the case of a pirate he had sentenced to a gruesome death.[1] A storm had destroyed a large pirate fleet as it anchored off the prov-ince's coast. Four or five thousand sailors drowned; imperial soldiers rounded up more than 800 survivors. Among them stood "a man who pretended to be mute, with short hair, named Wang Guili [王貴利]" (Jiao 1672, 116). Soon after, "interrogators revealed that he is actually *Lun* Guili [倫貴利— *italics added*]," the fleet's leader, who the state wanted for previous raids. Lun's story fit a regular pattern for pirates of China's southern coast at the time. He blamed his life of crime on Vietnamese pirates who "snatched him up" in 1794 while he was out chopping wood near his village in Chaozhou Prefec-ture and forced him to become a pirate. Apparently, he accepted his fate, and soon caught the attention of Chen Tianbao (陳添保, Vietnamese *Trần Thiên Bảo*), a powerful corsair who operated within the "water world" of the Tong-king Gulf that spans Vietnam and China (Murray 1987, 36; the term "water world" comes from Murray). Before long, Lun commanded a fleet of his own.

Chen Tianbao certainly shaped Lun Guili's fate, too. He worked for the Viet-namese "King of Annam [安南國王]" Nguyễn Huệ, who gave the Cantonese pirate money, arms, royal title, a Vietnamese wife and, most importantly, safe haven and bases of operation in Vietnamese seaports in exchange for his political allegiance. The king needed Chen, and more like him. Two decades earlier, he and his brothers launched a rebellion that engulfed the Vietnamese-speaking world in violence for almost thirty years. Both the brothers and also their rebellion came to be called Tây Sơn (西山), after the "Western Mountains" overlooking the Vietnamese seaport of Qui Nhơn where it all began. From 1773 to 1789, Huệ and his brothers destroyed their rivals and crushed an invasion by the Qing emperor of China, who accepted his fate and recognized the new Tây Sơn state. The child of one rival house survived, however. Nguyễn Ánh rose from the ashes, and in 1789 seized the maritime commercial center of Saigon. With his powerful navy, he threatened the entire Vietnamese coast, exposing the country's urban centers. Suddenly disadvantaged, the Tây Sơn court turned to Chinese pirates like Chen Tianbao. This only delayed the inevitable, it seems. In 1792 the Nguyễn navy burned most of the Tây Sơn fleet at Qui Nhơn (Dutton 2006, 222, 268). Nguyễn Huệ turned again to Chen for help, and he in turn recruited Lun Guili and others.

Proof of the young pirate's accomplishments lay before the governor and his court, in a batch of documents and copper seals that Qing troops rescued from his sunken fleet. They bore the title, "Luân Quý Lợi [Lun Guili], Commander in Chief of the Virtuous Fleet, Marquis of Tiến Lộc [Advancing Fortune]."[2] He had earned the honors after only three years of service.

Lun sailed his fleet to Zhejiang in order to help his Vietnamese overlord. Since this unholy alliance began, Chinese-born pirates like Lun seasonally raided China's coast for booty, part of which they handed over to the Tây Sơn, who used the proceeds to sustain their war against Nguyễn Ánh (Chang 1983, 57–58). Nature turned against Lun, however. Once in Zhejiang, he anchored his fleet of twenty-eight ships offshore and prepared for his raid. "Suddenly, a great wind struck the sea, and tore the ships apart." His fleet destroyed, Lun "clung to a piece of wood and drifted with the current" to a nearby island, where he hid (Ruan 1820, 2: 8).

It did not take long for provincial soldiers to find Lun Guili. The governor didn't take long to decide the pirate's fate, either. Granted summary powers to deal with pirates striking China from beyond the empire's reach in Vietnam, the governor ordered Lun to suffer execution by "a thousand cuts," a gradual flaying and dismemberment meant to maximize Lun's suffering in both life and afterlife.

What did collusion with the Tây Sơn give Lun Guili in order for him to risk life and afterlife? Lun has grown familiar to historians who study China's piracy crisis during the turn of the nineteenth century.[3] This literature uniformly sees men like Lun Guili in two ways: one, as part of a large-scale collaboration between Tây Sơn rebels, on the one hand, and "Chinese" pirates on the other (Antony 2003; Liu Ping 1998a, b; Murray 1987; Dutton 2006, 2, 19, 54, 200–201, 219–227); another, as a compact between Tây Sơn and "Vietnamese" pirates, albeit of Chinese origin (Chang 1983). The relationship was part of the bargain wherein Chinese pirates like Lun engaged in a swap with the Vietnamese Tây Sơn, an exchange that took place across the Sino-Vietnamese border. Nguyễn Huệ granted pirates a package of incentives that men like Lun Guili apparently couldn't refuse. In return, they offered their naval services, their political loyalty, and changed their hair and attire to "Vietnamese" style. How you wore your hair clothes apparently mattered a lot to the Tây Sơn. Attire certainly mattered to the Qing government. In the end, Vietnamese clothing and hairstyle helped to seal Lun's grim fate. Of course, piracy was a capital crime under Qing law, but during the 1790s foreign dress aggravated the crime's severity. Worried about the security threat that pirate collusion with the Vietnamese posed to their southern maritime provinces, the imperial court declared that any Chinese pirate arrested in "foreign" attire would be executed by slow slicing, summarily and without review (Murray 1987, 45). Lun could jettison his clothes, but the hair presented a problem, for every Chinese male knew that he must wear the Manchu queue or suffer execution. The marooned pirate understood this. "Fearing interrogation by others *because of his long hair* (italics added)," the stranded Lun immediately "used his own knife to cut [his] hair to half its original length" (Jiao Xun 1672, 116). Many pirates wore long hair, but the governor's report specifies that Lun married a Vietnamese wife and kept long hair according to "local" or native custom, not pirate norms (Ruan 1820, 2: 8). Another pirate, Liang Guixing, actually bore a chop that bore the words "allowed to grow hair" (*xuyou toufa* 蓄有頭髮; Murray 1987, 36). So this was no pirate hairstyle. What then did it signify?

The fact that Lun Guili wore Vietnamese attire does not mean that he had integrated into Vietnamese society. Even during the chaotic decades of civil wars, governments implemented policies that sought to control Chinese immigration to Vietnam, their status, and the terms of their integration into Vietnamese society. Chinese who sought to live in Vietnam during the 1790s had to choose from one of two options. In the first option, they could live in one of the many expatriate enclaves established in or near the country's key trading centers. Following precedent, the Tây Sơn government named these people *Đường Nhân*—in Chinese *Tangren* 唐人, meaning "Tang people"— while their rival Nguyễn Ánh changed the term to *Thanh nhân*—or "Qing people," *Qingren* 清人. People like Lun who opted to become subjects of a Vietnamese monarch, however, had to follow the second option and seek permission to join one of the country's Ming Loyalist or Minh Hương villages.

Who were the Minh Hương? The group first appeared in Vietnam during the mid-1600s, when Chinese merchant colonies across Asia began to assimilate Chinese exiles of China's Ming dynasty, which had fallen to Qing conquerors in 1644. The name "Minh Hương (in Chinese 明香)" literally means "Ming incense," and refers to the loyalty they maintained toward their vanished emperor. Some of these loyalists settled in central and southern Vietnam, where they offered their allegiance to the Vietnamese sovereign, who settled them in separate Minh Hương villages (*Minh Hương xã* 明香社)" located in or near the important seaports of his domain. Allowed to marry Vietnamese, the group quickly metamorphosed into a bureaucratic-merchant elite and, within a few generations, a distinct Sino-Vietnamese ethnicity.

Minh Hương evolved within the same maritime milieu as their Vietnamese rebel and Chinese criminal cousins. On the one hand, they were largely integrated into Vietnamese society through intermarriage. On the other hand, they remained embedded within Chinese society through kinship, marriage, native place, occupational guilds, and other institutions that spanned the Asian maritime. They used their ambiguous identity to their advantage, capturing powerful positions in Vietnamese government, diplomacy, and economy and dominating Vietnamese seaborne trade. Enterprises like trade and shipbuilding in which they prevailed made their interactions with pirates and smugglers inevitable. At the same time, Minh Hương lived among Vietnamese, fought with them throughout the Tây Sơn war, and exerted a profound influence on the war's outcome. Geographically speaking, all three inhabited the same port cities of the Vietnamese Tongking Gulf—the same place that one Qing official identified as the "rat hole" of Chinese piracy in the 1790s (Wei Yuan, quoted in Li 1976, 5). But they were also part of a much larger set of seaborne social currents that structured a "submerged history" of long-term continuity that periodically inspired "conspicuous histories" of market shifts, littoral warfare, political upheaval, and predatory entrepreneurship. Somewhere in this messy mix we find social groups with ambiguous identifies and ambidextrous cultural functions. Here we find the most important agents of change, at least in the case of Vietnamese history. The Minh Hương were exactly this sort of people. The Minh Hương evolved from these social currents. From them, rebellion, apocalypse, and political revolution came to Vietnam. Thanks to them, merchants became pirates, pirates became generals, and a new era in Vietnamese history unfolded.

For Chinese like Lun, there were many good reasons to join a Minh Hương village. Many Chinese did. The communities developed during the 1600s, when Ming loyalists organized their maritime resistance against the conquering Qing dynasty (Salmon 2003). When the Qing finally defeated them in 1683, recalcitrant loyalists migrated from their old base on Taiwan to Cochinchina, a *de facto* kingdom in southern Vietnam ruled by Nguyễn Ánh's ancestors during the seventeenth and eighteenth centuries (Chen 1960, 449–450, 454). There, they joined "tens of thousands" who had previously migrated there and settled in the Chinese seaport towns along the Vietnamese coast (Yu Jin 1669, 2: 37). The towns began to assume a Ming loyalist or "Minh Hương" identity around 1651. By 1698, a network of Minh Hương villages spanned southern Vietnam, and the Nguyễn lords of Cochinchina incorporated them into their state (Wheeler 2015).

During their formative years at the end of the seventeenth century, Minh Hương vassals extracted a host of privileges from their new Nguyễn lord that transformed their identity from political exiles into an elite class of foreign trading merchants, royal bureaucrats, and cultural authorities within Vietnamese state and society. At the peak of their power in the eighteenth century, the Minh Hương enjoyed a set of political privileges that included the right to hold positions of state and nobility and to intermarry with Vietnamese—just like Lun Guili, Chen Tianbao, and the other Chinese pirate-admirals of the Tây Sơn did. But that isn't all. Minh enjoyed the right to own land, to run Cochinchina's ports and their customs, and to govern the foreign merchant community. They also continued to enjoy status within the kingdom's expatriate Chinese communities, giving them access to the important institutions of Chinese trade in Cochinchina. As a consequence, their combined privileges exceeded those held by both Vietnamese and Chinese in the kingdom. Such privileges made the Minh Hương quite wealthy and powerful as a merchant-bureaucratic elite and cross-cultural broker between Vietnamese and Chinese societies and states. Their stake lay firmly anchored in Vietnamese interests, however. Ambitious Minh Hương invested their energies into advancing along Vietnamese, not Chinese, hierarchies: many in Lun's day held high-ranking bureaucratic and military positions in both the Tây Sơn and Nguyễn states. Many become well-respected scholars and poets in the Vietnamese community. Some served as diplomats to the Qing court, and in one case Minh Hương served as intelligence gatherers.[4] The people of the Minh Hương community were essential insiders, to two worlds, the Chinese and Vietnamese, not just one.

The Minh Hương also developed a distinct a Sino-Vietnamese culture, which had a lot to do with their open membership. Minh Hương maintained their identity as political exiles. However, in order to join a Minh Hương village, a person had to be Chinese and male; no proof of Minh loyalist ancestry was necessary. Intermarriage exerted an even greater influence, it seems. This greatly changed the community's ethnic content, even if they maintained their identity as political exiles. Culturally, the community integrated so intimately with Vietnamese society that they took on the attributes of a creole-like, Sino-Vietnamese ethnicity. As a result, Minh Hương assimilated many facets of Vietnamese culture thanks to intermarriage—including language and dress (Choi 2004, 38). This would explain why Qing interrogators described their turncoat prisoners like Lun as dressed in "Vietnamese" attire.

From the perspectives of Chinese pirates and Tây Sơn leaders, Minh Hương membership would have created a powerful incentive to join the rebels. Membership meant wealth and power to a man like Lun Guili, and a lot of it. Many Chinese wished to join a Minh Hương village—so why wouldn't a powerful pirate leader? This would have catapulted them from the lowest rungs and furthest margins of Chinese society to the apex of Vietnamese social and political hierarchies. He could transform himself into a respectable man, like many Chinese pirates of the past, like the pirates who joined the ranks of his enemy, Nguyễn Ánh. Membership offered opportunities for great wealth and political power, maybe enough to risk death by slow cuts. What better incentive could there have been to submit himself to a Vietnamese monarch and assume the harmless mantle of Ming loyalty?

The Minh Hương functioned as a group that interconnected with both Chinese and Vietnamese networks of loyalty through temple bonds—of clan, religion, and even loyalty to a long-dead dynasty. This produced an identity that shifted—not only for individual Minh Hương, but also for those who have observed them. This made them effective brokers of wealth, power, and culture within the larger Chinese world order. What produced them? The best place to begin is in Asia's eastern littoral, in the "social fields of the sea"—as both Jennifer Cushman and Fernand Braudel described it (Braudel 1972; Cushman 1993).

Charting the Streams of Collective Destiny

The Minh Hương of Vietnam evolved within the same human ecology that produced the so-called Chinese pirates of the South China Sea. Chinese pirate fleets anchored in the seaports of the Tongking Gulf, especially in the sites within Guangdong and central Vietnam where most Minh Hương and their ancestors lived or had lived. Reviewing this maritime environment and its long-term history recreates the context within which the intermingling societies of Minh Hương and Chinese pirates evolved. This may shed light on the ways in which the community may have enabled the Sino-Vietnamese pirates that plagued South China at the end of the eighteenth century.

Geographically speaking, the people of Lun Guili's world developed from two streams of maritime transhumance that ran along the coast of southern China and converged at the center of what today is called Vietnam. To find the first of these streams, draw a broad line across a map of Asia: Start from the Korean Straits, pass through the Strait of Taiwan and stop at the center point of Vietnam's "S"-shaped coast. Along this stream, sea ships moved commerce between Northeast, Southeast and South Asia and the world beyond. Most of these ships were Chinese, the majority of them from Fujian province that faced the Taiwan Strait, and for whom this long stream had become their commercial and social "fields of the sea" (Cushman 1993). Sailing along this ocean stream, ships anchored at major seaports along the South China coast, intersecting with an even greater streams of inter-coastal trade that integrated China's coastal urban centers. From Guangzhou, the southernmost of these centers, the great stream continued, tracing the coast until it reached Hainan Island.

At Hainan, the stream then split in two, and passed around the northern and southern ends of the Tonking Gulf. Ocean-going vessels turned south and sailed along Hainan's east coast until they reached the island's southern tip. From there, ships hopped across the open sea to Vietnam's central coast. For the sake of convenient reference—and solely for convenience—I will call this long stream between Fujian and central Vietnam "the Fujian Stream." While ocean vessels took the Fujian Stream, coasters continued west, squeezed between Hainan's north shore and the Leizhou Peninsula, and continued along the coast of the northern Tongking Gulf. We will call this coastal stream the Tongking Stream. Ships followed the shore's slow arc from west to south as they passed from Chinese into Vietnamese jurisdiction, meeting the Fujian Stream at the strategic shipping island of Culao Cham along Vietnam's Central Coast.

Merchant Chen helps us to understand how these two streams shaped circulation in the following 1775 interview by a Vietnamese official named Lê Quý Đôn:

> Then I asked, what is the lay of the sea routes? He responded: The sea routes are like the rim of a frypan. Hainan Island . . . is exactly in the pan's center . . . so that everyone can move quickly and remain close. (Lê Quý Đôn 1776, 233)

From here, both coasters and ocean vessels continued on into Southeast Asia, into the Chinese "water frontier" in the Gulf of Thailand (Cooke 2004).

In this area that Merchant Chen defined as "the pan," piracy perennially thrived. At the place where the Fujian and Tongking streams converged, coastal and oceanic ships merged and hugged the coast in order to avoid the dangerous shoals of the Paracels. This effectively concentrated coasters and ocean vessels into a single stream along one of the world's largest sea-lanes, which made them ready prey for the people who lived along the coast. Some form of maritime predation has thus thrived here for at least two millennia (Wheeler 2010). Robert Antony and Li Qingxin have begun to document piracy for the Tongking Gulf's northern waters in more recent times (Antony 2003; Niu Junkai and Li Qingxin 2011). While early piracy in the region has yet to be well documented, there are clear signs that military conflict typically took the form of naval battle and raids bent on plunder (Wheeler 2010), displaying characteristics that resemble a political economy of chiefdoms driven in large part by plunder that was similar in other parts of Southeast Asia (eg., Hall 1985; Junker 1999).

The piracy crisis that spanned the turn of the nineteenth century represents one among many reiterations of Asian piracy and smuggling in which central Vietnam played a role. Maritime predation and contraband commerce were as familiar to the people of the coastal stream as they were to the people of Fujian Stream—two societies with a long history of social interaction. From this, we can begin to understand the genesis of the Minh Hương and that of the so-called Chinese pirates of the Tây Sơn war two centuries later.

Vietnamese elites took advantage of the upsurge in piracy during the 1500's in order to expand their coastal power. For first Lord of Cochinchina, it became his path to dynastic power that would last for three centuries. His behavior reflected not only the long-term patterns of the coastal world he governed, but that of other coastal elites across littoral East and Southeast Asia. He forged alliances with many of the Fujianese armed traders who began to use central Vietnam as an offshore base where they could conduct trade between Japan and China (Li 1998, Chapter 3). They were part of a large informal commercial economy in which fleets of armed traders collaborated with a dense network of local fisherfolk, officials, elites, and merchants that penetrated the Chinese coast, as Lin Renchuan showed (Lin 1987; Lin 1990). Again, Lord Hoàng imitated a common pattern in sixteenth century coastal Asia, wherein a local political power offered sanctuary and other perquisites in exchange for services. It was also a pattern common to central Vietnam since long before Vietnamese settled the region (Hall 1985; Wheeler 2006b). While the Nguyễn lord did not depend upon them to provide military services, he did use them to help finance and supply his military endeavors, using commercial means to amass armaments, ships, cash, and other items needed to defeat his political rivals. More importantly, this offshore source of wealth offered the lord a political economy whose source lay offshore, beyond the reach of those who would try to prevent his attempt to create an autonomous domain. In this way, Nguyễn Hoàng had more in common with commercial warlords and entrepreneurial elites in places like Satsuma and Kyushu in southern Japan and China's south-coastal provinces.

The identity of the pirates, the privateers, and merchants was never very clear. All of them seemed to operate as some form of "military entrepreneur" or another (Gallant 1999; van Schendel and Abraham 2005), using military means to reach their commercial ends, or commerce (whatever its legal status) to realize political goals. This behavior would not have been inconsistent with the long history of "trade and raid" culture that characterizes the region's boat culture since prehistoric times.

As the political climate in China worsened in the 1600s, the Sino-Vietnamese water world once again turned chaotic and violent. This also led to the rise of another commercial warlord who, in his attempt to create an independent Chinese state at sea, set in motion a series of events that produced the Minh Hương of Vietnam.

The Manchu destruction of the Ming dynasty exerted a profound effect on commerce and politics in maritime East Asia. China's collapse led to the confederation of merchant, military, and political powers under the Ming Loyalist banner of Zheng Chenggong. Part merchant, part pirate, part warrior, the great militarized entrepreneur was literally a child of this growing transoceanic society, and grew to oversee a massive international maritime trade empire, making him well-suited to attempt building a Chinese political order at sea. In order to create a sustainable political economy, Zheng launched embassies to overseas countries like Cochinchina to establish trade relations and organized a system of merchants dedicated to nurturing intersea commerce, and fleets to both protect them and also destroy competitors. Zheng confederates soon dominated Chinese merchant enclaves all over maritime Asia, and occupied the strategic islands from which his "generals"—client military entrepreneurs, really—patrolled the South China Sea routes. Along this route, Zheng fleets bottled up major seaport areas like Longmen and the Pearl River Delta, perhaps to channel contraband commerce toward their merchant fleets, with the help of a covert network of fisherfolk, officials, gentry, and monks controlled by the family of the Qing emperor's viceroy (Peng 1957, 7–12). They used violence to enforce their own system of taxation and "permits" in the seas between Japan and Southeast Asia, and dealt ruthlessly with competitors. Several Zheng confederates occupied the ports and offshore islands in the Tongking Gulf zone; many of them operated simultaneously in the Longmen and Dong Nai areas, at the northern and southern ends of the Tongking region; many also, when faced with defeat, refused to forsake their Ming clothing or shave their heads, and fled to Vietnam, like the so-called pirates of the Tây Sơn era a century later.

One of these so-called generals was a privateer named Yang Yandi (in Vietnamese Dương Ngạn Địch) 楊彥迪. From his base in Longmen near the Vietnamese border in western Guangdong (now Guangxi), Yang's fleet patrolled the waters that flowed around, and beyond, the Tongking Gulf "frying pan," from Guangdong to the Gulf of Siam—in other words, the Tongking Gulf Region. As Zheng fortunes waned in 1670s, Yang and his confederates turned to outright raiding (Hayashi 17th c., 1: 327, 338, 351, 367, 398, 422, 439). He and other marauders from the northern gulf like Chen Shangchuan (陳上川, in Vietnamese Trần Thượng Xuyên) and Mo Jiu (莫九, better known by the Vietnamese transliteration of his name, Mạc Cửu) quickly emerged as important power brokers in the "water frontier" between the Mekong and

Siam, using strategies that would not have seemed all that out of place to armed traders or commercial warlords of centuries past. When the Qing navy forced Yang and his 200 ships to abandon their base in Longmen in 1682, the privateer simply moved his base "downstream," to the region of Dong Nai or Nong Nai at the mouth of the Saigon and Mekong rivers. When the Ming loyalists under the Zheng clan lost their last stronghold on Taiwan to the Qing the following year, these military entrepreneurs already forged an alliance with the Nguyễn court that would culminate in Vietnam's Minh Hương community (Wheeler 2015). Longmen had shifted from just beyond the northern frontier of the Vietnamese coastal highway to the southern frontier, a fact that historians do not perceive because it also migrates from one national history to another: from Chinese to Vietnamese.

When the Zheng regime collapsed in 1683, self-identified Minh Hương were already deeply invested in Cochinchinese commerce, state, and society. In addition to their intermediary role in sea trade and control of state customs, they staffed the Nguyễn bureaucracy and often acted as cultural, religious, and diplomatic intermediaries, both within Cochinchina as well as China and Japan—all countries that lay along the Fujian Stream (Wheeler 2007, 307–315). By the end of the 1600s, the Ming Loyalist communities (or *Minh Hương xã*) extended into the Cochinchina's own water frontier, which stretched from the Mekong Delta to the Gulf of Thailand's coast. Their influence spanned beyond the Vietnamese world into maritime Asia, through the two ocean streams that connected it, thanks to their control of the flow of rice and other commodities. They utilized their extensive and intricate networks of loyalty in order to control trade between Vietnam and the outside world, especially Siam, the Tongking Gulf, and the major ports of the South China coast. They provided both Cochinchina and Chinese governments with intelligence (e.g., Lê Quý Đôn 1776, 1:103; Wills 2001) and dominated the diplomatic discourse between the two states. In Hà Tiên, they operated as an autonomous entity under the Mạc clan, who settled there after winning Nguyễn patronage in 1700, and became a powerful intermediary in Siamese-Vietnamese relations during the eighteenth century (Chen 1979, 1536). Out of this milieu of armed traders came a new and powerful merchant-bureaucratic elite.

Cochinchina's Minh Hương community reached the peak of its power in the 1700s. Then suddenly, they played the initial hand in their own destruction, and the decimation of their ancestor's adopted country. In central Vietnam, which the Tây Sơn controlled for nearly three decades, Minh Hương leaders resurrected their villages, some of which had been destroyed during the initial phase of the war between 1771 and 1775, most notably the key shipping center of Hội An.[5] The Tây Sơn reaffirmed Minh Hương status and privilege as it existed during the Cochinchinese era, and apparently extended the system into the old territory of Tonking in the north (Trần Bá Chí 1992). The same holds true for the villages of the South or Mekong region, where Minh Hương were most numerous (Choi 2004: 38). After their initial decimation at the hands of Tây Sơn soldiers in 1778, Minh Hương communities quickly resurrected. When Nguyễn Ánh finally secured permanent power over the Mekong region and formed a government in Saigon in 1789, he fully restored the political and commercial status of Minh Hương, and placed individuals in high positions within his government and military. After all, he had to; they controlled the rice. Whatever the long-term outcome, Minh Hương had fully regained their powerful position as the broker between Vietnam and its maritime neighbors.

Complicating Case Scenarios from the Fujian Stream

Once we look at this world through the prism of Minh Hương society, and the ocean streams that created them, we see that their role in the Tây Sơn conflict was far more significant than anyone has realized or acknowledged. This challenges basic tenets of Vietnamese national history, all the while demonstrating the stream-shaped geography of the ocean region that created both of them. Three pirates illustrate this well. The first two examples profile Li Cai and Ji Ting, who lived in Cochinchina before the Tây Sơn uprising began and helped the early rebels to transform their local rebellion into a massive cataclysm. One of these Sino-Vietnamese Minh Hương merchants met his end while still embroiled in this political struggle, although he did so as a turncoat against the Tây Sơn. The other merchant, however, died as a pirate. The third profile describes a man who began his career as a pirate before he migrated to Vietnam in the middle of the Tây Sơn war. Instead of joining the Tây Sơn, he offered his services to their enemy and the war's ultimate victor, Nguyễn Ánh.

Li Cai and Ji Ting

Li Cai 李才 (Vietnamese Lý Tài, alias Li Azhi 李阿智) helped start the Tây Sơn Uprising. Typical among Minh Hương, Li was Fujianese. According to available biographical sources,[6] he migrated from Fujian to Hội An in order to work as a merchant. He must have been successful, because he reportedly conducted business with important members of the seaport's Minh Hương leadership there. This being the case, Li may have belonged to a Minh Hương commune before he encountered theTây Sơn, if not in Hội An than elsewhere. While the timing remains unclear, sometime before 1771 he moved to Qui Nhơn. Soon after, he helped spread disaster throughout the Vietnamese-speaking world.

In 1771 the three Nguyễn brothers launched their uprising in the hills west of Qui Nhơn. Two years later, they seized the port city. According to Vietnamese court historians of the nineteenth century, the brothers, once traders themselves, won the support of the port town's "Qing merchants 清商" (ĐNTL 178). At some point during the next year and a half, Tây Sơn leader Nguyễn Văn Huệ recruited Li and another Hội An merchant named Ji Ting (Tập Đình 集亭) to mobilize a Chinese land and naval force that they could lead north in a combined offensive with theTây Sơn; one aimed at overthrowing the Nguyễn lord of Cochinchina. Like Lun Guili, Ji Ting came from Chaozhou Prefecture in Guangdong. Like Li Cai, he migrated to Vietnam in order to become a merchant, not a pirate, travelling there in 1759 and settling in the port city of Qui Nhơn. He too appears to have been successful, and made friends with other merchants from Chaozhou and Huizhou prefectures in Guangdong. By the time the Tây Sơn seized Qui Nhơn in 1773, the town's Chinese merchants reportedly regarded Ji as their leader. This would explain why the Tây Sơn approached him to raise an army and navy. According to a report to the Qing Grand Council, Tây Sơn's brother Nguyễn Nhạc "hired Chinese Li Aji 李阿集 and Li Azhi 李阿智," AKA Ji Ting and Li Cai, "gave them official titles, and asked them to manage their navies and ships" in the northern offensive against the Nguyễn lord. Li and Ji began at once to mobilize, with the help of the Chinese community. Ji's named his force the Trung Nghĩa or Loyal and Righteous Army (忠義軍); Li's became known as the Hoa Nghĩa or Harmonious and Righteous Army (和義軍; GZYGX 655).

In May–June 1775, Li Cai and Ji Ting joined the Tây Sơn, and together they launched an amphibious advance north against the Nguyễn king of Cochinchina. For the first time in the dynasty's history, Nguyễn defenses fell into disarray and retreated, all the way to the kingdom's main seaport, Hội An. Disasters began to compound for the Nguyễn court. Hearing the news of the Nguyễn defeat, the Trịnh 鄭 lords of the rival Vietnamese state

of Tonking (*Đàng Ngoài* 塘外 or *Đông Kinh* 東京) seized their historic opportunity to destroy their longtime rival. They invaded Cochinchina, swept
south and snatched the Nguyễn capital Phú Xuân (near today's Huế). The
Nguyễn armies began to collapse. The royal court fled by boat to the distant
South. Two Nguyễn princes stayed behind and, with the support of another expatriate (or "Qing") Chinese merchant they raised an army to defend
Hội An against the coming Tây Sơn in advance. Their resistance held for two
months, but finally crumbled (*ĐNTL* 185). Trịnh and Tây Sơn forces met at
the Hai Vân Pass north of the port city, and the two sides settled on a kind
of detente. Ten years later, however, the Tây Sơn toppled the Trịnh, too. The
rebels controlled nearly all of Vietnam. Soon, however, the lone survivor of
fallen Nguyễn house, Nguyễn Ánh, returned to seek his revenge, and by 1802
destroyed the Tây Sơn and "restored" the Nguyễn house, but not before millions died of violence, starvation, and disease.

Li and Ji clearly influenced this convulsive event in Vietnamese history.
But their role was brief. Nguyễn Nhạc held Ji Ting responsible for the Tây
Sơn failure to advance against the Trịnh, so he removed Ji from leadership and
placed Li Cai in command of all Chinese forces, which Li banded together
into a single Hoa Nghĩa Army (Choi 2004, 36). Ji Ting fled to Guangdong,
and was later arrested by Qing officials as a pirate (*Qing Gaozong Shilu*, 996:
12–13; 998: 15–16; 999: 6–7; 1004: 31; *GZYGX* 1982: 656; Li 1976, 4). Li's
fortunes held out a little bit longer than his compatriot. With Ji gone, Li now
presided over an army that comprised nearly two-thirds of the entire Tây Sơn
military. Most of the Tây Sơn army, in other words, comprised Chinese, as the
missionary Labartette claimed. By the end of the year, however, Li Cai turned
on his Tây Sơn overlord, fled south and surrendered to a Nguyễn general
(Zheng Guangnan 2001, 26). Li arrived in time to help the Nguyễn repel the
Tây Sơn's first attack on Gia Định in 1776. Sources state that Li organized the
"Tang" Chinese colonists in the Mekong into a defending army, and specifically cites the role of both Minh Hương communities there (Zheng Guangnan 2001, 27, 28f63). Apparently, his betrayal proved so upsetting to the Tây
Sơn brothers that when they finally succeeded in seizing Gia Định in 1777,
they unleashed their soldiers against the Chinese populations in and around
Gia Định, massacring thousands (Choi 2004, 36). Soon after, Li died in a duel
with a pro-Nguyễn rival/ally (Dutton 2006, 202).

One finds no evidence that Li had ever been a pirate. The same cannot be
said for Ji, however. The official history of the Qing dynasty reports that, in

1776, Qing officers arrested two Chinese pirates, Ou Shengzu 歐盛祖 and Wang Sihai 王四海, in Fujian. Both of them confessed that they were accomplices of Ji Ting. Among their possessions, investigators found a Bình Định Jade Talisman (平定玉符) that belonged to Ji, clearly a gift that he received from his former Tây Sơn overlords. In another memorial submitted to the Qianlong Emperor, a Qing general reported that he had arrested several "pirates" and confiscated their properties. Interrogating their chief, Hong Ahan 洪阿漢, he discovered that the Tây Sơn had offered Li Aji 李阿集, AKA Ji Ting, an official title, a bribe, and a Vietnamese wife (Xu Wentang 2001, 5). Ji, whom sources consistently identify as a Qing subject, accepted (No such evidence exists for Li). While the Tây Sơn did not organize a deliberate campaign to raid China using Chinese pirates until 1792, the strategy to recruit Chinese pirate leaders began with Ji Ting and Li Cai nearly two decades earlier. In fact, it catalyzed a local rebellion into the cataclysm that decimated Vietnam. The move fit into a larger pattern that encouraged collaboration between coastal warlords and seaborne merchants *cum* pirates that dates back millennia on the Vietnamese central coast. These pirates came from one of the two streams that shaped Vietnamese society: one coastal and the other partly overseas. Most importantly, they raise questions about the conventional depiction of the Tay Uprising as a proto-nationalist, proto-revolutionary movement inspired by, and largely fought by, Vietnamese. Expanding the spatial context and then placing the pirates in a clearly defined set of transhumance patterns, derived from the human ecology of the South China Sea, reveal this.

He Xiwen (Hà Hỷ Văn) 何喜文

Mo Guanfu, like most of the pirates, joined the pirate cause, Tây Sơn vassalage and Minh Hương community in Vietnam well into the civil war. Mo, another Cantonese from eastern Guangdong along the Fujian Stream, arrived in Vietnam in 1788. In that year, a Chinese Ministry of Justice report states:

> Annan [Tây Sơn] chief commander Chen Tianbao (Trần Thiên Bảo 陳添保) persuaded the culprit Mo Guanfu (Mạc Quan Phù 莫觀扶), Zheng Qi (Trịnh Thất 鄭七) and others to surrender and pledge allegiance to [Tây Sơn-led] Annan. The Annan government bestowed the title of chief commander to both Mo Guanfu and Zheng Qi, and asked them to fight against Nông Nai 農耐 [the Tây Sơn's enemy, Nguyễn Ánh]. The culprit did not get along well with the foreign [Vietnamese] officials, so he went out to the

sea again to rob. By the first year of Jiaqing [1796], he had already robbed seventeen big and small ships in succession, and had recruited more than 1000 pirates. He fought with Fujianese pirate Huang Shengchang 黃勝長, and killed more than 600 pirates on Huang's ships. Realizing the culprit's skill and bravery, the [Tây Sơn] Vietanmese government bestowed on him the title of Lord of Donghai (Đông Hải 東海王), and kept him [in Vietnam] to fight against [the Nguyễn kingdom of] Nông Nại. In the sixth year of Jiaqing [1801], the culprit was caught by Nông Nại navies on the sea of Phú Xuân 富春 [near Hue] together with Liang Wengeng [Lương Văn Canh 梁文庚]. Nine ships in total were caught."[7]

By 1796, the Nguyễn regime of Đồng Nai or Nông Nại had begun to win the upper hand in the civil war after it seized the strategic port city of Qui Nhon. By 1801, the Tây Sơn leaders were all dead, and the war was over. After they established diplomatic relations with China, the victorious Nguyễn Ánh handed Mo and his confederates over to the Qing government in China, which executed Mo by slow slicing.

I have included this passage here because the arresting officer in this passage was a man named He Xiwen—pronounced *Hà Hỷ Văn* in Vietnamese.[8] Vietnamese historians paint the collaboration with Chinese pirates as entirely the work of the Tây Sơn. This is not true. Plenty of evidence demonstrates that many men from the same two streams that produced the better-known Chinese pirates allied with the Nguyễn instead of the Tây Sơn. He Xiwen demonstrates this because He, despite having died an immortalized hero, was a pirate.

He Xiwen deserves greater attention in studies of the Sino-Vietnamese piracy crisis of the 1790's. In most ways, his biography resembles those of most other Chinese pirates, except for two significant differences. First, his side won. Second, sources on piracy never mention him, most likely because his side won. As Vietnamese refugees of another civil war two centuries later put it, "only the losers are bandits"—or pirates. Given this moral dimension to Vietnamese historiography, Vietnamese sources do not associate him with piracy at all, and praise him as a great military hero. This is true of all Chinese "admirals" who served the Nguyễn, Minh Hương or not. Having gambled on the victorious faction, brigands like He Xiwen earned credit in posterity as virtuous soldiers and statesmen, to be venerated in imperial histories and local inscriptions for all Vietnamese to celebrate and emulate. Yet he clearly bears all the hallmarks of Gallant's pirate as "military entrepreneur," as many so-called pirates of his day were, judging from his biography.

He Xiwen's nineteenth-century biography contains several clues to his pirate past, despite its hagiographic rhetoric. His story begins in China, in Sichuan province far from the sea. There, he joined a White Lotus band, a Buddhist millenarian school whose uprising threatened the stability of the Qing. For reasons unknown, he somehow migrated to Fujian, where he joined a pirate band that belonged to the Tiandihui secret society and, according to his imperial biographers, "raided the coasts of Fujian and Guangdong" (ĐNLT, 2: 500). In 1786, for reasons unknown, he led his pirate fleet to the island of Pulo Condor. There, he came into contact with Nguyễn Ánh, then at the nadir of his power. The Chinese pirate offered to help, and Nguyễn Ánh accepted. They set sail for Long Xuyên, where Nguyễn Ánh began to recruit other pirate chiefs and plot his return to power (Murray 1987, 187n6). Nguyễn Ánh behaved no differently than his adversary did in his treatment of pirates like He, whom he granted military titles in return for his loyalty and military service. He soon distinguished his fleet in battle, using Pulo Condor as his base of operations from which he repeatedly attacked Tây Sơn fleets. In 1790, "He sent his warships past Qui Nhơn and Thuận Hóa to the North," to Lianzhou in the Tongking Gulf. Once there, they "drew the rebel's sea bandits" into battle, and successfully "brought their twenty-three ships to defeat." Two years later, his fleet led the naval first naval assault on Qui Nhơn, the heart of the Tây Sơn realm, and at the intersection of the coastal and Fujian streams. Thereafter he participated in the Nguyễn offensives that led to their victory over the Tây Sơn in 1801. He supervised the capture of many of his former Chinese compatriots, including many of the Tây Sơn generals we have just reviewed. Then, just as Nguyễn Ánh began to plan his final assault against the Tây Sơn , He suddenly "grew ill and died among his army." The king, "who loved him dearly, was forever full of regret" at this loss, and bestowed many honors on He and his family.

Nguyễn Ánh clearly loved his Chinese vassal. After victory over the Tây Sơn was complete, and he declared the new Nguyễn dynasty. Nguyễn Ánh, now the Gia Long Emperor, placed He's fleet in charge of the empire's coastal defense, "because of [He's] accomplishments in building such a powerful fleet" (ĐNLT, 2: 501). His family continued to play a role in Nguyễn government, including his son, Hà [Hỷ] Dương (C: He Xiyang 何喜揚), who served as the Superintendent of Chinese Shipping, or Cai phủ Tàu (該府艚), a position traditionally reserved for members of the Minh Hương community.

At the very least, He Xiwen's biography suggests that a more nuanced as-
sessment of the relationship between Vietnamese combatants and Chinese
pirates is in order. However extensive his relationship to Chinese pirates may
have been, Nguyễn Ánh's collaboration with them reflects a pattern of behavior that was millennia old in the Sino-Vietnamese water world. Such collaboration was more the norm than the exception, in other words. In her study
of Sino-Vietnamese piracy, Diane Murray reports that a number of pirates
captured in 1796 and 1797 bore seals given to them by Nguyễn Ánh (Murray
1987, 188n6). One wonders how many more of these profiles could be located in the Chinese imperial archives.

It should also be noted that Tây Sơn leaders worked against pirates when
different circumstances favored it. Qing court records reports a case in 1790,
in which Tây Sơn court officials sent their king a letter while he was visiting
China to celebrate the emperor Qianlong's birthday, to inform him that pirates from Vietnam had raided the ships of Cantonese fishermen Chen Zhao-
qiu 陳朝球 and others, in the Tongking Gulf (AKA Beibu wan 北部灣). A
Tây Sơn official named Phạm Quang Chương 范光章 successfully attacked
the pirates and released Chen and his fellow fishermen's ships. Emperor Qianlong praised Phạm and bestowed him with a length of satin in gratitude.
"Phạm Quang Chương's act of hunting down and cleaning up the pirates
. . . is truly laudable," the emperor wrote" (*Qing shilu,* Qianlong 55 (1790),
cited in Li Guangtao, 215). By the time this event occurred, the Tây Sơn had
already recruited the first of its pirates, Chen Tianbao. Alternating attitudes
toward pirates reflects a norm, not only in Sino-Vietnamese piracy, but piracy
throughout world history. Actually it was a strategy common to all coastal
power elites throughout the Asian littoral.

These curious "Chinese pirates" could tell us a lot about the functioning of
society in the Tongking Gulf region and its impact on political convulsions
in Vietnamese history like the Tây Sơn war, in ways that take us well beyond the typical nationalist theses. Most curious is their relationship with the
Minh Hương. Both groups lived along the Vietnamese littoral, but circulated
throughout a much wider region defined largely by the two streams outlined
here. In fact, their movements follow patterns that can really only be understood through regional models that in this case have yet to be built. As we have
seen, expatriate Chinese and Minh Hương merchants supported the Tây Sơn

rebellion in its early years. (In fact, the most surprising finding for Vietnamese historians will be the fact that maritime predators empowered the rise to
power of both the Tây Sơn brothers and Nguyễn Ánh, that is, Li Cai, Ji Ting
and He Xiwen.) Their support continued thereafter. This support necessarily
included the Chinese pirate-admirals. Geographically speaking, it is hard to
imagine how such large fleets could have avoided the country's largest merchant class, who monopolized shipping and trade in the very country where
they most likely fenced most of their stolen goods. Moreover, piracy was seasonal, and pirates like their merchant counterparts spent portions of the year
anchored in safe haven, which in this case meant the "rat hole" of Vietnam's
central coast, where Minh Hương lived and worked. The patterns remained
the same in both the 1600s and 1700s. The "logic" of their movements justify
the utility of a Tongking Gulf Region for fleshing out hitherto hidden history
in the largely invisible history of the Sino-Vietnamese water world along the
South China Sea's western littoral.

Large-scale piracy of the kind that developed during the 1790s in the waters of Vietnam and China required a large investment of capital to launch
and sustain. It was a large economic enterprise, in other words, that fed from
oceanic streams. Large pirate fleets grappled with the same challenges that any
large and complex organization faced, as David Starkey points out. Throughout world history, "substantial investments were needed to mount large-scale,
deep-water ventures" of the kind mobilized by the Chinese pirates described
above. The capital necessary "to purchase and equip vessels, procure armaments and provisions, and recruit labor came in some cases from legitimate
mercantile and government sources." Algerian merchants funded Turkish cor-
sairs, and American colonial governors backed Atlantic buccaneers (Starkey
1994, 115–116). Both Tây Sơn and Nguyen regimes patronized, protected,
and funded Chinese pirates (AKA armed traders or military entrepreneurs),
and Minh Hương were a part of both states (as they were a century before).

The key to understanding the role of the Minh Hương in the economy of
the Tongking Gulf zone (and South China Sea zone at large) may lie in the
routine of pirate economy. Underneath the pirate's age-old alternative job as
privateer, the work of capturing and redistributing goods continued, as it did
every raiding season. If they did not rely on merchants for cash, they certainly
depended upon them for supplies and redistribution, i.e. fencing goods. Here
we find the Minh Hương as an unavoidable intermediary. Soon after he seized
Gia Định in 1789, for example, Nguyễn Ánh discovered that he could not

import rice from Siam to supply his troops unless he went through the Minh Hương community (Choi 2004, 41). The populations of central and northern Vietnam relied heavily upon outside sources of rice; perhaps this explains in part why the Center seaport of Hội An resurrected so quickly, in 1778, only a few years after the rebels razed the city to the ground. One must not forget the role that shipbuilding communities play in the pirate economy, either. Chinese from Fujian encouraged another Chinese piracy crisis in the sixteenth century by "building large-hulled ships out of self interest [私造雙桅大船舵]" and selling them on the black market (Zheng Guangnan 1998, 376–379). Vietnam had become a large source of raw materials for shipbuilding in China by the late 1700's (Wheeler, forthcoming). Perhaps Minh Hương shipbuilders, most of whom claimed Fujianese ancestry, were doing the same (see an example of a shipbuilding family in Chen 1964). As Michael Pearson points out, pirates "are a varied lot." So are the principal agents of their economy. Merchants "were often happy to support piracy in order to acquire dubious, 'hot' goods" in the Indian Ocean (Pearson 2003, 126–127); the same can be said for pirate bands worldwide, throughout history, whether among the ancient Greeks or contemporary Somalis (e.g., Casson 1991; Murphy 2010).[9]

The economics of piracy help blur the lines of identity that state interrogators and present-day historians—with their historically earthbound perspectives—would like to enforce for their own agendas' sake. Their variety makes them hard to categorize, not so much because of their complexity but because the human ecology of the Sino-Vietnamese littoral in which all these people evolved possesses none of the geographical characteristics perceived by the boundary-conscious analysts who study them today. H. A. Ormerod, taking a cue from Aristotle, got it right when he likened the pirate to the nomad, the product of fisherfolk people "who live by hunting." Piracy was in fact a "manifestation" of a region's ecology, a mode of production and redistribution. To Peregrine Horden and Nicholas Purcell, it is "*cabotage* by other means" (Horden and Purcell 2000, 387). Or, as Braudel put it succinctly, simply "a way of making a living" (Braudel 1984). To all of them, this mode of production suggests habitat as much as criminality. Given its dynamic character, the form predation takes can vary constantly in both time and space (Anderson 1995, 194). As occupations varied, so too could identity. In Lun Guili's case we see an example of someone furiously working in vain to shed one identity for another, in response to the geographic and political predicament he faced on the shores of Zhejiang. The greater connectivity of the sea relative to land offered seafarers such advantages. Over time, an identity could quickly adapt to suit new exigencies. We see this in the heritage of the Minh Hương, as they metamorphosed from pirates to armed traders to armed insurgents a merchant-bureaucratic elite, in a way reminiscent of the Swahili of East Africa (e.g., Middleton 1994) or Huguenots of the Atlantic (Bosher 1995).[10] And very much like more familiar pirates documented in the Mediterranean.

And yet this agency unfolded within a specific ecology that created a long-term continuity. One does not perceive this too readily by looking at the Tongk-ing Gulf as a rim, but the faint outlines do appear when one follows the streams on which people and their boats traveled. Chinese pirates, Nguyễn lords, Tây Sơn rebels, and Minh Hương, too—evolved from the same water world where predations functioned intrinsically in everyday life. It thrived when sea com-merce was good, and it thrived when it it was bad. It always adapted, however (Anderson 1995, 181, 185–186). Minh Hương, having descended mostly from men who were at best military entrepreneurs, at worst pirates, understood this ambiguous world, and how to adapt to it in order to prosper within it.

Perhaps the Tongking Gulf best resembles the "narrow seas" into which Braudel divided the Mediterranean; however, looking at the Tongking Gulf from the shipboard up suggests a world whose geography may make more sense as a space of flows. For example, if we only look at small scale, endemic piracy in the gulf, which drew from local elements, the world looks more like a narrow sea. However, large-scale, episodic piracy drew from much wider streams than geography of basins can accommodate. The streams that sus-tained this occupation drew from as far as South China and Thailand, and possibly beyond. Networks of all kinds plugged into this great oceanic river, and from the river, extended far, wide, and deep, into land as well as sea space. If the Mediterranean constitutes a "zone of introversion," as Peregrine Horden has defined it, perhaps this unbounded zone constitutes a zone of extrover-sion. It will take a good deal more work to test such speculation, however. This is especially true with regard to the nature of the sea, where climatic, geophysical, and ecological processes contribute to regional unity more than the human elements overemphasized in most ocean studies (Lambert 2006, 482), not to mention this chapter. If we resist the urge to fit the gulf and its people into a model, and follow Braudel's practice of reconstructing society from the ground—or rather sea—up, then we can begin to perceive patterns quite different in shape and function from the Mediterranean, yet comparable in more fruitful ways to Braudel's visions of the Mediterranean, and to the visions of other ocean bodies.

Notes

1. Antony 2003, 40–41; Chang 1983, 57–59, 66–67, 69, 191; Jiao Xun 1672, 116–117, 118; Liu Ping 1998a; 1998b; Murray 1987, 39–45; Ruan Heng 1820, 1: 9–15; 2:1–14.

2. The full title is "*Thiện tau đội đại thống binh tiến lộc hầu Luân Quý Lợi* 善艚隊 大統兵進祿侯倫貴利." Jiao 1672, 116.

3. In addition to Robert Antony, Chung-shen Chang, George Dutton, and Diane Murray cited above, see also works by Liu Ping, Li Qingxin, and Zheng Guangnan, cited in this article. Chinese studies of piracy have long focused on the great sixteenth-century crisis under the Ming dynasty, but attention surrounding this later episode seems to be growing.

4. Two well-known scholars, diplomats, and court officials who lived during the period under discussion were Trịnh Hoài Đức 鄭懷德 and Trần Tiến Thành 陳踐誠, are both discussed below. In one case, we find the Mạc clan of Hà Tiên, a small island halfway between Vietnam and Siam along the coast of southern Cambodia (now part of Vietnam). Mạc Thiên Tú, the clan leader, supplied the Qing court with "excellent information" that it sought on the political situation in Burma and Siam at the time (Wills 2001).

5. Inscriptions and local documents (now lost) suggest that the Hội An community restored its community by 1778. Chen 1962–63, 14–16; Đào Duy Anh 1943, 253. In the 1790s, the number of registered males in Hội An reached 250, according to the village register. Nguyễn Thieu Lau 1941, 365.

6. Unless otherwise noted, all information in this section comes from Choi, 36–37; *Đại Nam thực lục*, 177–178, 182–185, 187–189; Dutton, 200–201; Murray, 35; Zheng Ruanming, 5–6, 26–33.

7. MQSLGB 1960, 第3本, 211, (刑部「為行在刑部寄到總督覺羅吉等奏」 移會) cited in Xu 2001, 13–14.

8. Information on He Xiwen comes from the following sources, unless otherwise noted: *ĐNLT*, 500–502; *ĐNTL*, 228, 470; Trịnh Hoài Đức c1820, 134; Zheng Ruanming, 19–21.

9. The comparisons between Somalia and Vietnam during the late seventeenth and the late eighteenth centuries are intriguing. For example, the role of weak states in the creation of piracy (Murphy 2010); its close interdependence with smuggling and international finance networks and its influence on market network formations (World Bank 2013: 51–76); and its role in facilitating the movement of rebels, AKA, terrorists (Freeman 2009).

10. Thanks to Alexander Woodside for this suggestion.

References

Abulafia, David. 2005. "Mediterraneans." In *Rethinking the Mediterranean,* ed. W. V. Harris. Oxford: Oxford University Press.

Anderson, J. L. 1995. "Piracy and World History." *Journal of World History* 6 (2): 175–199.

Antony, Robert. 2003. *Like Froth Floating on the Sea.* Berkeley: Institute of East Asian Studies.

Archer, K. 1993. "Regions as Social Organisms: the Lamarckian Characteristics of Vidal de la Blahe's Regional Geography." *The Annals of the Association of American Geographers* 83 (3): 498–514.

Bailyn, Bernard. 1951. "Braudel's Geohistory: a Reconsideration," *Journal of Economic History* 11 (3): 277–282, reprinted in Stuart Clark. 1999. *The Annales School: Critical Assessments.* London: Routledge.

Blank, Paul W. 1999. "The Pacific: A Mediterranean in the Making?" *Geographical Review* 89 (2): 265–277.

Blussé, Leonard. 1999. "Chinese Century: The Eighteenth Century in the China Sea Region." *Archipel* 58: 107–129.

Bose, Sugata. 2006. *A Hundred Horizons: The Indian Ocean in the Age of Global Empire.* Cambridge, MA: Harvard University Press.

Bosher, J. F. 1995. "Huguenot Merchants and the Protestant International in the Seventeenth Century." *The William and Mary Quarterly,* Third Series 52 (1): 77–102.

Braudel, Fernand. 1972. *The Mediterranean and the Mediterranean World in the Age of Philip II.* Vol. 1. New York: Harper & Row.

———. 1984. *The Perspective of the World: Civilization & Capitalism 15th–18th Century.* Volume 3. Trans. Siân Reynolds. New York: Harper & Row.

Braun, David. 2011. "Thawed Arctic Could Be a Sea of Cooperation, Iceland Minister Says." *National Geographic* [online], June 25, 2011. http://newswatch.nationalgeographic.com/2011/06/25/thawed-arctic-could-be-a-sea-of-cooperation-iceland-minister-says/ (accessed November 22, 2011).

Casson, L. 1991. *The Ancient Mariners: Seafarers and Seafighters of the Mediterranean in Ancient Times.* 2nd ed. Princeton: Princeton University Press.

Chang, Chung-shen Thomas. 1983. "Ts'ai Ch'ien, the Pirate King Who Dominates the Seas." Ph.D. thesis, University of Arizona.

Chaudhuri, K. N. 1985. *Trade & Civilisation in the Indian Ocean: An Economic History from the Rise of Islam to 1750.* New York: Cambridge University Press.

Chen Chingho. 1960, 1968. "Qingchu Zheng Chenggong zhibu zhi yizhi [The Migration of the Zheng Partisans to Southern Borders (of Vietnam)]." In *Xinya xuebao* (Singapore) 5(1) (1960): 433–459; 8(2) (1968): 413–486.

Chen Chingho (Trần Kinh Hòa). 1962–1963 "Mấy điều nhận xét về Minh-hương-xã và các cổ-tích tại Hội-an [Some Observations about the Village of Minh-huong and the Monuments at Faifo, Central Vietnam]," *Khảo-cổ tập-san,* 1: 1–33.

Chen Chingho, ed. 1964. *Zhengtian Mingxiangshe Chen shi zheng pu* [A Brief Study of the Family Register of the Trans, A Ming Refugee Family in Minh-Hương ha, Thua-thien (Central Vietnam)]. Hong Kong: University of Hong Kong, Centre of Asian Studies.

Chen Chingho. 1979. "Mac Thien Tu and Phraya Taksin: A Survey of Their Political Stand, Conflicts, and Background." In *Proceedings, Seventh IAHA Conference, 22–26 August 1977*, 1534–1575. Bangkok: Chulalongkorn University Press.

Choi Byung Wook. 2004. *Southern Vietnam under the Reign of Minh Mạng (1820–1841)* Ithaca, NY: Southeast Asia Program Publications, Cornell University.

Cooke, Nola, et al., eds. 2004. *Water Frontier.* Boulder: Rowman and Littlefield.

Cushman, Jennifer. 1993. *Fields from the Sea.* Ithaca, NY: Southeast Asia Program Publications, Cornell University.

Đào Duy Anh. 1943. "Pho-lo, premiere colonie chinois de Thua Thien," *Bulletin des Amis du Vieux Huế* 3: 249–265.

ĐNLT. 1995. *Đại Nam liệt truyền tiền biên* [Biographies of the Eminent in Dai Nam, ancestral edition]. Translated into *Quốc ngữ* and annotated by Tự Thanh Cao et al. Hanoi: Nxb. Khoa học xã hội.

ĐNTL. 2002. *Đại Nam thực luc tiền biên* [The Veritable Records of Đại Nam]. Compiled by the Imperial History Officers of the Nguyễn Court, ca. 1840s. *Quốc ngữ* translation. Hanoi: Nxb. Giáo dục.

Dodds, Klaus. 2010. "A Polar Mediterranean? Accessibility, Resources and Sovereignty in the Arctic Ocean." *Global Policy* 1 (3): 303–311.

Dutton, George. 2006. *The Tây Sơn Uprising: Society and Rebellion in Eighteenth-Century Vietnam.* Honolulu: University of Hawai'i Press.

Fawaz, Leila, and C. A. Bayly, eds. 2002. *Modernity and Culture from the Mediterranean to the Indian Ocean.* New York: Columbia University Press.

Freeman, Colin. 2009. "Pirates 'smuggling al-Qaeda fighters' into Somalia." *The Telegraph* (July 5). http://www.telegraph.co.uk/news/worldnews/piracy/5743328/Pirates-smuggling-al-Qaeda-fighters-into-Somalia.html (accessed December 28, 2014).

Gallant, Thomas. 1999. "Brigandage, Piracy, Capitalism, and State-Formation: Transnational Crime from a Historical World-Systems Perspective." In *States and Illegal Practices,* ed. Josiah McC. Heyman. Oxford: Berg.

Goitein, S. D. 1999. *A Mediterranean Society.* Berkeley: University of California Press.

Guillot, Claude, et al. 1998. *L'horizon nousantarien. Mélanges en homage à Denys Lombard.* 3 vols. Published as *Archipel* 56 (1998), 57 and 58 (1999).

Gulliver, Katrina. 2011. "Finding the Pacific World." *Journal of World History* 22 (1): 83–100.

GZYGX. 1982. *Gudai Zhong-Yue guanxi shi ziliao xuanbian* [Selected Materials on the History of Sino-Vietnamese relations]. Beijing: Zhongguo shehui kexue chubanshe.

Hall, Kenneth. 1985. "The Politics of Plunder in the Cham Realm of Early Vietnam." In *Art and Politics in Southeast Asian History*, ed. Robert van Neil, 5–16. Honolulu: University of Hawai'i Center for Southeast Asian Studies, Southeast Asia Paper no. 32.

Hamashita, Takeshi. 2008. *China, East Asia and the Global Economy: Regional and Historical Perspectives*, ed. Linda Grove and Mark Selden. London: Routledge.

Harris, W. V., ed. 2005. *Rethinking the Mediterranean*. Oxford: Oxford University Press.

Hayashi Razan (17th c.). 1958–1959. *Kai hentai* [The Transformation from Civilized to Barbarian], ed. Ura Ren-ichi. Tokyo: Toyo Bunko.

Herzfeld, Michael. 2005. "Practical Mediterraneans: Excuses for Everything, from Epistemology to Eating." In *Rethinking the Mediterranean,* ed. W. V. Harris, 45–63. Oxford: Oxford University Press.

Horden, Peregrine. 2005. "Mediterranean Excuses: Historical Writing on the Mediterranean since Braudel." *History and Anthropology* 16 (1): 25–30.

Horden, Peregrine, and Nicholas Purcell. 2000. *The Corrupting Sea*. Oxford; Malden, MA: Blackwell, 2000.

———. 2005. "Four Years of 'Corruption': A Response to Critics." In *Rethinking the Mediterranean,* ed. W. V. Harris. Oxford: Oxford University Press.

Jiao Xun 焦循 (19th c.). 1995. "Shenfeng dang kou ji 神風蕩寇記 [A Record of the Destruction of Pirates by Divine Wind]," and"Shenfeng dang kou houji 神風蕩寇後記 [An Afterword on the Destruction of Pirates by Divine Wind]. In *Diaogu ji wenlu* 雕菰集文錄, repr. in *Guochao wenlu xubian* 國朝文錄續編, *juan* 1672. Ed. Li Zutao 李祖陶. Shanghai.

Junker, Laura Lee. 1999. *Raiding, Trading, and Feasting: The Political Economy of Philippine Chiefdoms*. Honolulu: University of Hawai'i Press.

Kulke, Herman. 1999. "Rivalry and Competition in the Bay of Bengal in the Eleventh Century and its Bearing on Indian Ocean Studies." In *Commerce and Culture in the Bay of Bengal, 1500–1800*, ed. Om Prakash and Denys Lombard, 17–36. New Delhi: Manohar Publications.

Labartette. 1775. Letter to M. Boiret, July 21. In *Nouvelles lettres édifiantes*, vol. 6, p. 288. Paris, 1818.

Lambert, David, et al. 2006. "Currents, Visions and Voyages: Historical Geographies of the Sea." *Journal of Historical Geography* 32: 479–493.

Larguéche, Abdelhamid. 2000. "The City and the Sea: Evolving Forms of Mediterranean Cosmopolitanism in Tunis, 1700–1881." In *North Africa, Islam and the Mediterranean World,* ed. Julia Clancy-Smith. London: Frank Cass.

Latour, Bruno. 2010. *On the Modern Cult of Factish Gods*. Durham, NC: Duke University Press.

Lê Quý Đôn. 1776. *Phủ biên tạp lục* [Desultory Record of the Subjugated Border]. *Quốc ngố* translation by Đào Duy Anh Hanoi: NXB Khoa Học Xã Hội, 1977.

Li Guangtao. 1976. *Ji Qianlong nian pingding Annan zhi yi* [An Obligation to Record the Pacification of Vietnam in the Qianlong Years]. Taibei: Zhongyang yanjiuyuan lishi yuyan yanjiusuo.

Liszka, T. R., and L. E. M. Walker. 2001. *The North Sea World in the Middle Ages: Studies in the Cultural History of North-Western Europe.* Dublin: Four Courts Press.

Li Tana. 1998. *Nguyen Cochinchina.* Ithaca, NY: Southeast Asia Program Publications, Cornell University.

Lin Renchuan. 1987. *Mingmo Qingchu siren haishang maoyi* [Self-interested Maritime Trade in the Late Ming and Early Qing]. Shanghai: Huadong shifan daxue chubanshe.

———. 1990. "Fukien's Private Sea Trade in the 16th and 17th Centuries," translated by B. J. ter Haar. In *Development and Decline of Fukien Province in the 17th and 18th Centuries,* ed. E. B. Vermeer, 163–215. Leiden: Brill.

Liu Ping. 1998a. "Guanyu Jiaqing nian di Guangdong haidao di jige wenti [Problems in Guangdong Piracy during the Jiaqing Years]." *Xueshu yanjiu* 9: 78–84.

———. 1998b. "Qing zhongye Guangdong haidao wenti shensuo [The Problem of Mid-Qing Piracy]." *Qingshi yanjiu* 1: 39–49.

Lombard, Denys. 1990. *Le carrefour javanais: Essai d'histoire globale.* 3 vols. Paris: EHESS.

———. 1994. "On the Chinese Mediterranean." In *Asia Maritima: Images et réalité, 1200–1800,* ed. Denys Lombard and Rothermund Ptak. Weisbaden: Harrassowitz Verlag.

———. 1995. "Networks and Synchronisms in Southeast Asian History." *Journal of Southeast Asian Studies* 26 (1): 10–16.

Marino, John A. 2004. "The Exile and His Kingdom: The Reception of Braudel's *Mediterranean.*" *Journal of Modern History* 76: 622–652.

Middleton, John. 1994. *World of the Swahili: An African Mercantile Civilization.* New Haven: Yale University Press.

Murphy, Martin N. 2010. *Small Boats, Weak Sates, Dirty Money: Piracy and Maritime Terrorism in the Modern World.* New York: Columbia University Press.

Murray, Dian H. 1987. *Pirates of the South China Coast, 1790–1810.* Stanford: Stanford University Press.

Nguyễn Thieu Lau. 1941. "La formation et évolution du village su Minh Hương (Faifóo)," *Bulletin des amis du vieux Hué,* 28 (4). 359–367.

Niu, Junkai, and Li Qingxin. 2011. "Chinese 'Political Pirates' in the Seventeenth-Century Gulf of Tongking." In *The Tongking Gulf through History,* ed. Nola Cooke et al., 133–142. Philadelphia: University of Pennsylvania Press.

Pearson, Michael. 2003. *The Indian Ocean.* London: Routledge.

Peng Zeyi. 1957. "Qingdai Guangdong yanghang zhidu di qiyuan [The Origins of Guangdong's Sea Guild System in the Qing Era]." *Lishi yanjiu* I (1): 1–24.

Pérotin-Dumon, Anne. 1991. "The Pirate and the Emperor: Power and the Law on the Seas, 1450–1850." In *The Political Economy of Merchant Empires,* ed. James D. Tracy. 296–227. Cambridge: Cambridge University Press.

Reid, Anthony. 1993. *Southeast Asia in the Age of Commerce*. New Haven: Yale University Press.

Ruan Heng 阮亨 (comp.) 1820. *Yingzhou bidan* 瀛舟筆談 [Writings from Yingzhou] ([China, s.n.], Jiaqing 25), 1: 9–15; 2:1–14.

Salmon, Claudine. 2003. "Réfugiés Ming dans les Mers du sud vus à travers diverses inscriptions (ca. 1650-ca. 1730)." *Bulletin de l'Ecole française d'Extrême-Orient* 90: 177–227.

Spinks, Rosie. 2011. "Arctic Will Become 'More of a Mediterranean than a Frozen Border'." *The Ecologist*, October 19, 2011. http://www.theecologist.org/News/ news_analysis/1092213/arctic_will_become_more_of_a_mediterranean_than_a_ frozen_border.html (accessed November 22, 2011).

Starkey, David J. 1994. "Pirates and Markets." In *The Market for Seamen in the Age of Sail*, ed. Lewis R. Fischer, 59–80. St. John's, Newfoundland: International Maritime Economic History Association.

Sutherland, Heather. 2003. "Southeast Asian History and the Mediterranean Analogy," *Journal of Southeast Asian Studies* 34 (1): 1–20.

Thomson, Janice. 1994. *Mercenaries, Pirates and Sovereigns: State Building and Extraterritorial Violence in Early Modern Europe*. Princeton: Princeton University Press.

Trần Bá Chí. 1992. "Phố cổ Phù Thạch [The Ancient Quarter of Phù Thạch]." *Những phát hiện mới về Khảo cổ học*. Hanoi: Viện khảo cổ học, Ủy ban khoa học xã hội Việt Nam.

van Schendel, Willem, and Itty Abraham, eds. 2005. *Illicit Flows and Criminal Things: States, Borders, And the Other Side of Globalization*. Bloomington: Indiana University Press.

Warren, James F. 1981. *The Sulu Zone, 1768–1898*. Singapore: Singapore University Press.

———. 1998. *The Sulu Zone: The World Capitalist Economy and the Historical Imagination*. Amsterdam: VU University Press.

———. 2000. *The Global Eeconomy and the Sulu Zone: Connections, Commodities, and Culture*. Quezon City, Philippines: New Day Publishers.

Wheeler, Charles. 2006a. "Re-thinking the Sea in Vietnamese History: The Littoral Integration of Thuận-Quảng, Seventeenth-Eighteenth Centuries." *Journal of Southeast Asian Studies* 17 (1): 123–153.

———. 2006b. "One Region, Two Histories: Cham Precedents in the Hội An Region." In *Viet Nam: Borderless Histories*, ed. Nhung Tuyet Tran et al. Madison: University of Wisconsin Press: 163–193.

———. 2007. "Buddhism in the Re-ordering of an Early Modern World." *Journal of Global History* 3: 303–324.

———. 2010. "Maritime Subversions and Socio-Political Formations in Vietnamese History: A Look from the Marginal Center *(mien Trung)*." In *New Perspectives on* the History and Historiography of Southeast Asia, ed. Kenneth R. Hall. New York: Routledge.

———. 2015. "Interests, Institutions, and Identity: Strategic Adaptation and the Ethno-evolution of Minh Hương (Central Vietnam), 16th–19th Centuries." Itinerario, 39 (1).

———. Forthcoming. "The Case for Boats in Vietnamese History: Ships and the Social Flows that Shaped Nguyễn Cochinchina (Central Vietnam), 16th–18th Centuries." In Of Ships and Men: New Approaches in Nautical Archaeology, ed. Paola Calanca et al. Paris: Ecole française d'Extrême-Orient.

Wigen, Kären. 2006. "Oceans of History: Introduction." American Historical Review 111 (3): 717–721.

Wigen, Karen, and Martin Lewis. 2009. The Myth of Continents: A Critique of Metageography. Berkeley: University of California.

Wills, John E., Jr. 2001. ""Great Qing and Its Southern Neighbors 1760–1820: Secular Trends and Recovery from Crisis." Paper presented at "Interactions: Regional Studies, Global Processes, and Historical Analysis," Library of Congress, Washington, DC, March 3.

World Bank. 2013. Pirate Trails: Tracking the Illicit Financial Flows from Pirate Activities off the Horn of Africa. Washington, DC: The World Bank.

Xu Wentang et al., eds. 2001. Yuenan, Zhongguo yü Taiwan guanxi de zhuanbian [Changes in Vietnamese, Chinese and Taiwanese relations]. Taipei: Zongyang yanjiuyuan Dongnanya quyu yanjiu jihua.

Yu Jin 余縉 1669. "Shuguo xiaoshun shu 屬國效順疏 [Memorial on a Vassal State's Effective Obedience]." In Daguan tang wen ji, (repr. Beijing, 2009), 2: 37.

Zheng Guangnan. 1998. Zhongguo haido shi [History of Pirates in China]. Shanghai: Huadong Lidong daxue chubanshe, 376–379.

———. 2001. "Shilun Yuenan Huaren zai 'Xin-Jiu Ruan zhi zheng' zhong suo panyan di jiaose [A discussion about the personalities among Vietnamese Chinese who acted in the 'War between the New and Old Nguyễn'." In Yuenan, Zhongguo yu Taiwan guanxi chuanbian [Changes in Relations between Vietnam, China and Taiwan], ed. Xu Wentang, 3–36. Taibei shi: Zhongyang yanjiuyuan Dongnanya quyu yanjiu jihua.

2

The Original Translocal Society

Making Chaolian from Land and Sea

HELEN F. SIU and LIU ZHIWEI

In the last few centuries, a substantial stretch of river marshes (*sha* 沙) emerged in the middle of a major tributary of Xijiang , the largest river system on the western edge of the Pearl River delta in southern China. Eventually named Chaolian *xiang* (潮連鄉), the island community was built by generations of fishermen and settlers who fished, farmed, traded, and reclaimed river marshes. The history of settlement involved various groups who used symbolic and instrumental means to claim rights to the land, absorbed some newcomers while excluding others, created cultural identities, social institutions, and political alliances to become part of the late imperial order. They left material records—temples, ancestral halls, river-landings, neighborhood shrines, burial grounds, stone stele commemorating renovations of communal buildings, marking markets, and managing conflicts. Documents were varied—local gazetteers, literary writings, lineage genealogies, political petitions, official edicts, religious and ritual texts, trade and tax accounts.

A close reading of these materials reveals narrative traditions privileging real or imaginary authorities of a land-based, literati-dominated state formation. These forms marginalize certain populations and networks that were linked to maritime-based historical processes, which could have been significant to the local community. We hope to uncover the missing links and highlight cultural and political contingencies that have refused to be contained by dominant narratives on the delta's development and reevaluate Chaolian's place in it.[1]

Delta formations are not entirely geographical. They are conscious constructs in which local populations draw on meaningful resources of land and sea to make livelihoods and communities. In late imperial China, the reclamation of river marshes in the Pearl River delta necessitated sophisticated organization of capital and labor, and invoked multiple nexuses of legal-cultural authorities. Wealth generated from the land triggered competitive claims to settlement rights and intense ritual posturing based on lineage, markets, ethnicity, and religion. Conflicts and negotiations among imperial and local officials, settlers, and migrants took place in material and discursive forms. Who prevailed in the historical records? Were the interests of maritime-based, mobile populations largely buried in voluminous records that had favored farming and bureaucratic governing institutions?[2]

In multi-scalar terms, we would like to explore how the making of a "local" community such as Chaolian was embedded in layers of translocal political economies and moral imaginations. At a macro level, we identify historical turns of dynastic fortunes and juxtapose centralizing state impulses with the ebbs and flows of inter-regional trade in the delta system along the South China coast. At a micro level, we shall highlight local agency in "placemaking," as displayed in collective entrepreneurial strategies and individual personalities.[3]

As suggested in the introduction of this volume, we trace our intellectual roots to rich and diverse analytical traditions. On recentering oceans and river basins in our conceptual frameworks, and treating inter-connected littoral societies in their own right rather than as margins to territorial civilizations, Fernand Braudel (1995), K. N. Chaudhuri (1985), Philip Curtin (1984), and Takeshi Hamashita (2008) have blazed the trail. One ventures to connect the Mediterranean, the Indian Ocean, and the East and South China seas to highlight historically global processes that have shaped our understanding of continents and civilizations. Scholars have used historical and ethnographic details to connect spaces, cultures, societies, and economies across a broadly-defined Asia (Abu-Lughod 1989; Goody 1996; 2006; Lewis and Wigen 1997, 2005; Brook 2007; Blussé 2008; Zheng 2011). Like Eric Wolf who wrote *Europe and the People without History* (1982), their works challenge linear, Euro-centric conceptual schemas, and rigid continental divides. In calling for a new maritime geography and redrawing the lines for area studies, Wigen argues for "reimagining the globe by entertaining novel spatial configurations and regional schemes" (Wigen 1999).

Our study shares the spirit of this conceptual venture. We engage the above scholarship on three fronts. First, we delineate the making of Chaolian in the context of a developing Pearl River delta during the Ming and Qing dynasties whereby indigenous and migrant populations cultivated various cultural nexuses of power to become part of a land-based Chinese empire. This theme in fact has been presented in our previous works (Faure and Siu 1995; Siu and Liu 2006; Faure 2007). Second, we connect the resourcefulness of generations of local inhabitants to circuits of trade, transportation and "piracy" extending from the hills to river systems in coastal South China and Southeast Asia (Murray 1987; Tagliacozzo 2005; Chaffee 2008; Scott 2009; van Schendel 2005; Wheeler 2006; Siu 2000). These processes intertwined with agrarian-based institutions. In the future, we hope to explore similar processes of placemaking in other river deltas—the Yangzi River delta, the Mekong delta, the Red River delta, among others. This is to pinpoint crucial moments in their development to explain connectivity and divergence.

In this volume, Willem van Schendel intertwines physical scale with temporality, and stresses crucial historical junctures in placemaking. He describes four spatial moments in the development of Chittagong, the seaport at the eastern junction of several major rivers of the Ganges delta as they meet the Indian Ocean. This second largest city in today's Bangladesh assumed characters of being "thick" or "thin" places at various times, as people related to them with different emotions, identities and uses. We can detect similar moments in the making of Chaolian in relation to a maturing Pearl River delta over the centuries.

Spatial and temporal connectivity has not been confined to maritime regions. Our research considers historical trading empires in a broadly defined region that extends from North Asia to the Gulf region over land and sea. We incorporate works of colleagues who stress multi-scalar connections and the flow of material goods, ideas, populations, political alliances, and symbolic resources far beyond the Silk Road. In the same spirit, Peter C. Perdue, Matthew Mosca, Priya Satia, and Wen-chin Chang (all in this volume) highlight such processes over land that paralleled and intertwined with the fluidity over vast ocean spaces.

Theoretically, we would like to engage the Weberian turn in history and anthropology by shifting conceptual attention of territories, cultures, and populations from static, material, bounded categories to fluid, meaningful, and historically significant processes. Philip Abrams terms these processes "structuring" (Abrams 1982). Crossing the disciplinary boundaries of history and anthropology has gained conceptual traction (Dirks, Eley, and Ortner 1994; Gupta and Ferguson 1997; Wang 2003; Liu 2003; Crossley, Siu, and Sutton 2006; Siu 2009; Harper and Amrith 2012). We shall use historical and ethnographic materials to highlight "making Chaolian," and critically examine how local knowledge production (Geertz 1983) is intertwined with longitudinal genealogies of translocal powers from both land and sea (Wilfred and Tagliacozzo 2009).

The Pearl River Delta in the History of Southern China

In southern China, three major rivers—Xijiang (西江), Beijiang (北江), and Dongjiang (東江) came together at their lower reaches to form the Zhujiang (珠江). As the river meandered to reach the sea, sedimentation formed vast river marshes. Historians have long investigated who eventually settled in this vast region and transformed the delta into rich farmland as part of the extension of the imperial empire. One might expect that the location of the region in relation to power centers in northern China, and the continuous accumulation of river marshes made this delta region an open frontier. In fact, the presence of water-based local populations and tribal groups in the hills was well established by historical records and by a close reading of local folklore, customs, and rituals. Amidst the rise and fall of imperial dynasties, local populations, migrants, and military colonies built dikes to tame floods and made polders for farming. They used instrumental and symbolic means to engage translocal forces to position themselves (Faure and Siu 1995).

Unlike regions along China's southeast coast (Fujian), which became a part of the imperial system in the Song dynasty when religious affiliations remained a core cultural priority for making local society and identities (Dean and Zheng 2010a, 2010b), Guangdong and the Pearl River delta were targets of state-making during the Ming a few centuries later. A combination of state efforts to register populations for purposes of tax collection and governance dovetailed with local initiatives to engage mainstream cultural priorities of kinship and descent. It resulted in the formation of large lineage groups and the downward percolation of a literati tradition (Faure and Liu 2000; Faure 2007; Tan 1993).

Reclamation efforts were accelerated since the Ming as lineage and merchant trusts embarked on projects with increased scales in capital investment and labor organization. By the Qing, at the edges of the sands, market towns with a concentration of lineage trusts thrived on inter-regional rice trade and other cash crops (mulberry, cocoons, sugarcane, citrus, fan palm). They were also centers of merchant wealth. A rich ritual complex exerted powerful languages of inclusion and exclusion among an unsettled local population (Siu 1990; Liu 1995; Luo 1994). Taking into account the diversity of livelihoods, institutional organizations, cultural circulation, and ritual richness, the Pearl River delta in the late imperial period displayed the characteristics of both frontier and core of a regional system.[4]

The early twentieth century saw the end of the imperial order and the rise of new commercial interests linked to regional and overseas trade rather than land-based lineage estates. The founding of the Republic in 1911 with its political programs was supported by merchant capital in Guangzhou, Hong Kong, Macau, and their overseas networks. The following decades saw an influx of investments and new ideas in the region—the building of ports and railroad, the modernization of banks, charities, and business organizations, merchant political mobilizations, and the founding of co-educational schools with new curricula (Ching 2006; Chung 1998; Tsin 1999). Politically, republicans aspired to unify the new nation by fighting their way northward. Warlords rose and fell, and the Japanese military maintained a precarious balance of power with local bosses from the late 1930s on. Regional economy and society were further propelled to commercial interests overseas in the ebbs and flows of social strife, war, and revolution. Old folks in the region could still remember how they lived through those tumultuous but surprisingly "liberating" decades (Siu 1989, 2000). Lu Zijun wrote *Chaolian Xiangzhi* in such a historical context.

Compiling *Chaolian Xiangzhi* (潮連鄉志)

In 1946, Lu Zijun (Lu Xiangfu) [盧子駿], at age 79, compiled a township gazetteer of his native place while living in Hong Kong. He was a respectable teacher of Confucian classics. Although trained for literati tracks of the late Qing dynasty, he was known to have liberal views. A biographic sketch of him in 1904 described him as having studied in Japan in his youth. Through dialogue with Japanese counterparts, he believed in reforming the Chinese writing script in order to make comprehension easier for a broad reading public. While a tutor of Chinese language at the Zhang Family School in Macau, he created a newspaper for children.[5]

The imperial government had often commissioned scholars with academic and official titles to record geography, economy, customs, personalities of distinction, and literati achievements at the county level where state bureaucracy intersected local society. Gazetteers at the township level written with private

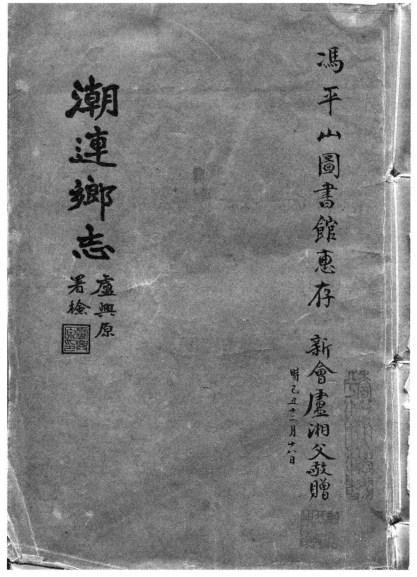

Chaolian Xiangzhi (1946). (Courtesy of The Society of Natives of Chaolian in Hong Kong)

Portrait of Lu Zijun (Lu Xiangfu) at age 79, from *Chaolian Xiangzhi*, 1946. (Courtesy of The Society of Natives of Chaolian in Hong Kong)

initiatives were rare. Back in 1908 when Lu compiled a genealogy of the Lu lineage in Chaolian, he was aware of valuable documentation of other lineage settlements in the township. During the following forty years, he resided in Hong Kong and only occasionally visited the township. As in other parts of China, the township had survived the fall of the Qing dynasty, warlord violence, the Japanese invasion, famine, and a prolonged civil war. He was anxious to thread together the community's settlement histories because elderly residents had passed on, and memories of hardships and accomplishments faded. It would be a pity, he claimed, if the meaning the place had for many generations vanished with the passage of time.

However "mapping" the place was difficult from the start. He discovered that details of Chaolian as a physical entity could hardly be found in official maps and records. Nature and geography were part of the story. The torrential flows of Xijiang regularly brought large quantities of silt. As the river slowed, local inhabitants built dikes and polders out of river mashes. The physical landscape continued to be transformed with the movement of the river and accumulated human efforts. Its representations in historical texts reflected an ambiguity. A map of the Kangxi period (seventeenth century) put the island on its edge in the sea. A map compiled in the Guangxu period (nineteenth century) had it closer to the landmass. Modern maps show Chaolian embedded in the middle of the Pearl River delta. Lu attributed two meanings to the island's name Chaolian. Both stressed its fluid positioning: high tides made it appear as an island in the middle of the river, and low tides exposed its connection to the river banks. Scholars gave it more literary eloquence, claiming that its shape resembled a lotus leaf floating with the currents. It took Lu great efforts to piece together fragments of information from regional gazetteers and local lineage genealogies. With help from colleagues, he was able to sketch a "map" of the island, with a less malleable physical territory and social landscape—hills, creeks, fields, river-landings, floodgates, village settlements, markets, ancestral halls, schools, temples, and shrines.

Lu was also meticulous about his sources for the gazetteer. Just as we consulted a variety of documentary and material sources in our own ethnographic research half a century later, Lu took sections from two county gazetteers of Xinhui (新會) to which Chaolian administratively belonged.[6] He then gleaned information from the genealogies of all the major surnames who had settled on the island—the Chen, Lu, Ou, Pan, Ma, Song, Chu, among others. He consulted private family records, examined rubbings from temple

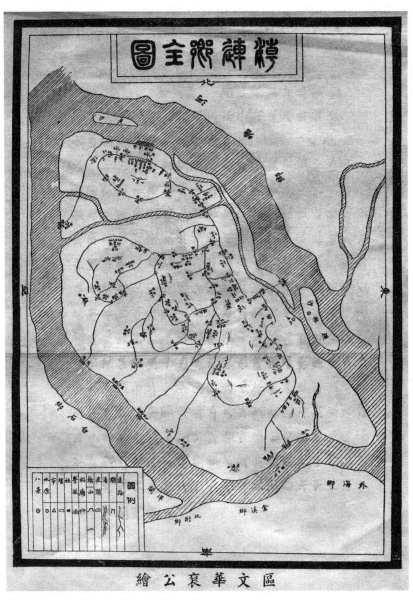

Chaolian mapped in the *Chaolian Xiangzhi*, 1946. (Courtesy of The Society of Natives of Chaolian in Hong Kong)

stele and historical monuments, and collected oral accounts from elders and contemporaries. Colleagues and fellow émigrés from Chaolian cooperated. So did native place associations and chambers of commerce in the region that thrived during the chaotic but open and dynamic decades of the Republican period. They contributed to Lu's effort in compiling and eventually publishing the township gazetteer. It is worth noting that the participants were well networked in Hong Kong, Macau, Guangzhou, and Shanghai, quite typical of populations in the trading communities in southern China during the first half of the twentieth century.[7]

Narrating Chaolian

In South China, lineage histories often mentioned a translocal origin of their founding ancestors. The majority of residents in the Pearl River delta would trace their ancestral history from a popular narrative that claimed that thirty-five surnames, in face of imperial wrath during the Song, migrated from Zhujixiang (珠璣巷) of Nanxiong (南雄) county in northern Guangdong. These migrants allegedly prospered into major lineages. Well-known Qing scholar Qu Dajun, for example, claimed that "Many ancestors of Guangdong's major lineages had migrated from Zhujixiang of Nanxiong. In fact there was a Zhujixiang in Xiangfu (Kaifeng, Henan). When Song officials accompanied the young emperor south, they did not forget their native roots, and use the name for where they settled in Nanxiong."[8] This narrative has long become the standard historical memory of major lineages in the delta.

Migration Charter and Lineage Formations

Lu followed such a standard narrative to describe how Chaolian had become a recognizable place, a process closely associated with a particular kind of lineage formation over the centuries in the region. He describes that before the Song dynasty (twelfth century), Chaolian was but an uninhabited patch of river marshes where fishermen occasionally moored. Migrants from the hills of northern Guangdong (Zhujixiang) made their way to the delta and eventually settled on the island. It was said that as descendants of officials and commoner families who fled to Guangdong to avoid the Mongol conquest at the end of the Song dynasty, they brought cultures and institutions of the Central Plains (Zhongyuan中原) to make local society. It was a route extending from

a political/cultural center to a peripheral region, and an outward movement
from a landmass to the water margins. However, he prefaced his narration
by pointing to a lack of systematic records in the official historiography, and
attributed patchiness in local documentation to difficulties in migration and
frontier settlement. It is ultimately up to the readers, he said, to trust the
"facts" or to treat them as make-believe (44).

Drawing on the genealogies of major lineages, which claimed settlement
rights on the island, Lu proceeded to describe two dozen surnames whose
descendants had built ancestral halls on the island from the Ming to the Republican period. All traced their origins to focal ancestors who had migrated
to the area since the Song dynasty. He singled out four major surnamed
groups (*daxing* 大姓) each occupying a distinctive settlement on the island.
They had eventually built ornate ancestral halls and compiled genealogies.
The documents included all key elements of the Confucian tradition as had
been locally propagated in the Ming and Qing. They highlighted the literati
accomplishments of male descendants, the filial piety of sons, the charitable
acts of mothers and wives, and the chaste conduct of widows. The Ou of
Fugang (富岡) village, a large and prosperous lineage settlement in Chaolian,
had compiled a thirteen-volume genealogy and built twenty-six ancestral halls
for various generations of ancestors, several schools and a charity funded by
income from lineage estates. Of equal importance in the social, political life of
the community was Lu's own lineage based in the village of Lubian (盧鞭). It
had also built twenty-seven halls, two schools located in its focal ancestral hall
named Dunben tang (敦本堂) and a communal granary. The Chens, spread
out in three village settlements, built twenty-eight halls. The smallest of the
four major surnames, the Pans, had twelve halls.

A distinguishing character of these surnamed groups was that lineage members had attained degrees in civil service examinations, and had risen high
in imperial officialdom during the late imperial period. Lu included detailed
biographical accounts of some of the officials and literati figures, closely following the narrative traditions of genealogies and gazetteers in late imperial
China. Some notable examples included Lu Ying (盧瑛) and Lu Rangde
(盧讓德). The biography of Lu Ying in *Chaolian Xiangzhi* was adapted from
the Lu lineage genealogy compiled by Lu Zijun. Based on materials from
the county gazetteer, Lu constructed an image of an ancestor who had attained literati ranks. The biography started with the civil service examinations
in early Ming, in which Lu argued that Lu Ying ranked first among those

in the township who had passed the provincial examinations. Moreover, he was the first in Xinhui county to become a provincial graduate *(juren)*. He stressed their literati achievements one shining upon the other ("後先輝映"). Lu also included the biography of the most prominent scholar–official of the Ou lineage, Ou Yue. He adopted Ou's biography from the county gazetteer entitled *Ou Yue zhuan* (區越傳), and copied a biographical essay, *xingzhuang* (行狀), from the Ou lineage genealogy. The former summarized Ou's official accomplishments. The latter, a more private biography, described in detail his character: he was filial to his stepmother, cultivated ritual and moral integrity; he treasured deep scholarly friendships; his writing styles and tastes displayed the character of famous scholar officials. Most importantly, Lu recorded Ou's efforts to establish the focal ancestor hall as cultivating self and family with a sense of propriety ("治身致家，悉准於禮").[9]

The message was well understood: that the settlers were not indigenous inhabitants (土著). Instead, their pedigree was traced from those considered Han from the cradle of civilization in northern China; they followed the teachings of neo-Confucians of the Song like Zhu Xi and a well-known Ming scholar from

A renovated ancestral hall in Chaolian. (Photo by Helen F. Siu)

the county, Chen Xianzhang; they worked hard to tame a water-based frontier, turned river marshes into fertile farmland, claimed settlement rights, registered themselves with the imperial government, and paid taxes as loyal subjects; their sons eventually obtained civil service examination degrees and were appointed officials; they set up ancestral estates, lived moral lives, worshipped their ancestors, performed all appropriate rituals, and kept their women folk virtuous. As the delta continued to expand due to natural sedimentation and by organized, large-scale reclamation from the Ming on, the lineages grew and their descendants prospered. A popular couplet that appeared on almost all ancestral halls, family tablets, and genealogies proudly pronounced that "ancestors sowed the seeds of foresight in their hearts, and generations were blessed with fields for cultivation" (心田先祖種，福地後人耕). Lu reinforced such a message in the way he narrated the history of Chaolian.

However, Lu did not hide his belief that the cradle of civilization had depended on rivers (such as the Yellow River in the Central Plains), and he observed that for Guangdong, dynamism came from the seas and coastal connections. He was comforted by the fact that Chaolian was at the heart of a vast delta crisscrossed by tributaries of the Xijiang linking land to sea. Over the centuries, he observed, the inhabitants were nurtured by such an environment. It broadened their horizons and enhanced their material well-being (Lu 1946, 3).

Dikes, Polders, and Merchant Capital

While the lineage tradition seems indisputable and linked to the settlement history of Chaolian, David Faure has given the narrative of lineage-building a different reading (1986, 2007). While acknowledging Freedman's seminal work on kinship and descent, his studies of the New Territories of Hong Kong and the delta demonstrate that lineage-building since the Ming involved processes of placemaking and settling in it. Settlement rights were the ultimate concerns, especially in the Pearl River delta in the Ming and Qing dynasties when local inhabitants, military colonies, migrant farmers, and traders vied for control of the maturing river marshes and actively positioned themselves in the expanding empire. We certainly share such perspective in our studies of the vast sands in Panyu and Xiangshan counties where institutions of imperial control were remote but stakes were high. The language of lineage, mixed with imperial metaphors and cultural/moral superiority, was one of power at that

juncture of state-building.[10] It was a discursive means shrewdly used by the
He of Shawan and by the He, Li, Mai lineages in Xiaolan to exercise dominance—to amass capital and labor for building agricultural infrastructure,
for controlling markets and trade routes, and for excluding competitors (Liu
1995; Siu 1990).

Although reclamations of the sands in Chaolian were not as massive and
capitalized as those in Shunde (Donghai shiliu sha 東海十六沙) or Xiangshan
(Xihai shiba sha 西海十八沙), Lu devoted a section of the gazetteer on the
building of dikes and polders by various lineages. He maintained that village
names, such as Lubian, Ganbian, Sunbian, Tanbian, Shangtan, indicated their
locations at the water margins. Reclamation over the centuries converted river
marshes into rich farmland for settlement. He listed six major ones that were
eventually linked to provide a degree of protection for the villages (Lu 1946,
72). From numerous legal suits filed with the county government, one could
detect bitter competition. Marking territorial boundaries was a tricky issue
and often disputed, as the sands shifted, the river changed courses, and new
sands formed against polders. A large strip of sands at the southern tip of the
island, Techeng Sha (特成沙) was presented in local folklore as dowry from
the Ou of Fugang to the Chen of Waihai across the waters. The story in fact
glossed over centuries of conflict over land rights between the two powerful
lineages.[11]

Flooding was an endemic problem for the settlers because the island was at
the lower reaches of the torrential Xijiang. From the amount of funds needed
to build and repair the massive dikes in the region, it was clear that merchant
capital across several counties was involved. Lu made an effort to record an
incident that had involved a merchant of the Lu surname in the early nineteenth century (twenty-first year of the reign of Jiaqing) whose ancestors were
said to have kin ties with the Lu of Beixiang village (北厢) in Chaolian. The
merchant, based in Shitou (石頭) in the neighboring Panyu county, was a
successful comprador for foreign traders. His sons staged a lavish ritual for
his tablet to be installed as a community leader of distinction. However, it
attracted the ire of literati members of the county, who filed a formal com-
plaint to the government and which led to an official investigation to have
his tablet removed. Lu felt that it was due to cultural conservatism, which
privileged the literati and looked down upon merchant wealth ("貴儒賤商"),
especially if the business was linked to foreign trade (1946, 74–76). Lu bent
over backwards to highlight the "charitable acts" of the merchant and his sons.

For example, they had donated hundreds of *mu* of land for his lineage and for community schools in Xinhui. Major sums were given to building dikes. His son Lu Wenjin (known in Western sources as Mowqua) contributed 40,000 taels to support the well-documented Sangyuan Wei (桑園圍) in Nanhai county, and another 133,000 taels for dikes in Xinhui. On top of it, he set aside over eight hectares of river marshes obtained after a lawsuit against another lineage to support future maintenance of the dikes, plus another 20,000 taels to settle the suit and build polders.[12] Lu did not elaborate on the real motivations for merchants to "donate" such sums except for lamenting the fact that these efforts were unappreciated by literati members of the community. However, one should note the aggressive intervention of merchant capital crossing county level boundaries to build the agricultural infrastructure of an increasingly commercialized delta by the early nineteenth century. In the literati narratives of making local society, the merchants were not given much recognition. Lu's effort to uncover and include their contributions seemed to have been haphazard at best, and was probably motivated by the fact that the merchant family in this case was remotely connected to his own lineage.

Community Rituals: The Cult of Hongsheng

Anthropologists and historians have long recognized that an important component of making place, confirming membership, attaching identities, and demonstrating power hierarchies was the performance of rituals. Lu's descriptions of popular beliefs and rituals in Chaolian wavered between respect (or tolerance) for local customs and slight disdain for the villagers' superstitions. On the list of twenty-three temples (*miao* 廟), one discerns the usual syncretistic world of deities with Buddhist, Daoist, and indigenous roots. Some, such as the Beidi, Huaguang, Huatuo, and Wenchang and Guandi, were tied to the imperial pantheon of gods worshipped by rural communities all over China. Others such as Tianhou, Fubo, and Hongsheng were located near dikes and river-landings and closely associated with rivers and the sea. There were also numerous neighborhood shrines (*she* 社) in the eight major village settlements.

Popular religion and associated rituals were given meanings far beyond individual acts of faith and worship (Wolf 1974; Ahern 1981; Watson 1985; Ward 1985). They were long used to demarcate spatial divisions and temporal rhythms of life, to affirm identities and social hierarchies, and to acquire political etiquette. Lu seamlessly wove the community's ritual complex of deities and temples into the island's lineage formations and their literati connections. He focused on the Hongsheng Miao (洪聖廟), a major community temple situated at the island's longest river-landing that could accommodate large boats from various markets in the Pearl River delta. A Ming dynasty temple with records of renovations through the centuries from the reign of Qianlong in the eighteenth century to Guangxu in the late nineteenth century, it was tied to the entire history of Chaolian. One side of the temple was flanked by the focal ancestral hall of the Ou lineage in Fugang. On the other side were the offices of the village alliance (*xiangyue* 鄉約) and communal school (*yixue* 義學).[13]

The deity, titled as Nanhai Guangli Hongsheng Zhaoming Longwang (南海廣利洪聖昭明龍王), was god of the South Seas. Folklore has it linked to the Nanhaishen Miao (南海神廟), popularly known as Boluo Miao (波羅廟) in historical Guangzhou. The temple in Guangzhou was founded in 594 A.D. on a waterfront at the outskirt of the city. Over the centuries, its major deity was given imperial titles and its socio-political position elevated. Among the major deities in the temple was a South Indian figure in a Chinese literati robe. Scholars believed that he was a foreign trader stranded in Guangzhou

Renovated Hongsheng Temple and Ou Lineage Hall today. (Photo by Helen F. Siu)

centuries ago when South Asians and Arabs from the Gulf region carried on thriving trade along the southeast cost (Long et al. 1984). There was probably significant cultural fusion among them and the local society.

From the various stone stele records in Chaolian's Hongsheng temple that Lu included in the gazetteer, it was clear that the deity was seen as a protector of coastal communities (from flood and pirates) as well as a patron for maritime trade. Hongsheng was in fact, worshipped mostly by the fishermen operating in inland rivers. Tianhou (Empress of Heaven 天后), on the other hand, was popular among coastal fishing communities. The founding myth of the temple in Chaolian was most revealing in identifying major stakeholders, the cultural strategies they employed, and the underlying tensions in community building. Stressing links with communities in the cradle of civilization in northern China, Lu recorded that the deity was brought back by a Lu lineage member from Beixiang village after he retired from office in Anhui Province in the Wanli reign of the Ming dynasty (1572–1620). As the Lu already had a family temple, the statue had to be put elsewhere. In the process of finding a site, it was rested in front of a local Tianhou Temple. It happened that the statue became too heavy to be lifted. After some deliberations with lineage and community leaders, Hongsheng was set up in the temple as the major deity, and Tianhou was moved to a small chamber to its side. The replacement of Tianhou with Hongsheng in the temple was significant. It probably reflected the dominance of the settlers over fisherfolk who had moored occasionally at the site. It could also have meant that the fisherfolk had transformed themselves into increasingly land-based communities and had begun to worship a less sea-based figure.

Over time, other deities were added, in particular, images representing two officials, Wang Lairen, governor, and governor-general Zhou Youde, who petitioned the Kangxi emperor to discontinue "the Great Clearance," a forceful relocation of coastal communities inland to cut off the supply lines of Ming loyalists (1662–1667).[14] Chaolian was considered outside the official line demarcating stable areas of rule. Its inhabitants were thus forced to move "inland," causing dislocations and conflicts. According to the gazetteer, villagers prayed to Hongsheng, and received a prediction that they would return home after 1,800 days. Subsequent to official Wang and Zhou's petition to the emperor, an edict in the eighth year of Kangxi allowed villagers to return home to resume their previous livelihoods. Villagers showed their appreciation for the official intervention by placing their images in the temple beside Hongsheng. The legend also gave Chaolian a proper "place" within the empire.

Nonetheless, the translocal and commercial linkages of the temple are worth noting. Over the centuries since its establishment, the temple went through numerous renovations, as recorded by more than a dozen stone stele on the side of the temple. A closer reading of the stele reveals that in earlier times, the contributors were individuals from major surnames, with a few from other parts of Guangdong who supposedly migrated during the dislocations in the Kangxi reign. The stele in the late Qing showed a more diverse composition of the patrons. Included were shops, river-landings, and non-local merchants, indicating a rise of commerce in the region. More interestingly, the contributions were often in silver dollars rather than taels. Silver dollars from the new world were common for trading in Guangzhou in the eighteenth and nineteenth century when Guangzhou carried a thriving foreign trade in tea, ceramics, silverware, furniture, and exotic curios fancied by clients from Europe, North America, Southeast Asia, and the Middle East.[15] To have the silver dollars used as contributions to local temple renovations indicated widespread use and the impact of foreign trade in daily life.

The Annual Birthday Parade of Hongsheng: Setting Boundaries

The annual parade of the deity to the various village settlements of the island was the biggest community event in Chaolian, funded by the major surnames. Lu described the preparations and the events in meticulous details (1946, 3393–3347). All the major surnames were involved. But the Lu, Ou, and Li lineages were given ritual priority because Hongsheng was believed to be the deity of the Lu, housed in a temple of the Ou and seated in a mobile throne provided by the Li ("盧家神, 歐家廟, 李家鑾輿"). The three surnames were also the wealthiest and their members most numerous. The event lasted for five days, with major rituals performed at the Lu, Ou, and Li settlements before a traveling statue of the deity was paraded to other settlements in the island along a fixed route from north to south. The route of the parade was set according to the sequence of petitions by various surname communities ("所到各姓，排日以分先後"), and roast pigs were used as ritual offerings. However, the powerful Lu, Chen, and Ou lineages offered cattle and lamb (太牢少牢), imitating ritual offerings by the royal courts to show off their elevated status.

Symbolisms of the parade were dominated by imperial metaphors. The deity was dressed in a Ming-style imperial robe, which was donated every ten years by the highest bidder in the robe society (龍袍會) of the Lu lineage in Lubian. At every designated site for greeting the deity, known as *yasheng* (迓聖), participants dressed themselves in literati style costumes, and followed the rituals of paying respect to high level imperial officials—formal pronouncements accompanied by gongs and drums and the firing of fire-crackers. Sacrificial offerings of roast pigs ranged from a few to a couple dozen per site. Other lineages also displayed offerings of cattle, lamb, fowl, and seasonal fruits. Lu mentioned that important lineage treasures were proudly displayed to show off the wealth of the lineages—bronze ritual artifacts, antique collections, paintings, precious stones, and jewelry. However, Lu lamented that with the passage of time and due to the chaotic decades of war and political strife, those display had become mere mirages and vague memories by the time he was writing.

The deity was accompanied by an elaborate entourage dressed as military guards and literati officials of the Ming-Qing variety; holding the deity's seal, banners, and other paraphernalia of authority. The parade was joined by brass bands with gongs and drums, and followed by colorful floats portraying figures in popular folklore. Financing these bands and ritual pavilions were merchant and native place associations named *ting guan* (亭舘). The bands came from regional cities in the delta where merchants conducted their trades.

It was customary for operas to be performed on make-shift stages during the birthday celebrations of local deities. Hongsheng's birthday parade was by far the most elaborate. Throughout the days of the parade, opera troupes from neighboring market towns were hired to entertain the deity. The most sought after troupe was based at the Jiqing Gongsuo (吉慶公所) of Guangzhou, which considered Chaolian an important source of business.[16]

In the last day of the parade, the deity was returned to the temple. At the 300-foot river-landing in front of the temple, the climax of the night's event was fireworks and shooting lucky rockets named *pao* (炮) by the organizers. Thousands gathered. Village toughs were hired by lineages and trade organizations at tremendous expense to take positions on land and boats, with the sole aim to grab many of the rockets' cores for a year of blessing from the deity. As in other territorial festivals, the annual birthday parade of Hongsheng was a truly extravagant event for Chaolian to come together as a community, to display its accomplishments, draw distinct territorial boundaries, reaffirm social hierarchy, and stage various languages of power and authority that connected it, in real and imaginary terms, to a land-based imperial order.[17]

Defending Chaolian

Once identified as the community deity, Hongsheng appeared in local folklore at its defender against outside intruders. The two major threats that Lu quoted at length from local documentation had come from the sea— the notorious pirate Zhang Bao in the reign of Jiaqing (early nineteenth century) and A Gun Zai in the Xianfeng reign (mid-nineteenth century). Both ravaged village communities along the coast and in the delta region for many years until defeated by government forces. At the height of their power, they attacked the county capital of Xinhui and neighboring Jiangmen, major cities in the western part of the delta. They both approached Chaolian across the river but were said to have been frightened off by efficacious acts of Hongsheng. On a stele for the renovation of the temple in late Qing, it was said that when Zhang Bao reached the island determined to plunder, officials were nowhere in sight. Anxious villagers prayed to Hongsheng and placed the deity's ceremonial boat onto the water in front of the temple. All of a sudden, an entire fleet with soldiers appeared, riding high winds and waves, sounding gongs and drums, and taking aim with cannons. Startled, the pirates sailed away in haste, and never returned. They later claimed that although they were not afraid of the inhabitants of Chaolian, its deity was to be avoided ("不怕潮連人, 只怕潮連神").

In the community's collective memory, a similar battle was forged against A Gun Zai. Around the mid-nineteenth century, peasant rebellions with different grievances swept across many provinces of China. In the south, related rebel groups were known as the Red Turbans (紅巾之亂). A Gun Zai was head of a local band menacing the delta. It was said that when the rebel/pirate approached the waters near Hongsheng temple, the ropes attached to the anchors of his fleet all snapped, and the boats drifted downstream for many miles. Afraid of incurring the deity's anger, he avoided Chaolian and attacked Jiangmen and its surrounding villages via land route. He was eventually defeated by government troops and village militia in these fortified sites (234, from a stele dated thirty-first year of the reign of Guangxu; also 286–291, copied from Lu lineage genealogies). Once again, the narrative cited divine power that sided with land-based communities with literati leadership and prevailed against disorderly elements from the sea.

Reading between the Lines

Lu's literati style of narrating Chaolian's history, and the discursive frame he used left some questions unanswered. We shall focus on two issues. First, who were the original local residents? It was clear from Lu's descriptions that fisherfolk and indigenous populations had congregated in the region before the migrants came. Lu mentioned them in the preface of the gazetteer but claimed that in the 600 years of settlement history, these original inhabitants disappeared without a trace (3). When the fisherfolk reappeared in documentary records cited by Lu, many were portrayed as pirates and bandits, and a threat to the community's established way of life. In the delta, fishermen were often labeled as "Dan" (蛋), a highly discriminated social category seen almost as an ethnic other. Popular legends described them as alien and physically unsavory. They mostly lived on boats because they were barred from building permanent dwellings on land. They were denied education and were not able to sit for civil service examinations. Their women were considered sexually promiscuous. In times of dynastic downturn, they were blamed for violent crimes and other social strife.

We have written on the shifting ethnic labels in the delta, and in particular, in Chaolian. In "Lineage, Market, Pirate and Dan: Ethnicity in the Pearl River delta of South China" (Siu and Liu 2006), it is argued that the Han-Dan divide was a result of the fluid political economy of sands reclamation in the Ming-Qing periods. In fact, most of the villages and market towns in the delta—with their entrenched lineage communities—were not built by migrants. Instead, there was a long process of creative self-differentiation among the indigenous populations that dovetailed with the downward percolation of state-making processes—military colonies, household registration, recording land and tax collection, plus other "civilizing" acts of the imperial bureaucracy. Winners used instrumental and symbolic means of a developing agrarian economy to gain their respective (culturally legitimate) places in the expanding polity, while losers were pushed to the margins. The losers appeared in historical records as tribal groups in the hills (such as the Yao), or as Dan in their boats. In our analysis, ethnicity should not be treated as an essentialized feature to define a population, but a language of power, a constructed label to

differentiate and discriminate. Labels for an ethnic hierarchy hardened precisely when an open "frontier" of river marshes allowed a great deal of room
for maneuver, resulting in intense competition among aspiring groups.

Gleaning the gazetteer and lineage genealogies from Chaolian, it appears
to us that the open "frontier" of a delta and its potential (and eventual) reclamation had allowed many of the mobile, water-based populations to become landed as settled agrarian communities. The rise of the lineages and the
disappearance of the original inhabitants in Lu's narrative were two faces of
the same process. This was further illustrated by his narrative concerning the
establishment of the Hongsheng cult (associated with delta communities in
transition from sea to land) and the marginalization of Tianhou (associated
with coastal fishermen).

The process was not without intense competition and conflict between settled villagers and newcomers. The Ou lineage of Zhigang at the southern tip
of the island was a case in point. As the Xijiang flowed from a northwestern
to a southeastern direction, new river marshes were formed at the island's
southern edges. Members of the Ou of Zhigang were late comers in Chaolian's
settlement history. Although they were numerous, and several lineage seg-
ments managed to build ancestral halls and eventually a focal ancestral hall,
the buildings were very modest compared to the ornate halls of the "major
surnames" in the northern part of the island (Lu, Ou, Pan, Chen). The Ou
lineage genealogies did not have a long list of literati figures or officials in the
imperial bureaucracy. In the Chaolian gazetteer and in our own ethnographic
encounters on the island, the village settlement was never fully recognized as a
respectable social entity. Despite some efforts by the Ou of Zhigang to claim
that its ancestors were related to the Ou of Fugang, the latter never acknowledged such claims. Instead, they argued that the two surnames were written
differently, signifying distance. The name of the village in local dialect is "Tsai
Mei" (豸尾) meaning "the tail of an insect."

Zhigang village was also marginalized in the island community's ritual
sphere. Popular saying ridiculed that "Tsai Mei villagers tried to imitate the
higher ups, but they grew the wrong kind of whiskers, and never learned
how to stage a ritual opera for the gods." The Chaolian gazetteer did describe
Zhigang's participation in the Hongsheng cult, that it received the deity on
the third day of the parade after the Chen's of Zishan. However, the descriptions were brief, and the deity did not stay overnight as in other village settlements. The gazetteer never mentioned Zhigang's claim that Hongsheng first

landed there, at a site where a Longpai (imperial dragon plaque) was situated, and that there was already a Tianhou temple nearby. It was also significant that the center of action for Hongsheng's visit took place not at the ancestral halls but near the river-landing and market. There were several days of operas, with a major stage extending a long way into the river. Hundreds of boats from the region congregated, including large ones from Guangzhou and Hong Kong. The boat people and the market traders contributed heavily to the festive funds (*huichang* 會嘗) managed by the Ou lineage in Zhigang. It was clearly an important festival for water-based groups in the delta region connected to the Zhigang market rather than to the priorities of the wealthy lineages at the northern part of the island. After the market declined at the turn of the century, festivities and contributions diminished. Old residents recalled that in the 1940s, the deity received audiences at the focal ancestral hall and the Weidong *zu,* a powerful segment hall in the Republican period. Operas were performed in front of the focal ancestral hall and not at the market, and that paintings and literati objects were displayed (Siu and Liu, 305–306).

The second issue centers on the positioning of the merchants and markets. Geographically, Chaolian was positioned in the middle of a shipping route that linked the Xijiang to ocean trade. Along the bank of the river on the island's west was Jiangmen, a large trading port in the western part of the delta. Xinhui local gazetteer (1908) described the regional markets as follows:

> Commerce in the region is concentrated in Jiangmen, and radiated to the county capital and rural markets in the vicinity. On its right, Jiangmen connects the core areas of Gaozhou, Leizhou, Qiongzhou, Yangjiang, Enping, Xinning, Heshan. On its left, it controls the major river and ocean routes. That is why it is equal in stature with Guangzhou and Hong Kong as a major market. Furthermore, with the opening up of Beijie as a foreign port, business thrives.[18]

Jiangmen was particularly important for Chaolian because it connected the southwestern region of Guangdong Province to the major commercial centers of the Pearl River delta. Situated at the juncture of Xijiang's river-to-ocean networks, the city's importance rivaled that of Guangzhou and Hong Kong. In 1904, the Qing government and Britain signed a treaty (續議通商行船條約) to make Jiangmen a port open for foreign trade. Parts of Xijiang in the vicinity of the city, along riverside neighborhoods such as Beijie of Jiangmen, Zhishan of Chaolian, and Liyushan of Waihai, were designated for foreign ships to moor. Such development further drew the livelihoods of Chaolian's residents into wider market networks and commercial environments.

Beijie, the area in Jiangmen lined with six piers for the transport of goods and passengers was locally known as the *yangguan* (Foreign Customs). The pier to Chaolian was located on its southern edge. In the early decades of the twentieth century, the area was lined with shops for grain, salt, medicinal herbs, wine and cooking sauces, dried fish, and other agricultural goods. In an interview conducted in 2012, an old resident recalled that during the Japanese invasion, the area was a site for intense battles between the Japanese and Nationalist troops. It was probably due to its strategic importance for river transport linking the western part of the Pearl River delta to Guangzhou, Macau, and Hong Kong. Today, the old vestiges are gone. A lone British-style mansion that was the home of the Asia Petroleum Company remained standing by the side of a four-lane motor road. Not far from Beijie is Dongdi, an internal river front of Jiangmen lined with ornate merchant houses, hotels, shops, and warehouses supporting a prosperous regional market during the Republican decades. Many natives of Chaolian

Restored merchant houses along Dongdi embankment, Jiangmen. (Photo by Helen F. Siu)

who were members of the Lu, Ou and Chen lineages owned properties and conducted businesses there.

Surprisingly, in Lu's narration, commerce was a crucial omission. Lu listed various markets (periodic and daily 墟市) on the island, but provided scant descriptions on the key players, their trade and operations, and their impact on Chaolian's community. However, between the lines of the gazetteer, and in the biographies of notable community figures he compiled, one can discern a growing commercial region and the social impact of merchants and markets. As mentioned in the earlier section of the paper on lineage building, merchant capital was heavily involved in building and maintaining dikes and polders. Native sons in market towns and cities in the delta provided some necessary resources. They put up the capital for establishing ancestral estates, paid enormous legal fees when land rights were disputed in court, and financed the labor intensive operations. When political negotiations with state officials were necessary, they mobilized vast social networks in merchant guilds, native place associations, charities and chambers of commerce.[19]

On the ritual front, the merchants also had a visible presence. The stone stele in the Hongsheng temple showed that merchants, owners of river-landings and shops made cash contributions to its renovations, and were major patrons of its festivities. They were particularly numerous by late Qing. During the parade of Hongsheng, the brass bands and ritual pavilions *(ting)* were largely financed by trade and native-place organizations in Guangzhou, Foshan, and later, Hong Kong. Investments in literati statuses were important channels for upward mobility. Merchants were known to purchase official degrees, or were given such honor for charitable acts in local communities. As part of cultivating literati pretensions, they were collectors of art works and objects.[20] It would not be surprising if many of the precious art objects displayed in the ancestral halls during the *yasheng* ritual for Hongsheng were merchant possessions. Moreover, an old river-landing in front of the temple and near the daily market of Xiangtou (巷頭) was owned by a Lu lineage estate. Lineage estates from the Ou of Fugang and the Lu of Lubian also successfully controlled public scales in the market in Zhigang. Fees were levied from traders in the markets and collected to support the communal school (義學) next to the Hongsheng temple. Both illustrated the close association between lineage, literati, and commercial interests.

Lu did not provide detailed coverage of commerce and transport in Chaolian although he listed the river-landings and markets, distinguishing daily markets from periodic ones. Xiangtou, where the Chen lineage settled, had a large daily market (市) lined with weaving and dyeing workshops, wholesale and retail enterprises for native cloth, and tea houses where local and regional traders conducted businesses. It was close to the island's largest river-landing near the Hongsheng temple that could accommodate boats bringing goods and buyers from different parts of the delta and Guangzhou. According to Lu, the area had the appearance of a small town (*xiao duhui* 小都會) during the time when native linen production and trade were at the height of their operation. However, native businesses declined after foreign manufactured fabrics became popular in the region in the early twentieth century.

Given the low status of Zhigang in the hierarchy of village settlements on the island, one might have been surprised to find a thriving periodic market there. Situated at the southern tip of the island, Zhigang was vulnerable in times of social unrest. However, its location was an asset in times of peace and commercial development. Lu acknowledged its significance in the regional economy as follows:

> Tsai Mei *xu*, situated near the river at Tsai Mei. Numerous sails gathered on the horizon. There were scores of shops. The market met on the first, fourth, and seventh day every ten days of the month. Buyers and sellers congregated at dawn, with animals, vegetables, and a wide range of other goods. There were public scales, and scale fees were collected from traders. They belonged to the communal school [*yixue*] of Chaolian, and the annual income was substantial. From the end of Guangxu, when commercial activities moved to Jiangmen, the market in Tsai Mei declined into insignificance. (1946, 80)

These descriptions were probably not exaggerated, and were corroborated by our interviews (in the 1990s) with elderly villagers whose families had engaged in large-scale processing of the agricultural products being marketed. Let me reproduce the descriptions we had written on the impact of commerce and water transport on village lives, which Lu did not cover in his narrative (Siu and Liu 2006, 304–305).

"Ou Wumao (who was eighty-five years old in 1991) and Ou Jinyao (who was seventy-five years old in 1991) asserted that in the time of their great grandfathers (in the Jiaqing period) there were twelve public scales auctioned out to established lineages. The Ou of Fugang and the Lu of Lubian controlled the scales and collected the fees. The Ou in Zhigang participated as partners in the auctions. Large factories were built near Shengping *she* around the market. Many, dominated by merchants from Guangxi, produced building materials from oyster shells dug in the shallow waters. There were factories producing thick twines for tugging boats. Most important of all, there were large quantities of *chongcai* (a root crop), collected from various *xiangs* (Hetang, Chaolian, and Guzhen) in the Xijiang system, which were sun-dried and salted at factories in Zhigang, and employed hundreds of women. Dan fishermen transported these products to places as far away as Chencun in Shunde county, Guangzhou, Foshan, and, later in the nineteenth century, to Hong Kong and Singapore.

The great-grandfather of Ou Jinyao and a brother operated two large factories, known as the Shangchang and Xiachang. They also 'traded' salt needed for processing the vegetables. The volume of chongcai marketed exceeded ten thousand *dan* (a hundred catties per dan) annually. Brokers came from as far as Taishan county, beyond the western edge of the delta. Although the Ou family did not engage in farming, the great-grandfather was able to build a house for himself, and a sizable one for his son when the latter married. The bride was from a rich family in the neighboring village of Hetang, and had bound feet. Prosperity lasted a few generations. The family finally closed one factory in the late Qing, when wholesale markets in Jiangmen replaced those in Zhigang. The second factory folded in the early years of the Republic because some members of the Weidong *zu* accused it of smuggling salt. It was only then that the family went into farming. The owners of two unusually large houses in Shengping *she* belonged to cousins of Jinyao's great-grandfather (brothers Shengjin and Shengyan) in Yuehu zu. They prospered in Zhigang processing chongcai and trading grain. The family donated grain for charity and bought titles around the time of the Tongzhi emperor (in the 1860s), and later set up gold and jewelry shops in Hong Kong and Singapore.

Ou Wumao's family also engaged in a variety of trades. His great-grandfather was a buyer in the wholesale grain market in Jiangmen. His grandfather manufactured twine and traded it up the Xijiang to Wuzhou. His father took up sericulture in Zhigang, trading cocoons in Rongqi in Shunde county. Family fortunes declined in the 1930s and especially during the Japanese occupation, when he rented land from local ancestral halls and Chen-surnamed landlords from Zhishan (also in Chaolian) to grow grain. It is ironic that his family came to farming in a roundabout way, after other options had been closed."

Such ethnographic details tell us more about Chaolian's connections to regional markets in the Pearl River delta, up the Xijiang to the neighboring province of Guangxi, and later to Hong Kong, Macau, and Singapore. The statuses of its residents were quite fluid. In times of peace, as shown by livelihoods in Zhigang, the water-based populations were successful transport workers, boat masters, and merchants. They accumulated wealth and social standing and some turned to other trades or land-owning. Only in times of economic downturn were they accused of being bandits and pirates, and often reduced to poor tenant farmers and bond servants for the established lineages. Their experiences were probably a later version of what the "established" lineages in the northern part of the island had gone through centuries back. Their settlement histories added layers of meaning to Chaolian as a place.

Uncovering the missing parts in Lu's narration of Chaolian, we have taken into account multiple channels of mobility and cultural resourcefulness in a delta environment. In various moments of state-making during the Ming and Qing, indigenous settlers in Chaolian maneuvered between land and sea, agrarian economy and regional markets, frontier ventures and imperial institutions. They made community, secured their respective places in it and acquired distinctive identities. As fishermen, farmers, merchants, minor officials, smugglers, bandits and pirates, many rose beyond discriminating labels to become "landed" at various junctures of late imperial history.

In the emerging sands of the Pearl River delta, there were hardly state institutions, but local populations were able to give the language of an agrarian-based orthodoxy a creative and complicit reading. Simultaneously, they were able to tap into commercial and transport networks of a growing agrarian economy in southern China. The lineages they built and the religious rituals they financed and performed provided authoritative means to generate capital, acquire land, mobilize a labor force to build polders, grow grain and other crops, enforce contracts in trade and transport, settle disputes and negotiate with officialdom. Over the centuries, they made an economically viable community that straddled multiple translocal networks, and cultivated politically respectable and culturally significant selves. In these structuring processes, they contributed to the expansion and consolidation of an imperial order on their own terms.

Notes

1. The Chaolian project has been a collective effort since the early 1990s, supported by the Wenner-Gren Foundation for Anthropological Research, Yale Council on East Asian Studies, and the Hong Kong Institute for the Humanities and Social Sciences.

We thank May Bo Ching, Kwok Leung Yu and numerous field research assistants from Hong Kong and China to keep our interests going on this small island. Director Ma Ruai of Chaolian *zhen* has been a most competent "partner" providing administrative support and fieldwork access, and sharing our enthusiasm to uncover historical and ethnographic materials. David Faure has always been a constant source of intellectual insights, humor and companionship. We also thank the Society of Natives of Chaolian in Hong Kong for permission to use a map, a cover page, and a photograph from *Chaolian Xiangzhi* (1946).

2. See Lewis 2006 on narrative strategies in ancient texts that "othered" the regional and local. On the dominating presence of bureaucracy associated with an agrarian empire like China, see classics by Karl Wittfogel on oriental despotism (1957), Etienne Balazs on bureaucratic society (1964); see Hsiao Kung-Chuan 1960 on efforts of the late Imperial state to "civilize" local society.

3. See Siu 2010 for a short summary of the themes of unity and diversity in Chinese anthropology.

4. This deviates somewhat from G. William Skinner's characterization of regional core and periphery. Skinner 1985.

5. See *The South China Collegian* (嶺南學生界), 1904, 8(23).

6. *Xinhui xianzhi* by Lin and Peng 1841, also *Xinhui xiangtuzhi* by Tan Biao et al 1908. Liu Zhiwei, David Faure and Siu conducted fieldwork in Chaolian from 1989 to 1995, and sporadically from then on to explore new documentary materials and to keep up with recent developments.

7. See a membership directory of Chaolian natives, *Lügang Xinhui Chaolian Tongxianghui huiyuan lu* (Hong Kong, 1947).

8. Qu Dajun, *Guangdong xinyu* 1700 (Repr., Zhonghua Shuju 1995, 49).

9. See Lu 1946, *Chaolian Xiangzhi,* volume 5, 107–112.

10. Faure and Liu argue that the building of local society in Fujian during the Song followed a language of religion that dovetailed with state-building at the time. For community formation in Guangdong, largely during the Ming, lineage pedigree became the language of power.

11. See the Ou lineage records on the Techeng Sha.

12. Lu was known to foreign merchants as Mowqua II. His position was second to 伍秉鑒, comprador for Jardine Matteson. Lu and Wu were chosen in 1813 by the Qing government to be head merchants but Lu's business suffered a decline from 1829 on. His descendants were said to have returned to Xinhui, but Xinhui County gazetteer did not include his biography. For more information, see Liang Jiabin, *Guangdong shisanhang kao* (The Thirteen Foreign Factories of Guangdong), Guangdong Renmin Chubanshe, 1999, 293–296; . See also Paul Van Dyke *The Canton Trade: Life and Enterprise on the China Coast, 1700–1845* (Hong Kong: Hong Kong University Press, 2007) on the thirteen foreign factories.

13. *Yixue* was a public institution in the township, an arena for the surnames in Chaolian to discuss community affairs. Since the Song dynasty, local officials had

promoted *yixue* as channels to disseminate education and civility in local society. In the Qing and Republican eras, special offices were set up to promote them. *Yixue* started with a civilizing mission but ended up as institutions for local self-government.

14. The edict was announced in 1622, and triggered revolts by coastal fishermen. After the revolts were put down, the government implemented the policy in five counties in the delta—Panyu, Shunde, Xinhui, Dongguan, Xiangshan. Populations outside a set boundary had to be forcibly moved inland.

15. See Crossman 1991; Wilson and Liu 2003 on the China export trade at the time.

16. For a contract of the Jiqing guild, see *Cantonese Opera Costumes* (粵劇服飾) by Hong Kong Cultural Museum, 55–56, Hong Kong Leisure and Cultural Services Department, 2005.

17. For comparison, see Choi Chi-cheung's work on Hongsheng's birthday celebrations by the fisherfolk in Kau Sai village of Hong Kong. See also Siu 1990 on the chrysanthemum festivals of Xiaolan in the neighboring county of Xiangshan from the late eighteenth to the late twentieth centuries.

18. Tan Biao et al, 1908. *Xinhui Xiangtuzhi,* vol 15, 145.

19. See Mann 1987 on merchant-state dynamics; Faure 1989, and 2007 on the operations of lineage estates as business corporations in Guangdong, Siu 2000 on the close relationship between merchant, lineage, and literati operations in late imperial and early Republican China.

20. See Brook 1998; Clunas 1991/2004 on commercial culture and connoisseur material objects.

References

Abrams, Philip. 1982. *Historical Sociology.* Ithaca: Cornell University Press.

Abu-Lughod, Janet. 1989. *Before European Hegemony: The World System A.D. 1250–1350.* New York: Oxford University Press.

Ahern, Emily Martin. 1981. *Chinese Ritual and Politics.* Cambridge: Cambridge University Press.

Balazs, Etienne. 1964. *Chinese Civilization and Bureaucracy.* Edited with an introduction by Arthur F. Wright; translated by H. M. Wright. New Haven: Yale University Press.

Blussé, Leonard. 2008. *Visible Cities: Canton, Nagasaki, and Batavia and the Coming of the Americans.* Cambridge, MA: Harvard University Press.

Braudel, Fernard. 1995. *The Mediterranean and the Mediterranean World in the Age of Philip II.* Berkeley: University of California Press.

Brook, Timothy. 1998. *The Confusions of Pleasure: Commerce and Culture in Ming China.* Berkeley: University of California Press.

———. 2007. *Vermeer's Hat: The Seventeenth Century and the Dawn of the Global World.* New York: Bloomsbury.

Chaffee, John. 2008. "At the Intersection of Empire and World Trade: The Chinese Port City of Quanzhou (Zaitun), Eleventh-Fifteen Centuries." In *Secondary Cities and Urban Networking in the Indian Ocean Realm C. 1400–1800*, ed. Kenneth Hall, 99–122. Lanham, MD: Lexington Books.

Chaudhuri, K. N. 1985. *Trade and Civilisation in the Indian Ocean: An Economic History from the Rise of Islam to 1750*. Cambridge: Cambridge University Press.

Ching May Bo 程美宝. 2006. *Diyu wenhua yu guojia rentong: wanqing yilai "Guangdong wenhua" guan de xingcheng* 地域文化與國家認同: 晚清以來 "廣東文化" 觀的形成 [Regional Culture and National Identity: The Evolution of the Idea of 'Guangdong Culture' since the Late Qing]. Beijing: Shenghuo Dushu Xinzhi Sanlian Shudian.

Chung, Po-Yin, Stephanie. 1998. *Chinese Business Groups in Hong Kong and Political Changes in South China*. London: Macmillan.

Clunas, Craig. 1991/2004. *Superfluous Things: Material Culture and Social Status in Early Modern China*. Honolulu: University of Hawaii Press.

Crossley, Pamela Kyle, Helen F. Siu, and Donald S. Sutton, eds. 2006. *Empire at the Margins: Culture, Ethnicity, and Frontier in Early Modern China*. Berkeley: University of California Press.

Crossman, Carl. 1991. *The Decorative Arts of the China Trade: Paintings Furnishings and Exotic Curiosities*. Woodbridge, Suffolk, UK: Antique Collector's Club.

Curtin, Philip. 1984. *Cross-Cultural Trade in World History*. Cambridge: Cambridge University Press.

Dean, Kenneth, and Zheng Zhenman. 2010a. *Ritual Alliances of the Putian Plains: Vol. 1: Historical Introduction to the Return of the Gods*. Leiden: Brill.

————. 2010b. *Ritual Alliances of the Putian Plains: Vol. 2: A Survey of Village Temples and Ritual Activities*. Leiden: Brill.

Dirks, Nicholas, Geoffrey Eley, and Sherry Ortner, eds. 1994. *Culture/Power/History: A Reader in Contemporary Social Theory*. Princeton: Princeton University Press.

Faure, David. 1986. *The Structure of Chinese Rural Society: Lineage and Village in the Eastern New Territories, Hong Kong*. Hong Kong: Oxford University Press.

————. 1989. "The Lineage as Business Company: Patronage versus Law in the Development of Chinese Business," The Second Conference on Modern Chinese Economic History, Vol. 1:347–376. Taibei: Institute of Economics, Academic Sinica.

————. 2007. *Emperor and Ancestor: State and Lineage in South China*. Stanford: Stanford University Press.

Faure, David, and Helen Siu, eds. 1995. *Down to Earth: The Territorial Bond in South China*. Stanford: Stanford University Press.

Faure, David 科大衛, and Liu Zhiwei 劉志偉. 2000. "Zongzu yu difang shehui de guojia rentong: Ming-Qing huanan diqu zongzu fazhan de yishixingtai jichu" 宗族與地方社會的國家認同————明清華南地區宗族發展的意識形態基礎,

[Lineage and State Affiliation in Local Society: The Ideological Basis of Lineage Development in Ming Qing South China]. *Lishi yanjiu* 歷史研究 3: 3–14.

Geertz, Clifford. 1983. *Local Knowledge: Further Essays in Interpretive Anthropology.* New York: Basic Books.

Goody, Jack. 1996. *The East in the West.* Cambridge: Cambridge University Press.

———. 2006. *The Theft of History.* Cambridge: Cambridge University Press.

Gupta, Akhil, and James Ferguson. 1997. *Anthropological Locations: Boundaries and Grounds of a Field Science.* Berkeley: University of California Press.

Hamashita, Takeshi. 2008. *China, East Asia and the Global Economy.* Edited by Linda Grove and Mark Selden. London: Routledge.

Harper, Tim, and Sunil Amrith. 2012. "Introduction: Sites of Interaction," *Modern Asian Study,* 46 (Special Issue 02): 249-257

Hong Kong Cultural Museum 香港文化博物館. 2005. *Yueju fushi* 粵劇服飾 [Cantonese Opera Costumes]. Hong Kong: Leisure and Cultural Services Department.

Hsiao, Kung-chuan. 1960. *Rural China: Imperial Control in the Nineteenth Century.* Seattle: University of Washington Press.

Lewis, Mark. 2006. *The Construction of Space in Early China.* Albany: State University of New York Press.

Lewis, Martin, and Kären Wigen. 1997. *The Myth of Continents: A Critique of Metageography.* Berkeley: University of California Press.

Liang Jiaben 梁嘉彬. 1999. *Guangdong shisanhang kao*廣東十三行考 [The thirteen hongs in Guangdong]. Guangzhou: Guangdong Renmin chubanshe.

Lin Xingzhang et al. 1841. *Xinhui Xianzhi* [Xinhui County Gazetteer].

Lingnan xueshengjie. 1904. 嶺南學生界 [*The South China Collegian*], 8: 23.

Liu, Zhiwei. 1995. "Lineage on the Sands: The Case of Shawan." In *Down to Earth: The Territorial Bond in South China,* ed. David Faure and Helen Siu. Stanford: Stanford University Press.

Liu Zhiwei 劉志偉. 2003. "Diyu shehui yu wenhua de jiegou guocheng: Zhujiang Sanjiaozhou yanjiu de lishixue yu renleixue duihua" 地域社會與文化的結構過程：珠江三角洲研究的歷史學與人類學對話 [Regional Society and the Structuring of Culture—A Dialogue between History and Anthropology in the Study of the Pearl River Delta]. *Lishi yanjiu* 歷史研究 1: 54–64.

Long Qingzhong 龍慶忠 et al. 1984. *Nanhai shen miao* 南海神廟 [Temple of the God of South Seas]. Guangzhou: Guangzhou shi wenhua ju.

Lu Zijun 盧子駿. 1946. *Chaolian Xiangzhi* 潮連鄉志 [Chaolian Township Gazetteer].

Luo Yixing 羅一星. 1994. *Ming Qing Foshan jingji fazhan yu shehui bianqian* 明清佛山經濟發展與社會變遷 [Economic Development and Social Change of Foshan during Ming and Qing]. Guangzhou: Guangdong renmin chubanshe.

Mann, Susan. 1987. *Local Merchants and the Chinese Bureaucracy, 1750–1950.* Stanford: Stanford University Press.

Murray, Dian. 1987. *Pirates of the South China Coast 1790–1810*. Stanford: Stanford University Press.

Perdue, Peter C. 2003. "A Frontier View of Chineseness." In *The Resurgence of East Asia: 500, 150 and 50 year Perspectives*, ed. Giovanni Arrighi, Takeshi Hamashita, and Mark Selden, 51–77. London: Routledge.

Qu Dajun 屈大均. 1700. *Guangdong xinyu* 廣東新語 [New narratives on Guangdong]. Repr., Beijing: Zhonghua shuju 1995.

Scott, James. 2009. *The Art of Not Being Governed: An Anarchist History of Upland Southeast Asia*. New Haven: Yale University Press.

Siu, Helen. 1990. "Recycling Tradition: Culture, History and Political Economy in the Chrysanthemum Festivals of South China." *Comparative Studies in Society and History* 11 (2): 32–62.

———. 2000. "The Grounding of Cosmopolitans: Merchants and Local Cultures in South China." In *Becoming Chinese: Passages to Modernity and Beyond, 1900–1950*, ed. Wen-hsin Yeh, 191–227. Berkeley: University of California Press.

——— 蕭鳳霞. 2009. "Fansi lishirenleixue" 反思歷史人類學 [Reflections on Historical Anthropology]. *Journal of History and Anthropology* 歷史人類學刊, 7 (2): 105–137.

———. 2010. "Unity and Diversity: Explaining Culture and History." In memory of G. William Skinner. *Taiwan Journal of Anthropology* 8 (1): 65–76.

Siu, Helen F., and Liu Zhiwei. 2006. "Lineage, Market, Pirate and Dan: Ethnicity in the Sands of South China." In *Empire at the Margins: Culture, Ethnicity and Frontier in Early Modern China*, ed. Pamela K. Crossley, Donald Sutton and Helen Siu, 285–310. Berkeley: University of California Press.

Tagliacozzo, Eric. 2005. *Secret Traders, Porous Borders: Smuggling and States along a Southeast Asian Frontier, 1865–1915*. New Haven: Yale University Press.

Tan Biao 譚鑣 et al. 1908. *Xinhui xiangtuzhi* 新會鄉土志 [Xinhui Local Gazetteer].

Tan Dihua 譚棣華. 1993. *Qingdai Zhujiang Sanjiaozhou de shatian* 清代珠江三角洲的沙田 [The Sands of the Pearl River Delta in the Qing]. Guangzhou: Guangdong renmin chubanshe.

Tsin, Michael. 1999. *Nation, Governance, and Modernity in China: Canton 1900–1927*. Stanford: Stanford University Press.

Van Dyke, Paul. 2007. *The Canton Trade: Life and Enterprise on the China Coast, 1700–1845*. Hong Kong: Hong Kong University Press.

van Schendel, Willem. 2005. "Spaces of Engagement: How Borderlands, Illegal Flows and Territorial States Interlock." In *Illicit Flows and Criminal Things: States, Borders, and the Other Side of Globalization*, ed. Willem van Schendel and Itty Abraham, 38–68. Bloomington: Indiana University Press.

Wang Mingke 王明珂. 2003. *Qiang zai Han Zang zhijian* 羌在漢藏之間 [Qiang between the Han and Zang]. Taipei: Luan Ching.

Ward, Barbara E. 1985. *Through Other Eyes: Essays in Understanding "Conscious Models"—Mostly in Hong Kong*. Hong Kong. Boulder, CO: Chinese University Press; Westview Press.

Watson, James. 1985. "Standardizing the Gods: The Promotion of T'ien Hou (Empress of Heaven)." In *Popular Culture in Late Imperial China*, ed. David Johnson, Andrew J. Nathan, and Evelyn S. Rawski, 292. Berkeley: University of California Press.

Wheeler, Charles. 2006. "Re-thinking the Sea in Vietnamese History: The Littoral Integration of Thuận-Quảng, Seventeenth-Eighteenth Centuries." *Journal of Southeast Asian Studies* 17 (1): 123–153.

Wigen, Kären. 1999. "Culture, Power, and Place: The New Changing Landscapes of East Asian Regionalism." *American Historical Review* 104 (October): 1183–1201.

———. 2005. "Cartographies of Connection: Ocean Maps as Metaphors for Inter-area History." In *Interactions: Transregional Perspectives on World History*, ed. Jerry H. Bentley, Renate Bridenthal, and Anand A. Yang, 150–166. Honolulu: Hawaii University Press.

Willford, Andrew and Eric Tagliacozzo, eds. 2009. "History and Anthropology: Strange Bedfellows." In *Clio/Anthropos: Exploring the Boundaries between History and Anthropology*, 1–26. Stanford: Stanford University Press.

Wilson, Ming, and Liu Zhiwei. 2003. *Souvenir from Canton—Chinese Export Paintings from the Victoria and Albert Museum*. Shanghai: Shanghai Classics Publishing House.

Wittfogel, Karl. 1957. *Oriental Despotism: A Comparative Study of Total Power*. New Haven: Yale University Press.

Wolf, Arthur. 1974. *Religion and Ritual in Chinese Society*. Stanford: Stanford University Press.

Wolf, Eric. 1982. *Europe and the People without History*. Berkeley: University of California Press.

Zheng, Yangwen. 2011. *China on the Sea*. Leiden: Brill.

3

Spatial Moments

Chittagong in Four Scenes

WILLEM VAN SCHENDEL

The river meets the ocean in a blaze of blue and green. No wonder people have made this spot their home for millennia: the fishing is good, the soil is fertile, and flood-free hillocks make it a safe home-site. But its greatest boon is a natural harbor, excellent for deep-water anchorage. Maritime trade goods have flowed through this location from the earliest recorded time.

The people who lived here turned this spot into a distinct place—or rather a succession of places—whose importance waxed and waned, as did its visibility in the historical record. Over the ages it bore many names, such as Pentapolis, Sudkawan, Porto Grande, Xatigam, Bengala, Chottogram, Saitagong, and Islamabad.[1] But the name that stuck is Chittagong and I will use it here. The etymology of the word is unknown; even so, there is no dearth of fanciful explanations.[2] Today, Chittagong is Bangladesh's prime seaport and its second city—it has over four million inhabitants. The city's name extends to the entire coastline (Chittagong district) and the uplands to the east (the Chittagong Hills).

In this chapter I examine how people turn a location into a place, and I do so by presenting four vignettes of Chittagong. The term "place" has many uses. Here I follow a practice among geographers who distinguish between space and place. Space refers to the physical, three-dimensional expanse in which we live our lives and to aspects such as location, position, proximity, distance, and movement. Space can be mapped, as can our position in it. Place, on the other hand, is a social concept. Place is created by people: it is lived experience; it is the ways in which people use and imagine space. Social practices make places and, in turn, the places we live in become embedded in us—there can be "no place without self and no self without place" (Casey, 2001, 684).[3]

"Placemaking" processes are continuous and therefore the histories of places matter. Contemporary places embody earlier incarnations even if people discount them or are unaware of them. There are physical elements: we live with old bridges, tunnels, and roads that have reduced distances between locations; our predecessors have cleared forests and drained lakes to create today's agricultural land; and old embankments protect us against floods. But placemaking involves much more; it encompasses what localities mean to us, how we imagine their histories, and what we feel about them. These immaterial, subjective elements are just as important.

One way of exploring the varying importance, emotional appeal and usefulness of place to people is by distinguishing between "thick" and "thin" places (Casey 2001; Duff 2010). Thick places are places to which we are committed because they enhance our sense of meaning, belonging and connectedness:

The location of Chittagong, marked by a white dot. (Courtesy of The Bay of Bengal Large Marine Ecosystem Project)

they provide us with enriching experiences. Thin places lack this specificity; they are of fleeting importance to us or leave us cold.[4] Places may oscillate between thickness and thinness over time and for specific social groups or individuals. They are the temporary outcomes of both everyday social practices and (sometimes antagonistic) planned interventions.[5]

This chapter is consciously tentative in its exploration of placemaking in Chittagong. It seeks to link concepts developed by sociospatial theorists with historical evidence about a particular location. This is important because "lively debates on the spatiality of social relations occur regularly in the social sciences. However, these debates often run their course without major impact on empirical inquiries into matters spatial, especially where they appear too abstract, abstruse, or one-dimensional to bear on concrete research."[6] How can we use sociospatial theory in empirical enquiries? And can we devise a language that is up to the task of dealing with *histories* of placemaking?

Beyond changes in thickness and thinness, the vignettes I present here explore what could be called dimensions of placemaking. Recent attention to these has been a response to "the kind of neoliberal-tsunami version of globalisation which totally erases place [and makes it] very difficult to think place in a progressive way" (Massey et al. 2009, 411). Jessop et al. (2008) propose to study sociospatial relations as made up of four relationally intertwined dimensions: places, territories, scales, and networks. In studying any of these, each of the others should be taken into account. Thus places must be explained as products of local histories and practices and, concurrently, of territorial, scalar, and network relations in the wider world.

This is a tall order. Applying such theoretical directives to empirical research requires a width of scope as well as a grasp of detail that is hard to muster. The following sketches fall far short of exploring all dimensions equally or adequately. They are merely a way of testing how productive this approach to placemaking may be. We observe Chittagong at four points in time: 1600, 1900, 1950, and 2010 CE.

1600: Asian Trade Hub

In the early seventeenth century Chittagong was, by all accounts, a very distinctive place. It was also extraordinarily different from the place that we now call Chittagong. I will briefly sketch the placemaking actions that shaped Chittagong by considering the dimensions of network, territory and scale.

Network

Most of what we know about Chittagong in the early 1600s is a result of it having been a node in commercial networks, especially brisk regional trade across the eastern Indian Ocean (Van Galen 2002, 153–157). Chittagong was the most prominent northern port in a 'polycentric networked realm' that linked coastal towns in Sri Lanka, Indonesia, Malaysia, Thailand, Burma/ Myanmar and Bangladesh and India.[7] Like other coastal ports, it played host to a plurality of trade groups and sojourners from across the region, just as Chittagonians could be found in many other ports.[8]

Why was Chittagong so prominent as an entrepôt in this networked realm? Its significance was hardly fortuitous: it acted as the gateway to another polycentric commercial network stretching to the north and east. This comprised the trade routes connecting the sea with the uplands of Tibet, Yunnan, northern Burma, Assam, Tripura, and the Chittagong hills (Stargardt 1971; Yang, 2004; Mukherjee 2009). Here communication routes focused on the region's many rivers, although in the mountainous areas land routes were also important. Thus Chittagong's own river, the Karnaphuli, brought down cotton, timber, and other forest products from the Chittagong hills. But the giant Brahmaputra was much more important. This 2,900 km-long river runs from the Tibetan plateau across the eastern Himalayas and through the plains of Assam and the Bengal delta to the sea. Where this river breaches the Himalayas, it flows very closely to other major rivers: the Sittang (allowing access to Burma), the Mekong (flowing through Thailand, Laos, Cambodia and Vietnam), the Yangzi (running east through central China) and the Yellow river (providing access to northern China). Thus the Brahmaputra formed the westernmost link of a vast nexus of waterways connecting South, Southeast and East Asia.[9]

In the 1600s the Brahmaputra flowed through the eastern part of Bengal and acted as a major thoroughfare for goods, ideas and people (its course would change drastically in the late eighteenth century).[10] Its mouth was close to Chittagong, the only stable seaport in the changeable landscape of the active delta. Rice and agarwood were among many commodities that passed from the interior through Chittagong to overseas destinations.[11]

Chittagong acted as the principal swivel between these two grand commodity circuits—the seaborne Eastern Indian Ocean network and the river-borne Brahmaputra-and-mountains network. For this reason, a great variety of people chose to make Chittagong a focal point of placemaking. These networks were not sharply bounded; rather they were regional constellations of dense trade routes that were open to actors from farther afield. Thus Chinese traders visited the port of Chittagong to buy cotton textiles and horses from Bengal and sell ceramics but there are no indications that they settled there (Chakravarti 1999; Sen, 2006; Hall 2010).

On the other hand, traders from the west, especially Persians and Arabs, had long formed communities in this port town (Subrahmanyam 1988, 308; Prakash 2004 451). By 1600 they were being crowded out by traders from even farther away: Portuguese traders had arrived in Chittagong some eighty years before. They soon ran a trading post and customs house there and they became prominent in the cowry trade, a very old connection between the seaborne and river-borne networks. Cowries are small shells that were used as currency in Bengal, northeastern India, parts of Burma and Yunnan. The bulk of these shells came from the Maldive Islands (located to the southwest of Sri Lanka) and passed through Chittagong on their way to users in the interior (Vogel and Hieronymus 1993; Yang 2004; Boomgaard 2008; Deyell 2010).

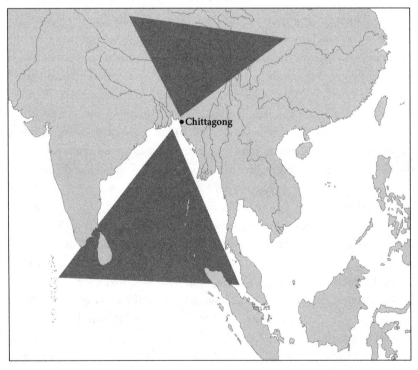

Chittagong astride the seaborne and riverborne networks. (Map by Willem van Schendel)

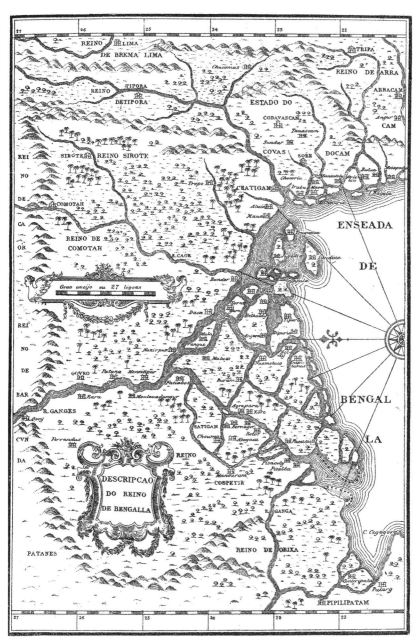

The first Portuguese map of Chittagong ("Chatigam") and surroundings, ca. 1550. On this map east is on top and north to the left. (João de Barros, *Ásia de João de Barros: dos feitos que os portugueses fizeram no descobrimento e conquista dos mares e terras do Oriente, Vol 4. [Quarta década]* Lisbon, 1777–88, II, 451)

The networks that shaped Chittagong were not just commercial. With trade
came cultural pluralism. In 1600, Chittagonians must have spoken many languages. Among them were Persian and Portuguese—prominent languages of
seaborne trade—as well as Arakanese, Chittagonian and Bengali.

Religious pluralism was also marked. Chittagong found itself at the inter-
section of four major religio-cultural realms: Buddhist, Islamic, Hindu, and
Christian. Theravada Buddhism linked the town with Arakan, Burma, and Sri
Lanka in the south; its largest Buddhist temple was located on Rangmahal hill
(Qanungo 1988, 636). Through its Muslim inhabitants it was part of the Islamic
cultural sphere of Persianized and Arabicized communities in coastal South and
Southeast Asia and, increasingly, Islamic communities in the Bengal delta and
Ganges valley. Chittagong was a point of embarkation to Mecca (Eaton 1993,
87). Hindu religious practices connected Chittagonians to vernacular communities to the west, in Bengal and down the eastern coast of India.[12] Christianity
in the form of Portuguese Catholicism was a vigorous newcomer.

We do not know exactly how these worldviews and vernaculars met and
mingled in Chittagong's dynamic cultural mix of the early 1600s but they
have left many traces in the city's cultural practices. Some examples of this are
the Chittagonian language (*Chatgaia buli* or *Chatgan bhasa,* which is spoken
today by more than 10 million people), and is an Indo-Aryan language related to Bengali, peppered with Arabic, Persian, and Portuguese expressions.
By the early 1600s communities of Christians had developed, some of them
Portuguese-speaking, and today Chittagong town still has its "Firingi Bazar"
(Frankish [= Portuguese] Market) neighborhood (Campos 1919, 90, 100–
111). And in another neighborhood, Badarpatti, lies the symbolic tomb of
fifteenth-century Persian Islamic preacher Badr Shah, who became the focus
of an extensive coastal network of pilgrimage and cross-religious worship that
persists today.[13]

Territory

Chittagong's residents and sojourners—participants in complex, far-flung
networks of commerce and culture—turned this anchor point into a distinct
place. But there was another dimension to placemaking here: territory. Chittagong is located in a long narrow coastal plain squeezed between the ocean to
the west and hills to the east. The southern part of this plain is usually referred
to as Arakan, the northern as Chittagong. Historically, state formation in the

Chittagong plain has been unstable. The town itself never became the centre of a strong state; instead, it was variously seized by states emerging in Arakan (to the south), Tripura (to the northeast), or Bengal (to the northwest). In 1600 it had been under Arakanese rule for about half a century (Leider and d'Hubert 2011). Territorial power pointed south and its manifestations were noticeable to the inhabitants of Chittagong. The town was the seat of an Arakanese governor, a large naval garrison controlled it, and it was a mint that trilingual coins (Arakanese, Arabic, Bengali) that circulated in the local economy (Bodhinyana 2001). The Arakanese state depended heavily on revenues from Chittagong's long-distance trade as well as from local textile production and agriculture (Van Galen 2002, 155–157). Territorial control proved difficult, however, because of the power of the Portuguese who sometimes formed alliances with Arakanese power holders and sometimes turned against them. For a while they established their own stronghold on the nearby island of Sandwip, drawing some trade away from Chittagong (Mukherjee 2008; Roy 2011).

Scale

The actions of networking communities and territorial power holders were significant in making Chittagong the place it was in 1600. But how significant? What do we miss when we apply these lenses? Introducing a scalar dimension reveals how much more could be done. Shifting down, we may discover numerous small-scale commercial networks that played a role; for example, exchanges between townspeople and local peasants and fisherfolk,[14] or between people in the plains and those in the nearby hills. And shifting up, we can frame placemaking in Chittagong town in terms of an expanding capitalist world system.

Scale is also important in exploring cultural networks. The Arakan-Chittagong plain can be understood as a small cultural arena that stood apart from the larger units of Bengal and Burma and sustained local cultural expressions and experiences.[15] Scaling up, the Arakan-Chittagong plain can be seen as belonging to a much larger cultural realm beyond the "Indian" heartland. Whether we see it as a frontier between Arid and Monsoon Asia (Gommans 2002), or follow Mukherjee's suggestion that Bengal was divided between a western part (the Gangetic region) that was culturally 'Indic' and an eastern part (the Brahmaputra region) that was not, Chittagong was clearly on the non-Indic, Monsoon side of the division.[16]

In the early 1600s Chittagong was a highly networked, multicultural and open place. As a major trade entrepôt it was meaningful not only to its inhabitants but also to those who visited it—and even to some halfway around the world, who had only heard of it, such as the Portuguese poet Camões (1997 10, cxxi). In other words, at this time Chittagong was a 'thick' place.

1900: Colonial Town

Three hundred years later, in the early 1900s, Chittagong was still a notable urban center with a good seaport but it had become a different, and in many ways 'thinner' place. The maritime networks that had sustained it had collapsed, major ecological change had affected its position, and its cultural context had changed dramatically. Territorial aspects had eclipsed networks in making Chittagong a place, and we shall consider these first.

Territory

There had been major physical changes in the Bengal delta, transforming the geography of the territory itself. The clear distinction between the delta's eastern and western halves had become blurred because in 1787 the enormous Brahmaputra River had suddenly shifted its channel westwards and now joined the Ganges upstream.[17] This allowed for much easier communications between the northeastern regions and the southwestern delta, favoring port cities in the west, notably a purposeful newcomer, Kolkata (Calcutta).[18] The eastern delta, which receives heavier monsoon rains and was now much more densely populated than in 1600, had lost its commercial edge but was still an enormously productive agricultural region.

For Chittagong town the westward pull was strengthened by state formation. From the mid-seventeenth century the town had been incorporated into states whose power emanated from the western delta—the Mughal Empire (from the 1660s to the 1720s), the semi-independent "Nawabi" state of Bengal (from the 1720s to the 1750s), and British India (from the 1750s onwards). The earlier southward orientation towards Arakan had withered away as Arakan ceased to be a power, especially after it was invaded by Burma (1784) and then annexed to British India (1826).

By 1900 Chittagong found itself surrounded by British-held territories. The entire eastern Indian Ocean had become a "British sea" because almost all its coasts were British colonies and British sea power was unchallenged. In this

Imperial troops on parade in Chittagong, 1939. (Courtesy of the Goadby Collection, Centre of South Asian Studies, University of Cambridge)

great new imperial ensemble, Chittagong had been allocated two minor roles, one territorial and the other commercial. It was ruled from Kolkata (Calcutta) in the western Bengal delta, a city that had become the capital of British India in the late eighteenth century. Chittagong had been made part of the province of Bengal and it was now the headquarters of a division (group of districts) in eastern Bengal as well as of the district of Chittagong.[19] Arakanese governors had been replaced by British and Bengali officials. Military personnel from all over India were stationed here. In the second half of the nineteenth century Chittagong had acted as a springboard for imperial expansion: military expeditions left from here to subdue and annex the Chittagong Hill Tracts (1860) and the Lushai Hills (1895, now Mizoram).

Network

As a port, Chittagong had lost much to Kolkata, which the British had developed as Bengal's chief port. They had not developed road connections between Eastern Bengal and Kolkata, however, so Chittagong served as a feeder port, mainly for coastal vessels carrying agricultural produce to Kolkata, but also industrial and agricultural goods from Bengal to Burma.[20] And Chittagong port still played a role in the dwindling cowry trade.[21]

But now, around 1900, Chittagong's fortunes were beginning to change. Two very valuable export crops had come up—tea in Assam and jute in eastern Bengal—and these could be traded more easily through nearby Chittagong than through faraway Kolkata. In addition, important oil and coal reserves had been discovered in Assam. This prompted the government to revive the ancient Brahmaputra-and-mountains network by constructing the

Assam-Bengal Railway and improving Chittagong's port.[22] By the 1920s the value of trade passing through the port had quadrupled (Mukherjee 2003). Chittagong was now a hub of colonial extraction: its main commercial role lay in expediting the flow of export crops to the metropolis.

Chittagong's changing fortunes were also reflected in a drastically altered cultural mix. The trading communities from around the Eastern Indian Ocean—which had been so prominent in 1600—had disappeared, as had the Persians and Portuguese. The Arakanese presence was gone. In its place had come British overlords and Bengali administrators (who considered Chittagong a hardship posting)[23] and European traders with Bengali helpers. Most Bengalis now thought of Chittagong as an inalienably Bengali town and they considered the Chittagonian language a rustic or "impure" form of the Bengali language. There were also other new groups, notably the Marwaris (a north Indian commercial group), who dominated banking. Their presence showed clearly how Chittagong's networks of orientation had changed: the Marwaris outcompeted their rivals, the Chettiars, who came from the South Indian areas previously closely linked to Chittagong.

Religious networks also revealed Chittagong's new orientation. Buddhism was much less in evidence. There were still Buddhist minorities in Chittagong district (notably Barua, Rakhaing, Marma, and Chakma) but Chittagong town had lost its Buddhist flavor. The hill that had housed the main Buddhist temple in 1600 was now the site of the town's hospital. Old Christian connections had also weakened, although a small Catholic community tracing its origins to Portuguese contacts remained in town.[24] The British had established new Christian connections, however. Visitors to Chittagong could not fail to notice their churches and missionary and educational institutions.

Meanwhile, two religious networks had been strengthened in Chittagong town, both resulting from Bengalization. The first was Islamic. A major change since 1600 had been the rise of Islam as an identity marker in eastern Bengal, linked to the clearing of forests and the spread of agriculture (Eaton 1993). Chittagong lay at the far outreach of this development. By 1900 almost half of the Bengali inhabitants of the town considered themselves Muslims. Another religious network that rose to importance in Chittagong town was Hinduism, the faith of many Bengali service holders, traders, and professionals, as well as of others, such as the Marwaris. By 1900 Hindus made up a little less than half the population of Chittagong town (Ahmed 1981, 3).

Scale

We can look at the new territorial arrangements and networks from different vantage points, scaling up or down. Thus the process of Bengalization that had transformed Chittagong since the early 1600s can be understood as part of a larger eastward expansion of the "Indic" cultural sphere. Chittagong's cultural connections with the "non-Indic" regions to the south and east were now greatly diminished but the boundary was close by: a mere fifty kilometers to the east and some hundred to the south Buddhism and several local religions flourished, as did languages and customs not understood by Bengalis—who had developed the pejorative term *Magh* for these non-Bengali neighbors.

If we scale up we can also see the trade that flowed through Chittagong as an example of the worldwide reach of European resource extraction under conditions of empire. As a seaport of British India, Chittagong exemplified transformations that had occurred all over the colonized world. It exported two new cash crops that had changed the lives of millions of producers in the interior. Tea was produced mainly on British-owned plantations in Assam— by 1900 the world's leading tea exporting region—and was sent down the specially built railway to Chittagong. There were also tea plantations along the railway track (notably in Sylhet district) and around Chittagong town. From here British shipping companies transported the tea to Britain. Smallholders in eastern Bengal provided virtually all of the world market with jute, a plant whose fibers were used for sacks, rope, curtains, burlap, and carpets. From Chittagong jute was shipped to processing mills in Dundee but by 1900 the Scottish jute industry was being overtaken by jute mills in Kolkata, so jute from Chittagong was often processed there.

Scaling down, we can look at how these different forces had affected placemaking in Chittagong. The layout of the city now followed colonial precedents. There was a small European elite connected with government, the port, the armed forces, the railways, the jute and tea trade, and edu-cation. Their offices and houses were grouped together in European-style buildings and they ran the socially exclusive and racially restricted Chit-tagong Club.[25] The most coveted locations were the tops of the town's small hillocks.[26] The "white town" was dispersed on the hilltops with the "native town" located along the river.[27] In 1878 the highest district official gave this description:

[Chittagong] consists of a loosely arranged network of streets along the river, and up a creek, the old Porto Grande of the Portuguese. Here there is a large Roman Catholic cathedral and bishop's residence of masonry, round which cluster the houses of the Portuguese, built of mat and thatch, and raised, as are all the houses in these parts, on stout piles, thus leaving under the house an open space of some three feet high, which is a receptacle of garbage and refuse of all kinds. Large warehouses belonging to the English, French and native merchants line the bank of the river, and the rest of the space is occupied by the huts of the native (principally Musulman) population, with one or two large, handsome brick mosques. The whole of this quarter is shrouded in rich vegetation, palms, plantains, mangoes and other trees . . . amidst which gleam pools of black and stagnant water . . . On each of [the] hills is a European house surrounded by casuarina trees . . . There are also large courthouses and public offices, a big Protestant church, schools and post office . . . I have never seen so lovely a place to look at, nor one so loathsome to live in. (Beames, 1961, 276–277)

Since then, the railway had arrived and, in true British-Indian fashion, provided housing for its personnel in the "Railway Colony." The newly expanded port had jetties for seagoing vessels and claimed much of the riverside land. This was a focus of interest for Chittagonians who were looking for jobs on ships, an age-old occupation that had by now led some to settle in port cities such as Liverpool, London, and New York.[28]

1950: Pakistan's Lifeline

By the middle of the twentieth century there was yet another distinct twist to placemaking in Chittagong—and once again it was unanticipated territorial change rather than commercial networking that occasioned it.

Territory

In 1947 British rule ended and Chittagong became a part of Pakistan. This new state consisted of two separate territories, 1,500 km apart: West Pakistan (today Pakistan) and East Pakistan (today Bangladesh). Chittagong was East Pakistan's only seaport. In an age in which air traffic was still limited and expensive—and rail and road connections between East and West Pakistan impossible across hostile Indian territory—Chittagong was of absolutely vital

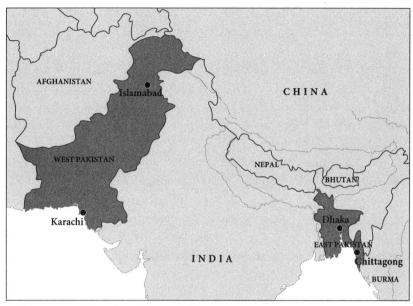

Chittagong and Karachi—Pakistan's lifeline, 1947–1971. (Map by Willem van Schendel)

importance to Pakistani communications.[29] Goods and people traveling between the two wings took the 5,000 km shipping route from Chittagong to Karachi, around the southern tip of India.[30]

Chittagong's new position led to rapid expansion; it annexed surrounding villages and began to be thought of as a city rather than a town (Rizvi 1970, 459–460). For the first time attempts were made at urban planning. The Chittagong Development Authority, created in the 1950s, assigned certain tasks to certain neighborhoods: for example, government offices and staff quarters in Agrabad and heavy industries in Kalurghat. The port grew and the Pakistan Navy established a gunboat squadron there.[31] Industrial activities multiplied as Chittagong turned into East Pakistan's commercial dynamo. It hosted East Pakistan's only oil refinery as well as jute and cotton mills, tanneries, and match and metal re-rolling factories.

Network

British rule had ended with the partition of British India into Pakistan and India. This had great consequences for Chittagong's trade networks. To start with, the Brahmaputra-and-mountains connection was lost. Its main colonial manifestation had been the tea trade, which collapsed because Assam fell to India and the railway connection was severed.[32] Second, the jute trade was in disarray because the Kolkata jute mills were out of reach in India. East Pakistan feverishly set out to create an industry of its own to process the jute it grew (Van Schendel, 2005, 157–160). Some new jute mills were set up in Chittagong. Third, the British-era financial networks faded as most Marwaris, being Hindus, left Pakistan for India.

Chittagong's new commercial ties were with faraway West Pakistan. These soon turned out to be largely extractive. Economic disparities between the two wings widened over the years despite the fact that jute from East Pakistan, exported from Chittagong, earned the country two-thirds of its foreign exchange (Sobhan, 1962). West Pakistan's government was accused of treating East Pakistan as an internal colony, with Chittagong as its commercial bridgehead. The city certainly saw an influx of West Pakistani businessmen, bureaucrats, and technicians. Its industries and shipping companies were largely owned and managed by newcomers from West Pakistan or abroad and they ran largely on local labor.

Chittagong's social and cultural mix had undergone great change. Three groups that had dominated the scene during British rule were no longer important. British administrators and Marwari bankers had faded but the most devastating social effect was the disappearance of many local Hindus. The partition of Pakistan and India had impelled them to leave Chittagong and settle in India, never to return. This robbed the city of much professional expertise and cultural capital and turned it into a Muslim-majority place.

New people appeared in Chittagong and began to shape the city. Immigrant groups of Muslims—notably 'Muhajirs' (members of Urdu-speaking trading elites from North India who settled in Pakistan after 1947) and Punjabis from West Pakistan—now took over the roles formerly held by British, Marwaris, and Chittagonian Hindus. They soon clashed with the local elite in a conflict of interests that expressed itself in a politics of language. This conflict, and the Bengali language movement it produced, was noticeable all over East Pakistan but it had a local flavor in Chittagong. Here fragmentation and politicization among the business community was strikingly expressed by the fact that the city had no less than six different Chambers of Commerce (Kochanek 1993, 130).

Two other immigrant groups appeared on the scene as well. The first were Western expatriates connected with various development programs, a community that would grow considerably in the decades to come (Andrews et al. 1992). The other group was quite different but would also grow over the years. They were Muslim refugees from Arakan, known as Rohingyas.

Scale

By the 1950s the nation-state had emerged as a crucial placemaker in Chittagong. National planning efforts increasingly affected how the city developed but Chittagong hardly became a strictly planned space. Many other actors were involved in shaping the new Chittagong, from immigrant laborers seeking living space to entrepreneurs seeking new opportunities for trade or industrial production. Countless individual activities interacted with and reworked state plans, leading to a place that appeared disorderly and makeshift. Even so, there was an atmosphere of hope and expectation: Chittagong seemed to be on a roll.

National attempts at placemaking were also shaped by larger-scale actions and ideas, such as the emergence of an international set of social engineers who worked from theories of "modernization" or "development." Pakistan government policies became heavily dependent on these development experts and the financial aid they commanded, first mainly from the United States and later through the World Bank's Aid-to-Pakistan consortium. Thus Chittagong's transformation and infrastructural change also reflected the insights and practices of an international "modernization industry."

2010: Bangladeshi Metropolis

Today Chittagong hardly resembles the city of the 1950s. Caught up in another twist of state formation as well as in a global intensification of networks, it has taken on yet another persona.

Territory

Tensions between the two wings of Pakistan exploded in 1971 when the government ordered a military crackdown to quell East Pakistani unrest. This backfired. What followed became known as the Bangladesh Liberation War and by late 1971 East Pakistan had turned into the independent state of Bangladesh. The warring parties—Pakistan's armed forces, Bangladeshi freedom fighters, and an Indian invasion force—wreaked havoc in Chittagong. In the early 1970s it was a desolate, chaotic place. But its location guaranteed it a quick recovery and a future as Bangladesh's only stable seaport. Chittagong began to reinvent itself and by the early twenty-first century it had become a novel place.

Hugely expanded, its port now handled 80 percent of the imports and exports of a country of 150 million inhabitants. Chittagong's territorial orientation had changed once again. No longer twinned with Karachi as East Pakistan's gateway to West Pakistan, it had now become ancillary to territorial decision-making in the new national capital, Dhaka. The two cities had never before been so directly in competition with each other. Whereas Dhaka represented political and administrative power, Chittagong was the industrial and commercial powerhouse, with about 40 percent of the heavy industries located in or near it. As placemaking in Chittagong came to depend on policies emanating from Dhaka, many Chittagonians developed a sense of being ill-treated and neglected. It was a classic case of resentment-yet-attachment between a country's commercial hub and its center of power. Chittagonians can be heard saying things like "We make the money and they spend it."

Network

By 2010 Chittagong had turned into a city that was holding its own in an increasingly integrated world economy. Network and territory closely meshed in what was now the main outlet of a country that was experiencing economic growth to the tune of 6 percent a year. No longer focused on specific regions, its networks spanned the world. Its exports (ready-made garments, jute products, leather, and shrimp) went largely to the United States and Europe. Its imports (machinery, chemicals, iron and steel, textiles, foodstuffs, petroleum products, and cement) largely came from China, India, and the Gulf.

There were many new connections as Chittagong's competitive advantage—abundant cheap and pliable labor—attracted investors from all over the world. For example, it now boasted a Korean Export Processing Zone. Korean capital also played a role in a new industry that had turned Chittagong into a major recycling center: shipbreaking. It came up in the 1980s and flourished as end-of-life ships were stripped and their waste products repackaged and re-used.[33]

Beyond the economic networks there were the geo-political ones—China invested in the construction of two new seaports that many considered to be part of its naval strategy to control a "string of pearls" around the Indian Ocean.[34]

This prospect is of considerable military concern to India, as is the possibility that the ancient Brahmaputra-and-mountains connection could be revived if plans were to materialize to construct a road and railway from Kunming in southwest China through Burma/Myanmar to Chittagong (Singh 2010; Paul 2010; Pandit 2010). In a parallel development, reconnection of the more western parts of the Brahmaputra-and-mountains region now seemed poised to come about. Landlocked Nepal and Bhutan—wanting to be less dependent on Indian ports—had long eyed Chittagong as an alternative. Similarly, for decades traders in Northeast India had pleaded for access to nearby Chittagong port. For different political reasons, both the Indian and the Bangladesh government had blocked such trade—driving it underground as goods were smuggled—but by the 2010s they seemed to relent (Rahmatullah 2011; Hasan 2011).

Chittagong's new networks also included international education. The public University of Chittagong, established in 1966, had a national scope. In 2008 a more international initiative came to fruition when the private Asian University for Women opened its doors in Chittagong. It was geared to providing women from South and Southeast Asia and the Middle East with a North-American style of higher education.

The city's social and cultural mix had undergone considerable change. The Muhajirs and Punjabis, who had been dominant till 1971, had been killed during the Liberation War or had fled to Pakistan; Bengalis had taken their place. As a result Chittagong was now more Bengali than ever. Bengalis—not necessarily locals—dominated its commercial and administrative life, and the city's elite had become an important player in Bangladeshi national affairs. The number of expats linked to aid, trade, industry, and international organizations had risen, as had the number of Rohingya refugees from Burma; both now formed distinct communities in the city.

Scale

In half a century the city saw its population increase tenfold, to over 4 million people in 2010. City planners were unable to make much of a mark on placemaking: dense settlements developed haphazardly as hills were flattened to accommodate newcomers and poorly-constructed apartment blocks went up—particularly risky in an earthquake and cyclone zone.

The new Chittagonians were mostly poor; they were refugees from rural stagnation who were unable to find steady jobs in the city and formed communities in vast slums of their own creation. Many tried to scale up by participating in new labor migration opportunities. Following an all-Bangladesh trend, they sought employment abroad, especially in the Gulf and Southeast Asia. The remittances they sent home changed Chittagong and shaped its appearance in many ways, from construction activities (houses, mosques) to the setting up of a range of enterprises.

Conclusion

These four snapshots from Chittagong's long past fall far short of providing even a potted history of the city—they skip many crucial events, twists, and transformations that occurred in between these four moments.[35] The snapshots are intended merely to help us think about how people create places out of spaces and how we can re-inscribe place into our notions of globalization.

First, in these vignettes Chittagong appears as four places successively blossoming in a single location. In other words, places are moments, "spatial moments [that] come into being and continue being made at the meeting points of history, representation, and material practice" (Raffles 2002, 7–8). Such meetings involve clashes, negotiations, compromises, and adjustments as people construct places out of a range of resources: human as well as non-human, and material as well as discursive.[36]

Second, we have seen that, for various participants, the "thickness" of a place varies with the outcome of these negotiations. For example, over time Chittagong became "thicker"—affectively a more significant place—for Bengalis as they emerged as the dominant group in the city. The Muhajir immigrants who arrived in Chittagong after 1947 had a different experience. Before 1947 Chittagong had meant nothing to most of them but now they threw themselves into contributing to a new Pakistani version of the city: more Muslim, Urdu-speaking, modern and dynamic than ever before. They invested ample wealth, labor, and emotion into this venture of turning Chittagong into a "thick" place where they belonged and to which they were committed. And yet, a quarter of a century later, the Pakistani place they had helped create had disappeared and their contributions were denounced. Expelled from Bangladesh, they were left with fading feelings of nostalgia and recrimination as the Chittagong of yesterday thinned out in their minds.[37]

This distinction between thick and thin places is essential to remind us of the subjective and discursive nature of placemaking, which cannot be grasped by simply applying the dimensions of scale, network and territory. In this chapter we have only been able to give a cursory glance at how people experience, imagine, embody, enact, and interpret these dimensions, what meanings and emotions they derive from places and how these feed into their placemaking behavior. Other contributions to this volume (notably Perdue, Limbert, Siu, and Tsu) develop this approach to place more fully. In doing so, they point to the need for sociospatial theory to incorporate the subjectivities underlying placemaking and thus to engage more fully with empirical work on place in history, anthropology, and literature. They also invite a dialogue with recent work in human geography employing concepts such as 'relational placemaking,' 'positionality' and 'habitus' (Casey 2001; Duff 2010; Pierce, Martin, and Murphy 2011).

Third, the thickness or thinness of a place may be less related to a person's physical presence than in the past. Earlier, those whom force of circumstance forced to leave a place generally lost the capacity, but not necessarily the disposition, to shape it. Belonging would turn into longing, giving rise to an émigré mindset. This tension between disposition and placemaking (or between habitus and habitation)[38] has been explored for certain moments—e.g. decolonization and Partition (Chakrabarty 1996)—but it remains undeveloped for others. Today this tension is modified by frequent long-distance face-to-face communication by virtual means. New social media allow many migrants to feel intimately connected with the places they have left behind and to remain actively involved in placemaking through remittances, day-to-day decision-making and other practices. In other words, long-distance placemaking has entered a new phase.

Fourth, this development underlines the value of understanding places multi-dimensionally, as transitory products of local histories, practices and imaginations, and, concurrently, of territorial, scalar and network relations in the wider world. Chittagong's four configurations show, however, that we need to approach multi-dimensionality flexibly because the different dimensions may not be equally important to explain how places are constructed. Their roles change over time and differ locally. For example, the territorial dimension emerged as being extremely significant for Chittagong in its recent embodiments. Unanticipated quirks of state formation influenced placemaking here more than some currently popular approaches—flows, rhizomatic inter-connectivity, network geographies, or rescaling—allow for.[39]

Finally, this chapter has sought to demonstrate the usefulness of comparative studies of placemaking, the unending creation of spatial moments. We can do so by looking at one location across time, as we have done here, or at different coexisting locations.[40] Both approaches highlight how the impact of the different dimensions on the production of place varies. When we study place, scale, network, and territory jointly, we are reminded of the local bumpiness of social space and the inadequacy of undifferentiated notions of the global.

Notes

1. The second-century Egyptian Ptolemy speaks of Pentapolis; fourteenth-century Moroccan adventurer Ibn Battuta refers to it as Sudkawan; sixteenth-century Portuguese sources speak of Porto Grande, Xatigam, and Bengala; Bengalis have long called it Chottogram; Saitagong is the Arakanese appellation; and seventeenth-century administrators named it Islamabad. For these and several other names (some of which are disputed), and various spellings, see Yule (1903, 58, 85–86, 203–204, 649) and Gerini (1897).

2. For example, that the name Chittagong comes from the Arabic word *shat* (delta) prefixed to *ganga* (Ganges) (Bernoli in 1786); that it derives from "the *chatag,* which is the most beautiful little bird I ever saw" (Jones in c. 1792); that it refers to the earthen lamp *(chati)* lit by the town's guardian saint Badr Pir to rid it of evil spirits (Khan in 1871); that it is from the Sanskrit *Chaturgrāma* ("four villages") or *Saptagrāma* ("seven villages") (Yule in 1886); that it refers to an inscription in Arakanese ("Tsit-ta-gung," presumably "there shall be no war") on a lost tenth-century victory monument; and so on. See Yule (1903, 204); Khan (1871, 27), cited in Serajuddin (1998, 356); Ali (1967); Comstock et al. (1847).

3. Theorists have proposed various terms to express the lived, experiential aspects of space, e.g., "thirdspace" (Soja) and "place-world" (Casey). Casey (2001, 683, 688) describes space as "the encompassing volumetric void in which things (including human beings) are positioned" and place as "the immediate environment of my lived body—an arena of action that is at once physical and historical, social and cultural . . . places come to be embedded in us; they become part of our very self, our enduring character, what we enact and carry forward."

4. In somewhat similar vein Marc Augé (1992; 1995) described these as "non-places" and distinguished them from "anthropological places."

5. See the wide-ranging discussions following the publication of de Certeau (1980/84).

6. Jessop et al. (2008, 389).

7. Hall (2010, 111) describes this as the "Bay of Bengal network" for the period up to 1500 CE.

8. "In this context, 'place' must be understood as an anchor point, a settlement spot where a number of people gathered 'temporarily' or 'permanently'—with the implication that 'permanently' is really temporary, and subject to better opportunities elsewhere, or an ultimate return to the ethnic homeland" (Hall, 2010, 117).

9. Not all these rivers were easily navigable in the region where they flowed most closely together—western Yunnan and eastern Tibet—but, even so, in this mountainous region their valleys provided crucial corridors for the movement of people and goods.

10. The Brahmaputra flowed past Mymensingh in north Bengal and then east of Dhaka. In 1787 it suddenly changed course, found a channel west of Dhaka and merged with the Ganges in central Bangladesh. This had huge consequences for commercial activities in eastern Bengal and for trade flows to and from the port of Chittagong.

11. Bengal as a whole, but especially the eastern sector, was so productive that by the sixteenth century it had become the world's major exporter of rice. "There is such a quantity of rice," observed the Frenchman, François Pyrard, after spending the spring of 1607 in the eastern port of Chittagong, " . . . that, besides supplying the whole country, it is exported to all parts of India, as well to Goa and Malabar, as to Sumatra, the Moluccas, and all the islands of Sunda, to all of which lands Bengal is a very nursing mother, who supplies them and their entire subsistence and food. Thus, one sees arrive there [Chittagong] every day an infinite number of vessels from all parts of India for these provisions . . ." (Eaton, 2009, 200). On agarwood or aloeswood, see Mukherjee (2006).

12. On the transformation from a rootless "Sanskrit cosmopolis" to vernacular cultural forms in Southern Asia in the period 1000–1500, see Pollock (1998; 2000).

13. "The inhabitants of Chittagong venerate him as their guardian saint . . . His name is invoked by the boatman of eastern Bengal along with other five saints called *Panch Pir*. He is the immortal patron saint of seamen along the coastline as far south as the Malayan Peninsula and further. The . . . Buddhist kings of Arakan settled some villages in *waqf* on his tomb and they used to come for pilgrimage to the holy dead and offer presents. The people of Tenasserim in Myanmar call him Madra and to the native of Akyab he is known as Buddah Auliya or Buddah Sahib. In Chittagong, people call him in various names, Badr Alam, Badar Auliya, Badar Pir or Pir Badar and Badar Shah" (Hossain, 2003). See Serajuddin (1998) and Hall (2010, 123).

14. For a distinction between "port cities" and "littoral societies," see Pearson (2006).

15. These units themselves were far from monolithic. Roy (2011, 121) argues that seventeenth-century Bengal was a "fragmented polity" and that "a notion of "Bengal" as a meaningful unit in global economic history cannot be sustained.'

16. Mukherjee (2009, 115) introduces the term "Indic" for the western reaches of the Bengal delta and "Sinic" for its eastern reaches and the areas stretching from there to Yunnan. It might be good to look for a term other than Sinic because of its association with (Han) Chinese-ness. If this region was largely "beyond the pale of Hinduism," as Mukherjee asserts, it was also beyond the pale of Chinese-ness. For the time being, this non-Indic, non-Sinic and non-Burmese place (covering the space that we know today as eastern Bangladesh; the Rakhine, Chin, and Kachin states of Burma; and Northeast India) remains without an agreed name. I refer to it as the Brahmaputra-and-mountains region here.

17. For additional changes in the water flowing through various branches of the Ganges, see Eaton (1993, 195–198).

18. This is how a European visitor described Chittagong in the early 1700s: "Xatigam is a Town that borders on *Bengal* and *Arackan*, and its Poverty makes it a Matter of Indifference whom it belongs to. It was here that the *Portugueze* first settled in *Bengal*, but the Dangers their Ships run in coming thither in the South-west Monsoons, made them remove to the *Bandel* at *Hughly*. The *Mogul* keeps a *Cadjee* or Judge in it, to administer Justice among the *Pagan* and *Mahometan* Inhabitants, but the Offspring of those *Portugueze* that followed the Fortune of *Sultan Sujah*, when he was forced to quit *Bengal*, are the domineering Lords of it. It is not so fertil in Corn as *Bengal*, and has but few Cotton Manufactures, but it affords the best Timber for building, of any Place about it . . . The Government is so anarchical, that every one goes armed with Sword and Pistol, and Blunderbuss, nay, even Priests are obliged to go armed, and often use their Arms to as bad Ends as the licentious Laity, and some of the Priests have died Martyrs to villainous Actions" (Hamilton 1744, II, 25–26).

19. Chittagong's commercial orientation made it very different from most provincial towns in Bengal, which were dominated much more by administrative and landholding interests. See Islam (1980).

20. On poor connections between the eastern and the western delta, see Munshi (1992, 526–530) and Ahmed (1974, 237–242).

21. In the early nineteenth century Malcolm (1839, 133–134) had described Chittagong as follows: "The streets are in good order, and the bazaar abundantly supplied with every sort of domestic and foreign produce. The town includes 12,000 people, and immediately adjacent are many populous villages . . . About three hundred vessels, chiefly brigs of from forty to a hundred tons, are owned in the place, and many vessels from other places resort there. The chief exports are rice and salt. I saw lying at anchor several large Maldive boats, of indescribable construction. These vessels, with a deck made of thatch, venture annually, during this fine season, from those distant islands, bringing cowries, tortoise-shell, cumela, cocoa-nuts and coir for rope; and carry away rice and small manufactures."

22. Khan (2002), Munshi (1992, 537–541). The town received an additional, if temporary, boost when the province of Bengal was split in two, making Chittagong

the main port of the new province of Eastern Bengal and Assam from 1905 to 1911. For an analysis of the forces behind this policy, see Ludden (2012).

23. In the late nineteenth century, "Chittagong, being very unhealthy, was regarded as a penal station, and all the worst men in the Services were sent there . . . In addition to the officials there were some merchants and tea-planters, rough, rowdy bachelors, hardly fit society for ladies or gentlemen" (Beames, 1961, 292). Sudha Mazumdar—wife of a Bengali official posted to "remote," "'distant" Chittagong—provides a critical portrait of upper-class life in the town in the 1920s (1977, 189–200).

24. "The men dressed in a white calico shirt, white trousers and a crimson sash round the waist; the women in a cotton gown with black mantilla and a parasol of some vivid colour. Down in the native town, close along the river bank, they kept shops where they sold bad liquor to the sailors, and the back rooms were kept for immoral purposes by the women. Brawls were frequent, and the two English constables, with a native force of police, had enough to do to keep the peace in those unsavoury slums." Beames describing this community in 1878 (1961, 287, see also 297–300).

25. This institution still exists. See http://www.chittagongclubbd.com/history.htm

26. This is how a British official, posted to Chittagong in 1878, described his arrival by boat from Kolkata: "a mass of English, French and Yankee ships—long lines of godowns on piles—a jetty—a flagstaff—roofs peeping over the trees—fringe of palm above them, and above that again a lot of curious little hills each with a crown of tall casuarina trees and a bungalow. In the extreme distance, faintly seen through the haze, the blue mountains of Burma—*voilà* Chittagong" (Beames, 1961, 276).

27. The preference of "British gentlemen" for Chittagong's hilltops is attested to as early as the late eighteenth century (Van Schendel 1992, 123).

28. Although for centuries ships that took to sea from Chittagong must have had men from the town and the surrounding villages serving as crew, the evidence is fragmentary. By the early 1900s a clear pattern had emerged: "Seamen who hail from Sylhet, Noakhali [two northern districts] and Chittagong form the bulk of the engine-room crew, while the deck crew consists mainly of people coming from Noakhali and Chittagong" (Desai 1940, 22).

29. "Port facilities were inadequate to handle more than a fraction of the traffic required by the new country. Transport facilities between the two Wings were practically non-existent. The whole transport system had to be re-oriented . . . Chittagong was the only seaport of East Pakistan at the time of independence, and had a capacity of only half-a-million tons a year; by 1955 its capacity had been expanded to over 2 million tons a year . . . At partition the country had practically no shipping of its own. Since then seven national shipping companies have been formed, and there are now 20 Pakistani merchant ships in commission, with a dead weight tonnage of about 180,000 handling about a million tons between East and West Pakistan, plus some Haj traffic and tramp services" (Government of Pakistan 1957, 485–486, see also 495, 499).

30. Travelers between the two port cities were almost certain to pass through Karachi's new transit point, aptly named "Chittagong Colony" (Naqvi, 2006).

31. During the Second World War fear of a Japanese invasion had led the British authorities to follow a "denial policy," which included the destruction of boats and the dismantling of workshops and some installations of Chittagong's port (Government of Pakistan 1957, 487). Allied forces also constructed an airfield at Chittagong from which numerous flights over "The Hump" (the eastern Himalayas), to southwestern China, were carried out. In retaliation, Japanese air raids caused extensive damage in Chittagong. Chittagong also played a vital part (as the Indian Ocean supply point for southwestern China) in Allied plans to revitalize the overland Brahmaputra-and-mountains connection by means of railway connections, oil pipelines and the "Stillwell Road" across The Hump.

32. See van Schendel (2005) for information about illegal trade continuing across the officially closed borders between East Pakistan and India.

33. "[S]teel plate from the ships provides 90% of the steel used in Bangladesh and is turned into reinforcing rods for the concrete making the new houses and apartments springing up in Bangladeshi cities; ship chandlery is resold to equip the coastal fishing fleet; and electric motors and components are reconditioned and sold to land- based industries with, for instance, ships' boilers and compressors being used in dyeing fabric and generators to power the factories producing garments for the clothes export sector. Indeed the proud boast of the industry is that 99% of an end-of-life ship is 'recycled'" (Gregson et al. 2010, 848). See also Park (2009).

34. A second port is being planned in Sonadia Island to the south of Chittagong (Devichand 2010).

35. Among these are the town's occupation by the British (1757), a soldier's rebellion (1857), the Chittagong Armoury Raid (1930), the famine of 1943, Allied military build-up during World War II, the Bangladesh Liberation War (1971) and several devastating cyclones.

36. For a recent analysis of complex struggles over space and history in another Asian port, see Sutherland (2011).

37. By contrast, those Muhajirs who could not leave do continue to experience Chittagong as a 'thick' place, albeit radically different from pre-1971. Most Muhajirs were staunch supporters of a united Pakistan and were pro-Pakistani during the Bangladesh Liberation War. After the war those who could not flee to (West) Pakistan were herded into camps as hated collaborators. Today these camps still exist and, in Chittagong alone, are home to thousands of stateless and despised refugees (Sholder, 2011, 47–48).

38. By linking the concepts of "habitus" and "habitation," Casey (2001, 487) suggests a relationship between dispositions and placemaking: "If habitus represents a movement from the externality of established customs and norms to the internality of durable dispositions, habitation is a matter of re-externalization—of taking the habitus that has been acquired and continually re-enacting it in the place-world."

39. For an even more extreme case of territory trumping other dimensions, see Van Schendel (2002).

40. The two can be combined as well. Thus contemporary sources as well as later historians have described Arakanese, Portuguese, and Dutch military-commercial activities in seventeenth-century Chittagong as "piracy." Wheeler (on Vietnam) and Siu (on southern China)—both in this volume—analyze the complex interplay of 'piracy' and state formation in coastal localities, inviting comparison with Chittagong at different moments in time, including the present (today, Chittagong-bound ships frequently fear attacks by pirates (van Schendel, 2005, 274–275, 291–292)).

References

Ahmed, Rafiuddin. 1981. *The Bengal Muslims 1871–1906: A Quest for Identity*. Delhi: Oxford University Press.

Ahmed, Sufia. 1974. *Muslim Community in Bengal, 1884–1912*. Dacca: S. Ahmed/ Oxford University Press.

Ali, S. M. 1967. "Arakan Rule in Chittagong (1550–1666 A.D)." *Journal of Asiatic Society of Pakistan* 12 (3): 333–351.

Andrews, Margaret W., et al., eds. 1992. *Letters from Chittagong: An American Forestry Couple's Letters Home, 1952–54*. New Delhi: Arnold Publishers.

Augé, Marc. 1992. *Non-lieux: Introduction à une anthropologie de la surmodernité*. Paris: Seuil.

———. 1995. *Non-Places: An Introduction to Supermodernity*. London: Verso.

Beames, John. 1961. *Memoirs of a Bengal Civilian: The Lively Narrative of a Victorian District Officer*. London: Chatto & Windus.

Bodhinyana, U. 2001. "An Outline of the Arakanese Rule in Southeast Bengal During 16th and 17th Century AD." *Arakanese Research Journal* 1. http://www.narinjara. com (accessed June 14, 2011).

Boomgaard, Peter. 2008. "Early Globalization: Cowries as Currency, 600 BCE-1900." In *Linking Destinies: Trade, Towns and Kin in Asian History*, ed. Peter Boomgaard, Dick Kooiman and Henk Schulte Nordholt, 13–27. Leiden: KITLV Press.

Camões, Luís de. [1572]. 1997 *Os Lusíadas*. Lisbon: Publicações Europa-America.

Campos, J. J. A. 1919. *History of the Portuguese in Bengal*. Calcutta: Butterworth & Co.

Casey, Edward S. 2001. "Beyond Geography and Philosophy: What Does It Mean to Be in the Place-World?" *Annals of the Association of American Geographers* 91 (4): 683–693.

Chakrabarty, Dipesh. 1996. "Remembered Villages: Representation of Hindu-Bengali Memories in the Aftermath of Partition." *Economic and Political Weekly* (August 10): 2143–2151.

Comstock, G. S., et al. 1847. "Notes on Arakan." *Journal of the American Oriental Society* 1 (3): 219, 221–258.

De Barros, João. 1777–1788. *Ásia de João de Barros: dos feitos que os portugueses fizeram no descobrimento e conquista dos mares e terras do Oriente, Vol 4. (Quarta década).* Lisbon.

De Certeau, Michel. 1980. *L'invention du quotidien, vol. 1. Arts de faire.* Paris: Union générale d'éditions.

———. 1984. *The Practice of Everyday Life.* Berkeley: University of California Press.

Desai, Dinkar D. 1940. *Maritime Labour in India.* Bombay: Servants of India Society.

Devichand, Mukul. 2010. "Is Chittagong one of China's 'string of pearls'?" *BBC News,* May 17. http://news.bbc.co.uk/2/hi/business/8687917.stm (accessed November 26, 2011.)

Deyell, John S. 2010. "Cowries and Coins: The Dual Monetary System of the Bengal Sultanate." *The Indian Economic and Social History Review* 47 (1): 63–106.

Duff, Cameron. 2010. "On the Role of Affect and Practice in the Production of Place" *Environment and Planning D: Society and Space,* 28: 881–895.

Eaton, Richard M. 1993. *The Rise of Islam and the Bengal Frontier, 1204–1760.* Berkeley: University of California Press.

———. 2009. "Shrines, Cultivators, and Muslim 'Conversion' in Punjab and Bengal, 1300–1700." *The Medieval History Journal* 12: 191–220.

Gerini, G. E. 1897. "Notes on the Early Geography of Indo-China." *Journal of the Royal Asiatic Society of Great Britain and Ireland* July: 551–577.

Gommans, Jos. 2002. "Burma at the Frontier of South, East and Southeast Asia: A Geographic Perspective." In *The Maritime Frontier of Burma: Exploring Political, Cultural and Commercial Interaction in the Indian Ocean World, 1200–1800,* ed. Jos Gommans and Jacques Leider, 1–7. Leiden: KITLV Press.

Government of Pakistan. 1957. *The First Five Year Plan 1955–60.* Karachi: National Planning Board.

Gregson, N., et al. 2010. "Following Things of Rubbish Value: End-of-life Ships, 'Chock-chocky' Furniture and the Bangladeshi Middle Class Consumer." *Geoforum* 41 (6): 846–854.

Hall, Kenneth R. 2010. "Ports-of-Trade, Maritime Diasporas, and Networks of Trade and Cultural Integration in the Bay of Bengal Region of the Indian Ocean: c. 1300–1500." *Journal of the Economic and Social History of the Orient* 53: 109–145.

Hamilton, Alexander. 1744. *A New Account of the East Indies . . . ,* 2 vols. London: C. Hitch and A. Millar.

Hasan, Rabiul. 2011. "Nepal First to Use Ctg Port: Takes Its Goods From Morocco Thru Chapainawabganj." *The Daily Star,* July 17. Hossain, Shamsul. 2003. "Badr Auliya." In *Banglapedia: National Encyclopedia of Bangladesh,* ed. Sirajul Islam and Sajahan Miah, I, 359. Dhaka: Asiatic Society of Bangladesh.

Islam, M. S. 1980. "Life in the Mufassal Towns of Nineteenth-Century Bengal." In *The City in South Asia: Pre-Modern and Modern,* ed. Kenneth Ballhatchet and John Harrison, 224–226. London: Curzon Press

Jessop, Bob, Neil Brenner, and Martin Jones. 2008. "Theorizing Sociospatial Relations." *Environment and Planning D: Society and Space* 26: 389–401.

Khan, Hamidullah. 1871. *Ahadith ul-Khwanin*. Calcutta.

Khan, Misbahuddin. 2002. *History of the Port of Chittagong, 1888–1947*, 2 vols. Dhaka: International Centre for Bengal Studies.

Kochanek, Stanley A. 1993. *Patron-Client Politics and Business in Bangladesh*. New Delhi: Sage.

Leider, Jacques, and Thibaut d'Hubert. 2011. "Traders and Poets at the Mrauk U Court: Commerce and Cultural Links in Seventeenth-Century Arakan." In *Passageways: The Northern Bay of Bengal Before Colonialism*, ed. Rila Mukherjee, 77–111. New Delhi: Primus Books.

Ludden, David. 2012. "Spatial Inequity and National Territory: Remapping 1905 in Bengal and Assam." *Modern Asian Studies* 46: 483–525.

Malcolm, Howard. 1839. *Travels in South-eastern Asia, Embracing Hindustan, Malaya, Siam, and China; with a Full Account of the Burman Empire*. Oxford: Oxford University Press.

Massey, Doreen, Human Geography Research Group, Sophie Bond and David Featherstone. 2009. "The Possibilities of a Politics of Place Beyond Place? A Conversation with Doreen Massey." *Scottish Geographical Journal* 125 (3–4): 401–420.

Mazumdar, Shudha. 1977. *A Pattern of Life: The Memoirs of an Indian Woman*. Edited by Geraldine H. Forbes. New Delhi: Manohar Book Service.

Mukherjee, Hena. 2003. "Assam Bengal Railway." In *Banglapedia: National Encyclopedia of Bangladesh,* ed. Sirajul Islam and Sajahan Miah, I, 311–312. Dhaka: Asiatic Society of Bangladesh.

Mukherjee, Rila. 2006. *Strange Riches: Bengal in the Mercantile Map of South Asia*. New Delhi: Foundation Books.

———. 2008. "The Struggle for the Bay: The Life and Times of Sandwip, an Almost Unknown Portuguese Port in the Bay of Bengal in the Sixteenth and Seventeenth Centuries." *Revista da Faculdade de Letras—História* (Porto) 3 (9): 67–88.

———. 2009. "Mobility in the Bay of Bengal World: Medieval Raiders, Traders, States and the Slaves." *Indian Historical Review* 36 (1): 109–229.

Munshi, Sunil Kumar. 1992. "Transportation and Communication." In *History of Bangladesh 1704–1971. Volume Two: Economic History*, ed. Sirajul Islam, 519–541. Dhaka: Asiatic Society of Bangladesh.

Naqvi, Abbas. 2006. "Falling Back." *Daily Times* (Lahore), December 17.

Pandit, Rajat. 2010. "China Eyes Rail Link to Chittagong." *The Times of India,* September 18. http://articles.timesofindia.indiatimes.com/2010–09–18/india/28237001_1_chittagong-port-yunnan-province-india-and-china (accessed November 24, 2011.)

Park, Bong-Nam. (Director). 2009. *Iron Crows* [Film documentary]. Frontline News Service. Paul, Manas. 2010. "Bangladesh Welcomes Indian Investment in Chittagong: Foreign Minister." *Defence Pakistan*, November 11. http://www.defence.

pk/forums/bangladesh-defence/81365-bangladesh-welcomes-indian-investment-chittagong-foreign-minister.html (accessed October 29, 2011).

Pearson, Michael N. 2006. "Littoral Society: The Concept and the Problems." *Journal of World History* 17: 4353–4373.

Pierce, Joseph, Deborah G. Martin, and James T. Murphy. 2011. "Relational Place-Making: The Networked Politics of Place." *Transactions of the Institute of British Geographers* NS 36: 54–70.

Pollock, Sheldon. 1998. "The Cosmopolitan Vernacular." *The Journal of Asian Studies* 57 (1): 6–37.

———. 2000. "Cosmopolitan and Vernacular in History." *Public Culture* 12 (3): 591–625.

Prakash, Om. 2004. "The Indian Maritime Merchant, 1500–1700." *Journal of the Economic and Social History of the Orient* 47 (3): 435–457.

Qanungo, S. B. 1988. *A History of Chittagong*. Chittagong: Signet Library.

Raffles, Hugh. 2002. *In Amazonia: A Natural History*. Princeton, NJ: Princeton University Press.

Rahmatullah, M. 2011. "Connectivity Issue: Political Leaders Set the Tone." *The Daily Star*, March 28.

Rizvi, S. N. H., ed. 1970. *East Pakistan District Gazetteers: Chittagong*. Dacca: East Pakistan Government Press.

Roy, Tirthankar. 2011. "Where is Bengal? Situating an Indian Region in the Early Modern World Economy." *Past & Present* 213: 115–146.\

Sen, Tansen. 2006. "The Formation of Chinese Maritime Networks to Southern Asia, 1200–1450." *Journal of the Economic and Social History of the Orient* 49 (4): 421–453.

Serajuddin, Asma. 1998. "Badr Pir and his *Dargah* at Chittagong: A Study in the Architectural Extension of Pirism." In *Contributions to Bengal Studies: An Interdisciplinary and International Approach*, ed. Enayetur Rahim and Henry Schwarz, 344–358. Dhaka: Pustaka.

Sholder, Hannah. 2011. *Housing and Land Rights: The Camp-Dwelling Urdu-Speaking Community in Bangladesh*. Dhaka: Refugee and Migratory Movements Research Unit (RMMRU).

Singh, Prashant Kumar. 2010. "China-Bangladesh Relations: Acquiring a Life of their Own." *China Report* 46 (3): 267–283.

Sobhan, Rehman. 1962. "The Problem of Regional Imbalance in the Economic Development of Pakistan." *Asian Survey* 2 (5): 31–37.

Soja, E. W. 1996. *Thirdspace: Journeys to Los Angeles and Other Real-and-Imagined Places*. Oxford: Blackwell, 1996.

Subrahmanyam, Sanjay. 1988. "A Note on Narsapur Peta: A 'Syncretic' Shipbuilding Centre in South India, 1570–1700." *Journal of the Economic and Social History of the Orient* 31 (3): 305–311.

Sutherland, Heather. 2011. "Whose Makassar? Claiming Space in a Segmented City." *Comparative Studies in Society and History* 53 (4): 791–826.

van Galen, Stephan. 2002. "Arakan at the Turn of the First Millennium of the Arakanese Era." In *The Maritime Frontier of Burma: Exploring Political, Cultural and Commercial Interaction in the Indian Ocean World, 1200–180*, ed. Jos Gommans and Jacques Leider, 151–162. Leiden: KITLV Press.

van Schendel, Willem. 2002. "Stateless in South Asia: The Making of the India-Bangladesh Enclaves." *The Journal of Asian Studies* 61 (1): 115–147.

———. 2005. *The Bengal Borderland: Beyond State and Nation in South Asia*. London: Anthem Press,.

———, ed. 1992. *Francis Buchanan in Southeast Bengal (1798): His Journey to Chittagong, the Chittagong Hill Tracts, Noakhali and Comilla*. Dhaka: University Press Limited.

Yule, Henry. 1903. *Hobson-Jobson: A Glossary of Colloquial Anglo-Indian Words and Phrases, and of Kindred Terms, Etymological, Historical, Geographical and Discursive* (new edn., edited by William Crooke, B.A.).

4

War and Charisma

Horses and Elephants in the Indian Ocean Economy

ALAN MIKHAIL

Indian Ocean trade involved much more than just spices and textiles.[1] Between 1200 and 1800, live animals were regularly in motion on ships between South Asia and the Middle East. Many different kinds of animals were in demand for many different kinds of reasons, and their histories of trade therefore illuminate many different economic processes. Two of the most important of these animals were horses and elephants. Horses were moved primarily from the Arabian Peninsula and southern Iranian coast to India to fuel military confrontations between various rival states in the subcontinent. They were also often shipped on from India to China and Southeast Asia. Elephants went in the opposite direction. They were shipped from India to various parts of the Middle East (and beyond) as objects of fascination and wonder that were used by imperial powers to project ideas of sovereignty, alliance, kingship, and universality. Horses thus drove a military economy while elephants fueled a charismatic economy. Both of these very different animal economies stretched across Asia—from Istanbul and Cairo in the far west to China in the far east. This chapter examines the horse and elephant trades to understand aspects of the history of the Indian Ocean economy, the political uses of live animals by late medieval and early modern states, and connections between the Middle East, South Asia, and beyond.

The War Horse Economy

While India's role in Indian Ocean trade was usually that of supplier, it was also of course an important consumer of goods coming from elsewhere. One of the largest and most lucrative import markets in India was for horses from the Arabian Peninsula and the southern Iranian coast. The two main threads of this trade to South Asia began in the Yemeni port city of Aden and around the Persian Gulf island of Kish. The port city of Hormuz on the Persian Gulf near Kish was the largest trading site for horses destined for South Asia.[2] Egypt was a secondary trading link of the Aden-India trade, and China[3] and Southeast Asia[4] were secondary links of the Kish-India trade. Most of these horses from the Persian Gulf and Arabian Peninsula were funneled through the ports of Goa, Bhatkal, and Cannanore (today's Kannur in Kerala) to the Deccan Kingdom of Vijayanagara.

Arabian and Persian horses were renowned for their strength, size, and speed and were indeed used for centuries by the leaders of south India's independent kingdoms to gain a comparative military advantage over their

Horse from Ottoman translation of Qazvīnī's *'Aca'ib ül-Mahlukat.* (Walters Art Museum, Ms. W.659, 76b, Images for Academic Publishing)

enemies.[5] Poems from the Sangam Period in South India (third century BCE to third century CE), for instance, mention the importation of white Persian horses via ship to ports in the southeast. While most horses exported from the Persian Gulf went to India, many also made their way farther east to China, either directly or via secondary trade links between the subcontinent and China. During the Tang dynasty (early seventh to early tenth century), horses were sent to China from the Persian Gulf as tribute.[6] Chinese traders in the Indian Ocean were especially keen to break into the region's maritime horse trade. For example, the twelfth-century Guangzhou customs official Zhou Qufei wrote from Kollam on the Malabar Coast that Arabian horses were regularly found there and were of the highest quality. A few years later in 1225, another customs official, Zhao Rugua, wrote about the Indian Ocean horse trade from various areas he visited on the Persian Gulf coast. In Oman, he made special note of the exchange of horses, pearls, and dates for cloves, cardamom, and camphor from South Asia.[7] He also visited the tiny Persian Gulf island of Kish and commented that its chief export was its "fine horses."[8]

The horse trade from the Persian Gulf to India (and then on from India to China) increased markedly in the thirteenth and fourteenth centuries. The primary reason for this upsurge in trade was the Mongol conquests of the thirteenth century.[9] Parts of Iran became central administrative zones of the Ilkhanid Empire, and because of the close familial and, in turn, economic relationships between Ilkanid and Yuan rulers, trade between Central Asia and China exploded in this period.[10] Horses moving from Iran and Central Asia to China were a major component of this trade.[11] And this traffic in horses would continue into the fifteenth[12] and sixteenth centuries.[13] Increased desire for Iranian horses in China benefitted the maritime horse trade to and from India.[14] As various military confrontations during the fourteenth century interrupted trade along the Silk Road, the route by sea became an increasingly preferred alternative. The two most famous Ilkhanid historians, Rashid ad-Din Fazlallah and Vassaf al-Hazrat, both wrote of Indian envoys sent to Kish exclusively to make arrangements for the export of horses to southern India. According to these writers, roughly 10,000 horses, brought from various parts of Iran, were taken annually from Kish to the Pandya dynasty in southeast India.[15] Historians generously estimate that ships in this period could carry up to 100 horses. Thus in the thirteenth century, at least 100 ships a year carried horses from Kish to southeast India—representing an obviously enormous investment in capital and maritime resources.

Marco Polo, writing in roughly this period, offers a description of these ships and of the commerce in horses between Hormuz and India.[16] Of this trade, he writes, "The country [Persia] is distinguished for its excellent breed of horses, many of which are carried for sale to India, and bring high prices, not less in general than two hundred Tours pounds. . . . The traders of these parts convey the horses to Chisi [Kish], to Ormus [Hormuz], and to other places on the coast of the Indian Sea, where they are purchased by those who carry them to India."[17] When in southeast India years later, Marco Polo saw the other end of this horse trade and describes some of what continually fueled it. "No horses being bred in this country, the king and his three royal brothers expend large sums of money annually in the purchase of them from merchants of Ormus, Diufar, Pecher, and Adem [Hormuz, Doha, Sohar, and Aden], who carry them thither for sale, and become rich by the traffic, as they import to the number of five thousand, and for each of them obtain five hundred *saggi* of gold, being equal to one hundred marks of silver. At the end of the year . . . perhaps not three hundred of these remain alive, and thus the necessity is occasioned for replacing them annually."[18]

Marco Polo also offers clues about the rickety ships that made the horse trade possible. "The vessels built at Ormus [Hormuz] are of the worst kind, and dangerous for navigation, exposing the merchants and others who make use of them to great hazards."[19] Concerned for his safety, Marco Polo therefore decided to travel overland to China from Hormuz, making the long journey through Central Asia and then on to Beijing. On his return trip, however, Marco Polo, perhaps still aching from his earlier overland saddle ride, came back from China to Hormuz by ship. Beyond fears for his safety, his earlier decision to go overland from Hormuz to Beijing may have partly been influenced by the dozens of horses onboard these ships. He writes that horses were loaded on to vessels on top of the ship's cargo with little to protect either the horses' hooves or the merchandise underneath them.

Perhaps as well he found this mode of transport less than desirable because of the intense smell that many observers noted about these ships and their equine passengers. For example, 'Abd al-Razzaq Samarqandi, Timurid ambassador to Calicut in the middle of the fifteenth century, vividly describes how the stench of the ship he boarded in Hormuz with a group of horses nearly made him faint with illness.[20] Elsewhere, we read that horse merchants covered the decks of their ships with a certain straw (that the Portuguese called the straw of Mecca) known to grow near the Omani cities of Muscat and

Qalhat that would soak up horse urine and manure to help get rid of the smell.[21] Periodically during their trips, merchants would throw the saturated straw overboard and replace it with fresh reserves kept on board. Offering further details about the transportation of horses on ships leaving from Hormuz and Muscat, a Portuguese Augustinian Friar who lived in Hormuz in the 1590s wrote that horses were bled before being loaded onto ships to make them more tame and docile.[22] They were then packed very tightly into the ship's galleys to make sure they could not move during the journey and were thus made to stand for the entire trip from the Persian Gulf coast to India.

In addition to the occasionally smelly and—for the humans but especially for the horses—seemingly uncomfortable unity of commerce provided by the Pax Mongolica, another significant reason the horse trade took off in the fourteenth century was military rivalry among the independent states of the Deccan.[23] As already noted, about 10,000 horses were moved annually from Hormuz to Pandya. The majority of these animals were utilized for military purposes. In the fourteenth century, the southern Vijayanagara and Bahmani Empires would vastly eclipse the Pandyas in the southeast in the numbers of horses they imported to support their frequent wars of conquest.[24] The military value the Vijayanagara state attached to its importation of horses from Iran in the fourteenth century, for which it gladly paid high prices, is made abundantly clear by the numerous carvings of warriors on horseback found in palaces and temples from the period.[25] Indeed, the Vijayanagara king Krishnadeva Raya made patently clear that the importation of horses—and, of course, the use of South and Central Asian elephants, whose imposing bodies in 'Abd al-Razzaq Samarqandi's words "bent the earth, and created quakes the world over"—were strategic military goals that should be encouraged to ensure his kingdom's domination of its enemies.[26] He wrote:

> A king should improve the harbours of his country and so encourage its commerce that horses, elephants, precious gems, sandalwood, pearls and other articles are freely imported . . . Make the merchants of distant foreign countries who import elephants and good horses attached to yourself by providing them with villages and decent dwellings in the city, by affording them daily audience, presents and allowing decent profits. Then those articles will never go to your enemies.[27]

In line with its king's advice, Vijayanagara, the capital of which was the largest and most important city in pre-colonial peninsular India, emerged as one of the most militarized of the Deccan empires, owning chiefly to its ability to import large numbers of horses from the Persian Gulf (and elephants from more northern areas in the subcontinent and from Central Asia) and its ability to take advantage of several new equine warfare technologies for its cavalry.[28] These new technologies included "the foot-stirrup providing greater support for the rider, better harnesses allowing more control over the horse, high saddles with pommels, and nailed horseshoes."[29] The Bahmani Empire, one of Vijayanagara's main rivals in the south, was quick to replicate these technologies, thus spurring a fourteenth-century arms race for more horses, better riding equipment, and more sophisticated cavalry techniques.

Competition for horses and for control of the horse trade was not only about warfare, however.[30] It was also of course about money. By the end of the fourteenth century, the import of horses from Hormuz and Aden had been regularized to the point that several merchant families were able to make huge windfall profits from the horse trade on India's southwestern coast.[31] The fifteenth century indeed saw several large-scale military confrontations over control of the now lucrative Indian Ocean horse trade.[32] For example, Chaul and Dabhol, two cities established by Firuz Shah of the Bahmani Empire as important horse trading posts at the start of the fifteenth century, were consistently under attack by various forces hoping to take control of their commerce.[33] Goa as well was subject to several military incursions in the fifteenth century aimed at seizing control of its lucrative horse trade. When Goa was captured at the end of the fifteenth century by the Adil Shahi dynasty of Bijapur, it was estimated that the business of importing horses from Hormuz alone netted the impressive sum of approximately 100,000 pardaos a year.[34] Horses from Hormuz, as well as from the Arabian Peninsula, were sold in Goa and then distributed throughout the Vijayanagara Empire in southern India. In 1512 Afonso de Albuquerque, the Portuguese governor in India, wrote to his king that "the trade in horses yields incredible profits, because bringing them from Hormuz and from the coast of Arabia to Goa it is possible to gain 300, 400 or 500 percent."[35] As further evidence of the scale of this commerce, consider the observation of another Portuguese writer in the first quarter of the sixteenth century who estimated that the emperor of Vijayanagara held over 20,000 horses in his imperial stables.[36] In addition to their important military purposes, these horses were used to patronize government administrators and provincial elites throughout the empire.

When the Portuguese captured Goa in 1510, they quickly moved to try to take advantage of the established Indian Ocean horse trade that ran through the port city.[37] Indeed, to more tightly control equine commerce, they tried to funnel all horse-trading vessels on the Malabar Coast through Goa, pursuing and capturing ships that tried to import horses elsewhere on the coast.[38] In 1546, for example, Portuguese ships chased and captured the ship of Khwaja Sofar of Gujarat as he attempted to bring horses directly from Hormuz to Gujarat.[39] The Portuguese eventually relented on their monopolization attempts and made some concessions in the 1540s.[40] Rulers in Cannanore were thus allowed to send four ships annually to Hormuz to collect horses and other goods. Similarly, Ibrahim Adil Shah I of the Adil Shahis of Bijapur successfully concluded a contract with the Portuguese in 1546 that allowed him to import twelve horses every year from the Arabian Peninsula; a subsequent agreement in 1548 increased this number to fifteen. In an even earlier treaty from 1539, Burhan Nizam Shah I, the Nizam Shahi rule of Ahmadnagar, was allowed to import one hundred horses a year directly from Hormuz. And in 1534 a contract was signed between the Portuguese in Goa and the rulers of Gujarat about the movement and import of horses from Hormuz. Rival leaders of the Adil Shahi and Vijayanagara Empires constantly jockeyed for Portuguese favor in the sixteenth century, hoping to be able either to buy horses from the Europeans at favorable prices or to import them directly from Hormuz and Aden. The virtual Portuguese horse monopoly in Goa meant they could play rival Deccan empires off of one another by allowing or preventing access to horses while at the same time making a handsome profit for themselves. The Portuguese charged customs duties on those bringing horses (as well as other goods of course) to Goa and were therefore able to control the prices of horses in India. For instance, it was estimated that the sale of horses to Vijayanagara between the years 1544 and 1546 garnered the Portuguese 60,000 fanoes.[41] To give a further example of how lucrative this trade could be, upon his death in Goa in 1546, a wealthy Portuguese horse merchant named Rui Fernandes had amassed a small fortune of 4,000 pardaos from his equine import business. (The price of a single horse in the first half of the sixteenth century ranged between 325 and 400 pardaos.)[42]

Portuguese horse merchants not only had to contend with local political forces in south India, but also with those ultimately in charge of their supply—the Safavid shahs in possession of Hormuz and the Ottoman sultans in control of Aden.[43] Like all players in the Indian Ocean horse trade, these empires were obviously also keen to make their own profits. Shah Tahmasp of the Safavid Empire, for example, was known for charging excessive taxes on the export of horses from his southern port city.[44] Similarly, the Ottomans charged high fees for the export of horses and other goods from the port of Aden, and in the sixteenth century they, rather unsuccessfully it turns out, even attempted to institute an outright ban on the export of horses from Ottoman Basra.[45] Arrangements were eventually made to allow the Portuguese to pay lower export duties in exchange for permitting independent trade between Ottoman and Safavid merchants and Gujarati traders and those farther south on the western coast.[46] The Portuguese however still attempted to control the Indian Ocean horse trade by forcing as many ships as possible to dock in their stronghold of Goa. The city thus became a critical hub of the global horse economy where Arab and Persian horse traders had established connections and spent a great deal of time; some of them even built homes for themselves, as was suggested above. In the sixteenth century, anywhere from four to ten boats a year brought horses from the Arabian Peninsula to Goa, and eight to twenty ships brought horses from Hormuz. Indeed, as the major account of the reign of the sixteenth-century Mughal emperor Akbar, *Ain-i-Akbari,* makes clear, horses from the Ottoman and Persian worlds continued to play a central role in Mughal warfare throughout the sixteenth century.[47]

Thus various political powers in South Asia—Pandya, Vijayanagara, Portuguese, Mughal—and the Middle East—Ilkhanid, Ottoman, Safavid—tapped into the Indian Ocean horse trade for economic and political purposes driven by the military need for these animals in South India.[48] For over a millennium, from antiquity well into the early modern period, the power provided by the strong muscles of horses found in the markets of Aden and Kish connected Middle Eastern pastoral economies to South Asian military ones.

The Charismatic Economy

Alongside this military economy in horses, there was another very different kind of Indian Ocean animal economy. Various empires imported elephants and other charismatic megafauna from India to help evidence rival claims to universal sovereignty in the late medieval and early modern worlds. These wondrous creatures were rare and unknown enough to be constructively and creatively deployed by imperial sovereigns in the Muslim world and beyond in their symbolic and military rivalries against one another. Political leaders thus used these charismatic animals to impress upon foreign travelers and their domestic subjects alike their abilities to command, control, and display nature's bounty.

A large bulk of India's elephant exports ended up in Egypt, either for domestic purposes or to be moved on to Europe, Istanbul, or elsewhere. India and Egypt had, of course, been linked through trade for millennia.[49] They were the two final nodes of the Indian Ocean world, with Egypt playing an important role as one of the primary way stations for goods from India, and points further east, moving to Europe and the Mediterranean. In the early modern period of Ottoman rule in Egypt, the province's role in this commercial network only expanded as European and Ottoman trade with South Asia and other parts of the Indian Ocean world greatly increased to feed growing tastes throughout the Mediterranean for Indian spices, textiles, and much more.[50] Many Egyptian merchants in the Ottoman period indeed made their fortunes largely by tapping into Indian Ocean trade, either directly or through intermediaries who purchased Indian goods for the Egyptian market in Aden, Jidda, or elsewhere along the Red Sea coast.[51] There thus emerged in Egypt, as most everywhere else, a robust demand for Indian imports—spices, finished goods, and textiles.[52] India's animal wealth was an important component of this demand.

Moreover, even before the Portuguese rounded the Cape of Good Hope at the end of the fifteenth century, many of India's animals found their way to European courts. As with most items of trade from South Asia to Europe, these creatures moved through the Middle East. For example, in the summer of 802 the famed Harun al-Rashid facilitated the movement of an Indian elephant, later to be named Abul Abaz, to the residence of the Emperor Charlemagne.[53] As trade between India and the Ottoman Empire and Europe intensified in the sixteenth century with the increased use of seaworthy vessels and Ottoman-Portuguese rivalry in the Indian Ocean, more and more animals were in transit between South Asia and the Ottoman Empire to feed both Ottoman and European animal sensibilities which had by this point been whetted to the sight of elephants as well as rhinos, tigers, lions, and other animals.[54] As the historic hinge of this trade between Asia and Europe, Egypt was an overland pinch-point for many of these animals, ensuring that Egyptians were regularly exposed to the fantastic spectacle of these creatures as they moved between the Red and Mediterranean Seas.[55]

After the Ottomans conquered Egypt in 1517, the province immediately came to function as the very lifeline of the empire to the Indian Ocean.

Controlling Egypt threw the empire into the Indian Ocean for the first time in its history, leading to growing rivalry between the Ottomans and the Portuguese for control of trade to and from India and thereby also leading to the increasing importance of the connection between Egypt and the subcontinent. It was thus primarily through Egypt that the Ottomans were connected to early modern Indian Ocean animal circulation networks like the ones centered around the horse and elephant trades.

The driving force behind the Ottoman consumption of charismatics like elephants was their use of these animals in the imperial menagerie, royal processions, and other venues of self-conscious imperial stagecraft. Egypt had been part of a globalized economy in charismatic megafauna long before the early modern period, and the Ottomans were neither the first nor the last imperial power in Egypt to create a collection of animals.[56] Indeed, the world's earliest known evidence of a sovereign cultivating and maintaining a

Elephant from Ottoman translation of Qazvīnī's 'Aca'ib ül-Mahlukat. (Walters Art Museum, Ms. W.659, 109a, Images for Academic Publishing)

menagerie for political purposes comes from ancient Egypt from around 2500 BCE in the form of inscriptions at the Saqqara cemetery depicting collections of gazelles, oryx, addax, ibis, falcons, cheetah, hyenas, and mongooses.[57] Hatshepsut's (r. 1490–1470 BCE) renowned menagerie in Thebes included elephants and leopards imported from India and monkeys and a giraffe from Somalia. In addition, later wall paintings depict the delivery of antelope, a giraffe, cheetahs, and monkeys to pharaoh. And even later, the Ptolemies created one of the ancient world's most extensive zoological collections and are purported to have organized the largest animal procession ever to that date: 96 elephants, 24 lions, 14 leopards, 14 oryx, 16 cheetahs, 14 wild asses, and hundreds of domesticated animals.[58] Charismatic megafauna had thus been collected by sovereigns—in Egypt and obviously elsewhere as well—for a very long time indeed.

Still, by all accounts the Ottoman menagerie in Istanbul was one of the early modern world's largest and most diverse.[59] One historian has gone so far as to say that "the best royal zoo in early modern times was found in the Ottoman capital."[60] At any given time, the menagerie on the grounds of the Topkapı Palace was home to elephants, lions, leopards, tigers, rhinoceroses, dogs, horses, birds, and many more creatures. Over the course of the sixteenth century, the number of animals in the menagerie ranged anywhere between 35 and 200.[61] Visitors to the sultan were always quick to comment on what he kept on the palace grounds. For example, an accountant for the British Levant Company named John Sanderson, who lived in Istanbul at the end of the sixteenth century, was floored by the mysterious beasts he regularly saw in the city. Of one of them that came to the capital from Ethiopia via Egypt he wrote, "The admirablest and fairest beast that ever I sawe was a jarraff, as tame as a domesticale deere and of a reddish deere colour, whitebrested and clovenfooted. He was of a very great hieth; his forelegs longer then the hinder; a very longe necke; and headed like a cambel, except two stumps of horne one his head."[62] Sanderson later watched Sultan Mehmed III lead his armies out of Istanbul on the Hungarian campaign of 1595. Of this military procession he wrote, "The jarraff before spoken of, beinge prince of all the beasts, was ledd by three chaines of three sondry men stalkinge before him. For it is the custome that, the Great Turke in person goinge on warefare, most or all in generall the cheefe men and beasts attend him out of the citie."[63] That the Ottoman menagerie was impressive was clear enough to Sanderson and all others who visited Istanbul.[64]

Also clear to these visitors was that Istanbul's animals almost always came to the city from elsewhere—chiefly from Egypt, India, Iran, and East Africa. In the words of Thomas Gainsford, a British diplomat who joined the Istanbul embassy in 1607, "Under the [palace's] walls are stables for seahorses called *Hippopotami,* which is a monstrous beast taken in *Nilus,* Elephants, Tygres, and Dolphines: sometimes they have Crocadiles and Rhinoceros: within are Roebuckes, white Partridges, and Turtles, the bird of *Arabia,* and many beasts and fowles of Affrica and India."[65] Thus again, before and continuing throughout the early modern period, the global trade in charismatic megafauna was largely an Indian Ocean affair centered mostly around animals originating from the Indian subcontinent moving to the Ottoman Empire, Iran, East Africa, China, and elsewhere.[66]

In both Istanbul and Cairo—the two largest cities in the Ottoman Empire— South Asian elephants played an active role as instigators of imagination, projections of imperial authority, and symbols of Ottoman attempts to manage and come to terms with nature. In these and other important ways, the history of elephants in these two Ottoman cities reflects wider early modern uses of and ideas about the animal in the Muslim world, South Asia, Europe, and beyond. One of the principal reasons behind the demand for Indian elephants in the Ottoman Empire and also in Safavid Iran was their dual use as diplomatic gifts leaders gave both to cement alliances and to project their imperial power to rivals in the early modern world.[67] For example, in 1738, the post-Safavid leader of Iran, Nadir Shah, as part of his efforts of rapprochement with the Ottoman Empire, sent the Ottoman sultan Mahmud I an Indian elephant.[68] The gifting of elephants was a common practice in South Asia and was likely a practice exported from the subcontinent to the Ottoman and Safavid worlds.[69] Indeed, there is a long tradition in South Asia of the gifting and use of elephants as signs of power and prestige,[70] and, as evidenced by the major accounts of the reigns of several Mughal rulers, elephants continued to play a significant role in South Asian society and politics in the early modern period.[71] This centrality and symbolic power of elephants was surely not lost on Ottoman and Safavid visitors to the Mughal court.[72] For example, when the Ottoman admiral Seydi 'Ali Reis arrived to the Mughal court in October 1555, Humayun greeted him with a retinue of 400 elephants and several thousand men.[73] By adopting the largely South and Central Asian practice of gifting elephants, the Ottomans and Safavids thereby attempted to appropriate the near-universal prestige of the animal in order to generate their own symbolic capital by bestowing or displaying the beast to their rivals.[74]

In 1531, for example, envoys of Charles V to Süleyman's court were especially awed by the sight of two elephants and a number of beautiful horses in the first courtyard of the palace.[75] For their part, the Ottomans' rivals—including Charles V himself—also used elephants to good effect as part of their imperial competition for authority and power in the early modern world. When Charles V's nephew Maximilian II was sent from Spain to take up residence in Vienna in the early 1550s, he was given an elephant to mark and celebrate his new appointment.[76] This South Asian pachyderm most likely originated in either Kerala or Sri Lanka and was sailed first to Portugal and then to the Spanish capital Valladolid in 1551. In a letter accompanying the elephant upon his arrival in Spain, another of Maximilian's uncles, John III of Portugal, suggested to his nephew, "I think you should name the animal and give it the name of the deadly enemy of the West as well as of your splendid home, namely Sultan Suleyman. In this way he will become your slave and will be properly humiliated. As your show animal, he will move to your residence in Vienna, named after the Sultan who wanted to destroy it!"[77] In this rather direct statement of early modern imperial rivalry played out through the possession of an elephant, Süleyman the pachyderm thus fulfilled two roles for Maximilian in Vienna—a spectacle of delight and wonder for the city's residents and a symbolic reminder of the pacification of the Ottoman enemy on the other side of the city's gates.[78]

Another envoy to Süleyman's court, Ogier Ghiselin de Busbecq, a Flemish diplomat who served as ambassador to Istanbul for Holy Roman Emperor Ferdinand and who penned a well-known account of the empire in the sixteenth century, was thoroughly enamored of an elephant he saw perform in the Ottoman palace.[79] "When this *Elephant* was bid to dance, he did so caper or quaver with his whole Body, and interchangeably move his Feet, that he seem'd to represent a king of Jig; and as for playing at Ball, he very prettily took up the Ball in his Trunk, and sent it packing therewith, as we do with the Palm of the Hand."[80] No doubt this imposing creature undertaking such nimble, agile, and intricate contortions impressed upon the sultan's visitors the gravity of their impending audience with a sovereign who could make ferocious creatures perform such wondrously light-footed acts.

Similarly, a Habsburg representative sent to Edirne in 1628 took special care to note his marvel at two elephants that performed for him during his meal with Ottoman officials.[81] These elephants were possibly those that had been sent to Istanbul a few years earlier in November 1620 as a gift from the Safavid Shah ʿAbbas I. This gift package included four Indian elephants, two large tigers, and a rhinoceros.[82] The Ottoman sultan thus reused these diplomatic gifts from one of his rivals to great effect to awe visitors to his own protected domains. The shadow of God on earth obviously wanted his rival sovereigns to see that his shadow spread over much more than just the earth's human creatures.

Further evidence of elephants in the Ottoman capital demonstrates some of the various other public uses they served. Illustrations of the circumcision ceremonies of Ahmet III's sons in 1720, for example, show several extremely elaborately adorned elephants participating in the festivities.[83] There is some scholarly debate about whether or not these miniature depictions represent actual living elephants that were present during the circumcision ceremony. Some of these creatures were clearly fantastical. One elephant is, for instance, shown shooting fireworks from its nostrils.[84] At the very least, not at all surprisingly given the steady presence of the animal in Istanbul for centuries, the image of the elephant, if not the real-life breathing being itself, was quite familiar to the city's residents in the early eighteenth century.[85] This was obviously a result of the many gifts of living elephants made to sultans over the preceding two hundred years. It was additionally a result of the knowledge of the elephant form as seen in other guises—most importantly as depicted in many well-known Mughal miniature paintings and in elephant figurines that were popular in early modern Europe and that were often gifted to the Ottomans in the sixteenth and seventeenth centuries.[86] The ambassador Busbecq, for example, brought to Süleyman from Emperor Ferdinand the gift of a clock mounted on an elephant figurine.[87] Large numbers of this popular style of clock have survived and, indeed, seem to have been quite common imperial gifts throughout the Mediterranean in the sixteenth century.[88] Furthermore, the elephant clock is a device that taps into a much older scholarly tradition of such machines in the Muslim world; in point of fact, device manuals from various periods discuss elephant clocks.[89]

Despite these numerous earlier examples of elephants (and of the elephant form) in Istanbul, only beginning in the late 1730s did the sultan consistently have an elephant in his menagerie at Topkapı Palace.[90] In a firman and accounting book from March 1739, the sultan writes that the daily stipend to be given to elephant keepers *(filbanan)* to cover both their salaries and the

maintenance of the animals in their charge was 510 akçes.[91] This money was
to be taken from the customs revenues of Istanbul and was further specified
as totaling 15,300 akçes a month.[92] Later cases confirm that these allowances
from Istanbul's customs revenues for elephants and their keepers held steady at
these levels (510 akçes per day for a total of 15,300 akçes per month) through
September 1739[93] and then on through March 1740.[94] Most of this money
went to feeding the elephants.[95] Every day the palace kitchen provided each
elephant with one kıyye (1.28 kg) of sugar, one kıyye of butterfat, and fourteen kıyye of bread.[96]

By all accounts, being an elephant attendant was quite a comfortable life
indeed. A series of cases from 1742 makes this abundantly clear and gives us
a further breakdown of the resources put toward the upkeep of elephants in
the Ottoman capital. At the beginning of this year, there were fourteen men
put in charge of one elephant.[97] The head elephant keeper *(filcibaşı)* was given
a monthly salary of 7.5 guruş, and the other thirteen elephant keepers were
each paid four guruş per month.[98] In October 1742, the number of elephant
keepers was decreased from thirteen to eleven[99] and was then again reduced
down to ten in December of that year.[100] In addition to their normal salaries,
these men also received daily rations of salt, onions, chickpeas, rice, bread,
firewood, wax, and other necessities.[101] The total amount earmarked for elephant handlers' provisions was 45 akçes a day.[102] As before, all of these monies
were taken from Istanbul's customs revenues and were distributed by the head
of the palace stables *(mirahor ağa).*[103]

There is no evidence that Ottoman elephant handlers received any formal
training in how to care for or control Istanbul's elephants. It seems reasonable
to imagine that perhaps a mahout (an elephant handler) accompanied elephants on their journey from the subcontinent and then remained in Istanbul
for at least some time to care for the creatures in their new home and to teach
others how to properly tend to them.[104] As will be seen, this was often the case
with Indian elephants that came to Egypt in the eighteenth century.[105] There
is, moreover, some evidence suggesting that elephant handlers were in demand
in Istanbul since Ottoman authorities occasionally sought them out and paid
for their travel to and maintenance in the city.[106]

Imports of elephants to the Ottoman capital continued throughout the
eighteenth century. In December 1778, for example, an elephant was sent
to the sultan as a gift from the ruler of Jalbār, pointing again to the fact that
most elephants in the Ottoman Empire came from South Asia.[107] For reasons

unstated, Sultan Abdülhamid I decided to send this elephant to Edirne.[108] Perhaps he was content with the elephants already in the menagerie; perhaps he
felt that the imperial hunting residence in Edirne could have used an elephant;
or perhaps he simply did not want to deal with the expense and administrative
overhead of keeping another elephant in the capital. Whatever the case may
have been, this creature was sent to Edirne in the care of a low-ranking imperial official known as the *kışlak emini*.[109] This man was charged with ensuring
that the elephant comfortably settled into his new home and had sufficient
amounts of food and drink. Moreover, five days after the elephant was sent to
Edirne, the sultan authorized fifty guruş to also be sent to the former Ottoman
capital to support the animal's upkeep.[110] Later in the spring of 1818, another
group of Indian elephants came to the Ottoman capital—this time as a gift
from the Qajar court—and a new cadre of five elephant handlers was hired to
look after them.[111]

Cairo was the other major destination for elephants arriving to the
Ottoman Empire. Crossing the Indian Ocean, sailing up the Red Sea, and
finally docking in Suez or other of Egypt's Red Sea ports, some of these
creatures continued overland through Egypt only to get on other ships on
the Mediterranean coast to travel to Istanbul and elsewhere.[112] Others stayed
on in Egypt, almost always in Cairo, and came to play important roles in the
cultural and political life of the city in the early modern period. In 1512, for
example—just a few short years before the Ottoman conquest of Egypt—four
elephants were sent to Cairo by an unnamed "king of India" *(malik al-hind)*
as a gift to the Mamluk sultan Qansuh al-Ghawrī.[113] When the ship carrying
these animals from India arrived to Suez in November of that year, it was
found that only two of the elephants had survived the trip. These two survivors
were immediately led from the Red Sea coast to al-Ghawrī's court and entered
Cairo with great pomp and circumstance.[114] All of Cairo came to watch the
elephants as they were paraded through the city's gates and then through the
center of the Mamluk capital accompanied by a stream of drummers and
horn players. On their backs they wore red velvet sashes, and their trunks were
overlaid with ornate metalwork. It was said to be a day of great delight as the
city celebrated these "two wondrous creatures" *('azīmān al-khalqa)*.

This celebratory moment was a welcome respite from the general sense of
foreboding that hung over Cairo in the 1510s.[115] The Ottomans had already
made clear their desire to capture Egypt in this period, and al-Ghawrī was
busy with plans to thwart these Ottoman threats through a possible alliance

with the Safavid shah.[116] Thus as a show of friendship and in an attempt to placate the Ottoman sultan against attacking the Mamluk Empire, al-Ghawrī sent one of his two recent elephantine acquisitions as a gift to Ottoman sultan Selim I.[117] He dispatched the animal to Istanbul, along with a few other delicacies from Egypt, with one of Selim's envoys who had come to Cairo bearing a rather less cheerful gift for al-Ghawrī—the head of his vassal Ala al-Dawla whom the Ottomans had just defeated in Syria and a fethname (declaration of war) formally proclaiming Ottoman intentions to conquer the Mamluks.[118] Selim received the elephant in Istanbul where, as in Cairo, it occasioned great wonder and excitement among the city's residents.[119] The four elephants in this account—two of whom died while at sea, one of whom stayed in Cairo, and the other who went to Istanbul—moved along the Indian Ocean's established trade networks—networks that again had circulated animals, and of course spices and other goods, for over a millennium.[120]

Moreover as this case also shows, elephants played important symbolic and tactical roles in the careful political maneuverings and diplomatic negotiations among the major empires of the early modern world—in this case between the Ottomans, Safavids, and Mamluks on the eve of the Ottoman conquests of Egypt and Syria. al-Ghawrī likely sought to elicit from Selim the same kind of awe and wonder that residents of Istanbul and Cairo experienced upon seeing elephants in the hopes that this reaction would cause Selim to at least reconsider his military plans. Unsurprisingly, and unluckily for al-Ghawrī, his elephant gift did nothing to stop Ottoman armies from taking his territory.

Beyond these tales of imperial conquest, the two elephants that arrived alive in Egypt from India also help to illuminate how early modern Ottoman subjects, and those soon to be subjects of the empire, experienced the few charismatic megafauna they encountered over the course of their lives. The epic procession of elephants through Cairo or imperial ceremonies that included them such as circumcision festivals or celebrations of military victories were all rather rare occasions for Ottoman urbanites. The sight of elephants during these events exposed residents of various Ottoman cities to marvels of creation they had never before seen. Elephants allowed Cairenes and Istanbulites to experience what to them must have seemed like an enormous anomaly—even freak or abnormality—of nature and also to engage with a living creature that had come from oceans away. These animals thus expanded the ecological, fanciful, and geographic horizons of these humans' imaginations. They, moreover, also performed an important recreational function for Cairenes.

The history of an elephant sent from India to Egypt in 1776 suggests some of these recreational roles.

> During this year came a group of Indians with a small elephant which they brought to al-'Aynī Palace. They put him into the big barn. The people rushed to this spectacle. At the gates servants stood who took money from the sightseers. Likewise the Indian grooms of the elephant collected a great deal of money. The people would bring him pastries and sugar cane and they would amuse themselves observing him sucking the cane and eating it with his trunk. The Indians would address him in their language and he understood their words. Whenever they presented him to a grandee, they would say something to him and the elephant would go down on his knees and salute with his trunk.[121]

As borne out by this passage, Indian mahouts themselves, not Ottoman or Egyptian merchants in South Asia, were the ones who most often brought elephants to Egypt.[122] Thus, as with the horse trade, it was typically locals who controlled the export and transport of charismatic animals. This points both to the importance of the animal trade to local economies throughout the Indian Ocean trading world and also helps to explain something of the circulation of people and knowledge between places like Egypt and India.[123] Moreover, the presence of Indian mahouts in Egypt further suggests that Egyptians, much like Istanbul's elephant keepers, did not have much experience or expertise in handling elephants and therefore largely had to rely on the knowhow of the Indian experts who accompanied the animals.[124]

Most importantly, this passage relates the experiences of wonder, amazement, and spectacle Egyptians enjoyed with this elephant.[125] They brought him food, were dazzled by the way his handlers controlled him, and were impressed by the respect he showed Egyptian elites.[126] Thus the most important thing about the presence of elephants in Egypt was the true awe and spectacle they offered—beings rarely, if ever, seen by most Egyptians that changed their sense of the world around them.[127] This early modern economy of elephants and other charismatic creatures was therefore one based on uniqueness, splendor, novelty, imagination, and celebration, not on strictly quantifiable economic benefits derived from transport, hauling, or other laboring forms of animal productivity.

The history of elephants in Ottoman Cairo and Istanbul therefore points to a certain Indian Ocean economics and early modern aesthetics of the human-animal world and also to the role of animals in the politics of early modern imperial rivalries. Recognizing the political potential of megafauna charisma, Ottoman officials in Egypt and Istanbul consciously deployed elephants and other animals to impress upon their rivals and subjects their imperial power and ability to tame and display nature. Significantly, these means of displaying animals were not meant to illustrate the sovereign's animalistic conquest and subjugation of nature, but rather his capacity to stage and harness the wonders of the natural world in controlled spectacles like processions or imperial ceremonies. The sovereign was the sponsor of this marvel and amazement, not a brute attempting to dominate it. Fantastic creatures such as elephants were thus symbols of how human political authority could harmoniously assemble the wonders of the natural world and reconcile its often violent and random forces. While humans indeed succeeded in bringing elephants halfway around the world from India to the Ottoman Empire, only elephants could arrest the imagination of an entire city, make all its inhabitants stop in amazement, and expand these people's worldviews beyond anything they could have ever envisioned.

Within the general trade economy of the Indian Ocean, horses were exchanged for elephants—weaponry for wonder. This traffic in live animals illuminates the intersections of the environmental and economic history of the early modern Indian Ocean world—a commercial network that spread from Istanbul and Cairo in the far west to China in the far east. Human relationships with various kinds of animals were obviously central to the function of large-scale land-based agrarian empires of the sort that ruled throughout the Middle East, South and Central Asia, and China during the late medieval and early modern centuries. The stories of the horse and elephant trades show that animals also had important roles to play on the oceans. Beyond this, these animals' histories also help to elucidate some of the history of human perceptions of animal utility. Nonhuman animals functioned as both material military tools of combat and more abstract sources of imagination and wonder.

Around these different aspects of the human-animal relationship, whole economies of trade and exchange emerged across Asia and the Indian Ocean. The horse trade, for example, supported an entire political economy of warfare in southern India. The presence of elephants in Istanbul created an intricate administrative infrastructure of upkeep, care, and maintenance—an economy fueled by the Ottoman dynasty's use of elephants to demonstrate its abilities to command, control, and display the natural world. Moreover, smaller, more local economies such as those of horse breeding in Iran or elephant training in India were also sustained by the global animal trade. Indeed, the Asia-wide commercial networks examined in this chapter tied together dozens of localized economies, encompassing their human actors and the knowledges they and their nonhuman counterparts together produced. The movement of South Asian elephants from India to the Middle East also led to the movement of human mahouts and the knowledge of how to handle elephants. For their part Persian horse traders brought their animal commodities to the western coast of India, with some settling there permanently. The Indian Ocean animal economy was thus also an economy of human movement and knowledge circulation.

Notes

This chapter is informed by earlier discussions presented in Alan Mikhail, *The Animal in Ottoman Egypt* (Oxford: Oxford University Press, 2014).

1. The literature on Indian Ocean trade is obviously enormous. Most useful for me have been K. N. Chaudhuri, *Trade and Civilisation in the Indian Ocean: An Economic History from the Rise of Islam to 1750* (Cambridge: Cambridge University Press, 1985); Chaudhuri, *The Trading World of Asia and the English East India Company, 1660–1760* (Cambridge: Cambridge University Press, 1978); Sanjay Subrahmanyam, *The Political Economy of Commerce: Southern India, 1500–1650* (Cambridge: Cambridge University Press, 1990); Subrahmanyam, ed., *Merchants, Markets and the State in Early Modern India* (Delhi: Oxford University Press, 1990); Ashin Das Gupta, *The World of the Indian Ocean Merchant, 1500–1800: Collected Essays of Ashin Das Gupta*, comp. Uma Das Gupta (New Delhi: Oxford University Press, 2001); James C. Boyajian, *Portuguese Trade in Asia under the Habsburgs, 1580–1640* (Baltimore: Johns Hopkins University Press, 1993); C. A. Bayly, *Imperial Meridian: The British Empire and the World, 1780–1830* (London: Longman, 1989).

2. For his part, Marco Polo described Hormuz as an "eminently commercial" port "frequented by traders from all parts of India." Marco Polo, *The Travels of Marco Polo the Venetian*, trans. W. Marsden, rev. T. Wright, ed. Peter Harris (New York: Alfred A. Knopf, 2008), 48–49. Basra in Iraq was also an important Persian Gulf horse-trading city.

3. See for example the following account of horses, elephants, and other items being traded from Sri Lanka to China in the thirteenth century: Zhao Rugua, *Chau Ju-Kua: His Work on the Chinese and Arab Trade in the Twelfth and Thirteenth Centuries, entitled Chu-Fan-Chi*, trans. Friedrich Hirth and W. W. Rockhill. 2 vols. (New York: Paragon Book Reprint Corp., 1966), 73.

4. William G. Clarence-Smith, "Elephants, Horses, and the Coming of Islam to Northern Sumatra," *Indonesia and the Malay World* 32 (2004): 271–284.

5. While my focus here is primarily on the horse trade fueled by military considerations, another arena in which horses were clearly essential in the early modern period and long before as well was in the maintenance of systems of post. On the administration of the Ottoman post system, see Colin Heywood, "The Ottoman *Menzilhane* and *Ulak* System in Rumeli in the Eighteenth Century," in *Türkiye'nin Sosyal ve Ekonomik Tarihi, (1071–1920): Birinci Uluslararası Türkiye'nin Sosyal ve Ekonomik Tarihi Kongresi Tebliğleri,* ed. Osman Okyar and Halil İnalcık (Ankara: Meteksan Şirketi, 1980), 179–186; Heywood, "Some Turkish Archival Sources for the History of the Menzilhane Network in Rumeli during the Eighteenth Century (Notes and Documents on the Ottoman Ulak, I)," *Boğaziçi Üniversitesi Dergisi* 4–5 (1976–1977): 39–54; Heywood, "The Via Egnatia in the Ottoman Period: The Menzilḫānes of the Ṣol Ḳol in the Late 17th/Early 18th Century," in *The Via Egnatia under Ottoman Rule (1380–1699): Halcyon Days in Crete II,* ed. Elizabeth Zachariadou (Rethymnon: Crete University Press, 1996), 129–144. On the use of horses and pigeons in the Mamluk post system, see Housni Alkhateeb Shehada, *Mamluks and Animals: Veterinary Medicine in Medieval Islam* (Leiden: Brill, 2013), 59–67. On post in the Muslim world more generally, see Adam J. Silverstein, *Postal Systems in the Pre-Modern Islamic World* (Cambridge: Cambridge University Press, 2010); Gagan D. S. Sood, "'Correspondence is Equal to Half a Meeting': The Composition and Comprehension of Letters in Eighteenth-Century Islamic Eurasia," *Journal of the Economic and Social History of the Orient* 50 (2007): 172–214.

6. Ralph Kauz, "Horse Exports from the Persian Gulf until the Arrival of the Portuguese," in *Pferde in Asien: Geschichte, Handel Und Kultur,* ed. Bert G. Fragner, Ralph Kauz, Roderich Ptak, and Angela Schottenhammer (Vienna: Österreichischen Akademie der Wissenschaften, 2009), 131. See also Christopher I. Beckwith, "The Impact of the Horse and Silk Trade on the Economies of T'ang China and the Uighur Empire: On the Importance of International Commerce in the Early Middle Ages," *Journal of the Economic and Social History of the Orient* 34 (1991): 183–198.

7. Zhao Rugua, *Chinese and Arab Trade,* 133.

8. Ibid., 134.

9. Kauz, "Horse Exports from the Persian Gulf," 131–132. For a comparison between Song and Mongol horses in the warfare of the thirteenth century, see Valerie Hansen, *The Open Empire: A History of China to 1600* (New York: W.W. Norton, 2000), 347–348.

10. See for example Priscilla Soucek, "Ceramic Production as Exemplar of Yuan-Ilkhanid Relations," *RES: Anthropology and Aesthetics* 35 (1999): 125–141.

11. Yokkaichi Yasuhiro, "Horses in the East-West Trade between China and Iran under Mongol Rule," in *Pferde in Asien: Geschichte, Handel Und Kultur,* ed. Bert G. Fragner, Ralph Kauz, Roderich Ptak, and Angela Schottenhammer (Vienna: Österreichischen Akademie der Wissenschaften 2009), 87–97; S. Jagchid and C. R. Bawden, "Some Notes on the Horse Policy of the Yüan Dynasty," *Central Asiatic Journal* 10 (1965): 246–268.

12. Roderich Ptak, "Pferde auf See: Ein vergessener Aspekt des maritimen chinesischen Handels im frühen 15. Jahrhundert," *Journal of the Economic and Social History of the Orient* 34 (1991): 199–233.

13. See for example the following on horses going from Samarkand to China: Li Gouxiang, Yang Chang, Wang Yude, et al., eds., *Ming Shi Lu Lei Zuan: She Wai Shi Liao Juan* (Wuhan Shi: Wuhan Chu Ban She: Xin Hua Shu Dian Jing Xiao, 1991), 1063–1087. On the Ming horse trade, see Morris Rossabi, "The Tea and Horse Trade with Inner Asia During the Ming," *Journal of Asian History* 4 (1970): 136–168.

14. On the importance of horses for military and economic relations between China and India in various periods, see Ranabir Chakravarti, "Early Medieval Bengal and the Trade in Horses: A Note," *Journal of the Economic and Social History of the Orient* 42 (1999): 194–211; Bin Yang, "Horses, Silver, and Cowries: Yunnan in Global Perspective," *Journal of World History* 15 (2004): 294–300.

15. Kauz, "Horse Exports from the Persian Gulf," 133.

16. For a useful economic analysis of Marco Polo's comments about the horse trade on the Indian coast, see Ranabir Chakravarti, "Horse Trade and Piracy at Tana (Thana, Maharashtra, India): Gleanings from Marco Polo," *Journal of the Economic and Social History of the Orient* 34 (1991): 159–182.

17. Marco Polo, *Travels of Marco Polo,* 43. This passage is also cited in Kauz, "Horse Exports from the Persian Gulf," 132–133.

18. Marco Polo, *Travels of Marco Polo,* 258.

19. Ibid., 50.

20. Kauz, "Horse Exports from the Persian Gulf," 134–135. For an analysis of 'Abd al-Razzaq Samarqandi's travel text, see Muzaffar Alam and Sanjay Subrahmanyam, *Indo-Persian Travels in the Age of Discoveries, 1400–1800* (Cambridge: Cambridge University Press, 2007), 54–82.

21. Rudi Manuel Loureiro, "Portuguese Involvement in Sixteenth Century Horse Trade through the Arabian Sea," in *Pferde in Asien: Geschichte, Handel Und Kultur,* ed. Bert G. Fragner, Ralph Kauz, Roderich Ptak, and Angela Schottenhammer (Vienna: Österreichischen Akademie der Wissenschaften, 2009), 141.

22. Ibid.

23. Kauz, "Horse Exports from the Persian Gulf," 132; Alam and Subrahmanyam, *Indo-Persian Travels,* 67. See also Velcheru Narayana Rao and Sanjay Subrahmanyam, "Notes on Political Thought in Medieval and Early Modern South India," *Modern Asian Studies* 43 (2009): 175–210.

24. Michael Gorgas, "Animal Trade between India and Western Eurasia in the Sixteenth Century—The Role of the Fuggers in Animal Trading," in *Indo-Portuguese Trade and the Fuggers of Germany, Sixteenth Century,* ed. K. S. Mathew (New Delhi: Manohar, 1997), 196–197.

25. Carla M. Sinopoli, "From the Lion Throne: Political and Social Dynamics of the Vijayanagara Empire," *Journal of the Economic and Social History of the Orient* 43

(2000), 377–380; John M. Fritz, "Vijayanagara: Authority and Meaning of a South Indian Imperial Capital," *American Anthropologist* 88 (1986): 44–55.

26. Fritz, "Authority and Meaning." For 'Abd al-Razzaq Samarqandi's take on elephants and more generally on the importance of elephants in Vijayanagara, see Alam and Subrahmanyam, *Indo-Persian Travels,* 76–77. On elephants in Vijayanagara, see also Gorgas, "Animal Trade between India and Western Eurasia," 206–211.

27. A. Rangasvami Sarasvati, "Political Maxims of the Emperor Poet, Krishnadeva Raya," *Journal of Indian History* 6 (1925): 69, 72, cited in Catherine B. Asher and Cynthia Talbot, *India before Europe* (Cambridge: Cambridge University Press, 2006), 77.

28. On the importance and history of the city of Vijayanagara, see Anna Libera Dallapiccola, ed., with Stephanie Zingel-Avé Lallemant, *Vijayanagara, City and Empire: New Currents of Research.* 2 vols. (Stuttgart: Steiner Verlag Wiesbaden, 1985); Anila Verghese and Anna L. Dallapiccola, eds., *South India under Vijayanagara: Art and Archaeology* (New York: Oxford University Press, 2011); Fritz, "Authority and Meaning;" Asher and Talbot, *India before Europe,* 59–60 and 63; Alam and Subrahmanyam, *Indo-Persian Travels,* 67–79.

29. Asher and Talbot, *India before Europe,* 59.

30. Horses were also used effectively for didactic and symbolic purposes in several South Indian histories written in this period. Sanjay Subrahmanyam, "Reflections on State-Making and History-Making in South India, 1500–1800," *Journal of the Economic and Social History of the Orient* 41 (1998): 382–416.

31. Generally on trade in early modern southern India, see Subrahmanyam, *Political Economy of Commerce.*

32. Gorgas, "Animal Trade between India and Western Eurasia," 196–206.

33. Ibid., 198; Loureiro, "Portuguese Involvement in Sixteenth Century Horse Trade," 138–139.

34. Gorgas, "Animal Trade between India and Western Eurasia," 198.

35. Quoted in Loureiro, "Portuguese Involvement in Sixteenth Century Horse Trade," 139.

36. Gorgas, "Animal Trade between India and Western Eurasia," 203; Loureiro, "Portuguese Involvement in Sixteenth Century Horse Trade," 138.

37. Loureiro, "Portuguese Involvement in Sixteenth Century Horse Trade," 137–143.

38. Ibid., 139; Gorgas, "Animal Trade between India and Western Eurasia," 202–205. See also Pius Malekandathil, "Maritime Malabar and a Mercantile State: Polity and State Formation in Malabar under the Portuguese, 1498–1663," in *Maritime Malabar and the Europeans, 1500–1962,* ed. K. S. Mathew (Gurgaon: Hope India Publications, 2003), 197–227; Ashin Das Gupta, *Malabar in Asian Trade: 1740–1800* (Cambridge: Cambridge University Press, 1967).

39. Gorgas, "Animal Trade between India and Western Eurasia," 201.

40. The details of the following concessions are outlined in ibid., 202–205.

41. Ibid., 203.

42. Ibid., 204.

43. On Safavid trade in the Persian Gulf, see Willem Floor, *The Persian Gulf: A Political and Economic History of Five Port Cities, 1500–1730* (Washington, DC: Mage Publishers, 2006).

44. Gorgas, "Animal Trade between India and Western Eurasia," 201–202. On the uses of horses (and other animals) in Safavid royal pageantry, see Willem Floor, "The Talar-i Tavila or Hall of Stables, a Forgotten Safavid Palace," *Muqarnas* 19 (2002): 19–63.

45. Hedda Riendl-Kiel, "No Horses for the Enemy: Ottoman Trade Regulations and Horse Gifting," in *Pferde in Asien: Geschichte, Handel Und Kultur,* ed. Bert G. Fragner, Ralph Kauz, Roderich Ptak, and Angela Schottenhammer (Vienna: Österreichischen Akademie der Wissenschaften, 2009), 43–49.

46. Gorgas, "Animal Trade between India and Western Eurasia," 201–202.

47. Abul Fazl 'Allami, *The Ain i Akbari,* vol. 1, trans. H. Blochmann (Frankfurt am Main: Institute for the History of Arabic-Islamic Science at the Johann Wolfgang Goethe University, 1993), 132–142, 215, 233–234. Horses from Iraq and Turan were well-known in Mughal India into the seventeenth century as well. See the following discussion involving emperor Jahangir just before his death in 1627: Mutribi al-Asamm Samarqandi, *Conversations with Emperor Jahangir,* trans. Richard C. Foltz (Costa Mesa: Mazda Publishers, 1998), 37. For an analysis of the Indian Ocean and Persian Gulf horse trade in the eighteenth and nineteenth centuries, see Hala Fattah, *The Politics of Regional Trade in Iraq, Arabia, and the Gulf, 1745–1900* (Albany: State University of New York Press, 1997), 159–183.

48. For a useful holistic treatment of the three major empires of the early modern Muslim world, see Stephen F. Dale, *The Muslim Empires of the Ottomans, Safavids, and Mughals* (Cambridge: Cambridge University Press, 2010).

49. See for example S. D. Goitein and Mordechai Akiva Friedman, *India Traders of the Middle Ages: Documents from the Cairo Geniza, "India Book"* (Leiden: Brill, 2008); Ian Shaw, "Egypt and the Outside World," in *The Oxford History of Ancient Egypt,* ed. Ian Shaw (Oxford: Oxford University Press, 2000), 308–323; R. Stephen Humphreys, "Egypt in the World System of the later Middle Ages," in *Islamic Egypt, 640–1517,* vol. 1, *The Cambridge History of Egypt,* ed. Carl F. Petry (Cambridge: Cambridge University Press, 1998), 445–461; Bernard Lewis, "The Fatimids and the Route to India," *Revue de la Faculté des Sciences Économiques de l'Université d'Istanbul* 11 (1949–1950): 50–54.

50. See for example the following cases of Venetian merchants in Egypt working to secure transport of spices, gold, and textiles from South Asia: Archivio di Stato di Venezia (hereafter ASV), Miscellanea Documenti Turchi, 554 (Evahir N 952/26 Nov.–5 Dec. 1545); ASV, Miscellanea Documenti Turchi, 714 (Evahir L 961/19–28 Sep. 1554); ASV, Miscellanea Documenti Algeri, Egitto, Marocco, Persia, Tripoli, Tunisi, 1,

Documenti Egitto 1 (10 § 877/10 Jan. 1473). The following case concerns Armenian merchants in Egypt and their trading links across the eastern Mediterranean: ASV, Miscellanea Documenti Turchi, 1050 (Evahir R 1001/25 Jan.–3 Feb. 1593). For an analysis of Armenian trading networks in the early modern period, see Sebouh David Aslanian, *From the Indian Ocean to the Mediterranean: The Global Trade Networks of Armenian Merchants from New Julfa* (Berkeley: University of California Press, 2011). For an example of the commerce in salt between Venice and the Ottoman Balkans, see the Ottoman letter included in the following: ASV, Senato, Deliberazioni, Costantinopoli, 1 (Evahir L 965/6–15 Aug. 1558).

51. 'Abd al-Raḥman al-Jabartī, *'Abd al-Raḥman al-Jabartī's History of Egypt: 'Ajā'ib al-Āthār fī al-Tarājim wa al-Akhbār*, ed. Thomas Philipp and Moshe Perlmann. 4 vols. (Stuttgart: Franz Steiner Verlag, 1994), 4: 283; Nelly Hanna, *Making Big Money in 1600: The Life and Times of Isma'il Abu Taqiyya, Egyptian Merchant* (Syracuse: Syracuse University Press, 1998), 34–35, 58, 77.

52. On Egyptian demand for Indian products, see al-Jabartī, *'Ajā'ib al-Āthār*, 1: 50, 52, 553; 2: 120, 329–330; 4: 233.

53. Gorgas, "Animal Trade between India and Western Eurasia," 195–196.

54. Ibid., 195–225.

55. Humphreys, "Egypt in the World System of the later Middle Ages," 449; Janet L. Abu-Lughod, *Before European Hegemony: The World System A.D. 1250–1350* (New York: Oxford University Press, 1989).

56. Generally on the history of menageries, see R. J. Hoage and William A. Deiss, eds., *New Worlds, New Animals: From Menagerie to Zoological Park in the Nineteenth Century* (Baltimore: Johns Hopkins University Press, 1996).

57. This summary of ancient menageries comes from R. J. Hoage, Anne Roskell, and Jane Mansour, "Menageries and Zoos to 1900," in *New Worlds, New Animals: From Menagerie to Zoological Park in the Nineteenth Century*, ed. R. J. Hoage and William A. Deiss (Baltimore: Johns Hopkins University Press, 1996), 8–15. For a broad perspective on the history of various diplomatic roles played by charismatic megafauna, see Liliane Bodson, ed., *Les animaux exotiques dans les relations internationales: Espèces, fonctions, significations* (Liège: Université de Liège, 1998). For a popular account of the political role of charismatics across time and space, see Marina Belozerskaya, *The Medici Giraffe: And Other Tales of Exotic Animals and Power* (New York: Little, Brown and Company, 2006).

58. Generally on the Ptolemaic zoo, see Harry M. Hubbell, "Ptolemy's Zoo," *The Classical Journal* 31 (1935): 68–76.

59. For a very general short sketch of the collection, see Metin And, *16. Yüzyılda İstanbul: Kent—Saray—Günlük Yaşam* (İstanbul: Yapı Kredi Yayınları, 2011), 129–132.

60. Thomas T. Allsen, *The Royal Hunt in Eurasian History* (Philadelphia: University of Pennsylvania Press, 2006), 204.

61. And, *16. Yüzyılda İstanbul*, 129.

62. John Sanderson, *The Travels of John Sanderson in the Levant, 1584–1602: With his Autobiography and Selections from his Correspondence,* ed. Sir William Foster (London: Hakluyt Society, 1931), 57, also cited in Gerald MacLean, "The Sultan's Beasts: Encountering Ottoman Fauna," in *Looking East: English Writing and the Ottoman Empire before 1800* (New York: Palgrave Macmillan, 2007), 152. For more on giraffes in Istanbul in the sixteenth century, see And, *16. Yüzyılda İstanbul,* 132. For a seventeenth-century Arabic travel account to Ethiopia commissioned by the Amir of Yemen al-Mutawakkil ʿAla Allah Ismāʿīl ibn al-Qāsim, see Sharaf al-Dīn al-Ḥasan ibn Aḥmad ibn Ṣāliḥ al-Yūsufī al-Jamālī al-Ḥaymī, *Riḥlat al-Ḥaymī ilā Arḍ al-Ḥabasha,* ms. 35 B (Veneranda Biblioteca Ambrosiana, Milan).

63. Sanderson, *Travels in the Levant,* 59–60, also cited in MacLean, "The Sultan's Beasts," 153.

64. For various travelers' comments about Istanbul's animal collection, see And, *16. Yüzyılda İstanbul,* 129–132.

65. Maclean, "The Sultan's Beasts," 153.

66. For an analysis of India's central role in the early modern Eurasian economy, see Stephen Frederic Dale, *Indian Merchants and Eurasian Trade, 1600–1750* (Cambridge: Cambridge University Press, 1994).

67. The same was true in earlier periods and in different places as well. At the end of the tenth century, for example, the clearly very impressed court of the Chinese Emperor Taizong asked a visiting Arab embassy how it captured elephants. One of the ambassadors replied, "To capture elephants, we use decoy elephants to get so near them that we can catch them with a big lasso." Zhao Rugua, *Chinese and Arab Trade,* 117–118.

68. Hedda Reindl-Kiel, "Dogs, Elephants, Lions, a Ram and a Rhino on Diplomatic Mission: Animals as Gifts to the Ottoman Court," in *Animals and People in the Ottoman Empire,* ed. Suraiya Faroqhi (Istanbul: Eren, 2010), 280. This elephant came to Istanbul during a period of intense administrative correspondence and military maneuvering between the Ottoman Empire and Iran. Animals were integral to this back and forth between the two imperial states as they aided in the movement of various envoys and emissaries sent from Ottoman lands to Iran. In 1731, for example, 500 mules were collected to move men and equipment toward the Iranian border. Başbakanlık Osmanlı Arşivi (hereafter BOA), Cevdet Askeriye 16011 (3 M 1144/8 Jul. 1731). And in 1735 and 1741, arrangements had to be made to move barley and other foodstuffs for the horses and other animals transporting the sultan's troops and emissaries to the Ottoman eastern front. BOA, Cevdet Askeriye 28573 (29 C 1148/16 Nov. 1735); BOA, Cevdet Hariciye 3089 (2 Ra 1154/18 May 1741).

69. On the gifting of elephant in early modern South India, see Gorgas, "Animal Trade between India and Western Eurasia," 206–211.

70. On the material and symbolic importance of elephants in pre-Mughal South Asia, see Thomas R. Trautmann, "Elephants and the Mauryas," in *India, History*

and Thought: Essays in Honour of A. L. Basham, ed. S. N. Mukherjee (Calcutta: Subarnarekha, 1982), 254–281; Simon Digby, *War-horse and Elephant in the Delhi Sultanate: A Study of Military Supplies* (Oxford: Orient Monographs, 1971).

71. See for example the relevant sections of Babur, *The Baburnama: Memoirs of Babur, Prince and Emperor,* trans. and ed. Wheeler M. Thackston, intro. Salman Rushdie (New York: Modern Library, 2002); Jahangir, *The Jahangirnama: Memoirs of Jahangir, Emperor of India,* trans. and ed. Wheeler M. Thackston (Washington, DC: Freer Gallery of Art; New York: Oxford University Press, 1999); Abul Fazl 'Allami, *Ain i Akbari.*

72. On the roles of elephants and other animals in the Mughal court, see Annemarie Schimmel, *The Empire of the Great Mughals: History, Art and Culture,* trans. Corinne Attwood, ed. Burzine K. Waghmar (London: Reaktion Books, 2004), 213–223; Asok Kumar Das, "The Elephant in Mughal Painting," in *Flora and Fauna in Mughal Art,* ed. Som Prakash Verma (Mumbai: Marg Publications, 1999), 36–54. See also Sujit Sivasundaram, "Trading Knowledge: The East India Company's Elephants in India and Britain," *The Historical Journal* 48 (2005): 27–63. For their part, rulers of Aceh in the early modern period also learned a great deal about the royal uses of elephants from the Mughals. Clarence-Smith, "Elephants, Horses, and the Coming of Islam," 274 and 279.

73. For an account of Seydi 'Ali Reis's visit to the Mughal court, see Alam and Subrahmanyam, *Indo-Persian Travels,* 111–120. See also Palmira Brummett, "What Sidi Ali Saw," *Portuguese Studies Review* 9 (2002): 232–253; Giancarlo Casale, *The Ottoman Age of Exploration* (New York: Oxford University Press, 2010), 120–123.

74. Generally on Ottoman-Mughal relations, see Naimur Rahman Farooqi, *Mughal-Ottoman Relations: A Study of Political and Diplomatic Relations between Mughal India and the Ottoman Empire, 1556–1748* (Delhi: Idarah-i Adabiyat-i Delli, 1989); Bernard Lewis, "The Mughals and the Ottomans," in *From Babel to Dragomans: Interpreting the Middle East* (New York: Oxford University Press, 2004), 108–114; Alam and Subrahmanyam, *Indo-Persian Travels,* 298–303. On the related topics of the Ottomans in the Indian Ocean and Ottoman-Portuguese rivalry there, see Salih Özbaran, *Ottoman Expansion towards the Indian Ocean in the 16th Century* (Istanbul: Bilgi University Press, 2009); Özbaran, *The Ottoman Response to European Expansion: Studies on Ottoman-Portuguese Relations in the Indian Ocean and Ottoman Administration in the Arab Lands during the Sixteenth Century* (Istanbul: Isis Press, 1994); Özbaran, "A Turkish Report on the Red Sea and the Portuguese in the Indian Ocean (1525)," *Arabian Studies* 4 (1978): 81–88; Özbaran, "Ottoman Naval Power in the Indian Ocean in the 16th Century," in *The Kapudan Pasha, His Office and His Domain: Halcyon Days in Crete IV,* ed. Elizabeth Zachariadou (Rethymnon: Crete University Press, 2002), 109–117; Casale, *Ottoman Age of Exploration;* Casale, "The Ottoman Administration of the Spice Trade in the Sixteenth-Century Red Sea and Persian Gulf," *Journal of the Economic and Social History of the Orient* 49 (2006): 170–198; Anthony Reid, "Sixteenth-Century Turkish Influence in Western Indonesia,"

Journal of South East Asian History 10 (1969): 395–414; Michel Tuchscherer, "La flotte impériale de Suez de 1694 à 1719," *Turcica* 29 (1997): 47–69.

75. Reindl-Kiel, "Animals as Gifts to the Ottoman Court," 279–280.

76. Karl Saurer and Elena Hinshaw-Fischli, "They Called Him Suleyman: The Adventurous Journey of an Indian Elephant from the Forests of Kerala to the Capital of Vienna in the Middle of the Sixteenth Century," in *Maritime Malabar and the Europeans, 1500–1962*, ed. K. S. Mathew (Gurgaon: Hope India Publications, 2003), 153–164; Annemarie Jordan Gschwend, *The Story of Süleyman: Celebrity Elephants and Other Exotica in Renaissance Portugal* (Philadelphia: Pachyderm, 2010).

77. Saurer and Hinshaw-Fischli, "They Called Him Suleyman," 154–155.

78. Both during his life and after his death in 1553, Süleyman was beloved in Vienna. Homes decorated their facades with elephant motifs; "to the elephant" became a popular name for coffeehouses, guesthouses, and other businesses; stories, verse, and legends developed around Süleyman, his life, and his journey to Vienna; artists depicted him; and several of the city's leading scientists began to write about elephants. Ibid., 159–160.

79. Not surprisingly, the Ottomans were not the first to employ elephants as tools to display royal power in Istanbul. Connected to the sixth-century Byzantine Hebdomon Palace was a large cistern—known later as *fil damı* (elephant stable)—that housed a group of elephants who were brought to the palace on certain special occasions. Other such historic elephant stables were known throughout the city. Some of them were eventually converted into mosques—the mosque of the Tekke of Hekim Çelebi in Koska, for example. Hafız Hüseyin Ayvansarayî, *The Garden of the Mosques: Hafız Hüseyin Ayvansarayî's Guide to the Muslim Monuments of Ottoman Istanbul,* trans. Howard Crane (Leiden: Brill, 2000), 101.

80. MacLean, "The Sultan's Beasts," 151.

81. Reindl-Kiel, "Animals as Gifts to the Ottoman Court," 280.

82. About the tiger, the fourteenth-century Persian scholar Qazvīnī had this to say: "it is a tyrannical and arrogant animal, very strong, swift, a [good] jumper, and of handsome appearance. Its back is extremely weak, and gives way if it feels but a slight degree of pain. It and the snake are close friends, but it is at enmity with all other animals. When it kills its prey it sleeps three days and nights, and on the fourth day it goes forth to hunt again." Hamd Allāh Mustawfī Qazvīnī, *The Zoological Section of the Nuzhatu-l-Qulūb of Hamdullāh al-Mustaufī al-Qazwīnī,* ed. and trans. J. Stephenson (London: Royal Asiatic Society, 1928), 35. For an illuminating study of the human-tiger relationship in parts of Southeast Asia, see Peter Boomgaard, *Frontiers of Fear: Tigers and People in the Malay World, 1600–1950* (New Haven: Yale University Press, 2001).

83. Suraiya Faroqhi, "Exotic Animals at the Sultan's Court," in *Another Mirror for Princes: The Public Image of the Ottoman Sultans and Its Reception* (Piscataway: Gorgias Press; Istanbul: Isis Press, 2009), 96–97.

84. During celebrations of the entry of Süleyman the elephant to Trent while on his way to Vienna in late 1551, there were likewise wooden sculptures of the animal constructed in which fireworks were shot out of the fabricated elephant's nostrils. Saurer and Hinshaw-Fischli, "They Called Him Suleyman," 156.

85. For a useful comparative analysis of the role of elephants in Britain in roughly the same period, see Christopher Plumb, "'Strange and Wonderful': Encountering the Elephant in Britain, 1675–1830," *Journal for Eighteenth-Century Studies* 33 (2010): 525–543.

86. On Mughal elephant paintings, see Das, "The Elephant in Mughal Painting." Another example of the very clear connection the Ottomans drew between elephants and India is found in Deli Birader's sixteenth-century account of bestiality. "It is said that in India, people fuck elephants. When they desire an elephant, one man climbs on the shoulders of another. Then they put not only their cocks into the elephant's vagina, but their balls." Selim Sirri Kuru, "A Sixteenth-Century Ottoman Scholar, Deli Birader, and His Dāfiʿüʾl-ġumūm ve Rāfiʿüʾl-humūm," (Ph.D. dissertation, Harvard University, 2000), 254. For the Ottoman writer, this tale is related as a sign of the anomalous wonder of both interspecies sex and India.

87. O. Kurz, *European Clocks and Watches in the Near East* (Leiden: Brill, 1975), 28–29; Faroqhi, "Exotic Animals," 97. For further discussion of the ubiquity of elephant imagery in Europe, see Robert Elena Hinschaw-Fischli, "Some Italian and German Representations of India in the Early Renaissance—with a Predilection for Elephants," in *Maritime Malabar and the Europeans, 1500–1962*, ed. K. S. Mathew (Gurgaon: Hope India Publications, 2003), 165–196.

88. Kurz, *European Clocks and Watches*, 29.

89. Perhaps the most famous text from this genre is al-Jazarī's *Book of the Knowledge of Mechanical Devices* completed in 1206, which outlines in great depth and detail the construction and proper function of an elephant clock. Abī al-ʿIzz Ismāʿīl al-Jazarī, *al-Jāmiʿ bayna al-ʿIlm wa al-ʿAmal al-Nāfiʿ fī Ṣināʿat al-Ḥiyal*, ed. Aḥmad Yūsuf al-Ḥasan, with ʿImād Ghānim, Mālik al-Mallūḥī, and Muṣṭafā Taʿmurī (Aleppo: Jāmiʿat Ḥalab, Maʿhad al-Turāth al-ʿIlmī al-ʿArabī, 1979). For an English translation of this text, see Ismāʿīl ibn al-Razzāz al-Jazarī, *The Book of Knowledge of Ingenious Mechanical Devices: Fī Maʿrifat al-Ḥiyal al-Handasiyya*, trans. Donald R. Hill (Dordrecht: Reidel, 1974). See also Kurz, *European Clocks and Watches*, 8–9. The operation of an elephant clock is described as follows. When the half-hour strikes, "the bird on top begins to sing, the cupola turns, the man at the top left moves his arm, the falcon drops a metal pellet from his beak into the mouth of the upper dragon, the two dragons move, and the pellet finally lands in the small vase, the mahout moves his ankus [elephant goad] and beats the drum on the elephant's head, while the scribe turns and indicates the hour on a scale." Ibid., 9.

90. Faroqhi, "Exotic Animals," 98–99. A second elephant was acquired by the sultan's menagerie at some point in the middle of 1740s, but nothing is known about how it came to Istanbul.

91. BOA, Cevdet Saray 6683 (29 Za 1151/10 Mar. 1739). For comparative purposes, consider that the average daily wage of a janissary in 1600 was around three

akçes. Baki Tezcan, *The Second Ottoman Empire: Political and Social Transformation in the Early Modern World* (Cambridge: Cambridge University Press, 2010), 205.

92. There is some discrepancy in this citation of the total monthly amount to be spent on the elephant and his handlers. The sum of 15,300 akçes assumes a thirty-day month, but this case specifically states that a month it to be considered as having only twenty-nine days. Clearly this assumption of a shorter month was not factored into the calculation for the monthly total.

93. BOA, Cevdet Saray 7256 (2 C 1152/6 Sep. 1739).

94. BOA, Cevdet Saray 4499 (29 Z 1152/28 Mar. 1740).

95. For comparative purposes, see the following account of the amounts and kinds of foods elephants were given in Vijayanagara: Gorgas, "Animal Trade between India and Western Eurasia," 206.

96. BOA, Cevdet Saray 4301 (2 Z 1159/16 Dec. 1746). See also Faroqhi, "Exotic Animals," 98.

97. BOA, Cevdet Saray 6410 (29 N 1154/8 Dec. 1741); BOA, Cevdet Saray 2067 (26 L 1154/4 Jan. 1742); BOA, Cevdet Saray 2274 (4 Ca 1155/7 Jul. 1742).

98. BOA, Cevdet Saray 6410 (29 N 1154/8 Dec. 1741); BOA, Cevdet Saray 2067 (26 L 1154/4 Jan. 1742).

99. BOA, Cevdet Saray 5842 (22 Ş 1155/22 Oct. 1742).

100. BOA, Cevdet Saray 3559 (11 L 1155/9 Dec. 1742).

101. BOA, Cevdet Saray 6410 (29 N 1154/8 Dec. 1741); BOA, Cevdet Saray 2067 (26 L 1154/4 Jan. 1742). See also Faroqhi, "Exotic Animals," 98.

102. BOA, Cevdet Saray 6410 (29 N 1154/8 Dec. 1741); BOA, Cevdet Saray 2067 (26 L 1154/4 Jan. 1742); BOA, Cevdet Saray 5842 (22 Ş 1155/22 Oct. 1742); BOA, Cevdet Saray 3559 (11 L 1155/9 Dec. 1742).

103. BOA, Cevdet Saray 6410 (29 N 1154/8 Dec. 1741); BOA, Cevdet Saray 2067 (26 L 1154/4 Jan. 1742); BOA, Cevdet Saray 2274 (4 Ca 1155/7 Jul. 1742).

104. Intimating that handlers were often Muslim, Suraiya Faroqhi suggests that the prospect of being able to perform the pilgrimage during the journey from South Asia to the Ottoman Empire would be good incentive for a mahout to travel such a long distance with his charge. Faroqhi, "Exotic Animals," 98.

105. It was also the case with the elephant Süleyman whose mahouts brought him from South Asia to Vienna in 1552. Saurer and Hinshaw-Fischli, "They Called Him Suleyman," 157–159 and 162.

106. BOA, Cevdet Saray 8605 (5 Ra 1191/13 Apr. 1777). This case concerns the problem of dealing with the personal effects (which totaled 36.5 guruş) of an elephant handler on his way to Istanbul.

107. BOA, Cevdet Saray 6016 (22 Za 1192/12 Dec. 1778). Suraiya Faroqhi identifies Jalbār as an "Indian principality." Faroqhi, "Exotic Animals," 99. The name may refer to the town of Chalbar in modern-day Afghanistan.

108. For a later case about transporting an elephant from Egypt to Edirne, see BOA, Cevdet Dahiliye 10256 (28 Ca 1235/13 Mar. 1820).

109. In discussing this case, Suraiya Faroqhi points to the use of this minor official to accompany the elephant as evidence of Sultan Abdülhamid I's indifference toward the animal. Faroqhi, "Exotic Animals," 99.

110. BOA, Cevdet Saray 6483 (27 Za 1192/17 Dec. 1778).

111. BOA, Cevdet Saray 6778 (19 C 1233/26 Apr. 1818). Each of these handlers was paid thirty guruş a month.

112. For an example of the gifting of an elephant and other animals to the Mamluk sultan from the ruler of the Dahlak Archipelago in the Red Sea at the end of the fourteenth century, see Shehada, *Mamluks and Animals,* 72.

113. Reindl-Kiel, "Animals as Gifts to the Ottoman Court," 279; Celia J. Kerslake, "The Correspondence between Selīm I and Ḳānṣūh al-Ġawrī," *Prilozi za Orijentalnu Filologiju* 30 (1980), 227–228.

114. Muḥammad ibn Aḥmad ibn Iyās al-Ḥanafī, *Badā'i' al-Zuhūr fī Waqā'i' al-Duhūr,* ed. Muḥammad Muṣṭafā. 5 vols. (Cairo: al-Hay'a al-Miṣriyya al-'Āmma lil-Kitāb, 1982), 4: 284.

115. For useful accounts of Egypt in this period, see Carl F. Petry, *Twilight of Majesty: The Reigns of the Mamlūk Sultans al-Ashrāf Qāytbāy and Qanṣūh al-Ghawrī in Egypt* (Seattle: University of Washington Press, 1993); Petry, *Protectors or Praetorians?: The Last Mamlūk Sultans and Egypt's Waning as a Great Power* (Albany: State University of New York Press, 1994).

116. On Ottoman-Mamluk relations, see Emire Cihan Muslu, "Ottoman-Mamluk Relations: Diplomacy and Perceptions," (Ph.D. dissertation, Harvard University, 2007); Kerslake, "Correspondence between Selīm I and Ḳānṣūh al-Ġawrī," 219–234. On the emergence and history of the Ottoman-Safavid rivalry, see Adel Allouche, *The Origins and Development of the Ottoman-Ṣafavid Conflict (906–962/1500–1555)* (Berlin: K. Schwarz Verlag, 1983); Jean-Louis Bacqué-Grammont, *Les Ottomans, les Safavides et leurs voisins: Contribution à l'histoire des relations internationales dans l'Orient islamique de 1514 à 1524* (Istanbul: Nederlands Historisch-Archaeologisch Instituut te Istanbul, 1987); Maḥmūd Ḥasan 'Abd al-'Azīz al-Ṣarrāf, *Ma'rakat Chāldārān, 920 H/1514 M: Ūlā Ṣafaḥāt al-Ṣirā' al-'Uthmānī al-Fārisī: al-Asbāb wa al-Natā'ij* (Cairo: Maktabat al-Nahḍa al-Miṣriyya, 1991).

117. Generally on the role of gift giving in Ottoman-Mamluk relations, see Muslu, "Ottoman-Mamluk Relations," 182–209.

118. The dispatch of a fethname with the head of one of an enemy sovereign's allies had many precedents in the Muslim world and, importantly, was not always a symbol of aggression or confrontation. On these points and for a discussion of an earlier fethname sent to Mamluk Egypt with a severed head, see Matthew Melvin-Koushki, "The Delicate Art of Aggression: Uzun Hasan's *Fathnama* to Qaytbay of 1469," *Iranian Studies* 44 (2011): 193–214.

119. For later examples of elephants being sent from Egypt to Istanbul, see the following three cases: BOA, Cevdet Saray 2152 (28 R 1233/7 Mar. 1818); BOA, Cevdet Dahiliye 10256 (28 Ca 1235/13 Mar. 1820); BOA, Cevdet Maarif 3798 (16 C

1235/31 Mar. 1820). In all three of these cases, the elephants sent from Egypt to Istanbul likely came from India, but only the final two cases state this explicitly.

120. For an argument that the Ottoman conquest of Egypt was largely motivated by Ottoman desires to benefit from Egypt's established Indian Ocean trade links, see Casale, *Ottoman Age of Exploration*, 25–29.

121. al-Jabartī, *'Ajā'ib al-Āthār*, 2: 2.

122. Another example of Indians accompanying animals to Egypt was the case of the embassy sent by Tipu, Sultan of Mysore, to the Ottoman Empire at the end of the eighteenth century. One of Tipu's chief objectives in dispatching this mission was to secure the support of Ottoman sultan Abdülhamid I for his military efforts against the British in India. The delegation left Tipu's court for Istanbul in 1785 and stopped in Egypt on their way back home in the summer of 1788. According to al-Jabartī, Tipu's men took many gifts to Istanbul. Along with a pulpit made of aloe wood, gold, and silver and a large couch that could seat six, they arrived in the Ottoman court with two birds who purportedly spoke Hindi and impressed all who saw them. For al-Jabartī's accounts of the delegation's visit to Cairo and Istanbul and his description of the talking birds, see al-Jabartī, *'Ajā'ib al-Āthār*, 2: 263–264; 3: 107–108. On Tipu's delegation to the Ottoman Empire more generally, see Yusuf Hikmet Bayur, "Maysor Sultanı Tipu ile Osmanlı Pâdişahlarından I. Abdülhamid ve III. Selim Arasındaki Mektuplaşma," *Belleten* 12 (47) (1948): 617–654; Iqbal Husain, "The Diplomatic Vision of Tipu Sultan: Briefs for Embassies to Turkey and France, 1785–86," in *State and Diplomacy under Tipu Sultan: Documents and Essays,* ed. Irfan Habib (New Delhi: Tulika, 2001), 19–65; Alam and Subrahmanyam, *Indo-Persian Travels*, 314–327.

When Napoleon invaded Egypt, he had designs for an alliance with Tipu against the British. In early 1798, there were reportedly French plans to send a force of over 10,000 troops from Suez to India to help Tipu fight the British. Two events in May 1799, however, ensured that this alliance never materialized—the defeat of Napoleon's armies at Acre and Tipu's death during a battle against British forces. Generally on Tipu's reign, see Irfan Habib, ed., *Confronting Colonialism: Resistance and Modernization under Haidar Ali and Tipu Sultan* (London: Anthem, 2002); Aniruddha Ray, ed., *Tipu Sultan and His Age: A Collection of Seminar Papers* (Kolkata: Asiatic Society, 2001); Kate Brittlebank, *Tipu Sultan's Search for Legitimacy: Islam and Kingship in a Hindu Domain* (Delhi: Oxford University Press, 1997).

Also noteworthy is Tipu's use of tiger symbolism to project his sovereignty. Many of his kingdom's banners, coins, weapons, and seals incorporated tiger motifs, and he came to be known as the Tiger of Mysore. He maintained a menagerie of tigers in his palace at Seringapatam and, quite famously, commissioned a moving and sounding mechanical sculpture of a tiger atop a British soldier taking a bite out of the man's white flesh. Kate Brittlebank, "Sakti and Barakat: The Power of Tipu's Tiger, An Examination of the Tiger Emblem of Tipu Sultan of Mysore," *Modern Asian Studies* 29 (1995): 257–269; Maya Jasanoff, *Edge of Empire: Lives, Culture, and Conquest in the*

East, 1750–1850 (New York: Vintage, 2006), 177–180; Lawrence James, *Raj: The Making and Unmaking of British India* (New York: St. Martin's Press, 1997), 68.

123. For another example of the maritime commerce between India and Ottoman Egypt in this period, see BOA, Mühimme-i Mısır, 9: 71 (Evail Z 1189/23 Jan.-1 Feb 1776).

124. For a discussion of Indian mahouts in Mamluk Egypt, see Shehada, *Mamluks and Animals*, 174–175 and 192–193.

125. For an earlier example from the seventeenth century of how Egyptians similarly amused themselves with a young elephant calf, see Evliyâ Çelebi bin Derviş Mehemmed Zıllî, *Evliyâ Çelebi Seyahatnâmesi*, ed. Seyit Ali Kahraman, Yücel Dağlı, and Robert Dankoff. 10 vols. (Istanbul: Yapı Kredi Yayınları, 2011), 10: 442.

126. A Briton resident in Istanbul at the end of the sixteenth century wrote of a giraffe who was similarly made to kneel for amusement by his handlers. Maclean, "The Sultan's Beasts," 152.

127. In the early nineteenth century, a few decades after the previous account from 1776, another group of three elephants was brought to Cairo from India. Rumor preceded their actual arrival in the city. On June 16, 1817, word got out that the ship carrying these animals from the subcontinent was in Jidda and would soon leave this port for its final destination in Suez. With a buzz of anticipation in the air, the three elephants that, like so many other elephants before them, had begun their journey in India entered Cairo on Thursday, July 10, 1817. al-Jabartī describes the scene. "The three elephants arrived from Suez, one of which was bigger than the other two though it was the middle in age. They were brought into Cairo through Bāb al-Naṣr, passed through the center of the city, and went out through Bāb Zuwayla by al-Aḥmar Street on the way to Kara Maydān. Adults and children alike along with soldiers and Dalāt, mounted and on foot, rushed to look at the elephants, trailing behind them and crowding the market. The large elephant bore a wooden howdah on its back." al-Jabartī, *ʿAjāʾib al-Āthār*, 4: 389–391. Although this account gives no information about the identities of those who brought the elephants to Cairo from India, the mention of the animals' ages clearly suggests that those handling them knew a great deal about them. There are several other commonalities between this passage and the previous account. Like the elephant brought to Egypt in 1776, these three also clearly elicited a degree of awe, fantasy, and wonder from onlookers as they were paraded through Cairo. Moreover, in both cases, the animals were displayed in a palace or other royal structure.

References

Archival Sources

Archivio di Stato di Venezia
    Miscellanea Documenti Algeri, Egitto, Marocco, Persia, Tripoli, Tunisi, 1, Documenti Egitto, 1

Miscellanea Documenti Turchi, 554, 714, 1050
Senato, Deliberazioni, Costantinopoli, 1
Başbakanlık Osmanlı Arşivi
    Cevdet Askeriye, 16011, 28573
    Cevdet Dahiliye, 10256
    Cevdet Hariciye, 3089
    Cevdet Maarif, 3798
    Cevdet Saray, 2067, 2152, 2274, 3559, 4301, 4499, 5842, 6016, 6410, 6483, 6683, 6778, 7256, 8605
    Mühimme-i Mısır, 9

Manuscript Sources

Veneranda Biblioteca Ambrosiana, Milan
    al-Ḥaymī, Sharaf al-Dīn al-Ḥasan ibn Aḥmad ibn Ṣāliḥ al-Yūsufī al-Jamālī. *Riḥlat al-Ḥaymī ilā Arḍ al-Ḥabasha.* Ms. 35 B.

Published Primary Sources

Abul Fazl 'Allami. 1993. *The Ain i Akbari.* Translated by H. Blochmann. 3 vols. Frankfurt am Main: Institute for the History of Arabic-Islamic Science at the Johann Wolfgang Goethe University.

Babur. 2002. *The Baburnama: Memoirs of Babur, Prince and Emperor.* Translated and edited by Wheeler M. Thackston. Introduction by Salman Rushdie. New York: Modern Library.

Evliyâ Çelebi bin Derviş Mehemmed Zıllî. 2011. *Evliyâ Çelebi Seyahatnâmesi.* Edited by Seyit Ali Kahraman, Yücel Dağlı, and Robert Dankoff. 10 vols. Istanbul: Yapı Kredi Yayınları.

Hafız Hüseyin Ayvansarayî. 2000. *The Garden of the Mosques: Hafız Hüseyin Ayvansarayî's Guide to the Muslim Monuments of Ottoman Istanbul.* Translated by Howard Crane. Leiden: Brill.

Ibn Iyās al-Ḥanafī, Muḥammad ibn Aḥmad. 1982. *Badāʾiʿ al-Zuhūr fī Waqāʾiʿ al-Duhūr.* Edited by Muḥammad Muṣṭafā. 5 vols. Cairo: al-Hayʾa al-Miṣriyya al-ʿĀmma lil-Kitāb.

al-Jabartī, ʿAbd al-Raḥman ibn Ḥasan. 1994. *ʿAbd al-Raḥmān al-Jabartī's History of Egypt: ʿAjāʾib al-Āthār fī al-Tarājim wa al-Akhbār.* Edited by Thomas Philipp and Moshe Perlmann. 4 vols. Stuttgart: Franz Steiner Verlag.

Jahangir. 1999. *The Jahangirnama: Memoirs of Jahangir, Emperor of India.* Translated and edited by Wheeler M. Thackston. Washington, DC: Freer Gallery of Art; New York: Oxford University Press.

al-Jazarī, Ismāʿīl ibn al-Razzāz. 1974. *The Book of Knowledge of Ingenious Mechanical Devices: Fī Maʿrifat al-Ḥiyal al-Handasiyya.* Translated by Donald R. Hill. Dordrecht: Reidel.

————. 1979. *al-Jāmiʿ bayna al-ʿIlm wa al-ʿAmal al-Nāfiʿ fī Ṣināʿat al-Ḥiyal.* Edited by Aḥmad Yūsuf al-Ḥasan, with ʿImad Ghanim, Malik al-Malluḥi, and Muṣṭafa Taʿmurī. Aleppo: Jāmiʿat Ḥalab, Maʿhad al-Turāth al-ʿIlmī al-ʿArabī.

Kuru, Selim Sirri. 2000. "A Sixteenth-Century Ottoman Scholar, Deli Birader, and His Dāfiʿüʾl-ğumūm ve Rāfiʿüʾl-humūm." Ph.D. dissertation, Harvard University.

Li Gouxiang, Yang Chang, Wang Yude, et al., eds. 1991. *Ming Shi Lu Lei Zuan: She Wai Shi Liao Juan.* Wuhan Shi: Wuhan Chu Ban She: Xin Hua Shu Dian Jing Xiao.

Mutribi al-Asamm Samarqandi. 1998. *Conversations with Emperor Jahangir.* Translated by Richard C. Foltz. Costa Mesa: Mazda Publishers.

Polo, Marco. 2008. *The Travels of Marco Polo the Venetian.* Translated by W. Marsden. Revised by T. Wright. Edited by Peter Harris. New York: Alfred A. Knopf.

Qazvīnī, Ḥamd Allāh Mustawfī. 1928. *The Zoological Section of the Nuzhatu-l-Qulūb of Ḥamdullāh al-Mustaufī al-Qazwīnī.* Edited and translated by J. Stephenson. London: Royal Asiatic Society.

Sanderson, John. 1931. *The Travels of John Sanderson in the Levant, 1584–1602: With his Autobiography and Selections from his Correspondence.* Edited by Sir William Foster. London: Hakluyt Society.

Zhao, Rugua. 1966. *Chau Ju-Kua: His Work on the Chinese and Arab Trade in the Twelfth and Thirteenth Centuries, entitled Chu-Fan-Chï.* Translated by Friedrich Hirth and W. W. Rockhill. 2 vols. New York: Paragon Book Reprint Corp.

Secondary Sources

Abu-Lughod, Janet L. 1989. *Before European Hegemony: The World System A.D. 1250–1350.* New York: Oxford University Press.

Alam, Muzaffar, and Sanjay Subrahmanyam. 2007. *Indo-Persian Travels in the Age of Discoveries, 1400–1800.* Cambridge: Cambridge University Press.

Allouche, Adel. 1983. *The Origins and Development of the Ottoman-Ṣafavid Conflict (906–962/1500–1555).* Berlin: K. Schwarz Verlag.

Allsen, Thomas T. 2006. *The Royal Hunt in Eurasian History.* Philadelphia: University of Pennsylvania Press.

And, Metin. 2011. *16. Yüzyılda İstanbul: Kent—Saray—Günlük Yaşam.* Istanbul: Yapı Kredi Yayınları.

Asher, Catherine B., and Cynthia Talbot. 2006. *India before Europe.* Cambridge: Cambridge University Press.

Aslanian, Sebouh David. 2011. *From the Indian Ocean to the Mediterranean: The Global Trade Networks of Armenian Merchants from New Julfa.* Berkeley: University of California Press.

Bacqué-Grammont, Jean-Louis. 1987. *Les Ottomans, les Safavides et leurs voisins: Contribution à l'histoire des relations internationales dans l'Orient islamique de 1514 à 1524*. Istanbul: Nederlands Historisch-Archaeologisch Instituut te Istanbul.

Bayly, C. A. 1989. *Imperial Meridian: The British Empire and the World, 1780–1830*. London: Longman.

Bayur, Yusuf Hikmet. 1948. "Maysor Sultanı Tipu ile Osmanlı Pâdişahlarından I. Abdülhamid ve III. Selim Arasındaki Mektuplaşma." *Belleten* 12 (47): 617–654.

Beckwith, Christopher I. 1991. "The Impact of the Horse and Silk Trade on the Economies of T'ang China and the Uighur Empire: On the Importance of International Commerce in the Early Middle Ages." *Journal of the Economic and Social History of the Orient* 34: 183–198.

Belozerskaya, Marina. 2006. *The Medici Giraffe: And Other Tales of Exotic Animals and Power*. New York: Little, Brown and Company.

Bodson, Liliane, ed. 1998. *Les animaux exotiques dans les relations internationales: Espèces, fonctions, significations*. Liège: Université de Liège.

Boomgaard, Peter. 2001. *Frontiers of Fear: Tigers and People in the Malay World, 1600–1950*. New Haven: Yale University Press

Boyajian, James C. 1993. *Portuguese Trade in Asia under the Habsburgs, 1580–1640*. Baltimore: Johns Hopkins University Press.

Brittlebank, Kate. 1995. "Sakti and Barakat: The Power of Tipu's Tiger, An Examination of the Tiger Emblem of Tipu Sultan of Mysore." *Modern Asian Studies* 29: 257–269.

———. 1997. *Tipu Sultan's Search for Legitimacy: Islam and Kingship in a Hindu Domain*. Delhi: Oxford University Press.

Brummett, Palmira. 2002. "What Sidi Ali Saw." *Portuguese Studies Review* 9: 232–253.

Casale, Giancarlo. 2006. "The Ottoman Administration of the Spice Trade in the Sixteenth-Century Red Sea and Persian Gulf." *Journal of the Economic and Social History of the Orient* 49: 170–198.

———. 2010. *The Ottoman Age of Exploration*. New York: Oxford University Press.

Chakravarti, Ranabir. 1991. "Horse Trade and Piracy at Tana (Thana, Maharashtra, India): Gleanings from Marco Polo." *Journal of the Economic and Social History of the Orient* 34: 159–182.

———. 1999. "Early Medieval Bengal and the Trade in Horses: A Note." *Journal of the Economic and Social History of the Orient* 42: 194–211.

Chaudhuri, K. N. 1978. *The Trading World of Asia and the English East India Company, 1660–1760*. Cambridge: Cambridge University Press.

———. 1985. *Trade and Civilisation in the Indian Ocean: An Economic History from the Rise of Islam to 1750*. Cambridge: Cambridge University Press.

Clarence-Smith, William G. 2004. "Elephants, Horses, and the Coming of Islam to Northern Sumatra." *Indonesia and the Malay World* 32: 271–284.

Dale, Stephen F. 1994. *Indian Merchants and Eurasian Trade, 1600–1750.* Cambridge: Cambridge University Press.

———. 2010. *The Muslim Empires of the Ottomans, Safavids, and Mughals.* Cambridge: Cambridge University Press.

Dallapiccola, Anna Libera, ed., with Stephanie Zingel-Avé Lallemant. 1985. *Vijayanagara, City and Empire: New Currents of Research.* 2 vols. Stuttgart: Steiner Verlag Wiesbaden.

Das, Asok Kumar. 1999. "The Elephant in Mughal Painting." In *Flora and Fauna in Mughal Art,* ed. Som Prakash Verma. Mumbai: Marg Publications.

Das Gupta, Ashin. 1967. *Malabar in Asian Trade: 1740–1800.* Cambridge: Cambridge University Press.

———. 2001. *The World of the Indian Ocean Merchant, 1500–1800: Collected Essays of Ashin Das Gupta.* Compiled by Uma Das Gupta. New Delhi: Oxford University Press.

Digby, Simon. 1971. *War-horse and Elephant in the Delhi Sultanate: A Study of Military Supplies.* Oxford: Orient Monographs.

Farooqi, Naimur Rahman. 1989. *Mughal-Ottoman Relations: A Study of Political and Diplomatic Relations between Mughal India and the Ottoman Empire, 1556–1748.* Delhi: Idarah-i Adabiyat-i Delli.

Faroqhi, Suraiya. 2009. "Exotic Animals at the Sultan's Court." In *Another Mirror for Princes: The Public Image of the Ottoman Sultans and Its Reception* Piscataway: Gorgias Press.

Fattah, Hala. 1997. *The Politics of Regional Trade in Iraq, Arabia, and the Gulf, 1745–1900.* Albany: State University of New York Press.

Floor, Willem. 2002. "The Talar-i Tavila or Hall of Stables, a Forgotten Safavid Palace." *Muqarnas* 19: 19–63.

———. 2006. *The Persian Gulf: A Political and Economic History of Five Port Cities, 1500–1730.* Washington, DC: Mage Publishers.

Fritz, John M. 1986. "Vijayanagara: Authority and Meaning of a South Indian Imperial Capital." *American Anthropologist* 88: 44–55.

Goitein, S. D., and Mordechai Akiva Friedman. 2008. *India Traders of the Middle Ages: Documents from the Cairo Geniza, "India Book."* Leiden: Brill.

Gorgas, Michael. 1997. "Animal Trade between India and Western Eurasia in the Sixteenth Century—The Role of the Fuggers in Animal Trading." In *Indo-Portuguese Trade and the Fuggers of Germany, Sixteenth Century,* ed. K. S. Mathew. New Delhi: Manohar.

Gschwend, Annemarie Jordan. 2010. *The Story of Süleyman: Celebrity Elephants and Other Exotica in Renaissance Portugal.* Philadelphia: Pachyderm.

Habib, Irfan, ed. 2002. *Confronting Colonialism: Resistance and Modernization under Haidar Ali and Tipu Sultan.* London: Anthem.

Hanna, Nelly. 1998. *Making Big Money in 1600: The Life and Times of Isma'il Abu Taqiyya, Egyptian Merchant.* Syracuse, NY: Syracuse University Press.

Hansen, Valerie. 2000. *The Open Empire: A History of China to 1600*. New York: W. W. Norton.

Heywood, Colin. 1976–77. "Some Turkish Archival Sources for the History of the Menzilhane Network in Rumeli during the Eighteenth Century (Notes and Documents on the Ottoman Ulak, I)." *Boğaziçi Üniversitesi Dergisi* 4–5: 39–54.

———. 1980. "The Ottoman *Menzilhane* and *Ulak* System in Rumeli in the Eighteenth Century." In *Türkiye'nin Sosyal ve Ekonomik Tarihi, (1071–1920): Birinci Uluslararası Türkiye'nin Sosyal ve Ekonomik Tarihi Kongresi Tebliğleri*, ed. Osman Okyar and Halil İnalcık. Ankara: Meteksan Şirketi.

———. 1996. "The Via Egnatia in the Ottoman Period: The Menzilḫānes of the Ṣol Ḳol in the Late 17th/Early 18th Century." In *The Via Egnatia under Ottoman Rule (1380–1699): Halcyon Days in Crete II*, ed. Elizabeth Zachariadou. Rethymnon: Crete University Press.

Hinschaw-Fischli, Robert Elena. 2003. "Some Italian and German Representations of India in the Early Renaissance—with a Predilection for Elephants." In *Maritime Malabar and the Europeans, 1500–1962*, ed. K. S. Mathew. Gurgaon: Hope India Publications.

Hoage, R. J., and William A. Deiss, eds. 1996. *New Worlds, New Animals: From Menagerie to Zoological Park in the Nineteenth Century*. Baltimore: Johns Hopkins University Press.

Hoage, R. J., Anne Roskell, and Jane Mansour. 1996. "Menageries and Zoos to 1900." In *New Worlds, New Animals: From Menagerie to Zoological Park in the Nineteenth Century*, ed. R. J. Hoage and William A. Deiss. Baltimore: Johns Hopkins University Press.

Hubbell, Harry M. 1935. "Ptolemy's Zoo." *The Classical Journal* 31: 68–76.

Humphreys, R. Stephen. 1998. "Egypt in the World System of the later Middle Ages." In *Islamic Egypt, 640–1517*. Vol. 1, *The Cambridge History of Egypt*, ed.Carl F. Petry. Cambridge: Cambridge University Press.

Husain, Iqbal. 2001. "The Diplomatic Vision of Tipu Sultan: Briefs for Embassies to Turkey and France, 1785–86." In *State and Diplomacy under Tipu Sultan: Documents and Essays*, ed. Irfan Habib. New Delhi: Tulika.

Jagchid, S., and C. R. Bawden. 1965. "Some Notes on the Horse Policy of the Yüan Dynasty." *Central Asiatic Journal* 10: 246–268.

James, Lawrence. 1997. *Raj: The Making and Unmaking of British India*. New York: St. Martin's Press.

Jasanoff, Maya. 2006. *Edge of Empire: Lives, Culture, and Conquest in the East, 1750–1850*. New York: Vintage.

Kauz, Ralph. 2009. "Horse Exports from the Persian Gulf until the Arrival of the Portuguese." In *Pferde in Asien: Geschichte, Handel Und Kultur*, ed. Bert G. Fragner, Ralph Kauz, Roderich Ptak, and Angela Schottenhammer. Vienna: Österreichischen Akademie der Wissenschaften.

Kerslake, Celia J. 1980. "The Correspondence between Selīm I and Ḳānṣūh al-Ǧawrī." *Prilozi za Orijentalnu Filologiju* 30: 219–234.

Kurz, O. 1975. *European Clocks and Watches in the Near East.* Leiden: Brill.

Lewis, Bernard. 1949–50. "The Fatimids and the Route to India." *Revue de la Faculté des Sciences Économiques de l'Université d'Istanbul* 11: 50–54.

———. 2004. "The Mughals and the Ottomans." In *From Babel to Dragomans: Interpreting the Middle East.* New York: Oxford University Press.

Loureiro, Rudi Manuel. 2009. "Portuguese Involvement in Sixteenth Century Horse Trade through the Arabian Sea." In *Pferde in Asien: Geschichte, Handel Und Kultur,* ed. Bert G. Fragner, Ralph Kauz, Roderich Ptak, and Angela Schottenhammer. Vienna: Österreichischen Akademie der Wissenschaften.

MacLean, Gerald. 2007. "The Sultan's Beasts: Encountering Ottoman Fauna." In *Looking East: English Writing and the Ottoman Empire before 1800.* New York: Palgrave Macmillan.

Malekandathil, Pius. 2003. "Maritime Malabar and a Mercantile State: Polity and State Formation in Malabar under the Portuguese, 1498–1663." In *Maritime Malabar and the Europeans, 1500–1962,* ed. K. S. Mathew. Gurgaon: Hope India Publications.

Melvin-Koushki, Matthew. 2011. "The Delicate Art of Aggression: Uzun Hasan's *Fathnama* to Qaytbay of 1469." *Iranian Studies* 44: 193–214.

Muslu, Emire Cihan. 2007. "Ottoman-Mamluk Relations: Diplomacy and Perceptions." Ph.D. dissertation, Harvard University.

Özbaran, Salih. 1978. "A Turkish Report on the Red Sea and the Portuguese in the Indian Ocean (1525)." *Arabian Studies* 4: 81–88.

———. 1994. *The Ottoman Response to European Expansion: Studies on Ottoman-Portuguese Relations in the Indian Ocean and Ottoman Administration in the Arab Lands during the Sixteenth Century.* Istanbul: Isis Press.

———. 2002. "Ottoman Naval Power in the Indian Ocean in the 16th Century." In *The Kapudan Pasha, His Office and His Domain: Halcyon Days in Crete IV,* ed. Elizabeth Zachariadou. Rethymnon: Crete University Press.

———. 2009. *Ottoman Expansion towards the Indian Ocean in the 16th Century.* Istanbul: Bilgi University Press.

Petry, Carl F. 1993. *Twilight of Majesty: The Reigns of the Mamlūk Sultans al-Ashrāf Qāytbāy and Qanṣūh al-Ghawrī in Egypt.* Seattle: University of Washington Press.

———. 1994. *Protectors or Praetorians?: The Last Mamlūk Sultans and Egypt's Waning as a Great Power.* Albany: State University of New York Press.

Plumb, Christopher. 2010. "'Strange and Wonderful': Encountering the Elephant in Britain, 1675–1830." *Journal for Eighteenth-Century Studies* 33: 525–543.

Ptak, Roderich. 1991. "Pferde auf See: Ein vergessener Aspekt des maritimen chinesischen Handels im frühen 15. Jahrhundert." *Journal of the Economic and Social History of the Orient* 34: 199–233.

Rao, Velcheru Narayana, and Sanjay Subrahmanyam. 2009. "Notes on Political Thought in Medieval and Early Modern South India." *Modern Asian Studies* 43: 175–210.

Ray, Aniruddha, ed. 2001. *Tipu Sultan and His Age: A Collection of Seminar Papers.* Kolkata: Asiatic Society.

Reid, Anthony. 1969. "Sixteenth-Century Turkish Influence in Western Indonesia." *Journal of South East Asian History* 10: 395–414.

Reindl-Kiel, Hedda. 2009. "No Horses for the Enemy: Ottoman Trade Regulations and Horse Gifting." In *Pferde in Asien: Geschichte, Handel Und Kultur*, ed. Bert G. Fragner, Ralph Kauz, Roderich Ptak, and Angela Schottenhammer. Vienna: Österreichischen Akademie der Wissenschaften.

———. 2010. "Dogs, Elephants, Lions, a Ram and a Rhino on Diplomatic Mission: Animals as Gifts to the Ottoman Court." In *Animals and People in the Ottoman Empire*, ed. Suraiya Faroqhi. Istanbul: Eren.

Rossabi, Morris. 1970. "The Tea and Horse Trade with Inner Asia During the Ming." *Journal of Asian History* 4: 136–168.

al-Ṣarrāf, Maḥmūd Ḥasan ʿAbd al-ʿAzīz. 1991. *Maʿrakat Chāldārān, 920 H/1514 M: Ūlā Ṣafaḥāt al-Ṣirāʿ al-ʿUthmānī al-Fārisī: al-Asbāb wa al-Natāʾij.* Cairo: Maktabat al-Nahḍa al-Miṣriyya.

Saurer, Karl, and Elena Hinshaw-Fischli. 2003. "They Called Him Suleyman: The Adventurous Journey of an Indian Elephant from the Forests of Kerala to the Capital of Vienna in the Middle of the Sixteenth Century." In *Maritime Malabar and the Europeans, 1500–1962*, ed. K. S. Mathew. Gurgaon: Hope India Publications.

Schimmel, Annemarie. 2004. *The Empire of the Great Mughals: History, Art and Culture.* Translated by Corinne Attwood. Edited by Burzine K. Waghmar. London: Reaktion Books.

Shaw, Ian. 2000. "Egypt and the Outside World." In *The Oxford History of Ancient Egypt*, ed. Ian Shaw. Oxford: Oxford University Press.

Shehada, Housni Alkhateeb. 2013. *Mamluks and Animals: Veterinary Medicine in Medieval Islam.* Leiden: Brill.

Silverstein, Adam J. 2010. *Postal Systems in the Pre-Modern Islamic World.* Cambridge: Cambridge University Press.

Sinopoli, Carla M. 2000. "From the Lion Throne: Political and Social Dynamics of the Vijayanagara Empire." *Journal of the Economic and Social History of the Orient* 43: 364–398.

Sivasundaram, Sujit. 2005. "Trading Knowledge: The East India Company's Elephants in India and Britain." *The Historical Journal* 48: 27–63.

Sood, Gagan D. S. 2007. "'Correspondence is Equal to Half a Meeting': The Composition and Comprehension of Letters in Eighteenth-Century Islamic Eurasia." *Journal of the Economic and Social History of the Orient* 50: 172–214.

Soucek, Priscilla. 1999. "Ceramic Production as Exemplar of Yuan-Ilkhanid Relations." *RES: Anthropology and Aesthetics* 35: 125–141.

Subrahmanyam, Sanjay, ed. 1990. *Merchants, Markets and the State in Early Modern
India.* Delhi: Oxford University Press.

————. 1990. *The Political Economy of Commerce: Southern India, 1500–1650.*
Cambridge: Cambridge University Press.

————. 1998. "Reflections on State-Making and History-Making in South India,
1500–1800." *Journal of the Economic and Social History of the Orient* 41: 382–416.

Tezcan, Baki. 2010. *The Second Ottoman Empire: Political and Social Transformation in
the Early Modern World.* Cambridge: Cambridge University Press.

Trautmann, Thomas R. 1982. "Elephants and the Mauryas." In *India, History
and Thought: Essays in Honour of A. L. Basham*, ed. S. N. Mukherjee. Calcutta:
Subarnarekha.

Tuchscherer, Michel. 1997. "La flotte impériale de Suez de 1694 à 1719." *Turcica* 29:
47–69.

Verghese, Anila, and Anna L. Dallapiccola, eds. 2011. *South India under Vijayanagara:
Art and Archaeology.* New York: Oxford University Press.

Yang, Bin. 2004. "Horses, Silver, and Cowries: Yunnan in Global Perspective." *Journal
of World History* 15: 281–322.

Yasuhiro, Yokkaichi. 2009. "Horses in the East-West Trade between China and Iran
under Mongol Rule." In *Pferde in Asien: Geschichte, Handel Und Kultur*, ed. Bert
G. Fragner, Ralph Kauz, Roderich Ptak, and Angela Schottenhammer. Vienna:
Österreichischen Akademie der Wissenschaften.

5

Homemaking as Placemaking

Women in Elite Households in Early Modern Japan and Late Imperial China

MARCIA YONEMOTO

Throughout Confucian East Asia in the early modern period, especially for the social and political elite, the family or lineage (家 J: *ie*, Ch: *jia*) occupied a place of central importance. Its management and perpetuation required concerted efforts and frequent sacrifices on the part of all of its members, male and female, parent and child. Studying the *ie* / *jia* is complicated because it was simultaneously a physical entity (the household, occupying a discrete place in time), an abstract concept (the lineage, stretching from the past through the present, and extending into the future), and a symbolic marker (the home, uniting groups of related and unrelated people through their emotional and subjective attachments to place). The present chapter focuses on elite women's perceptions and constructions of home and family as a form of spatial and cultural placemaking. Women are integral to any understanding of the institution of *ie* / *jia* itself because they were, in practical terms, the producers of offspring and the managers of the household, but also because in ideological terms they were the rulers of the inner sphere of the home, which was the microcosm of the outer, public world, and the nexus of order in the community, state, polity, and cosmos. Elite women thus bore great responsibility not only for the well-being of their own families but for the stability of society at large. While studies of kinship and the family system have formed one of the

mainstays of historical research on this period, only in the past two decades
or so have the roles of elite women in the maintenance of household and lineage become the subjects of detailed study in the English-language literature.[1]
More recent still is scholarship on the regional and translocal differences in
the nature of family and lineage, focusing in particular on the distinctiveness
of marriage and inheritance practices across geographical regions and social
classes.[2] The present article adopts a different perspective in that it focuses on
women and the *ie / jia* in two ways: first, it defines the *ie / jia* as a gendered
place in historical time. In doing so, it follows recent theoretical scholarship
on the concept of place, viewing it as relational, socially constructed, and
engaged with issues of identity and subjectivity.[3] Secondly, it utilizes as sources the writings of educated women of the *bushi* (warrior or samurai) class
from mid-Tokugawa Japan and discusses these texts and what they say about
women's experiences of and within the *ie / jia* in relation to the comparatively
better-documented lives of women of the gentry class in late imperial China.[4]
Elite women in China and Japan form a natural translocal subject of inquiry,
for they shared many assumptions and values regarding home and family; indeed, their educations centered on the same body of classical Confucian texts.
Likewise, in terms of life experience and life cycle, women in both countries
were subject to similar expectations placed upon them by the patriarchal societies in which they lived: they were expected to be filial daughters, to marry,
to bear children and to educate and inculcate moral values in them, and to
faithfully serve the interests of their families until their deaths. At the same
time, women in both countries were able to undertake productive work, and
to indulge in intellectual and creative pursuits of their own while remaining
within the established family structure and performing their family duties.
Further, women often engaged in these endeavors alone, when their husbands
were away on official duty. I interpret the way women negotiated the boundaries between autonomy and authority, norms and exceptions, general practice
and local variation as a form of place-making, the conscious marking out of a
physical and symbolic sphere in which to nurture not only the family, but the
self. More specifically, I argue that elite women expressed this very localized
sense of place through the act of home-making. I define home-making, and
I examine it in the pages that follow, as a three-dimensional process: (1) establishing and managing the physical household, often in the face of frequent
moves to different locations; (2) perpetuating the lineage of the natal and/
or adoptive as well as the married family, and (3) preserving the memory of

home and the legacy of family, often by writing. These forms of home-making are both material and abstract, and they work along affinal as well as agnatic lines. Over time and across space, women crafted complex senses of home, whose physical locations seem to have mattered less than their emotional and symbolic resonance in daily life. In other words, by crafting durable senses of home within the often unpredictable and unstable worlds in which they lived, elite women in late imperial China and early modern Japan in created secure and meaningful places—spaces they could to some degree control and comprehend—for themselves and for their families.

The Household: Making and Remaking the Home

In contrast to the pervasive image emphasizing their cloistered immobility, women of the samurai class in mid-Tokugawa Japan and women of the gentry class in late imperial China moved frequently, and sometimes over considerable distances. While women had little or no choice with regard to many of these moves, such as joining a spouse's household upon marriage, following a husband to a new official posting, or fleeing natural disaster or political upheaval, women also moved voluntarily, in order to visit family and friends, to pay respects at temples and shrines, and to travel and sightsee. In other words, for elite women, physical mobility was more normative than it was anomalous. The peripatetic nature of elite women's lives made it such that the household itself frequently had to be moved and remade in a new location. Perhaps because of the challenges of home-making in distant and unfamiliar places, records of women's lives reveal the notion that while the household as a physical place was transient, the household as an abstract entity that represented ideas of "home" was strong and enduring. For such women, "home" was not solely a physical space, but a highly constructed imaginary entity, encompassing the native place, the natal family, and beloved family members and friends. In this section, I will show how elite women transformed residences in into well-run homes for their families not only through their skills at the myriad tasks that constituted household management, but through the conscious creation of a community of extended family networks that often transcended the home place.

Kuroda Tosako (1682–1753) was the wife of Kuroda Naokuni (1666–1735), a well-connected daimyo who administered numerous domains over his long career, and who by the time of his death in 1735 was receiving an official stipend of 30,000 *koku,* placing him in the lower ranks of the 260-odd daimyo.[5] Tosako's two diaries, *Ishihara-ki* (Record of Ishihara, 1717–18) and *Koto no hagusa* (Words of Leaves and Grasses, 1735–1758), both of which languished undiscovered in the archives until the 1980s, give scholars rare and important insights into the daily life of a daimyo wife.[6] Although they were not wealthy in terms of stipend, the Kuroda were rich in other ways, for they were *fudai* daimyo, hereditary allies of the shogunal house, and they also had close personal connections to the Tokugawa through marriage and adoption, which endowed them with considerable prestige and allowed them privileges that far exceeded their modest income. These connections ran in part through Naokuni, who was adopted as heir to his maternal grandfather, a *karō* in Tatebayashi domain, whose lord was the future shogun Tokugawa Tsunayoshi. From this position as heir to a favored retainer, Naokuni was betrothed as a youth to Tsunayoshi's infant daughter Tokumatsu, an alliance that unfortunately ended with the latter's death at the age of five. In 1702, at the age of twenty-six, he wed fourteen-year-old Tosako, who was the adopted daughter of Tsunayoshi's close adviser, the powerful Grand Councillor Yanagisawa Yoshiyasu (1568–1714) and his wife Sadako.[7] Tosako's illustrious family background served to consolidate Naokuni's political standing and his close ties to the highest levels of power in the shogunal system.

As was common for a woman of her status, Tosako moved her permanent residence more than half a dozen times in her long life, and she moved house temporarily several times more. The moves she made give us some insight into the tenuous nature of upper *bushi*-class women's attachments to any physical home space. Tosako's first move came as a young girl, when she left her natal family—she was born the daughter of Orii Masatoshi, a page to the fourth shogun Tokugawa Ietsuna—upon her adoption as the daughter of Yanagisawa Yoshiyasu. Such a move presented an appealing opportunity for the Orii, because Tosako could make a considerably more advantageous marriage as a Yanagisawa daughter, and thus indirectly bring benefit to her birth family, with whom she maintained contact throughout her life. When she wed Naokuni, Tosako moved to his primary residence in Edo, his upper mansion *(kami yashiki)* in Tokiwabashi, just outside the eastern gates of Edo Castle. But in 1717 the Tokiwabashi mansion was severely damaged by fire, and the family—primarily the women and children, since Naokuni was often away from Edo—was forced to move to the domain's slightly rustic lower mansion *(shimo yashiki),* located in Ishihara in the Honjō district, then considered the eastern hinterlands of Edo. They lived there for about a year until the upper mansion was repaired. Tosako moved several more times between various Edo residences, but in her later years the lower mansion at Ishihara became her retirement villa of sorts, where she lived more or less continuously from the time of her husband's death in 1735 until her own death in 1758.[8]

Tosako's diaries show that while the dislocations she experienced were sometimes upsetting to her, they were also opportunities to extend and deepen the family ties that made her various residences into homes. Her moves allowed her to enjoy new experiences and, importantly, motivated her to chronicle those experiences in writing. For example, when Tosako fled the fire that consumed the Kuroda upper mansion in 1717, she moved to Ishihara with a group of family members, including her three daughters, and her sister-in-law Nakayama Suzuko (born ca. 1675 and the widow of Naokuni's older brother Nakayama Naomichi). Tosako's mother-in-law lived in a separate residence nearby until she died in 1718. Tosako's diary, *Ishihara-ki,* recounts the drama of escaping the fire, the move to Ishihara, and the family's daily life there.

For Tosako, the material concerns of moving and setting up house do not feature prominently in her diaries; these matters would have been taken care of by servants or, if they were accomplished by Tosako herself, they did not merit mention in the diary. Rather, making a new home in Ishihara in 1717–18, when her husband was still alive and most of her children still at home, consisted not so much of routine chores but of taking advantage of the relative freedom of movement and anonymity the family enjoyed in this relatively undeveloped part of Edo. Indeed, for the women in the family, the yearlong stay in Ishihara was literally a breath of fresh air and an opportunity to explore the world much more freely than they could in Tokiwabashi, located as it was in the shadow of the shogunal castle. As Tosako wrote in her diary, "The Tokiwabashi house is immaculate and vast, while here in this house one feels much less restricted. Because it's the country out here, no one is watching us and we are able to go out from time to time to places nearby. I wonder whether it might not be a consolation to the girls [her daughters] to let them go out and see things."[9] Indeed, Tosako and her family got out and about with extraordinary frequency. Shiba Keiko has tallied up the excursions Tosako and her family members—mostly the women—made, and came up with a total of 117 trips over a one-year period; rarely did a few days go by that Tosako did not travel somewhere to do something or visit someone.[10] Many of the excursions were to nearby temples and shrines, in order to pray for the health

and well-being of family members, principally the immediate family and Naokuni's relatives, but also Tosako's own (adoptive) family, the Yanagisawa. Additionally, as the civic-minded wife of a daimyo, Tosako prayed for the "safety
of the realm" *(tenka anzen)*. She also visited the homes of relatives and friends,
tending to ailing family members, and staying for an extended time with her
daughter Toyoko after the birth of Toyoko's daughter, her first grandchild.

While Tosako's careful chronicling of these outings are in part a daily log of
activities in a new and different place, they also, importantly, constitute a carefully crafted narrative of complex familial relations, and of myriad obligations
that were social, political, and emotional in nature. In this respect, they resemble the travel accounts written by Chinese women in the late imperial period,
whose texts were "coded to display both their virtue and their learning," becoming, in the process, "'vehicles for expressing appropriate emotions.'"[11] At
the same time, some of Tosako's excursions were purely for pleasure—boating
and fireworks-viewing on the Sumida River in summer, for instance, which
the family did on half a dozen occasions. The participants in these outings
included Tosako and her daughters, sometimes joined by Tosako's mother-
in-law and her sister-in-law Suzuko, and of course a smattering of attendants.
Tosako's husband and sons-in-law only rarely joined in, emphasizing the ways
in which such outings functioned to replicate the already close cross-genera-
tional ties between women that had been established within the home. Tosako
makes little attempt to disguise such trips as dutiful, and this too echoes similar writings by Chinese women such as Wang Fengxian, wife of a magistrate in
Jiangxi Province in the early seventeenth century, who was interested neither
in "the logistics of traveling nor the famous sights on the way, but the minute
pleasures and moments of revelation on the road."[12]

Tosako's year in the lower mansion, and the diary she kept while there,
mark the beginning of what was to become a meaningful and lasting connection to Ishihara as a place. For although Tosako stayed only year in 1717–18,
she returned to the Ishihara *yashiki* in 1735, after the death of her husband
and the passing on of the household headship—and the right to residence
in the Tokiwabashi upper mansion—to Naokuni's heir Naozumi. And much
as *Ishihara-ki* was the document of her first and temporary stay in the lower
mansion when she was a young mother, wife, and daughter-in-law, her much
longer six-volume diary covering the years 1735 to 1753, *Koto no hagusa*, is
a chronicle of her return to Ishihara as a widow in her later years. In the latter text, the tone of Tosako's writing is quite different, as were her activities.

Purely pleasurable outings were few; instead, her thoughts and activities re-volve around preserving her husband's memory and, equally important, his reputation.

Wherever she lived, but especially in her later life at Ishihara, Tosako re-ceived guests constantly and relatives and friends took up temporary residence with her in Ishihara when for various reasons they were unable to stay in their own homes. Extending her generosity in this way was not only a personal act of friendship, it was an act of charity and benevolence—even a display of the economic well-being of her own household—that would not have gone unnoticed in the small world of the daimyo elite in Edo. Although Tosako says nothing about the mundane matter of how she funded her seemingly comfortable life, we know from other sources that Naokuni rose consistently in status, and thus in income, throughout his career. Indeed, his stipend dou-bled—from 15,000 to 30,000 *koku*—in the time he and Tosako were married. It is likely, though, that the Kuroda family's lifestyle was enabled as much by gifts and patronage received from their powerful relatives as it was by in-come alone. *Ishihara-ki,* for example, reveals the significant number of costly gifts—mostly rich fabrics for formal clothing—that were sent to Tosako by her own family, the Yanagisawa, and by Yanagisawa Yoshiyasu's patron, the shogun Tokugawa Tsunayoshi.[13] While ritually appropriate, these gifts were also useful and valuable, and no doubt facilitated the establishment and rees-tablishment of the Kuroda household.

The absence of direct discussion of financial matters in Kuroda Tosako's diaries is not surprising, for the crass nature of money matters was deeply distasteful to those raised in the upper echelons of the elite, whose members were taught to revere the "amateur ideal" of the leisured gentleman who de-voted his life to scholarship without thought of material gain. Tosako's silence regarding finances therefore does not necessarily stand as proof of the fami-ly's economic well-being, for the life of the gentleman scholar was, in eigh-teenth-century Japan as well as in China, as much ideal as it was reality. Even in the great gentry families of the Lower Yangxi, straitened financial circum-stances were the cause of great anxiety for women. Consider the case of Tang Yaoqing (1763–1831), the "talented woman" *(guixiu)* and matriarch of the Zhang family, and her remarkable daughters Qieying, Guanying, Lunying, and Wanying, whose life stories, spanning the late eighteenth and early nine-teenth centuries, are so vividly brought to life by Susan Mann.[14] The Zhang matriarch Yaoqing, like Tosako, moved frequently throughout her adult life.

Upon her marriage to Zhang Qi, she joined the Zhang household, but she did not leave their mutual home village of Changzhou until the age of thirty-five, when Zhang Qi moved his family to Anhui Province at the invitation of his accomplished elder brother Huiyan, who had received a post there.[15] Tang Yaoqing returned to live in her (and her husband's) native place of Changzhou on and off throughout her adult life, and her ties to it remained direct and immediate. Still, as Susan Mann writes, "Reading Yaoqing's story, one cannot help but be shocked at the dislocation suffered by 'successful' literati families like hers when the honor of an official appointment also meant a traumatic move to a strange part of the country."[16] Yaoqing and her family made a life in each of the new locales and yet, unlike the pleasurable escape experienced by Kuroda Tosako and her family, for the Zhangs each venture away was marked by trauma and unhappiness: in Huizhou, it was the death of Yaoqing's brother-in-law and the family's benefactor and, soon after, the death at age fourteen of Zhang Qi and Yaoqing's oldest and only son, Juesun. While in Anhui on a second sojourn, Yaoqing learned of the death of her own father. And in an incidence of savage misfortune, in the early phase of the extended family's move to Shandong, smallpox claimed four of Yaoqing's young grandchildren. It is no surprise that when Yaoqing was away from Changzhou, she longed for it and for the safety and comfort of family—her own and her husband's—that it represented. And yet Yaoqing died in Shandong, far from her native place, at the age of sixty-eight.

Throughout their many moves and misfortunes, Yaoqing and her daughters worked tirelessly in order to maintain the family's precarious hold on economic stability, albeit in discreet ways appropriate to their gender and class that did not draw undue attention to the family's dire straits. When her husband Zhang Qi was traveling, years would go by when Tang Yaoqing and the family received no news and no financial support from him, and even when he was home and contributing his earnings, it is unlikely that his income covered the family's routine expenses, much less the numerous acts of charity and costly performances of ritual devotion that Yaoqing undertook on behalf of her own and her husband's families.[17] Over the years, Yaoqing seems to have cobbled together several sources of independent income that were crucial to maintaining her family's standard of living: her own dowry money, the sale of her own and her daughters' fine embroidery, and monetary gifts from her Aunt Tang (her father's sister) and her own mother.[18] Indeed, maternal relatives on Yaoqing's side were crucial to the economic sustenance of the Zhang family. As Mann puts it: " . . . [I]n the Zhang family, financial support often traveled more readily through women's networks (marital, maternal, sororal) than through men's."[19] Tang Yaoqing was without doubt the primary household manager *and* provider in the Zhang family, and she and her daughters worked assiduously to ensure that the family's reputation did not diminish. Yet in her own writings and writings about her, this hard work and striving was transmuted into benign and gendered statements concerning thrift, diligence, and industry.

While pride, convention, and status consciousness would have combined to prevent both Tang Yaoqing and Kuroda Tosako from openly discussing their families' financial troubles in writing, this was not the case for Itō Maki (1797–1862), the wife of a low-ranking *hatamoto* in the early nineteenth century, who chronicled her and her family's financial difficulties in great detail in a series of letters written to her own parents. This cache of letters, like Tosako's diaries, was discovered only recently, and form the core of a fascinating study by the historian Mega Atsuko.[20] Like many enterprising women in the lower ranks of the samurai class in the late Tokugawa period, Maki was not born into the warrior class. Her father, Kobayashi Reisuke, was a doctor and scholar in Okamura in Mimasaka Province (present-day Okayama Prefecture). Maki was his eldest daughter, and received a solid education not only in the usual curriculum for girls and women, which emphasized the Japanese classics and calligraphy, but in the Confucian classics and in the Chinese scientific texts that were so important to her father and his work. Even if we accept that displacement was common among elite women in this period, Maki's life still represents an exceptionally high degree of mobility, both physical and social. In the course of her life, Maki became a member, by birth, adoption, or marriage, of no fewer than five different families, three of whom were unrelated to her by blood: her birth family (the Kobayashi, commoner physicians in Mimasaka Province); her first adoptive family (her paternal uncle, a commoner who had risen to *hatamoto* status in Edo, and his wife); her first husband's family (the Sugiura, *hatamoto* stationed in Kōfu); her second adoptive family (the Nakamura, who were *hatamoto*); and her second husband's family (the Itō, *hatamoto* stationed in Edo).[21] Perhaps in part because the epistolary genre is more explicitly descriptive than the classical style of Tosako's diaries and the poetic and lyrical texts of the Zhang women, the differences in the nature of household management among the lower ranks of the *bushi* class as depicted in Maki's letters are striking. From the time she came of age, Maki was deeply

concerned and directly involved in managing the material and especially bud-
getary aspects of her households. As was the case for both Kuroda Tosako and
Tang Yaoqing, in both of Maki's marriages her family's finances were greatly
aided by the support of her affinal relatives, most notably her paternal uncle,
Kobayashi Kōzaemon. Kōzaemon was an ambitious, upwardly mobile individual who in his late teens left home to serve as a clerk *(tedai)* to the *daikan* of
Kurashiki in Bitchu Province.[22] Although Kōzaemon, like the rest of his family, was of commoner birth, he eventually worked his way up into the samurai
class by merit, strategic selection of patrons, and not a little luck. Throughout
his life, his wealth and generosity exceeded his rather lowly rank, and he was
a sustaining force in the life of Maki, his adopted daughter/niece, and her
children. After Kōzaemon died, Maki noted that even though her second husband's stipend was slightly higher than that of her first husband, without her
uncle's help she could not make ends meet without borrowing at high interest
from moneylenders. Maki is explicit in her letters about their predicament:
she explains that her second husband Kaname had borrowed up to the legal
limit, and was hard-pressed to raise the money just to service—not to pay
off—their debts. Unlike Tang Yaoqing, however, Maki resolves these problems
not by more conventional forms of "women's work" such as taking in sewing,
but rather through what seems to have been a unique (and counterintuitive)
early modern Japanese tactic—adoption and strategic marriage alliances for
her children as a form of lineage maintenance, which could solidify a family's
standing economically, socially, and politically.

Lineage Maintenance: Securing
a Family's Place through Time

While recent scholarship has focused on the importance of women's roles in
household and lineage maintenance in late imperial China, this topic has yet
to be explored in detail with regard to early modern Japan. There are many
commonalities between the gentry families of late imperial China and the
warrior houses of Tokugawa Japan: both were under pressure to maintain a
standard of living appropriate to their social and political status while at the
same time suffering from diminishing economic resources; both were organized patrilineally, and their survival thus depended on the existence, in each
generation, of a suitable male heir; both in theory subscribed to the idea that
the interests of the patriline were at all times dominant; both dictated that

upon marriage women cut ties to their own parents and offered their loyalty and obedience solely to their in-laws, while in practice women often maintained important and lasting ties to their natal families; in both cases the male house-head was absent from home frequently and often for extended periods of time due to the requirements of his office; and in both cases, as we have seen, the day-to-day functioning of the household and, to a surprising degree, their economic viability depended upon the learning and the managerial and interpersonal skills of wives, daughters, and other female kin.

While these commonalities are compelling, perhaps even more telling are the differences in the ways that Chinese gentry families, on the one hand, and Tokugawa warrior families, on the other, responded to the challenges of maintaining their households and lineages across time. One key difference lay in the remarkable flexibility of the very principle of patrilineal descent in Tokugawa Japan, which was reflected in the widespread use of adoption—of men and women, adults and children, kin and non-kin. In late imperial China adoption was "widely used, and flexibly" within elite lineages, but the adoptee by the dictates of law and convention was supposed to come from within the kin group. Further, the adoptee was almost always a male kinsman who would serve as heir of the adopting family; adoption of a daughter's husband as heir, which was a very common form of adoption in Japan, was extremely rare in China.[23] In early modern Japan adoption of kin and non-kin was frequently and pragmatically deployed as a means not only to preserve but to improve a family's political, economic, and social standing, and women as well as men were adopted in order to accomplish these goals. It was not unusual for an individual to be adopted more than once, by completely unrelated families, if doing so could improve the status of the family of which s/he was a member. Another key difference lay in the acceptability of remarriage for women: in late imperial China the cult of the "chaste widow" was deeply entrenched in gentry families. Although in actual practice widows in China, especially in the lower social classes, seem to have deviated from the ideal of chastity, the freedom and seeming ease with which widows and even divorcées of the elite warrior class in early modern Japan remarried stands out as remarkable.[24]

Above and beyond her own history as an adoptee married to an adoptee, Kuroda Tosako's two diaries give evidence of her involvement in the alliances through marriage and adoption of her children and kin, alliances that served to secure the standing of both her husband's family and her affinal kin. Adoption was of great importance for the Kuroda house in part because Naokuni and Tosako's long marriage resulted in the birth of three daughters—Toshiko, Michiko, and Toyoko—but no sons. Of course, for men of Naokuni's standing there was the safety net provided by a concubine, and Naokuni did in fact have another daughter, Kumiko, and a son, Naoyuki, with his mistress. However, rather than making Naoyuki his heir, Naokuni and Tosako chose to adopt his nephew, Naomoto, the son of Naokuni's younger sister, at the age of sixteen as an in-marrying husband *(muko yōshi)* for his and Tosako's daughter Michiko.[25] Naomoto and Michiko, however, had only one daughter together before Naomoto's untimely death at the age of twenty-one. Far from allowing their daughter to languish in a state of chaste widowhood, within two months of Naomoto's death, Naokuni and Tosako adopted another in-marrying husband, this time a son of the Honda family, who took the name Kuroda Naozumi, and he became the second husband of Michiko and the new male heir to the family headship. For their part, Naozumi and Michiko, like Naokuni and Tosako, produced daughters in abundance—five in total—but no sons. Naozumi had three sons and two more daughters by concubines, but he bypassed his biological sons and instead adopted Naokuni's aforementioned son by a concubine, Naoyuki, as his heir. Naoyuki in turn adopted Naozumi's son Naohiro as *his* heir. The sisters, for their part, all married or were adopted into daimyo families (one was married into the Honda, the natal family of her father Naozumi).[26]

What should we make of this complicated history of multiple and interwoven adoptions and marriages? First, it is remarkable how important affinal ties are. Naokuni's line continued into the next generation not through sons, but through his daughter Michiko, for whom he adopted first his sister's son and then a non-kinsman as in-marrying husbands and heirs. In doing so he skipped over his own blood-related son by his concubine, as did his own adopted heir, Naozumi. This might have had to do with the relative ages of the heirs in question (and the biological sons did become heirs later, also by adoption), but there is certainly enough evidence of succession by infant and very young males in samurai families to suggest that youth alone did not rule out a male as heir. It seems possible that the Kuroda family's choices with regard to heirs had to do with a preference for keeping succession in the line of the principal wife, Tosako, rather than through children of a concubine, even if it meant effectively engineering succession through a daughter rather than a son. In other words, the preference for marrying in an heir as husband for a daughter was as much an indication of the value placed on her mother, the principal wife, as it was an expedient solution to the problem of having no suitable sons to inherit. Theoretically, following the oft-cited "Seven Rules for Divorce" that were popularized around this time in texts like *Onna daigaku takarabako* (The Treasure Box of Great Learning for Women, 1716) Naokuni was entitled to divorce Tosako because she did not bear a male heir, but clearly he did not do this. Naokuni's emotional ties to his wife notwithstanding, Tosako's importance to the family extended beyond herself, for continuing the line of descent through her blood kin ensured the continued favor of her family, the Yanagisawa, and through them, the shogunal house itself. This support, as discussed above, had very real effects on the family's fortunes.

If adoption and in-marrying husbands were integral to the preservation of the Kuroda, a daimyo lineage, it was even more the case for families much lower on the status scale within the warrior class, like Itō Maki's. The *hatamoto,* the group to which Maki's uncle and both her husbands belonged, were direct retainers of the Tokugawa shogun, and while this connection might have brought with it a certain amount of prestige, for the lower-ranking among them, life was a hand-to-mouth affair, in which indebtedness and financial worry were constant, and only vigilance and canny strategizing on the part of all members, male and female alike, could keep a family line from dying out. The letters written by Itō Maki to her parents are a vivid document of the daily, hands-on struggle for family standing and survival at the lower levels of the *bushi* class. Lineage success depended on many factors, not least of which was a family's luck in childbearings and its ability to marry its children well. The Kobayashi, however, like the Kuroda and the Zhang, were unlucky when it came to male heirs. Maki was one of four siblings: her older brother Tetsuzō, the family's heir, died at the age of twenty-five, at which point the heirship passed to her younger brother, Kyōzo. Kyōzo, however, fell victim to increasingly severe mental illness in his mid-twenties, and died in confinement in the family home at age thirty-nine. In the meantime, the family had arranged for succession to pass through Maki's younger sister O-Noe, whose husband Gunsuke was adopted as *muko yōshi,* and served as acting heir until their son Sōsuke came of age and officially undertook the duties of continuing the family's medical practice.[27]

As for Maki herself, it seems that she was positioned by her family for greater achievements: namely, marriage into the samurai class proper. This was accomplished through a roundabout process of adoption and marriage. As was mentioned earlier, at the age of sixteen or seventeen, Maki's father arranged for her adoption by her uncle Kōzaemon. By the time he adopted

Maki, Kōzaemon had attained *hatamoto* status, and was living in Edo earning a 150-*koku* stipend and occupying the position of Nikkō *fushin-yaku,* which involved him in the maintenance of the elaborate shrine to Tokugawa Ieyasu at Nikkō. Kōzaemon had a wide circle of influential friends, and ample spending money for gifts and amusements, but he too was unlucky in heirs: his first wife died bearing their only daughter, and the daughter herself died in 1807 at age of six. Kōzaemon remarried, but his second wife never bore him children. The adoption of Maki, therefore, was beneficial for both parties: on one hand, Kōzaemon gained a daughter for whom he might adopt in a husband and heir, though curiously, he never did do so. On the other hand, Maki, rather than remain a commoner scholar's daughter, gained *hatamoto* status through adoption by her uncle, and thus became a much more likely candidate for marriage into the *hatamoto* class, which would in turn ensure the samurai status of her descendants.

As planned, a few years after her adoption, in 1816 or 1817, Kōzaemon arranged for Maki to marry Sugiura Tamesaku, whose family were retainers serving in Kōfu Castle. Tamesaku's father's stipend was 150 *hyō,* making them among the lowest-ranking *gokenin.* However, Kōzaemon's personal wealth eased Maki and Tamesaku's finances. Maki and Tamesaku's first child, a daughter named Nao, was born in 1818, their son Seigorō in 1820. Then in 1823, Tamesuke took ill and died, leaving Maki a widow in her late twenties with two small children.[28] But as in the case of Kuroda Tosako's daughter Michiko, a second marriage was arranged for Maki, and it was a good one: her second husband was Itō Kaname, a lower-ranking member of the *ōban* corps with an income of 200 *hyō.*[29] In other words, not only was Maki able to remarry as a widow with two children, she remarried up. Furthermore, it is clear from records that Maki was married to Itō Kaname *not* as the adopted daughter of her uncle Kōzaemon but as the adopted daughter of one Nakamura Sōhei, whose family had been direct retainers of Tokugawa since beginning of their rule. Thus Nakamura Sōhei's status was higher than that of Kōzaemon, and in order to be married into a family of the Itō's status, Maki had to be adopted by the Nakamura first. This pattern of premarital adoption of both males and females in order to secure a more favorable marriage was common within the Tokugawa-period *bushi* class, and the fact that Maki's successive adoptions were arranged to compensate for her relatively humble birth seems to have been transparently obvious and known to all involved, and yet wholly unproblematic. Kaname, for his part, had been adopted into the Itō house as its heir, from another *ōban* house distantly related to them, the Doi. The Itō lineage was so riddled with adoption that, as Mega Atsuko puts it, "it would not be inappropriate to say that it was a house whose bloodline was in the process of being lost."[30] Kaname and Maki had two children together, who were also one boy and one girl: Tama, born in 1831, when Maki would have been around thirty-four or thirty-five years old, and Kinnojō, born in 1836, when Maki was forty.

Throughout this time, Maki's letters to her parents report details of the lives of the children (three of the four were living with her at the time of the correspondence), their growth, education, and talents. They also, as we have seen, chronicle the family's persistent money troubles. Maki's letters to her parents show clearly that adoption provided benefits not only in terms of status, but in terms of financial gain as well. For example, one of Maki and Kaname's strategies for easing their financial burden was to arrange for the early adoption of a thirteen-year-old boy as in-marrying husband for their five-year-old daughter Tama. The adoptive husband/son would bring with him a substantial dowry *(jisankin)* of eighty *ryō*. As reported in a letter by Maki to her parents, the boy, Heikichi, was the fourth son of Kaname's nephew Wakabayashi Ichizaemon (thus a first cousin once removed to his future wife, Tama). As Maki explains, they adopted Heikichi on a temporary basis *(kari yōshi)* for about a year, to see if the situation was workable, and when they saw that it was, the family then went through the formal procedures to adopt Heikichi legally, so he "can be called a member of the Itō house." It was made a condition of Heikichi's adoption that he would inherit the headship of the Itō house as the husband of Tama, superseding the rights of any boy born to Maki and Kaname subsequently (and making the adoption a more favorable option of Heikichi's birth parents). In fact, Maki was pregnant at the time and did give birth to a boy, Kinnojō. The circumstances suggest that this adoption was not due to worry about having a male heir, it was because of an immediate and pressing need for the adoptee's dowry money. As Mega Atsuko remarks, in this case the financial survival of the house trumped the biological prerogatives of the patriline.[31]

In the end, Tama's marriage plans turned out well for the Itō, if not for the hapless Heikichi, who disappeared from family records after several years, and is assumed to have died sometime after the marriage but before reaching adulthood, which left Kaname and Maki's son Kinnojō free to inherit the house headship. Tama, too, seems to have landed on her feet after the death of her cousin/husband. When she was sixteen, in 1846, negotiations began for her remarriage to a son of the Yōhara house, whose income and status was considerably higher than Itō Kaname's. However, the marriage plans were suspended because, as Maki put it in a letter to her parents, "the Yōhara son is not a good sort," and the family could not accept the engagement. The son himself had been adopted by the Yōhara with the intention of his becoming heir, but he had an affair and according to Maki he had an illegitimate child with a woman of "ill repute" whom he never married. It is not clear what exactly ensued in the six or so years between the end of the first engagement and Tama's eventual marriage in 1851, at age twenty-two, into the same Yōhara house, but it seems that she ultimately married not the unsuitable first candidate, but a *different* adopted son.[32]

Nao, the oldest child of Maki and first husband Tamesaku, was adopted by Itō Kaname after Maki's remarriage. As Itō's daughter, in 1834 or 1835 she was married to low-ranking samurai but the marriage failed almost immediately for reasons unknown, the couple divorced, and Nao returned home.[33] The divorce seems not to have damaged Nao's reputation, for at the end of 1835 Maki wrote that Nao was receiving marriage inquiries "from everywhere" but that she and Kaname had not yet decided on a candidate. In another letter in 1836 Maki writes: "Because O-Nao is thoroughly patient, I hope to soon arrange for her to marry a man of rank and live with him, perhaps a [man of the rank of] *ōban* or *ryōban* with whom she can live in a mutually beneficial relationship."[34] As in the case of Tama, and of Maki herself, one might think that a widow or a woman with a failed marriage might have to look for a second husband of a lower status than that of her own family, but Maki's letter reveals that she instead considered mates at the same or even higher rank (*ryōban* stipends were 300 *hyō*, while Ito's status of *ōban* earned 200 *hyō*).[35]

Finally, in 1857 negotiations began for the marriage of Maki's youngest child, Kinnojō, now the Itō household head. Maki wrote to her parents in 1857 that she hoped to find a bride for Kinnojō soon, so "things can get a little easier" for her with a daughter-in-law to take over the household chores. Maki was forty when Kinnojō was born, so she would have been sixty-two when he was preparing for marriage, and more than ready to retire and pass the rice paddle on to a younger woman.[36] The next year, she wrote that marriage talks had begun with a very wealthy high-ranking family, but after meeting the girl in person, Maki decided she was "not of good quality" and refused the opportunity. Besides, she wrote, "there are other good, attractive girls, so I will confer with their families."[37]

Maki's deep involvement in the marriages and adoptions of all her children are clearly described in her letters to her parents.[38] She expresses clear opinions about potential spouses, opinions that seem to have prevailed in the end. Of course Kaname, as the male head of household, was responsible for executing the formal marriage and adoption procedures, but it was clearly Maki herself who did the lion's share of planning and preparing for her children's marriages.[39] It was she who kept careful track of who married whom among families whose status was commensurate to that of the Itō. It was she who personally met and vetted potential mates, and assessed their personal qualities as well as the status implications of a union between the families. And it was she who performed the elaborate financial calculus to discern what costs and benefits a marriage alliance would accrue, and whether it was worth the risk. In short, she not only managed the household, she crafted the house-as-lineage.[40] As we shall see below, she also cultivated a sense of home centered on her natal family and village, one that she passed on to her children and that was preserved in her letters.

One wonders what Tang Yaoqing and her daughters would have thought of Kuroda Tosako and Itō Maki; one is tempted to say they would have found their actions, and the decisions made by their families, as incomprehensible at best and appalling at worst. Adopting non-kin, adopting in-marrying husbands for monetary gain, transparently utilizing adoption to enable social climbing, remarrying shamelessly after the death of a first husband—all of these would have struck the Zhang women as behavior utterly inappropriate to any person who wished to consider him or herself civilized.

At the same time, the Zhang women might have recognized glimmers of familiarity in the lives of Tosako and Maki. Families in Jiangsu, the province in which the Zhang native place of Changzhou was located, also engaged in a number of distinctive marriage practices, such as keeping a betrothed daughter at home until her husband was well-established in her career, and frequently having husbands marry into and reside with the wife/daughter's family (although the husbands were not adopted by the wife's family). These practices privileged women, and were thus viewed negatively by conservative critics in other regions.[41] Similarly, in the Pearl River Delta during the late imperial period, practices ranging from "marriage resistance" to the phenomenon of "delayed transfer marriages" allowed women to mitigate the demands of patrilocal marriage.[42] Yaoqing herself benefitted from these alternative marriage practices: she became engaged to Zhang Qi in 1780, when she was

seventeen years old, but they did not formally marry until Yaoqing was twenty-seven, a full ten years later. As we shall see, her daughters engaged in these
practices as well.

For Yaoqing, marrying her children well was a particular challenge, because
like Kuroda Tosako, she and Zhang Qi were favored by four daughters, but
only two sons, one of whom died as a teenager. While her husband was at
home for the marriage of their eldest daughter Qieying, he subsequently left
home for work and it fell entirely to Yaoqing to manage the immense task
of furnishing dowries and trousseaus, and of making wedding plans for the
younger three of their daughters.[43] The task was eased somewhat by the fact
that Yaoqing and Zhang Qi had decided early on, following the custom of
the region, to arrange an in-marrying husband for at least one of their daughters.[44] Their mates would be chosen from the wide circle of kin residing in the
"golden triangle" surrounding Changzhou, which was bordered by the Yangzi
River to the north and east and extended west and south to encompass the
area around Lake Tai.[45] In the end the husbands of both Lunying, the third
daughter, and Wanying, the youngest, came to live with the Zhangs, thus
sparing Yaoqing at least the effort and expense of organizing the elaborate
wedding ceremony parades that would have been required to transport the
brides, with great fanfare, to the residences of their husbands. Only the second
daughter, Guanying, required this, and to cover the enormous costs of such
an undertaking, Yaoqing embroidered not only for her own daughters but for
wealthy paying customers, and thus "she was up every night for months working in the light of the lamp near her sewing table, piecing silk and working
her designs."[46] The eldest daughter, Qieying, had married but like her mother
had done before her, she remained in her parents' home until her husband
had sufficiently established himself in an official position in Beijing. Qieying
did not leave her parents' home until she was forty years of age; after losing
her two children to smallpox, she had no further children of her own, instead
devoting herself to the rearing and education of her husband's son from a
previous marriage.

After Yaoqing's death, her daughters continued the work of managing the
Zhang lineage. Lunying, like her older sister Qieying, did not have more children of her own after the deaths of her young daughters in Shandong. Instead,
she and her husband adopted his nephew to continue her husband's line, and
they also adopted their niece, Wanying's third daughter, Cailan, to whom Lunying had always been close.[47] Youngest sister Wanying, who in the opinion

of her older sisters had made the best companionate marriage of all the female siblings, had four daughters and one son with her husband Wang Xi.[48] But in part because the family was well aware of the perils of having only a single son as heir, and also perhaps to mark her sister-in-law's "retirement" from childbearing, on Wanying's fortieth birthday, Yuesun's wife Mengyi gave her the "gift" of a concubine for her husband, who went on to bear three sons and a daughter by Wang Xi, making Wanying the "ritual mother" of nine children.[49] When Mengyi herself died in childbirth at age thirty-seven, leaving their beloved younger brother bereft, Qieying and Lunying stepped in to supervise the selection of a concubine for Yuesun. They eventually chose the daughter of a servant in the local magistrate's office named Li Luan, who was about the same age as Yuesun's daughter. Li Luan joined the family, was educated along with the younger Zhang cousins, and eventually became a treasured companion of Yuesun in his later years.[50] Qieying arranged the marriage of her niece Wang Caipin, Wanying's oldest daughter, into the Cheng family in nearby Wuxi.[51] Wanying's third daughter Cailan, after her adoption by Lunying, was married to a man named Lü Maorong but she died soon after the marriage, at which point Lü quickly remarried her younger sister Caizao. Finally, Wanying's only son and heir, Wang Chenbi, was married to his first cousin Zhang Xiangzhen, the daughter of Yuesun.[52] It is clear that the majority of these marriages and adoptions were accomplished through affinal ties, and that they were accomplished largely by the planning and social acumen of the women in the family. At every turn, the deep investment of the Zhang women in the maintenance of their natal lineage paid off in the lineage's survival; as Susan Mann aptly summarizes it, "Zhang Qi's line endured, in the end, through the will of its women."[53] She might well have been speaking of the Kuroda and Itō family lines as well.

Memory as Placemaking: Elite Women's Writing and Legacies of Home

One of the more notable commonalities among the women writers discussed here is the way they used writing to craft a meaningful sense of home. The notion of home, whether defined as the native place or as the family itself, provided women with comfort and consistency in the face of change and upheaval.

The connection to home was perhaps most naturally felt by the women of the Zhang family. Their native place, Changzhou, in the late imperial period was considered "one of the preeminent cultural centers for talented women poets."[54] Tang Yaoqing was a highly educated woman who was in great part responsible for her daughters' superb educations. All four Zhang daughters were recognized for their literary talents, but the two eldest were the best known: oldest daughter Qieying, became a celebrated poet and woman of letters in nineteenth-century Beijing, and second daughter Lunying's distinctive calligraphy was sought after by collectors throughout China and Korea. It was up to the family's women as well as its men to uphold the lineage's reputation for literary achievement, and while the women wrote, it was the Zhang men— Zhang Qi and especially his youngest son and heir Zhang Yuesun—who were in great part responsible for preserving, editing, and publishing the writings of their female kin.

While the Zhang women gained notoriety for their individual attainments, they also conformed to a type of "talented woman" who was characteristic of the great Jiangnan gentry lineages of which the Zhang were one. As members of this distinctive class, the Zhang were expected to maintain the family's roots in Changzhou by establishing an enduring ritual presence. Tang Yaoqing's final acts before she left Changzhou for the last time in order to join her husband in Shandong involved attending to rituals in honor of both her natal parents and her parents-in-law. After a delay of some years due to insufficient funds, Yaoqing somehow accrued enough funds to see to the building of a memorial arch for her mother-in-law, who had received in 1798 an official commendation from the imperial government as a chaste widow.[55] Yaoqing also attended to the ritual needs of her own parents, again managing to pull together enough money to purchase a gravesite and arrange for her parents' proper burial with ritual honors.[56] Only when these memorial duties were completed did she leave Changzhou. Throughout the years the Zhang spent away from their native place, Changzhou remained their touchstone, the locale for their most treasured memories of home and family. As was so often the case for elite women, the significance of the home place grew ever larger in mind and memory even as it became more distant and removed in time and space.

In the case of Kuroda Tosako, her diaries provided the means for her to craft a narrative of her own life and origins. She portrays herself as the wife and widow of Naokuni and as the mother, grandmother, and great-grandmother of their descendants, but also, critically, as a daughter of the Yanagisawa. The events Tosako recorded in her diary mark these various facets of her identity. She mourned Naokuni's death and the end of their forty-year relationship deeply, writing about how, because she was betrothed to him at the age of ten, he taught and raised her almost as if she were his child. In 1741, the seventh anniversary of Naokuni's death, Tosako applied for and received special permission from the bakufu to leave Edo—a privilege normally strictly denied to daimyo wives—in order to make a pilgrimage to Naokuni's grave at Nōninji, located in the town of Hannō in what is now Saitama Prefecture.[57] At the temple, she offered prayers to her late husband that included her promise to "never neglect your children and grandchildren, to carry on the family line, serve the state, and manage the household."[58] One can hardly imagine a more succinct statement of the duties of a devoted wife and widow. After Naokuni's death, Tosako took up residence once more at Ishihara, having given over the upper mansion to her daughter Michiko and her husband, the adopted Kuroda heir, Naozumi. At Ishihara, Tosako received numerous visitors, mostly family members, especially her married granddaughters, who often came and stayed with her for days at a time. Well into her old age, Tosako continued to make frequent outings, often to attend family events and rituals, such as the return of the daimyo—her son-in-law—to the Edo mansion at Tokiwabashi. She also maintained close ties with her own family, through visits with the Yanagisawa heir, her adoptive brother Yoshisato, until his death, and by holding memorials for her adoptive parents. Perhaps in line with her pledge to "preserve the family line" and to "serve the state," Tosako maintained the connections to other daimyo families that Naokuni had established, including an unusually close personal friendship with Matsudaira Katasada, daimyo of Aizu, to whom Naokuni had been a mentor. Other connections followed organically from the alliances of her daughters and granddaughters, who married into daimyo houses in Hitachi, Tanba, Iwaki, and Sanuki provinces. Finally, Tosako upheld her late husband's commitment to learning; Naokuni had studied with Ogyū Sorai and his disciple Dazai Shundai, and after Naokuni's death, Shundai frequently came to Ishihara to teach Naoyuki, the designated heir to his brother Naozumi, as Tosako listened in. Tosako also studied with Shinto scholars and Buddhist teachers, and altogether maintained an active literary and artistic life well into her later years.

Itō Maki, unlike either the Zhang women or Kuroda Tosako, had neither the wealth nor the influence to travel out of Edo to visit with her close relatives. Unlike them, she did not narrate her past in the form of a diary or in poems. Rather, her many letters are the only means through which she was able to sustain the personal relationships that meant the most to her, in particular the deep connection to her natal parents, the Kobayashi. In her letters, Maki repeatedly laments that "words cannot express" the regret she feels at not being able to see her parents in person or to do more to help them or her siblings, especially her troubled younger brother Kyōzō. A testament to the importance of the home place and all it represents comes in Maki's letter of 1849, which tells of her joy at looking at a map of Okamura that has been sent to her: "it's just like going home," she declared.[59] She enthusiastically received news of friends from childhood, and even though she had become a *hatamoto* wife, she yearned to write to old friends, all commoners, who remained in Okamura. But perhaps the strongest evidence of how much the home place mattered to Maki was the way in which she passed her attachment to it and to her natal family on to her daughters, in spite of the fact that neither of them ever went to Okamura or were able to meet their Kobayashi grandparents. In a New Year's card sent from Maki's oldest daughter Nao to her Kobayashi grandparents, she wrote about how much she wants to meet them. Younger daughter Tama, in a long letter written in 1833, revealed that Maki talked to her daughters a great deal about her childhood home. She wrote of how much Maki talked about her parents and her hometown, and that this made her want to meet them very badly. "But because I am a woman and it is a long trip, I cannot go," she wrote regretfully.[60] Tama even wrote that she wanted to move to be near the Kobayashi but her father's job would not allow it. Instead, she said, she wished to become a bird and fly to Okamura so she could at least lay eyes on them, even if from a distance.[61]

As the records by and about Tang Yaoqing, Kuroda Tosako, Itō Maki and their children suggest, keeping the family name and reputation alive, even as family members remained distant or passed away, was an important aspect of home-making on the part of elite women. Within a patriarchal and patrilineal system, women maintained households and lineages not only for their fathers, sons, and brothers, but for their mothers, daughters, and sisters as well. In this way, every elite family's continuity was by definition women's work.

Notes

1. See, e.g., Dorothy Ko, *Teachers of the Inner Chambers: Women and Culture in Seventeenth-Century China* (Stanford, CA: Stanford University Press, 1994); Susan Mann, *Precious Records: Women in China's Long Eighteenth Century* (Stanford, CA: Stanford University Press, 1997); Susan Mann, *The Talented Women of the Zhang*

Family (Berkeley: University of California Press, 2007); Anne Walthall, ed., *Servants of the Dynasty: Palace Women in World History* (Berkeley: University of California Press, 2008).

2. See, e.g., Bryna Goodman and Wendy Larson, eds., *Gender in Motion: Divisions of Labor and Cultural Change in Late Imperial and Modern China* (Lanham, MD: Rowman & Littlefield, 2005), and Helen F. Siu, ed., *Merchants' Daughters: Women, Commerce, and Regional Culture in South China* (Hong Kong: Hong Kong University Press, 2010).

3. See Tim Oakes and Louisa Schein, eds., *Translocal China: Linkages, Identities, and the Reimagining of Space* (London: Routledge, 2006), 19.

4. While my discussion of samurai-class Japanese women is based largely on my own research in primary sources, due to language constraints I engage the experiences of Chinese gentry women only through the secondary historical literature in English.

5. By definition, daimyo had to have a minimum stipend of 10,000 *koku*. By comparison, at the upper end of the wealth spectrum, the Maeda, largest of the "province-holding," or *kunimochi* daimyo, had a stipend of around one million *koku*.

6. Both texts can be found in Kuroda Tosako, *Ishihara-ki, Koto no hagusa: Daimyo fujin no nikki,* edited by Shiba Keiko (Tokyo: Katsura Bunkō, 2008). On Tosako's diaries, see also Marcia Yonemoto, "Outside the Inner Quarters: Sociability, Mobility, and Narration in Early Edo-Period Women's Diaries," *Japan Forum* 21: 3 (2009): 391–401.

7. Yoshiyasu and Sadako had three other daughters of their own, and two sons, but still adopted Tosako. In doing so, they may have been following an early Tokugawa practice of adopting daughters from powerful regional daimyo houses in order to solidify political alliances.

8. For biographical information on Tosako, see Shiba Keiko, "*Ishihara-ki* ni miru daimyō fujin no nichijō seikatsu," in *Edo jidai no onnatachi no sei to ai* (Tokyo: Katsura Bunkō, 2000), 95–117, reprinted in Kuroda. *Ishihara-ki, Koto no hagusa,* 301–323.

9. Kuroda, *Ishihara-ki, Koto no hagusa,* 4

10. Shiba, "*Ishihara-ki* ni miru daimyō fujin no nichijō seikatsu," 108–110.

11. Susan Mann, "The Virtue of Travel for Women in the Late Empire," in Goodman and Larson, eds., *Gender in Motion,* 61; embedded quote from Cynthia Brokaw in original.

12. Dorothy Ko, *Teachers of the Inner Chambers,* 221.

13. See Shiba, "*Ishihara-ki* ni miru daimyō fujin no nichijō seikatsu," 308.

14. Mann, *The Talented Women of the Zhang Family* (Berkeley: University of California Press, 2007).

15. Ibid., 17–18.

16. Ibid., 58.

17. Ibid., 60.

18. Ibid., 25–26, 59–60.

19. Ibid., 176.

20. Mega, *Bushi ni totsuida josei no tegami: binbō hatamoto no Edo kurashi* (Tokyo: Yoshikawa Kōbunkan, 2011); all subsequent references to and quotes from Maki's letters are from Mega's transcriptions into modern Japanese.

21. The dynamics of these adoptions and marriages, and the way each represented a move up in status for Maki, are discussed in greater depth in the next section.

22. The *daikan* was a bakufu official of *hatamoto* status; *tedai* was a commoner position, but clearly one from which an individual could work his way up. See Mega, *Buke ni totsuida*, 25–27.

23. Quote is from Ko, *Teachers of the Inner Chambers*, 194; on adoption in late imperial China, see also Ann Waltner, *Getting an Heir: Adoption and the Construction of Kinship in Late Imperial China* (Honolulu: University of Hawaii Press, 1990).

24. On widow chastity in late imperial China, see Janet M. Theiss, *Disgraceful Matters: The Politics of Chastity in Eighteenth-Century China* (Berkeley: University of California Press, 2004); on the frequency of divorce in early modern Japan, see Harald Fuess, *Divorce in Japan: Family, Gender, and the State* (Stanford, CA: Stanford University Press, 2004).

25. These adoptions occurred before the period covered in Tosako's diaries, so it is not known how much input she had into these decisions. But one would imagine, as the household manager, and the manager of ancestral worship, that she would have at least some influence, especially in who would join her own household. For these reasons I use the phrasing "Naokuni and Tosako chose . . ."

26. For genealogical records and relations between Kuroda family members, see tables in Kuroda, *Ishihara-ki, Koto no hagusa*, 359–373, and in Yonemoto, "Outside the Inner Quarters,"

27. Mega, *Buke ni totsuida*, 18–23.

28. Ibid., 27–33.

29. Oban corps were direct retainers of the shogun, whose job was to police the shogunal residences—Edo Castle in the capital, Nijo Castle in Kyoto, and Osaka Castle in Osaka. Oban corps rotated between Edo and these two latter locales every three years. See Mega, *Buke ni totsuida*, 36–37.

30. Ibid., 43.

31. Ibid., 48–51.

32. In a letter written in 1857 to her Kobayashi grandparents signed "Yohara Tama" Tama herself wrote that "in fourth month of (1851)" she moved to the Yohara house. Mega Atsuko speculates that her husband was probably a new adoptee into the Yōhara house, to replace or supersede the feckless son with the illegitimate child. Mega, *Buke ni totsuida*, 122.

33. Ibid., 117–118.

34. Ibid., 118.

35. Mega Atsuko notes that among commoners in the early modern period, divorce was not a "minus," and she concludes that divorce was not an obstacle to remarriage for *bushi* women either, in spite of the Confucian proverb that "a chaste wife does not have two husbands." Mega, *Buke ni totsuida,* 118–119.

36. Ibid., 123.

37. Mega remarks tartly that "then as now, we are in a world where women's beauty is an asset." Ibid.

38. I have not discussed here the complicated informal adoption arranged for Maki's eldest son from her first marriage, Seigorō, which was arranged by Maki's uncle Kōzaemon. On this, see ibid., 80–88.

39. Mega notes that although on the surface Kaname was arranging the marriage negotiations, in reality and in substance, it was Maki who did the work. Also, because Kaname was away on duty so much, Maki stood in for him as public representative of family. She even wrote correspondence on his behalf, due to an injury to his shoulder and hands that made him physically unable to write. Maki also handled relations with family, collected his *fuchimai* (salary rice) and in other ways acted as his representative. Ibid., 123–124.

40. Maki was also very concerned with succession within her own natal family, the Kobayashi; see ibid., 140–142.

41. See Mann, *Talented Women,* 87.

42. On marriage practices in South China, see Helen F. Siu, "Where Are the Women?: Rethinking Marriage Resistance and Regional Culture in South China," *Late Imperial China* 11 (2) (1990): 32–62.

43. Mann, *Talented Women,* 34.

44. Ibid., 32.

45. Ibid., 48.

46. Ibid., 34.

47. Ibid., 82.

48. Ibid., 111.

49. Ibid., 111.

50. On the fascinating later life and rise in status of this concubine, see ibid., 188–189.

51. Ibid.,157.

52. Ibid., 176–77.

53. Ibid., 123.

54. Ibid., 13.

55. Ibid., 36.

56. Ibid., 37.

57. In another sign of the importance of natal family relationships, Naokuni was buried at Nōninji, the ancestral temple of the Nakayama, his family of birth. His

father, Nakayama Naoharu, was also buried there. For Tosako's account of the trip, see Kuroda, *Ishihara-ki, Koto no hagusa*, 124–125.

58. Ibid., 126.

59. Mega, *Buke ni totsuida*, 158–159.

60. Ibid., 160.

61. Ibid.

References

Fuess, Harald. 2004. *Divorce in Japan: Family, Gender, and the State*. Stanford, CA: Stanford University Press.

Goodman, Bryna, and Wendy Larson, eds. 2005. *Gender in Motion: Divisions of Labor and Cultural Change in Late Imperial and Modern China*. Lanham, MD: Rowman & Littlefield.

Ko, Dorothy. 1994. *Teachers of the Inner Chambers: Women and Culture in Seventeenth-Century China*. Stanford, CA: Stanford University Press.

Kuroda Tosako. 2008. *Ishihara-ki, Koto no hagusa: Daimyo fujin no nikki*. Edited by Shiba Keiko. Tokyo: Katsura Bunkō, 2008.

Mann, Susan. 1997. *Precious Records: Women in China's Long Eighteenth Century*. Stanford, CA: Stanford University Press.

———. 2005. "The Virtue of Travel for Women in the Late Empire." In *Gender in Motion: Divisions of Labor and Cultural Change in Late Imperial and Modern China*, ed. Bryna Goodman and Wendy Larson. Lanham, MD: Rowman & Littlefield.

———. 2007. *The Talented Women of the Zhang Family*. Berkeley: University of California Press.

Mega Atsuko. 2011. *Bushi ni totsuida josei no tegami: binbō hatamoto no Edo kurashi*. Tokyo: Yoshikawa Kōbunkan.

Oakes, Tim, and Louisa Schein, eds. 2006. *Translocal China: Linkages, Identities, and the Reimagining of Space*. London: Routledge.

Shiba Keiko. 2000. "*Ishihara-ki* ni miru daimyō fujin no nichijō seikatsu." In *Edo jidai no onnatachi no sei to ai*. Tokyo: Katsura Bunkō.

Siu, Helen F. 1990. "Where Are the Women? Rethinking Marriage Resistance and Regional Culture in South China." *Late Imperial China* 11 (2): 32–62.

———, ed. 2010. *Merchants' Daughters: Women, Commerce, and Regional Culture in South China*. Hong Kong: Hong Kong University Press.

Theiss, Janet M. 2004. *Disgraceful Matters: The Politics of Chastity in Eighteenth-Century China*. Berkeley: University of California Press.

Walthall, Anne, ed. 2008. *Servants of the Dynasty: Palace Women in World History*. Berkeley: University of California Press.

6

Crossing Borders in Imperial China

PETER C. PERDUE

Many authors in this volume describe places located on borderlands, between different cultural zones and state divisions. In these borderlands, boundaries were porous, and a variety of peoples crossed them for legal and illegal purposes. The political scientist Joel Migdal describes the function of these boundaries as follows:

> Boundaries signify the point at which something becomes something else, at which the way things are done changes, at which 'we' end and 'they' begin, at which certain rules for behavior no longer obtain and others take hold . . . because boundaries connote the site at which things are done differently, of the limits to where things are done in one way, they are social constructions. And as the site where different ways of doing things meet, they are likely to be replete with tension and conflict.[1]

The "pirates" of the Tonkin gulf in Charles Wheeler's analysis were mainly traders from the southeastern coast of China, who linked communities in both the Vietnamese coast and their home towns. Matthew Mosca describes Kashmiri merchants who moved in and out of the Qing empire without restrictions, attracting the attention of officials and security services. Willem van Schendel's discussion of Chittagong also focuses on communities that span borders, highlighting distinctions between the resident border community, with its brokers, document producers, and officials, and the travelers who aimed to get through the border as conveniently as possible. As social spaces, these borders aroused different feelings among their residents and travelers. The psychological effects of border crossing need close attention, if we are to understand the effects of places on people and people on places.

What is it like to cross a border? In our world of constant air travel, passports, and security checks, border crossing is a routine, nearly uniform process, which may be tedious, but rarely produces anxiety (for those equipped with proper credentials). But in earlier times, and in certain parts of the world today, borders were not so evenly policed and regulated, and travelers nearly always faced danger, uncertainty, and self-doubt as they approached the edges of their familiar realms. Crossing borders had profound psychological effects, comparable to rites of passage. The journey took the traveler out of his zone of comfort into an alien realm, where he encountered delays, dangers, and foreign cultures, but also friends, comfortable inns, and a rewarding welcome, if he achieved his goal. Later he returned transformed and, fortunately for the historian, he often wrote about his experience.

Asian travelers faced the same obstacles and strange environments as travelers in the Western world, but we know much less about their experiences. Thousands of envoys and their fellow travelers arrived to pay tribute in Beijing each year, and their diaries have left ample documentation of their impressions, but most studies of China's relations with foreign peoples consider only the view from the court in Beijing. If we look at the experience of the travelers themselves as they went to Beijing, or when they negotiated with border guards, we get a different picture from the ideology of a "tributary system" promoted by the ritualists and the emperor's courtiers. Daily life on the borders encompassed diverse, unruly, and pragmatic adjustments that did not fit the stereotype of a loyal tributary. Borders were both sites of encounters of different peoples with different expectations and places where the abstract rules of ritual encountered the uncontrollable diversity of human behavior.

One did not have to travel very far to experience dislocation and alienation. China's borders were cultural rather than geographical. Travelers from Asia to the Chinese empire may have moved a relatively short distance, but their degrees of discomfort and alienation depended on the historical and cultural relations between their society and that of the empire. The Chinese empires called most of the visitors who came on diplomatic and economic missions "tributaries," but the uniform use of the term *gong* for "tribute" disguises multiple experiences and relationships. The concept of a "tribute system" endorsed by John K. Fairbank, L. S. Yang, and others implies a structured set of cultural and geographical relationships that did not match a constantly shifting multiplicity of encounters.[2]

This chapter describes four encounters on the Qing borders by merchants, tributary envoys, and exiled officials, in order to sketch the multiple opportunities and possibilities created by border interactions. These travelers generally kept diaries or wrote in a diary form in later memoirs. The chronological accounts of the journey created a structure that incorporated very disparate materials. The writer included concrete details about the weather, his health, and his feelings, alongside conversations with bystanders, both Chinese and from his own country, and reflections on classical texts related to the landscape through which he passed. Like any modern traveler, he mixed together immediate impressions with reflections filtered through historical knowledge and cultural biases. On the one hand, these accounts provide a distinct view of the empire itself, viewed by people who came from outside its territorial boundaries, or who were sent to the remote frontier from a career in the core. On the other hand, they also provide individual revelations about the cultural frameworks that extended beyond the core of China, while sharing elements with it.

Pak Chi-wǒn's Travel Diary

In 1780, the Korean scholar Pak Chi-wǒn (1737–1805) joined a tribute embassy to Beijing to celebrate the Qianlong emperor's seventieth birthday. He accompanied the Chief Envoy Pak Myongwǒn (1725–1795), his third cousin, on the orders of the Korean king Chongjo (r. 1776–1800). The embassy left Seoul on 5/25 (lunar date) crossed the Yalu River on 6/24, arriving in Beijing on 8/1. They left Beijing on 8/5 for Rehe, where they arrived four days later. After participating in the ritual celebrations, they returned from Rehe to Beijing, staying for nearly a month in the capital city. They left Beijing on 9/17 and arrived back in Seoul on 10/27.[3] Pak's *Rehe Diary* (Yŏrha Ilgi), a personal account of his journey, is now recognized as a classic of Korean literature. His wide-ranging curiosity about the scenes he viewed and the people he met gives a vivid picture of the society of southern Manchuria and the intellectual climate of Beijing.[4] His critical yet thoughtful stance toward the Manchu rulers of the Qing provides an unusual perspective on Qing society from a sympathetic outsider, and it represents an intervention in scholarly discussion of Korea's stance toward the Qing. Pak was one of the leading members of the Sirhak School, or School of Practical Learning, which was one of the dominant trends of thought in the mid-Chosŏn dynasty. Members of this school focused on improving the welfare of the Korean people through detailed empirical analysis of social conditions and specific policies addressing issues of rural poverty and official malfeasance. Pak drew on his experience in China to advocate learning certain practical measures from the Qing, rejecting the standard Korean categorization of the Qing as barbarians who had nothing to offer to the civilized culture of Korea. On the other hand, he detected considerable dissatisfaction among the Han Chinese literati whom he met, viewing them as chafing under political oppression and censorship by the Manchu court. Pak's dual attitude, facing both a Korean audience as an advocate of reform and a Chinese audience with sympathy toward their oppression, makes him a fascinating figure. He was someone who crossed a border, self-consciously reflected on cultural difference, and incorporated his personal experience into proposals for political and social change.

Crossing the Border

Pak begins his account with the date "24th day of the sixth lunar month of the third sixty-year cycle of the Gengzi (K: Kyongja) year" (Pak 1780, 1a). He explains that this date refers to the third cycle since the Chongzhen reign (1628–1644), the last emperor of the Ming dynasty. He cannot refer directly to the Chongzhen reign, because "soon we will be crossing the Yalu River and we want to avoid that term." The Manchus used Qing reign titles, but Ming scholars avoided this practice because they only recognized the Ming dynasty as Chinese. "The Manchus invaded China, displaced the Ming government, and enforced the Qing system, but this eastern land of ours, with its several thousand li extending at that time even across the Yalu River, preserved the Ming government's standards. This means that the Ming court still existed in the east, over the river" (Pak 2010, 2).

Pak has already prepared the reader for the double cultural encounter that he will reflect on throughout his journey. Korean scholars, regarding themselves as the true preservers of "Chinese" classical culture inherited from the Ming, were traveling into an alien land, where this civilization had been lost.

But they had to adapt to the new power controlling them by concealing their own practice of continuing the Ming calendar. He recognized that Koreans were not powerful enough to drive the Manchus out; they could only retain their cultural autonomy, while at the same time placating the powerful if dubiously legitimate rulers of the Qing. Later in his diary he debated with his fellow Korean travelers the legitimacy of Qing rule.

6/24
All morning it drizzled intermittently. In the afternoon we crossed the Yalu River, and rode about 30 li to Jiulian cheng where we camped. (Pak 1780, 1a; Pak 2010, 2)

The embassy made two significant crossings: the first at the Yalu River, the formal border between Korea and China, and the second at the willow palisade, the fence and guard posts separating Manchuria from both China and Korea. Crossing the Yalu River was primarily a struggle with nature, while crossing the palisade meant a conflict with humans. Heavy rains had swollen the river so much that an immediate crossing looked dangerous, but the envoys were in a hurry to get on their way. "Because the rains have greatly swollen the river, the jetty is nowhere to be seen. Even the sandy midstream island has disappeared. It would be impossible for the ferry's passengers to survive in such a rushing flood if the ferryman made the slightest mistake in traversing the river" (Pak 1780, 1b; Pak 2010, 3).

Pak also reflects on the causes of the Yalu River's turbulence by referring to records of its distant source. Most sources agreed that its source was in Paektu Mountain, and along with the Yellow and Yangzi Rivers, it was one of the "three great rivers of the world" (Pak 1780, 1a). He exhibits his provincial Korean pride by aligning the Yalu with the two great Chinese rivers as among the longest in the world, while also linking the high floodwaters with speculation that the rainy season has begun in Paektu Mountain far away. Although his trip is rooted in local geography, he is aware of distant effects from places he will never see.

He expresses his anxiety about the imminent crossing in a conversation with the equerries. After ten days of confinement in the inn, they were all impatient to depart. Pak, on the other hand, is resigned but fearful. "Though crossing the raging river still posed a danger, the day of departure had finally arrived and there was nothing we could do but leave . . . The trivial comment 'today we are really leaving' sounded more like a lamentation of the inevitability of departure rather than the pleasure of leaving." At the same time he turns back mentally and physically to the home he is leaving: "Gazing into the distance, I had had a sense of steaming heat. Quietly I turned away, looking back and trying to remember my home. . . . I could not help feeling sad, and the momentary urge to return home crept in. But to tell the truth, I had thought of this adventure as my 'grand tour', and often told myself it was a trip I must do at least once in my lifetime" (Pak 1780, 2a; Pak 2010, 4).

He makes one final gesture of farewell to his country, drinking glasses of Korean wine and pouring part of it on the pillars of the city wall, as he looks to the east and views the high mountains of Uiju shrouded in mist. He remembers a poem he often recited by a friend who had earlier crossed the border, including the line "Painful nostalgia for south of the river Ch'ŏngch'ŏng." Then he reflects on a story from the Warring States period, when Jingqing hesitated to cross the Yishui River, and the prince of Yan sent another man ahead of him. Through allusions to the classics, the landscape, and his companions together, Pak artfully portrays his hesitation in three different temporal perspectives.

Korean officials had to inspect the goods of all departing missions to prevent carrying of contraband goods. The travelers had to pass through three gates, each with increasingly severe punishments. Those who carried prohibited goods at the first gate were beaten with clubs and had their possessions confiscated. At the second gate, smugglers suffered sentence to exile, and at the third gate, decapitation. Severed heads dangled from the gate to reinforce the message. In fact, however, the inspection was quite perfunctory. The Governor of Uiju and his Registrar read out the names of the men, checked their appearance and their horses, and searched for evidence of "gold, pearls, ginseng, sable and excess silver bars" (Pak 1780, 3b; Pak 2010, 7). But in fact, many of the goods were not inspected, although the inspectors left much of the baggage strewn across the grass. Pak recognized that inspections were necessary, but also noted that "the dignity of those subjected to inspection is sometimes offended." Yet merchants of Uiju had already left earlier in the morning secretly and sneaked across the border to evade inspection.

The embassy comprised a total of 281 men and at least 55 horses. Five boats carried the company across the river, including the horses, goods, officials, documents, and servants (Pak 1978, 334). Pak notes the cheerful voices of the sailors who rowed the boat: "It was thanks to their skill and hard work that my boat moved like a comet across the waves. But the combination of water and speed made me as giddy as if a whole night had just flown by." To distract himself, he launched into a philosophical discussion with the chief interpreter, Hong Myŏngbok, asking him, "Do you know the route well?" Hong asked, "What do you mean?" Pak replied, "The route is not difficult to follow. It is there, over the river bank . . . The river is the border between the hill and us. Thus, if it is not the hill, it has to be the water. The ethics of all people and the law of all things in the universe are just like this water and the hill. Do not try to find the way anywhere else, as it is here" (Pak 1780, 4a; Pak 2010, 9). Hong was mystified, but Pak continued to expound on the moral Way as he crossed the river.

After they reached the other side, the group had a strange encounter with their first Chinese person. He was floating on a log in the middle of the river, accompanying felled timber down the river from Changbaek mountain. A border person in the most literal sense, his appearance marked the exact transition from the human world of Korea to that of China.

As soon as they reached the bank, they discovered that the boat before them had overshot the landing point and unloaded its cargo on a small island farther downstream. The sailors refused to bring these men up the river because the current was too strong. Punishments and threats of violence followed. The military official in charge of the crossing was forced to bare his buttocks and be flogged four times with a whip, and then to quickly move the stranded men back upstream. Like any move into a liminal zone, the crossing had created feelings of disorientation and disorder, as well as thoughts of moral transcendence, but order was quickly restored with the arrival of more military escorts.

Pak's second encounter with a local person revealed more of the new culture he had entered. He had learned one Chinese word (*Yue*), from the man on the logs, and used it to call a Chinese man to carry him on his back from his boat across the muddy shore. After the man put Pak down, he exclaimed, "If the mother of Heixuanfeng [the Black Whirlwind] was as heavy as this, he probably could not climb up the Yifeng mountain!" The interpreter "roared with laughter, and commented, 'That ignorant man does not know of Jiangge [a filial son of the Han dynasty who saved his mother by carrying her on his back], but knows about Li Kui [the Black Whirlwind, one of the immensely strong heroes of the vernacular novel *Shuihuzhuan,* which narrates the adventures of a band of righteous rebels in Shandong].'" Pak noted, "The sailor quotes from the romance or book of marvelous stories with ease as if they are part of his everyday speech" (Pak 1780, 5b; Pak 2010, 12). The sailor's comment revealed his intimate familiarity with Chinese vernacular novels, while the Korean scholar noted the parallel between the vernacular and classical traditions. The incident demonstrated that Koreans could bridge the cultural gap with China through their shared classical knowledge, while they could also gain access to popular knowledge that drew on classical precedents. Their sense of strangeness gradually wore off as they learned how to pay close attention to the new environment.

Pak's party then passed through the regions that had formerly been the location of the capital of the ancient Korean Goguryeo kingdom (37 BC–668 AD). He noted that "the soil looks fertile and well suited to cultivation" but the land appeared to be abandoned. He explained its desertion by assuming that the local inhabitants had fled during the Qing conquest in order to avoid having to shave their heads. (Even before the conquest, the Manchus had forced the entire Han population under their control to shave the front of their heads and wear a long pigtail.) Some had fled to Korea, and others had joined the Ming general who fought against the Qing, but most had been killed. In this "lonely place" however, the camps of the envoys and the shops of the merchants who flocked to serve them created new life. "Dense smoke from cooking, the sound of men talking and of horses neighing all generated the atmosphere of a lively village" (Pak 1780, 6a; Pak 2010, 13). The new activity of tributary relations overlaid itself in his consciousness on more deeply submerged layers: the ancient Goguryeo kingdom and the remnants of the dynastic wars of a century and a half ago.

Protected by military policemen from the threat of tigers, Pak felt more confident and secure in the tented camp than during the crossing. He commented on the great physical strength and comical appearance of the police guards. "They work harder than anyone else and eat more than anyone else among the servants in the retinue. The way they dress looks so droll that I nearly died from laughing the first time I saw them in their uniforms" (Pak 1780, 6b; Pak 2010, 14).

Two days later, the company moved on toward the willow palisade. Pak introduces the experienced Korean stableman, Tŭngnyong, who had traveled back and forth to Beijing since the age of fourteen, and was now guiding at least his thirtieth expedition. Tŭngnyong came from a scholarly family that had developed outstanding skill in Chinese, and he knew all the tactics necessary to get the travelers across the border. Others in the party also had extensive experience with the Chinese, and Pak the newcomer comes to recognize their value. They encounter five poor Manchu border guards along the river, and the Korean footmen yell at them to dismount and make way, shouting, "Do you know what kind of goods our lord had brought with him and what the wrapped documents are? It is written on that yellow flag, 'Goods to be presented to the emperor.' The Manchu guards, terrified, prostrate themselves and plead with the footmen to spare them from punishment with death. The footmen all laughed and forced the Manchus to prostrate themselves in the mud." Pak denounced his servants, saying, "I hear that you create all kind of commotion whenever you enter China . . . The way you behaved was abominable. From now on you should not provoke a commotion just for fun." They replied, "If we don't have a bit of fun like this, how do you expect us to break the monotony of a long, long journey?" (Pak 1780, 8b; Pak 2010, 19).

When he arrived at the palisade, the envoys pitched their tents and prepared for the necessary bargaining to allow them to cross into Manchurian territory. Then Pak learned about the underlying economic relationships that caused conflict at the border post. Many of the interpreters and porters, who had made the trip many times, greeted their Chinese counterparts through the fence, asking about their health. The Chinese in turn, asked them "Have you brought enough silver?" and "Are Mr. An and Mr. Han coming?" An and Han, two merchants from Uiju who traveled annually to Beijing, were the key intermediaries in the exchange of tribute and gift goods. The Korean government normally gave each of its officials gifts of ginseng, a packet for each of the thirty officials in the party, but on this trip the government allowed the officials to carry silver bars instead. The officials could profit from exchanging silver for goods in Beijing, with the aid of the Uiju merchants. The Uiju merchants also took orders from other merchants in Uiju who could not travel to Beijing. They "came to consider Beijing as the front gate of their house, their home away from home. They and the Chinese merchants came to understand each other well, and the rise and fall in commodity prices depended on this compact" (Pak 1780, 9b–10a; Pak 2010, 21). The Uiju merchants, who held a monopoly on the Korean Chinese trade, could easily manipulate prices in their favor, but the blame for unreasonably high prices usually fell on the officials who were granted trading rights. As Pak discovered, a great deal of contentious bargaining ensued at the border because of these relationships.

Once the gate was opened, "a crowd of Chinese choked the gate, all trying to pass through it at the same time. Their main reason was to assess the weight of the unloaded gifts and to scrutinize the luggage we were carrying on our

journey." The Chinese porters had the responsibility of carrying all the luggage
of the embassy to Beijing. A heated argument broke out between Tûngnyong
and the local officials about the exact number of items on the gift lists. The
local officials had added additional gifts to the list of required items, but the
Koreans had to negotiate to remove or reduce these supplementary items. If
the Korean negotiator had "weak negotiating skills, or if he was not fluent
enough in Chinese to rise to the occasion, we would have to meet all the
Manchurian demands, without being able to distinguish between what was
properly and what was wrongfully on the lists. Even worse, what was decided
this year would become a precedent for next year's visit." But the envoys,
in a hurry to get through the gate, pressed the interpreter to settle the dispute quickly. Tûngnyong forced a resolution by running up to one local man,
"grabbing him by the throat, threatening to hit him, and wildly swinging his
fist close to the man's face." He shouted, "on one visit you stole a moleskin cap
from my honored elder. The following year you drew my knife from my belt
and cut off the sheath's cord of my honored elder . . . Another time you were
going to steal my purse but you got caught . . . I will drag you, you rat faced
bastard, to the General of Fengcheng" (Pak 1780, 11a-b; Pak 2010, 25). The
old man begged forgiveness, and the local Manchurians settled for only a few
extra trivial goods. In fact, Tûngnyong had never had any of his property stolen last year, but his dramatic act intimidated the other Manchurians, making
them modify their demands. As his superior official recognized, "Tûngnyong
is resourceful . . . had he not done that the business would never be completed
and even after three days it would be difficult to pass through the gate" (Pak
1780, 12a, Pak 2010, 26).

Pak, relieved at finally reaching the heart of China, still felt a pang of anxiety and jealousy. "Once you enter this gate you are on Chinese soil and cut off
from all news of home. Feeling sad at the thought of leaving my homeland,
I looked towards the eastern sky for a short time, then turned around and
passed slowly through the gate" (Pak 1780, 12b; Pak 2010, 26).

Pak's diary artfully describes the personal experience of a first-time border
crosser, full of anxiety, expectation, excitement, and homesickness, while he
observes the contentious negotiations involved in getting the tribute embassy
through the Chinese barriers. The Koreans, who were the most experienced
and most reliable of China's tributary vassals, had devised techniques to extract
profit from their tribute missions, and they could even get away with a defi-
ant attitude toward subordinate border officials. Despite their fundamental

contempt for the current Manchu rulers, they also recognized a deep cultural tie to the Chinese classical tradition, and the most open-minded of them, like Pak Chi-wŏn, carefully looked for opportunities to learn from their giant neighbor.

Crossing the Border with 50,000 Sheep

In 1748 the experienced Central Asian trader Elianhuli and his companions approached the northwestern border of the empire at Hami on a tribute mission, bringing with them large herds of sheep, cattle, horses, sal ammoniac, raisins, rhubarb, and other trade goods. They, like the Koreans, had to struggle with border officials to be allowed into the empire, while they claimed to be following the conventional rituals of tribute presentation. Their experience displays analogous processes of investigation, resistance, negotiation, and eventual acquiescence by border officials. Crossing the northwestern border however, was even more difficult, because of the history of Qing and earlier dynastic relations with the peoples of the steppe.[5]

Elianhuli's mission included over one hundred Zunghar Mongols, Chinese and Turkic Muslims, and other traders from Central Asian oases. They were allowed to approach the border because the Yongzheng emperor had negotiated a truce during his military campaigns against the Zunghar Mongol state. Although the Yongzheng emperor (r. 1723–1735), like his father the Kangxi emperor (r. 1662–1722), regarded the Zunghar Mongols as a major threat to the empire, he lost a major battle with them and called for peace in 1734. The two sides did not sign a peace treaty, but a truce ensued. Both parties withdrew troops from the border and agreed on conditions for tribute missions. The Zunghars had always pressed for more trading rights in order to build up the resources of their state, but the Qing emperors resisted, while attempting to defeat the Zunghars militarily. Now the new Qing emperor, the Qianlong emperor (r. 1736–1795) decided to use the leverage of trade instead of military force. He would allow limited trading missions in exchange for the delimitation of a boundary that would restrain the expansion of the Zunghar state. For fifteen years, from 1739 to 1754, the two states engaged in regular trade and tribute relations. The Qing allowed three types of missions: formal diplomatic embassies sent to Beijing, border trade at the towns of Hami in Xinjiang and Suzhou in western Gansu, and presentation of "boiled tea" to lamas in Tibet, passing through Qing territory in Xining. The Qing expected to transform the nomads into non-militarized people through trading relations, just as many previous dynasties had done.

Regulations for the trading missions followed closely those negotiated with the Russians in 1727. The Zunghars offered for sale animals, furs, medicinal products and dried grapes in exchange for silk brocades, tea, rhubarb, and silver. Only one hundred men were allowed to trade at the border, and the missions could come only once every three years. They could stay only eighty days to conclude their business, and the quantity of trade goods had to be specified in advance. The Qing border officials policed the trade to prevent the export of gunpowder, metals, and weaponry.

The border trade, however, quickly boomed well beyond Qing expectations, increasing from 10,000 taels in 1738 to 105,000 taels in 1741. The Zunghar and Central Asian traders constantly argued for permission to bring more goods, and they brought private goods in addition to the officially permitted commodities. Trade in fact occurred more than once every three years, sometimes even twice in one year. Under pressure, officials reluctantly agreed to allow additional trade at Hami, 875 kilometers west of Suzhou. Every trade mission required extensive conflict and negotiation, as the Qing officials wavered in the face of insistent demands for trade. On the one hand, the emperor instructed border officials to "cherish guests arriving from afar" (*huairou yuanren*) in order to encourage peaceful relations, but on the other hand, the large numbers of animals and goods defied regulations and burdened the limited frontier markets.

Elianhuli and his wily caravan men flouted the regulations in almost every respect. They brought extra men, disguised as "doctors, cooks, and accountants," they tried to unload their surplus goods at high prices, and they pleaded for aid in disposing of sick animals, while all the while protesting that they depended heavily on the emperor's benevolence. Although the trade originated with the diplomatic truce in the Zunghar wars, in fact only 46 of the 136 men on the 1748 mission were Mongols; the large majority were Turkic Muslims. Certainly the trade missions brought revenue for the Zunghar state, but they also brought significant profits for the caravan traders who led them.

Elianhuli's successful struggle to cross the border and deliver his animals shows how frontiersmen arriving at the empire's borders could manipulate tribute regulations and rituals to serve their purposes. He arrived with 1,300 horses, 600 camels, 900 cattle, and 50,000 sheep, carrying three hundred loads of goods, including raisins and sal ammoniac. The border officer objected that no one wanted to buy raisins or *sal ammoniac*, but Elianhuli replied that the raisins were for eating, and they planned to sell the sal ammoniac along their route. They had not reported their arrival in advance, but he asked to speak directly with the high-ranking officer in Hami. He explained that the extra 36 men were doctors and accountants. The Anxi Provincial Commander-in-Chief reported this encounter to his superior, recognizing that it would cause trouble to prevent the group from trading, but that "barbarians are by nature crafty, and their words are not to be trusted."

One week later, Hami Division Commander Wang Neng'ai escorted the trading mission to Hami, crossing the border palisade and settling them in an open place to accommodate the animals and men. Elianhuli asked to sell his animals in Hami, instead of Suzhou, arguing that many of them were ill and would not survive the journey. The division commander replied, "You are supposed to sell them in Suzhou; how can we possibly do your trading for you? There are only a few official merchants in Hami, and no one wants your goods." Elianhuli replied, "But many of our animals are exhausted and worn out. If we drive them all the way to Suzhou, many will die in the heat, and . . . our common people will suffer." Exasperated, the division commander exclaimed, "You barbarians are always colluding in demands for charity!" and he scolded them for disobeying regulations.

In fact, Elianhuli had already practiced this scheme once before, unloading over ten thousand weak and exhausted animals in Hami, when he was granted a special exemption, but he had been warned not to do it again. The Suzhou officials also objected that they had reluctantly purchased over fifty thousand animals in the past, but their pastures were too small to accommodate such large numbers. The Hami official once again denounced Elianhuli: "You have been here several times, and you know that water and grass are scarce in Suzhou. Last time the commander allowed you to sell your animals at Hami. Because the road was so far and the animals were weak, it was unavoidable. How can you come again bringing so many weak, exhausted animals? You can't be trusted." Elianhuli replied that he was "deeply ashamed" for once again bringing such a large herd, that the Zunghars were "deeply grateful for the emperor's benevolence," and that his poor starving people eagerly took advantage of the promise of trade to "collect their animals to take advantage of the great emperor's benevolence . . . There was really no choice but to sell the animals at Hami and depend on the emperor's grace to save our lives" (Perdue 2005, 580).

The Qing officials knew that they were stuck in a quandary. The traders had clearly violated regulations, "but if we stick rigidly to the regulations, it will be difficult to keep these ten thousand or more exhausted animals alive. The poor barbarians will be devastated, and this will not carry out our emperor's policy of granting favor to distant peoples" (Perdue 2005, 581). They knew that the numbers of troops on the borders were being reduced, and they could not afford to cause unrest by depriving the pastoral peoples of income. In the end, they agreed to allow the traders to pasture their animals in order to build up their strength, then bring them to Suzhou for sale, and they could carry the sal ammoniac and raisins [their private trade goods] along with them.

Elianhuli had forced his way across the border in the face of Qing resistance, twisting the flexibility of the tribute trade regulations in his favor. Just like the Koreans and his Western successors in Canton fifty years later, he wanted to sell as much as possible, regardless of official restrictions. Unlike the Western traders, he did not directly challenge the customary norms of tribute trade: he constantly expressed his appreciation for the emperor's benevolence, he provided gifts for officials, and he urged the emperor to consider the welfare of his own people. Yet the implicit threat of war lay behind his mission's soothing words. Qing officials knew well that a renewal of war with the Zunghar state would undermine their efforts to soften up the pastoral peoples with trade, but it was always an available option. In the 1750s, the Qianlong emperor took advantage of a succession struggle among the Zunghars to launch military campaigns that destroyed the Zunghar state. But in this brief period of trading relations, the border was a site of tough, but peaceful negotiation over economic gain, and the experienced traders knew just how far they could push to gain their objectives.

An Exiled Scholar on the Frontier

> Autumn grain and spring wheat spread along the furrows
> It is green for several hundred miles down to the Crystal River
> The thirty-four military colony fields are interspersed like embroidery
> No need to transport millet out to the distant frontier.
>
> —Ji Yun, in Li Zhongzhi, ed., 2010, 144

The Chinese Hanlin scholar Ji Yun (1724–1805), like so many of his fellow literati, found himself embroiled in a case of corruption and banished to the frontier in Xinjiang in 1770. He spent only eighteen months there, returning in 1771, and on the way home he composed a series of poems about his experience in exile. By the time Ji Yun arrived a decade later, he had been appointed chief compiler of the *Siku Quanshu*, the great encyclopedic collection of classical works commissioned by the Qianlong emperor.[6]

Exile was a common experience for many Qing literati.[7] It was usually a short interruption in their official careers, a product of the uncertainties of patronage and factional politics in the court and the inevitable compromises that any working official had to make in the course of routine administration. The Qing forces had finally conquered Xinjiang in 1757, eliminating the rival Mongolian state of the Zunghars and establishing military rule over the region. Xinjiang provided vast new territories, sparsely settled with Turkic oasis farmers, awaiting settlement by migrants from the interior. Like Russia's Siberia, it was the perfect place for a penal colony. Military garrisons could clear its wide-open spaces with bonded labor, while literate prisoners could help in administration. Both scholar-officials and common criminals would find themselves mixed together there, thrust into an alien and challenging new landscape.

Soon after the conquest, the Qing rulers began to promote Xinjiang as an attractive destination for civilian settlement. They provided tax incentives, seeds, tools, carts, and animals to induce poverty-stricken farmers from northwest China to move to this distant frontier. They surveyed the availability of water in the oasis towns, and they transported experienced Uighur farmers from southern Xinjiang to northern Xinjiang to instruct the Han farmers in cultivation techniques.[8] By the time Ji Yun arrived, a decade later the settlement campaign had shown impressive results. Careful measurement of agricultural yields on military and civilian colony lands had revealed that the oasis soils, if well irrigated, supported astonishingly high yields.[9] Farmers of northwest China who suffered from constant drought could clear large, fertile fields, free of the insecurities of nature, in the open terrain of Xinjiang. Later, in the 1820s, the activist scholars Gong Zizhen and He Changling would argue strenuously for even more large scale immigration, incorporating Xinjiang as a province of the empire. Their recommendations were not heeded, and Xinjiang in fact turned out to be a difficult, costly, and insecure environment for Han and Muslim populations in the nineteenth century.

Ji Yun, however, observed the settlement process in its early phase of enthusiasm. His poetry reflects a wide-eyed awareness of the wonders of the landscape, recognition of the deep historical roots of the region and its radical difference from the core of China, and an activist attitude of developmentalism, aiming to transform the region into a productive, integral part of the empire.

In the preface to his poetry collection, he outlined his reasons for writing about his frontier experiences: "When I was banished for two years to Urumqi, I was so burdened with work on documents and registers that I had no time for poetry. In the twelfth month of 1770 I was pardoned, and in the second month of 1771 I packed my bags and returned home. In this season the snow was melting and the mud was thick. We could only travel in the deep night when the roads were frozen. In the lonely hostels during the day I had a great deal of free time, so I recalled the landscape and customs of my exile, and wrote descriptions of my former travels, as I rode from Balikun to Urumqi, in a set of 160 oems. As soon as a thought came to me I wrote it down; I did not make revisions. I called them 'Miscellaneous Poems from Urumqi.'"

He continued, "Urumqi was once a small part of the Western barbarian tribal region. In the past ten years since its conquest by sacred military might, the population has flourished, and their production has become abundant. This is the ultimate achievement of the Grand Unity of the empire. Liu Zongyuan [a Tang dynasty writer] once said, 'Only elegant writing can repay the state's benevolence.' Although I am now only a reprieved criminal, I used to work for the imperial court offices. Praising our flourishing age was my former occupation. Now I have personally traveled the border regions and written down my experiences, so all men here and abroad may know the Son of Heaven's supreme authority and virtue. He has opened up the farthest reaches of the northwestern lands, and the ancient sages cannot equal him. Now this is a land with ploughed fields and dammed rivers, where people sing and enjoy their leisure. They display the unprecedented achievements of our empire, and they have fulfilled their utmost desires. I will not only celebrate it with wine before candlelight but offer thanks to the friends whose fellowship has helped me. Written in the third month of 1771 by Ji Yun, the 'Old Historian of Hejian.'"[10]

Like the tributary envoys and traders, he spent only a short time in the region before returning to his more comfortable homeland, and he encountered strange sights, cultural difference, and a discomforting multiplicity of peoples well beyond the conventional framework of classical literati culture. But he embraced much of his experience and looked forward to the construction of an empire that incorporated diverse peoples harmoniously under its benevolent gaze.

The poetry of exile was a long-standing Chinese literary genre.[11] Famous poets from the Tang, who had spent time on the distant frontiers, established a tradition of mournful lament, looking retrospectively homeward from lands that they regarded as barren and backward. Exile implied futile, costly frontier wars, savage inscrutable barbarians, and painful separation from family and friends. On the other hand, exiled poets often described the stark landscapes of towering mountains, thundering rivers, and vast steppes in vivid detail. Ji Yun's collection of 160 poems follows the frontier exile tradition in its attention to landscape, but exhibits far greater enthusiasm than his predecessors. Unlike them, Ji Yun looks toward the transformation of the landscape, instead of seeing it as an ineradicable fact of nature. Ji Yun attached notes to each of his poems, pointing out geographic details and historical events associated with his scenes. These notes gave the poems a flavor of ethnographic detachment that complemented his subjective experience.

He enjoyed the bustling life of the city, its shops, its brothels, and the sounds of flute music in the evenings, and he boasted about the natural wonders of Xinjiang: the powerful mountain torrents and the winds that "blew men and horses around like whirling leaves" (Ji Yun 1937, 2, 4). For him this place of forlorn exile had become a site demonstrating the imperial mastery of nature and human society. The new conquests had given the Qing new powers to change nature: even the weather was warmer in Urumqi because of the growing population. The military colonies had brought abundant yields from verdant fields arranged in neat checkerboard patterns. Ji Yun added the domesticated frontier as a new trope to the Qing literary tradition.[12]

A central theme running through Ji Yun's poetry collection is the contrast between the natural marvels of the frontier and the progressive taming of sublime vistas by the empire's civilizing project. Towering peaks and violent winds and streams astound the traveler, but the progressive extension of cultivated fields, the building of dikes, and the growing vibrancy of urban life indicate the domestication of the wild frontier. Commercial contacts with the interior increase, as the local population develops increasingly Chinese tastes. Urumqi is not the same as the interior; Ji Yun continually contrasts distinctive features of his new settlement and the familiar scenes and experiences of his home. Yet, like Pak Chi-wŏn, he has a strong historical sense. He knows that this is a recently conquered land. Even the ghosts of repressed rebels still haunt the fields. Older ruined cities testify to ancient settlements, and classic texts describe sites in the Tang dynasty that he can visit. It is a land of multiple cultures, each with its separate economic value and social customs. But Ji Yun sees a trend toward cooperation and civilizing effects of literary culture. Military and civilian populations can work together to increase local prosperity, while merchants provide desirable Chinese goods from the interior. Ji Yun is an imperial poet who celebrates the beneficent influence of his emperor, recognizing that military occupation set the framework for the growth of peaceful coexistence.

Ji Yun saw the conspicuous military presence in the region as a force for peace and prosperity. He also remarked on the orderliness enforced by government allocation of land:

> The green fields and green plains have clear borders.
> The ridges parting the farmers' fields mean that they do not need to fight.
> In Jiangdu [in the Sui dynasty] they originally set up the equal field system
> But now it only survives here beyond the passes.[13]

The five disparate types of settlers of the region lived together peacefully:

> Households are registered in five categories
> Although they live together they do not associate with each other
> Among them they rely on village elders
> When there are disputes, the elders negotiate peace.[14]

The five categories of landholders were civilians recruited from the interior, merchants, military colonists and their families, voluntary civilian migrants, and criminal exiles who remained as commoner settlers. In Ji Yun's view, the frontier brought together diverse populations from the interior and showed them how to live together peacefully.

For the military colonizers, it was an idyllic time of peace:

> The signal fires have gone out, the deserts are green
> Bows and knives hang idly, only spring plowing matters
> Your five-year term of service is over in an instant
> These border guards do not fear traveling 10,000 *li*.[15]

Even the original Mongol inhabitants received some attention. Ji Yun described their rituals respectfully. He noted that the Ölöd Mongols every year worshipped at Tiger Peak, where they piled up rock cairns (*obo*) to mark sacred sites:

> Mist from afar blows across the green lotus
> The *obo* still preserve traces of ancient days
> You cannot reach the cloud-covered sacred mountain
> Every year they only worship at Tiger Peak.[16]

Ji Yun also traveled outside the city to inspect ancient ruins. He found an abandoned city where Buddhist temples and relics still remained. It might have been the remains of a Tang dynasty garrison. Again he noted the transition from war to peace:

> High moss-grown walls for ten *li* around
> When was this heroic defense built against Western barbarians?
> The traveler rests, gazing on a bone of the Buddha in a golden vase
> The pagoda instructs that one must follow Ashoka.[17]

These samples of Ji Yun's writing show that he saw frontier expansion as a pacifying, civilizing process. He did not neglect the military force needed to conquer and secure the borders, but he saw conquest over the long term as bringing peace, order, and new opportunities for the ambitious settlers and the military colonists in the region.

A Vietnamese Perspective on Borders

Lê Quý Đôn (1726–1784) was a high ranking Vietnamese scholar, who had traveled on a tribute mission to Beijing, and who endorsed the submission of the new Nguyen dynasty to the Qianlong emperor. As a contemporary of Ji Yun, he shared his Chinese counterparts' experience of the vastness of the empire and its great military and cultural power. As Liam Kelley has shown, Vietnamese envoys to the Qing court expressed in their poetic works great admiration for the "manifest civility" of the Chinese regime, and they viewed Qing China as a model for their project to create a more civilized society along Confucian lines.[18] On the other hand, since indigenous Vietnamese resistance had beaten back invasions by both the Ming and the Qing, they knew well the threat of their great northern neighbor and the need to stand on guard against it.

Lê Quý Đôn, like Ji Yun, contemplated ancient ruins in former border regions. In his verse, he too marked the change from war to peace, but emphasized the limits to imperial ambition:

Fort Cổ-lộng

Four hundred years—these walls have crumbled since.
Bean stalks and melon vines now sprout and thrive.
Limpid blue waves wash off King Trần's fierce wrath.
Spreading green grass can't hide Mu Sheng's shamed face.
Gold oxen, after rain, plow up some swords.
Cold birds, by moonlight, moan amidst the ruins.
Why must the empire's bounds forever stretch?
Nine districts formed the realm of Yao and Shun.[19]

Lê Quý Đôn meditates here on a fort built in Northern Vietnam by the Ming general Mu Sheng in the early fifteenth century.[20] The Yongle emperor (r. 1403–1424) had invaded Vietnam in 1406 and occupied the country. Trần Gián Định had proclaimed himself king and fought against the Ming forces, defeating Mu Sheng and forcing him to retreat to Fort Cổ-lộng in 1408. Eventually, the frontier warlord Lê Lợi drove out the Ming forces with a protracted guerrilla war, forcing them to make peace in 1427. Chinese forces did not cross the Vietnamese border again until 1788. Lê Quý Đôn, writing in the late eighteenth century, describes the conversion of battlefields into paddies, while noting that old swords still remain below the ground. The ruins evoke a vanished, futile war that contrasts with the abundance of peace. Lê openly questions the need for Chinese expansion, citing the ancient times of the sagely kings Yao and Shun, when the span of the empire was much smaller than either the Ming or the Qing. For Lê, the classics provided a model of a more modest empire, conscious of its limits, willing to respect other proud kingdoms on its borders, with equal claims to civilization. The famous eleventh-century poem attributed to Marshal Lý Thường Kiệt, rallying his troops against Chinese aggression, had expressed more resolute defiance:

The Southern emperor rules the Southern land
Our destiny is writ in Heaven's Book
How dare you bandits trespass on our soil?
You shall meet your undoing at our hands.[21]

On the other hand, Lê Quý Đôn unequivocally approved of the expansion of the Vietnamese kingdom to the south. His "Frontier Chronicles" (Phủ Biên

Tạp Lục) vividly described the new territories taken by the expanding Vietnam-ese state.[22] After the Trịnh lords conquered the Nguyễn rulers of the south in 1775, Lê served for six months in the new territories, collecting abundant detail in order to ensure that officials of the north would be well informed about the new lands they ruled. His *Chronicles* resemble Ji Yun's poems in "pursu[ing] the swarming details of economic and social life with a prodigal enthusiasm."[23] He, like Ji Yun, was a transient official, not a colonist. Yet both saw the frontier as a place that shaped one's character. It provided direct contact with real, if less "civilized" people who deserved moral government. The frontier expanded the cultural horizons of both men. Lê Quý Đôn, however, had a greater conscious-ness of limits than Ji Yun. He could not embrace unbounded expansiveness as a universal principle, especially not by Vietnam's giant neighbor to the north. Lê Quý Đôn's complex view recognized the contingency of border relations and the importance of local situations in boundary creation.

These four travelers crossed the imperial borders with similar motives of curiosity, fear, and desire for profit. Each of them used the opportunities given them by access to the Qing to obtain cultural and economic resources for their return to their home countries. The classical Chinese heritage provided all of them with historical analogies and empirical information, but their own ob-servations greatly supplemented and enriched their experience. Border cross-ing meant a personal journey into alien territory and return to familiar lands with new perspectives. Like their later Western visitors, these Asian travelers reflected upon the position of China in the wider world, and used what they learned of China to carry on dynamic interactions that shaped the relations of China and its neighbors.

Appendix

Hoang lũy đồi viên từ bách thu,
荒垒颓桓四百秋
Qua đằng đậu mạn phóng xuân nhu,
瓜藤豆蔓放春柔
Bich ba dĩ tẩy Trần vương hận
碧波 已洗陳王恨
Thanh thảo nan già Mộc Thạnh tu
青 草難遮木晟羞
Hoàng độc vũ dữ canh cổ kiếm
黃犢武雨余耕古劍

Hàn cầm nguyệt hạ táo tàn lâu
寒禽月下噪残樓
Phong cưởng hà sự cần khai tịch
封疆何用勤開辟
Nghiêu, Thuấn đưởng niên chỉ cửu châu.
堯舜當年只九州
Lê Quý Đôn, 1726–1784.
From *Lịch triều hiến chưởng loại chi* [tập 1], ed. Phan Huy Chú, Saigon
1972, vol.1, 150.

Notes

1. Joel S. Migdal, *Boundaries and Belonging: States and Societies in the Struggle to Shape Identities and Local Practices* (New York: Cambridge, 2004), 5.

2. John King Fairbank, ed., *The Chinese World Order: Traditional China's Foreign Relations* (Cambridge, MA: Harvard University Press, 1968); Lien-sheng Yang, "Historical Notes on the Chinese World Order," in *The Chinese World Order*, ed. Fairbank, 20–33; Nicola Di Cosmo, "Kirghiz Nomads on the Qing Frontier: Tribute, Trade, or Gift-Exchange?" In *Political Frontiers, Ethnic Boundaries, and Human Geographies in Chinese History*, ed. Nicola Di Cosmo and Don J. Wyatt (New York: Routledge-Curzon, 2003), 351–372; John E. Wills, Jr., ed., *Past and Present in China's Foreign Policy: From 'Tribute System' to 'Peaceful Rise'* (MerwinAsia, Portland, ME 2011).

3. Pak Chi-wǒn, *Yǒrha Ilgi (Rehe Riji)* [1780] 1956, Zhonghua Congshu, Taipei. Pak Chi-wǒn, *Yǒrha Ilgi (Nekka Nikki)*, trans. Imamura Yoshio (Tokyo: Heibonsha, 1978). Pak Chi-wǒn, *The Jehol Diary: Yorha Ilgi of Pak Chiwǒn (1737–1805)*, trans. Yang Hi Choe-Wall (Folkestone, Kent: Global Oriental, 2010), Marion Eggert, "A Borderline Case: Korean Travelers' Views of the Chinese Border (Eighteenth to Nineteenth Century)," in *China and Her Neighbours: Borders, Visions of the Other, Foreign Policy 10th to 19th Century*, ed. Sabine Dabringhaus, Roderich Ptak, and Richard Teschke (Wiesbaden: Harrassowitz, 1997).

4. On Pak's political views, see Dieter Eikemeier, *Elemente Im Politischen Denken Des Yǒn'am Pak Chiwôn (1737–1805)* (Leiden: Brill, 1970).

5. Peter C. Perdue, *China Marches West: The Qing Conquest of Central Eurasia* (Cambridge, MA: Harvard University Press, 2005), 258–265; 575–581; *Shiliao Xunkan* 25: 481–483ff.

6. Ji Yun, "Wulumuqi Zashi," (Shanghai: Shangwu Yinshuguan, 1937). Silvia Freiin Ebner von Eschenbach, trans. "Die Gedichte Des Chi Yün (1724–1805) Als Quelle Für Die Landeskunde in Ostturkestan Im 18. Jahrhundert," *Oriens* 33 (1992): 363–436; Li Zhongzhi, ed., *Ji Xiaolan Yu Siku Quanshu: Ji Xiaolan Wulumuqi Zashi Yizhu* (Beijing: Zhongguo Chuban Jituan Xiandai Jiaoyu Chubanshe, 2010).

7. Joanna Waley-Cohen, *Exile in Mid-Qing China: Banishment to Xinjiang, 1758–1820* (New Haven: Yale University Press, 1991).

8. James A Millward, *Beyond the Pass: Economy, Ethnicity, and Empire in Qing Central Asia, 1759–1864* (Stanford, CA: Stanford University Press, 1998). Perdue, *China Marches West,* 342–353.

9. Data on agricultural yields in ibid., 586–587.

10. Li Zhongzhi, ed., *Ji Xiaolan*, 125.

11. Gudula Linck, "Visions of the Border in Chinese Frontier Poetry." In *China and Her Neighbours: Borders, Visions of the Other, Foreign Policy 10th to 19th Century*, ed. Sabine Dabringhaus, Roderich Ptak, and Richard Teschke (Wiesbaden: Harrassowitz, 1997).

12. Perdue, *China Marches West,* 429.

13. Ji Yun, "Wulumuqi Zashi," 6. Li Zhongzhi, *Ji Xiaolan*, 151 poem #33.

14. Li Zhongzhi, *Ji Xiaolan*, 150 poem #32

15. Ibid., 149 poem #30

16. Ji Yun, "Wulumuqi Zashi," 5. Li Zhongzhi, *Ji Xiaolan*, 145 poem #26.

17. Ji Yun, "Wulumuqi Zashi,"3. Li Zhongzhi, *Ji Xiaolan*, 139 poem #16 (a variant text).

18. Liam C. Kelley, *Beyond the Bronze Pillars: Envoy Poetry and the Sino-Vietnamese Relationship* (Honolulu: University of Hawai'i Press, 2005).

19. Huynh Sanh Thông, *The Heritage of Vietnamese Poetry* (New Haven: Yale University Press, 1979), 15. See Appendix for original Chinese and Vietnamese text.

20. L. C. Goodrich, and Chaoying Fang, eds. *Dictionary of Ming Biography, 1368–1644.* 2 vols. New York: Columbia University Press, 1976, 361, 793–797.

21. Huynh, *The Heritage of Vietnamese Poetry,* 3.

22. Alexander Woodside, "Central Vietnam's Trading World in the Eighteenth Century as seen in Lê Quý Đôn's 'Frontier Chronicles'," in *Essays into Vietnamese Pasts,* ed. Keith Weller Taylor and John K. Whitmore (Ithaca, NY: Cornell University Southeast Asia Program Publications, 1995).

23. Ibid., 159.

References

Dabringhaus, Sabine, Roderich Ptak, and Richard Teschke, eds. 1997. *China and Her Neighbours : Borders, Visions of the Other, Foreign Policy 10th to 19th Century*. Wiesbaden: Harrassowitz.

Di Cosmo, Nicola. 2003. "Kirghiz Nomads on the Qing Frontier: Tribute, Trade, or Gift-Exchange?" In *Political Frontiers, Ethnic Boundaries, and Human Geographies in Chinese History,* ed. Nicola Di Cosmo and Don J. Wyatt, 351–372. New York: Routledge Curzon.

Ebner von Eschenbach, Silvia Freiin, and Ji Yun. 1992. "Die Gedichte Des Chi Yün (1724–1805) Als Quelle Für Die Landeskunde in Ostturkestan Im 18. Jahrhundert." *Oriens* 33: 363–436.

Eikemeier, Dieter. 1970. *Elemente Im Politischen Denken Des Yŏn'am Pak Chiwŏn (1737–1805)*. Leiden: Brill, 1970.

Fairbank, John King, ed. 1968. *The Chinese World Order: Traditional China's Foreign Relations*. Cambridge, MA: Harvard University Press.

Goodrich, L. C., and Chaoying Fang, eds. *Dictionary of Ming Biography, 1368–1644*. 2 vols. New York: Columbia University Press, 1976.

Haboush, JaHyun Kim. 2005. "Contesting Chinese Time, Nationalizing Temporal Space: Temporal Inscription in Late Choson Korea." In *Time, Temporality, and Imperial Transition: East Asia from Ming to Qing*, ed. Lynn A. Struve, 115–141. Honolulu: Association for Asian Studies and University of Hawai'i Press.

Ji Yun. 1937. *Wulumuqi Zashi*. Shanghai: Shangwu Yinshuguan.

Kelley, Liam C. 2005. *Beyond the Bronze Pillars: Envoy Poetry and the Sino-Vietnamese Relationship*. Honolulu: University of Hawai'i Press.

Migdal, Joel S. 2004. *Boundaries and Belonging: States and Societies in the Struggle to Shape Identities and Local Practices*. Cambridge: Cambridge University Press.

Millward, James A. 1998. *Beyond the Pass: Economy, Ethnicity, and Empire in Qing Central Asia, 1759–1864*. Stanford, CA: Stanford University Press.

Pak Chi-wŏn. 1780. (Repr., 1956) Yŏrha ilgi *(Rehe Riji)*. Taipei: Zhonghua Congshu.

Pak Chi-wŏn. 1978. *Yŏrha Ilgi (Nekka Nikki)*. Translated by Imamura Yoshio. Tokyo: Heibonsha.

————. 2010. *The Jehol Diary: Yŏrha Ilgi of Pak Chiwŏn (1737–1805)*. Translated by Yang Hi Choe-Wall. Folkestone, Kent: Global Oriental.

Perdue, Peter C. 2005. *China Marches West: The Qing Conquest of Central Eurasia*. Cambridge, MA: Harvard University Press.

Waley-Cohen, Joanna. 1991. *Exile in Mid-Qing China: Banishment to Xinjiang, 1758–1820*. New Haven: Yale University Press.

Wills, John E., Jr., ed. 2011. *Past and Present in China's Foreign Policy: From 'Tribute System' to 'Peaceful Rise.'* Portland, ME: Merwin Asia.

Yang, Lien-sheng. 1968. "Historical Notes on the Chinese World Order." In *The Chinese World Order: Traditional China's Foreign Relations*, ed. John K. Fairbank, 20–33. Cambridge, MA: Harvard University Press.

7

Kashmiri Merchants and Qing Intelligence Networks in the Himalayas

The Ahmed Ali Case of 1830

MATTHEW W. MOSCA

On the night of August 21, 1830, a Kashmiri merchant named Ahmed Ali penned an urgent petition to the East India Company's governor-general, explaining that he had been imprisoned by the authorities of the Qing empire on suspicion of spying for British India. This chapter uses his case as a microcosm through which to analyze the ambiguous status of Kashmir and Kashmiris in the worldview of Qing officials.[1] In part, it examines the case itself: the events leading to his arrest and the policy choices of the Qing state during this significant counter-intelligence operation and diplomatic incident. Here Qing official documents are complemented by the British Indian archives recently explored by John Bray (2011). More broadly, this chapter approaches Ahmed Ali's case as an instance of the evolving Qing efforts to manage frontier crossings in Tibet, complementing Peter C. Perdue's study of the frontier elsewhere in this volume. From this perspective, the case represents an instance in which the Qing state's efforts to assert centralized oversight over the flow of people and correspondence across the Himalayan frontier intersected with the complex web of relationships facilitating Kashmiri trade in Tibet—within the Kashmiri merchant community itself, and between that community and the two administrations it had to deal with, the Tibetan government and representatives of the Qing state sent from Beijing.

Ahmed Ali's case highlights the ambiguous status of Kashmir and Kashmiris in the spheres of commercial access, merchant identity, and political intelligence. Over the course of the eighteenth century the Qing state developed controls to limit European and Russian merchants to certain marts of trade on the frontier itself, notably Canton and Kiakhta. These controls were not, however, applied to traders arriving on other parts of the frontier from Central and South Asian homelands. Kashmiris, who represent perhaps the most extreme instance of this permissive Qing policy, lived and traded across much of Qing Inner Asia. Like other merchants enjoying relatively unrestricted access, notably Newari and "Andijani" traders, Kashmiris benefitted from the Qing state's vagueness about their place of origin and political allegiances. Yet, as comparable episodes embroiling their Newari (1788–93) and "Andijani" (1828–31) counterparts demonstrate, a political crisis could provoke analysis of their origins and loyalties and threaten to jeopardize their access to Qing markets.

How the Qing state understood Kashmir as a place and the relationship of Kashmiri merchants to that place, then, had both political and commercial implications. This understanding, in turn, influenced and was influenced by the ability of Kashmiris to escape state surveillance by avoiding being implicated in frontier disputes. Ahmed Ali's case, however, was only the clearest in a series of hints reaching Qing officials from 1790 onward that not only were many Kashmiri merchants based in British India, but that the Kashmiri homeland was in increasing contact with that power. The Kashmiri predicament was that of all South and Central Asian merchant communities trading with the Qing: increasingly, they were coming to serve as a commercial conduit connecting Qing territory to the British and Russian empires. Yet the Qing state as well as Kashmiri traders had reason to finesse the complications that might arise from a clearer perspective on their homeland's political identity. What appears at first glance to be evidence of a diminished Qing capacity to gather intelligence suggests, although it does not prove, a different interpretation: that the Qing state deliberately avoided elucidating Kashmiri ties to British India in order to have more flexibility in managing a convenient trade relationship.

Kashmiris in Qing Inner Asia

Kashmiri merchants were perhaps the most geographically dispersed foreign trading community within the Qing Empire, active throughout Tibet,

Qinghai, and Xinjiang. Their trade here predated Qing control, beginning at least as early as the start of the seventeenth century with trade in western Tibet. By 1700 they monopolized the export of prized goat wool to their homeland via Ladakh, and were becoming involved in the caravan trade between India and Central Asia across the Karakorams. In the eighteenth century, many Kashmiri merchants reached Lhasa via Patna and Kathmandu rather than Ladakh. During the reign of the Fifth Dalai Lama (1642–1682), if not before, some began to reside permanently in Lhasa and other central Tibetan cities that they had visited as traders for decades. Their descendants, faithful to Islam and their Kashmiri identity at the same time took local brides and spoke fluent Tibetan. From Tibet, some Kashmiris traded onward to Xining on the edge of China proper; by the first half of the nineteenth century, this may have extended to trading rhubarb up to the Russian border at Kiakhta (*QSL-DG*:37:483 [290.34b-35a]; 16/10/26). Individual traders may also have entered China proper.[2] Routes within the Qing Empire formed only part of a Kashmiri commercial network reaching westward through Afghanistan into Central Asia, and southward to the Coromandel Coast (Gaborieau 1973; Boulnois 2003).

Qing power in Inner Asia incrementally absorbed these outposts of Kashmiri trade, first in Xining, then Tibet with the expulsion of the Zunghar Mongols in 1720, and finally Yarkand and Kashgar, secured in 1759. During these conquests, Kashmiris attracted little scrutiny and were allowed to continue their pre-conquest activities. A brief review of the nomenclature applied to Kashmiris suggests that they were difficult to classify and track, and that the Qing state exerted little effort to do so.

Vagueness about the Kashmiri merchants' place of origin in the minds of Qing officials stemmed from the interplay of two factors: the terminological conflation of 'Kashmiri' and Muslims in general, and the fact that they entered Tibet from multiple directions. In Tibetan, Kashmiris were called *Kha-che*, a term that sometimes indicated Kashmiris *per se*, and sometimes all Muslims (Das 2000, 126; Jäschke 1998, 36–37). Qing officials and scholars had begun to adopt this term by 1721, when a military commander learned of a place called *Kaqi* (喀齊), whose people were traders (*FDYZ*, 250). In Gansu, also, a 1737 gazetteer of Suzhou listed among lands to the west "*Kaqi* [喀七], a Muslim country close to Tibet . . . [its merchants] frequently peddle their wares up to the outside of the [Jiayu] Gate, and they also market their wares outside Xining" (*CSX* 1967, 3:1289). By the mid-eighteenth century, Chinese sources began to follow Tibetan practice in applying *Kaqi* as a blanket term for all Muslims reaching Tibet, a usage close to another common term for non-Chinese Muslims, "turbaned people" *(chantou)*. One official early in the Qianlong period (1736–1796) commented that, "*Kaqi* lies southwest of Tashilhunpo, that is, where the turbaned Muslims [*chantou Huimin*] live . . . their tribes [*buluo*] are extremely numerous, and some of them have surrendered to the leader of the Zunghars . . . they come and go from Tibet as foreign merchants" (Chen 1969, 70). Here, Indian and Turkic Central Asian Muslim traders were clearly conflated under one rubric. Laconic mention elsewhere of "turbaned Muslim Kashmiris" *(chantou Huihui Kaqi)* could therefore be construed in either a strict or general sense (Zhang 1968, 67). One 1741 description of Tibet's commerce mentioned that "there are turbaned Muslims who peddle precious stones . . . there are Newaris and Muslims *(Baibu[3] Huimin)* who sell carpets, Tibetan brocade, *Kaqi* silk fabrics, all of which come from such places as Bhutan, Nepal, and India" (Jiao 1968, 124). Another contemporary source enumerated among merchants trading in Tibet "locals and various foreigners *(semuren)* from the Western Ocean *(Xiyang)*, the turbaned people *(chantou)*, the *Eluoelesu* (Orus, Russians?), and the Muslims *(Huihui)*" (XFX 1998, 548). Kashmiris certainly number among these "turbaned" and "Muslim" groups.

With the conquest of the Tarim Basin in 1759, the Qing state gained a new perspective on Kashmir. Immediately after the conquest, Kashmiri traders visiting Yarkand via Ladakh offered intelligence about developments in India (Mosca 2013, 78–79). Although Beijing's political interest in Kashmir soon lapsed, geographers in Xinjiang remained interested. One remarked of Kashmir in 1778 that "many of the rich merchants of Hindustan have homes in this place," and that, together with Andijan, it was the "homeland of merchants in the Western Regions" (Qi-shi-yi 2001, 96). However, authors in Xinjiang did not mention Kashmiri activity in Lhasa. Moreover, their terminology was different: not reliant on Tibetan mediation, they called Kashmir *Keshimi'er* (Manchu *Kesimir*) rather than *Kaqi*, and unlike in Tibet this term referred to Kashmiris *per se*, not to Muslims in general.[4]

A further shift in the nomenclature occurred between 1788 and 1793, when two Gorkha invasions placed Tibetan affairs under unprecedented scrutiny from Beijing. Although not directly involved, Kashmiris were caught up in the general surge in commentary. A joint memorial of 1789 laying out a framework for postwar trade regulations referred to them as *Kaqi fanhui* (卡契番回) and *Kaqi Huimin* (卡契回民) (QBJ 1992, 323). As state surveillance became stricter, the term *Keshimi'er* migrated from Xinjiang around 1791 and thereafter became standard in Qing official documents written in Tibet. While this implies that Kashmiris were being distinguished more clearly from other Muslims, and tied to a single homeland, there is no evidence of such a fundamental clarification influencing non- or semi-official geographic writing, even though most authors were Qing officials writing privately. In a private postwar essay, one *amban* observed that "there are the Newaris and the Kashmiri Muslim group [*Kaqi Huizhong* 卡契回眾] who frequently come to Tibet to trade; some among them came and settled in Tibet in years past and make a living by trade," adding that they should be kept under strict control and protected from harassment by Tibetan and Qing soldiers (Song-yun 1992, 65). His colleague commented more vaguely about "turbaned people" trading in Tibet, adding that some lived there permanently (He-ning 2002, 664). The 1796 *Wei-Zang tongzhi*, a gazetteer of Tibet, gave one entry to the "turbaned people" *(chantou)*, also called Kashmiri *(Keshimi'er)*, and described them as "Muslims of the Western Regions" *(Xiyu Huimin)* with a homeland southwest of Nepal. A separate entry was given to *Kaqi*, regarded as "a large Muslim tribe south of Bhutan," although this term was described as "also another name for the turbaned people" (*WZTZ*, 256). A Chinese scholar in Tibet in the 1790s explained that "turbaned people" were Muslims *(Huihui)*, mostly Kashmiri or Andijani, some having lived in Tibet for a long time. It is unclear if this author equated Kashmiri *(Keshimi'er)* with *Kaqi*, a term he used elsewhere and defined simply as "the name of the tribe of Muslims" *(Kaqi, Huihui buluo zhi ming)* (Zhou 2006, 3, 15).

No official inquiry into the geographic origins and political allegiances of Kashmiris took place before 1800, but at least one Kashmiri informally transmitted political intelligence. This was a merchant, resident in Further Tibet,[5] who was awarded by the Qianlong emperor a hat button of the fifth rank and accompanying peacock feathers for his diligence in aiding wartime logistics (*QKJ* 1992, 751). This man, called A-qi-mu-ju-e-er in Chinese sources, impressed Zhou Ailian, a private secretary involved in commissariat affairs, as a widely traveled polyglot. The Kashmiri explained to Zhou that although India was a land of immense wealth, real power had been taken from its *Kaqi* king (i.e., Mughal emperor) by two high officials of the Western Christian religion *(Xiyang Tianzhu jiao)*, who handled all matters of revenue, "only using this country's monarch and its dynastic name to bring the various tribes [*buluo*] to submission" (Zhou 2006, 40).

In Qing sources, then, Kashmiris blended with all Muslim traders from Central Asia as *chantou,* and with all Indian Muslims as *Kaqi.* Only *Keshimi'er* gave them a more specific geographic origin, but the relationship between these identities remained ambiguous. Into the 1830s, Qing observers remained vexed by how to understand the origins of a diasporic trading community whose individual members were resident in many lands.

Foreign Merchants and State Security in Inner Asia

Descriptions of Kashmiris and their origins were cursory and sometimes contradictory in part because they had never received close state scrutiny. To understand the potential impact of such scrutiny, we can consider the Qing investigations of Newari merchants during the two Qing-Gorkha wars, and of Andijani merchants in the wake of the Jahangir incursion into Xinjiang. In these cases, Beijing moved vigorously against foreign merchants when the empire's security seemed to be at stake, but allowed pragmatic economic concerns to temper its policy.

Before 1788, the southern frontier of Tibet lay almost entirely beyond the oversight of the Qing court, which perceived no threat from that direction. Local Tibetan administrators, nominally supervised by Qing *ambans,* determined what foreigners could cross the border. This changed only when the turmoil of the Gorkha wars persuaded Qianlong that greater central oversight was needed, a conclusion that hewed to a middle ground between other potential policies of greater leniency or harshness.

When the Gorkhas invaded Tibet in 1788, it was initially assumed that the Newaris (Tib. *Bal po;* Chinese *Balebu*), whose conquest by the Gorkhas was then unknown in China, had inexplicably turned aggressive. Almost immediately, the *amban* Qing-lin ordered the arrest of the leader of the Newari trading community and two servants, but took no action against ordinary traders (*QBJ* 1992, 19–20, 110). Qianlong criticized even this response as hasty, explaining that although the headman would deserve to be executed if he were indeed a spy, his detention without such proof was unwarranted. Rather, he and other Newaris should simply be prohibited from returning home during the war "without authorization *(si)*" (*QBJ* 1992, 24). Qing-lin assigned the investigation to a high-ranking Tibetan cleric and his underling, who found 98 Newari merchants, some of whom had lived in Tibet for twenty years. The head merchant was exonerated and allowed to stay in Tibet after the war (*QBJ* 1992, 46, 278).

During this first invasion Qing officials relied entirely on Tibetan counterparts for information about Newari merchants. It was the retired Tibetan chief minister Rdo ring Pandita who initially arrested and took custody of the head trader (*QBJ* 1992, 110). Other inquiries were delegated to a high-ranking Tibetan cleric and a governor *(sde pa)* (*QBJ* 1992, 46). It is not surprising, then, that the trade regulations drafted at the end of the first war placed foreign merchants under Tibetan administration—presumably formalizing prewar practices. Previously, Newaris and Kashmiris had been able to come and go without oversight. Now it was mandated that a foreign headman should formally be sent from their home country to manage the community jointly with a suitable Tibetan governor *(sde pa)* to prevent abuses and disputes. These headmen were to report annually on comings and goings. At the apex of supervision was a member of the Tibetan council of ministers *(bka'-blon)*, who would in turn report abuses to the Qing *amban* (*QBJ* 1992, 323).

A more interventionist response followed the second, larger Gorkha invasion of Tibet in 1791. Qianlong feared that Newari traders would spy on Qing military movements, and at the start of the campaign ordered secret investigations to find spies and suspicious people, who would be sent to Beijing. Other Newaris were to be expelled forever, even if Nepal surrendered (*QKJ* 1992, 82, 86). But things were not so simple: it was soon learned that some Newari families had lived in Lhasa since the Kangxi period, had thousands of dependents, and in some cases Tibetan wives, making mass deportations difficult and potentially dangerous (*QKJ* 1992, 111). Qianlong's response to this news was to presume that some merchants had grown loyal to Tibet and thus become potential sources of intelligence about their ancestral homeland (*QKJ* 1992, 114). Interviews with a community leader ascertained the key fact that Newaris were distinct from the Gorkha rulers who had conquered the Kathmandu Valley (*QKJ* 1992, 290). Qianlong suspended his expulsion order, partly to coax intelligence from these traders, planning to revisit their status after the war (*QKJ* 1992, 329). Crisis had led to a more granular understanding of the politics and ethnic composition of once-obscure Nepal.

After the war the Qing government studied trans-Himalayan trade and generated regulations that remained in force for decades to come. As the war was ending, Qianlong decided to prohibit Newari trade: those who wished to remain in Lhasa would be naturalized, enrolled on the population registers and "permanently regarded as ordinary subjects in Tibet *(yong zuo Zangnei minren)*. Others would be deported under guard and the frontier closed (*QKJ*

1992, 602–603). It was later acknowledged that such a closure would perforce require a halt to Kashmiri trade because it relied primarily on routes through Gorkha territory (*QKJ* 1992, 745). But as relations improved and Tibet's reliance on trade became clearer, Qianlong relented and instead opted for a new control regime even stricter than that for Russian trade at Kiakhta. Commercial oversight would be removed from Tibetan ministers (*bka'-blon*) and *ambans* would henceforth take personal responsibility for inspecting and supervising cross-border commerce (*QKJ* 1992, 668). In place of the pre-1788 lack of supervision, and the never-implemented reforms of 1789, supervision over foreign merchants would now be directed from Beijing.

From 1793, a series of interlocking control mechanisms were applied to both Newaris and Kashmiris. A population register was to be made for both communities, kept on file in the *ambans'* office. New checkpoints staffed by Qing military officers were to be established on the two major routes into central Tibet, at Dingri for the road from Kathmandu, and at Gyantse for the road from Bhutan. Merchants entering Tibet had to report to these posts for permission, and upon arrival in Lhasa to be duly entered into the register. Those wishing to depart had to apply through their community headmen for permits from the *ambans,* to be inspected during transit through these same posts. A similar pass-based system would manage religious travel into and out of Tibet (*QKJ* 1992, 700–701).

These regulations asserted Qing control over Tibet's foreign intercourse, with imperial officials sent by Beijing, not local administrators, supervising—and, if necessary, interdicting—human traffic across the Himalayas into Tibet. Foreign testimony confirms that this right was maintained: both Thomas Manning in 1811–12 and Evariste Huc in 1846 found that it was the Qing *ambans* rather than Tibetan authorities that took a lead role in investigating their presence and determining their expulsion (Markham 1971, 275–277; Huc 1927, 193). Still, Tibetan authorities retained day-to-day control: most Kashmiri and Newari imports were taxed in Lhasa, not at the border, by the Accounts Department (Tib. *rtsis-khang,* Ch. *shang-shang*) of the Tibetan government, although this process too now came under *amban* supervision (*QKJ* 1992, 738). In short, under ordinary circumstances Newari and Kashmiri merchants would continue to supervise themselves, interact with the Tibetan administration in matters of taxation and commercial law, and deal with the Qing state only when crossing the frontier, or when involved in political cases.

Between 1788 and 1793, Kashmiris escaped the scrutiny applied to Newari merchants, although new regulations devised to control Newari trade also applied to them. Their position was similar during a second episode of frontier unrest, the Khoqandi-backed invasion of Jahangir that devastated southern Xinjiang. In 1828 the Jiaqing emperor approved a plan to end trade with Khoqand, along lines similar to those proposed for Tibet in 1791: foreigners of long residence would be given the option of entering the population register as ordinary subjects, the rest would be expelled. Kashmiris were explicitly acknowledged not to have aided the enemy, but those who remained within the Qing realm would nonetheless be restricted to non-commercial occupations (Na-yan-cheng 1995, 847). Non-resident Kashmiris arriving from abroad would henceforth be limited to trade fairs near the border, essentially applying something close to the Kiakhta model to Xinjiang (Newby 2005, 135–152). This restrictive trading order collapsed in 1831, after a second Khoqandi invasion, but it is a further reminder that security concerns could lead harsh controls to be imposed on trade that had previously been largely unregulated by Beijing.

Recruiting Ahmed Ali: 1814–1817

East India Company interest in trade with Tibet, dating back to the 1760s, increased after 1809, when it extended its control over northern India up to the Sutlej and gained access to new parts of the Himalayan foothills. In 1812, the Company employee William Moorcroft crossed the Niti Pass to Gartok, the principal administrative center of western Tibet (Alder 1985, 134–156). With the conquest of Kumaon during the 1814–16 war with Nepal, the Company gained direct access to the edge of Tibet. Getting in, however, proved almost impossible for Britons, and between 1816 and 1818 several Company employees were turned back at the frontier. This, coupled with the fear that undue pressure on Qing Tibet might harm British trade at Canton, made the Company seek less obtrusive agents to promote commerce between India and Tibet.

As early as George Bogle's 1774 mission to the Panchen Lama, the utility of Kashmiris for relations with Tibet had been evident to the East India Company (Lamb 2002, 117, 153). Often headquartered in Company territory, but enjoying unimpeded access to Tibet, Kashmiris offered a means of gaining information and promoting commerce without eliciting concern in Beijing. In western Tibet, with justified fears that the British were trying to break their goat wool monopoly, Kashmiri merchants seem to have been hostile (Moorcroft 2005, 106). However, at least one among those trading between Patna and central Tibet through the Kathmandu Valley was tentatively willing to aid the Company. This was Ahmed Ali, in his early twenties when the Anglo-Nepal war broke out in 1814. He was an acquaintance of Moorcroft, and had briefly served the Company in some capacity collecting tax and opium revenues.[6] Asked to recruit potential intelligence assets for the impending conflict, Moorcroft approached Ahmed Ali. Although the Company's immediate interest was Nepal, the Kashmiri was also in a position to offer information about Tibet based on his firm's two centuries of trade in Lhasa and its high-level connections (he claimed) with that city's Tibetan and Qing authorities. Indeed, he boasted of inside access to diplomatic correspondence between the ruler of Nepal and the Qing emperor (Alder 1985, 192–197; Bray 2011, 319–323).

In 1815, having "drawn upon himself the resentment of the other Kash-meereean Merchants who traffic from Patna to Lassa by his having been active in the British cause," Ahmed Ali approached the Company with an offer to promote Indian goods in Tibet as its agent. The governor-general and his staff, wary that the Kashmiri might improperly presume upon any formal status to pursue private commercial ends, refused him an official appointment but were willing to assist at arm's length in an ostensibly private venture. During negotiations Ahmed Ali was issued instructions specifying the parameters of his mission and inquiries, which he later termed his *sanad* or commission, but he ultimately declined the offered terms. When he had second thoughts in 1817, he was told that the Company now wished to leave the expansion of trade "to the operation of natural Causes" (Bray 2011, 323–327). Still, in the end Ahmed Ali did gather information about Tibet. It is possible that Moorcroft—with a record of privately recruiting intelligence agents—made arrangements to keep the project alive.[7] Ahmed Ali later told his Qing inter-rogators that Moorcroft supplied him with a blank notebook. However, he was aware of Moorcroft's death when he set off for Tibet, so it is unlikely that a purely personal arrangement was his sole motivation (LFZZ: Deposition of Ahmed Ali). After his release Ahmed Ali maintained that he was fulfilling his 1816 commission. Although technically a dead letter, he presumably believed that the Company would still reward him for the information it had once sought (IOR: Hodgson to Prinsep, June 26, 1831).

Commercial Catastrophe: Ahmed Ali Visits Tibet

Ahmed Ali, although his family firm had long traded in Lhasa, was no old Tibet hand. He spoke no Tibetan and ran the Lhasa branch through Abdullah, a Kashmiri agent first hired by his father.[8] This branch was run as a partnership, with shares belonging to Ahmed Ali, his brother Ashraf Ali, Abdullah, and unnamed creditors in India. In 1820, Abdullah returned to India from Lhasa and announced a wish to retire. Three years later he was persuaded to return to Tibet together with Ashraf, who would run the operations of the house. After two years of losses, Ashraf came back with a letter from Abdullah summoning Ahmed Ali to Lhasa himself. Taking along his brother, Ahmed Ali reached that city in the summer of 1827, apparently for the first time (LFZZ::592:8; A.A. deposition). The first order of business was to settle the accounts of the branch and divide its assets, something that recent losses made difficult. Based on what a Kashmiri headman described to Qing authorities as "Muslim custom" (although Ahmed Ali claimed to be unfamiliar with the practice), he was expected to sign in advance a statement that accounts had been settled, to be held in trust by the local community leaders during the actual audit. This led to a later disagreement: Ahmed Ali claimed that despite his receipt no settlement was in fact made, while Ashraf and Abdullah maintained that a fair settlement was concluded in the presence of the local Kashmiri leaders (LFZZ: Depositions of A.A., Ashraf Ali, Abdullah). To the British, Ahmed Ali later complained that his agent and brother had embezzled large sums of money from him, but this charge was not recorded in Chinese documents.

By now Ahmed Ali, deprived by the dispute of his two closest associates, needed a new way to conduct business in unfamiliar Tibetan surroundings. A Tibet-born Kashmiri then living in his shop, called in Chinese documents Zha-ma-er-zu, recommended the services of his elder brother Fazl-ullah Fukro. An employment contract was drawn up, Fazl-ullah was summoned from Further Tibet, and new dealings commenced (LFZZ: Deposition of A.A.). Ahmed Ali by then faced legal as well as commercial woes. Although he had given Ashraf a share of the property, Ahmed Ali himself had kept control of the portion due to partners back in India. Ashraf felt that he could not return to Patna without these funds, lest he be dunned by creditors of the house, and therefore brought suit against his brother in the Finance Department of the Tibetan government, which had jurisdiction over the Kashmiri community (Gaborieau 1973, 25). Ahmed Ali countersued, alleging that he was still owed money. One of Fazl-ullah's jobs was to act as Ahmed Ali's agent in a proxy lawsuit *(baokong),* in return for a fee of one thousand silver *taels.* A Tibetan official, together with a leader in the Kashmiri community, reviewed the accounts and not only found Abdullah's figures sound, but determined that the former agent was still owed 2,831 *taels* of silver. Ashraf, however, was found to have improperly overspent during his previous sojourn in Tibet and to owe the house 10,000 "silver coins," presumably rupees. (To the British, Ahmed Ali alleged that Ashraf and Abdullah had bribed the judges to obtain this verdict) (IOR: Petition of A.A., Aug. 21, 1830.) Ashraf believed that he could pay this amount from his share of the house's investment put out for sale in Qinghai (Ahmed Ali acknowledged maintaining a "Kothee" [*kothi,* commercial premises] at "Selling" (Xining) (IOR: Petition of A.A., Aug. 21, 1830)). When these goods were brought back to Lhasa, however, Ashraf fretted over Ahmed Ali's insolvency and together with Abdullah requested a Tibetan minister *(bka'-blon)* to impound and liquidate them, so that the cash could be returned to India. This move evidently bankrupted Ahmed Ali, who was losing money under Fazl-ullah's new management. With his shop empty and subsistence difficult, he abandoned his shop and lived off charity at Lhasa's mosque (Ch., *Jiangdagang gongsuo,* Tib., *Rgyang-mda'-khang*). Fazl-ullah pursued him, demanding payment for another debt, and Ahmed Ali shot back that Fazl-ullah ought to return to him the funds given for the botched management of the court case. An argument between the two men dragged on for several months.[9] These commercial and legal disputes, played out in the Kashmiri community and Tibetan courts, did not yet concern Qing authorities.

To Catch a Spy: The Mechanics of Qing Counterespionage

All this time, Ahmed Ali was pursuing inquiries about Tibet and China. His confession to Qing authorities allows his activities to be reconstructed. When Abdullah had returned to India in 1820 Ahmed Ali had quizzed him about Tibetan affairs and had notes of their conversations taken down by a third party. He also copied notes about Tibetan route distances and dating systems made by Ashraf Ali during his earlier trip. After his own arrival in Lhasa, Ahmed Ali recorded his observations and responses to questions he posed to his new employee Fazl-ullah. Also copied was a questionnaire given by the Company's Resident in

Kathmandu, "Gardner sahib" *(Gare'erla'er sahaibu),* to a Tibet-bound Kashmiri merchant named Habib-ullah. As Gardner's successor Brian Hodgson later
explained, members of the Residency not uncommonly tried to find Kashmiri
agents to prosecute their inquiries (IOR: Hodgson to Swinton, Sept. 2, 1831).[10]
In this case Habib-ullah left Lhasa before finishing his task, leaving his instructions behind (LFZZ: 592:9–10; Deposition of A.A.).

Ahmed Ali's inquiries in Tibet seem to have been guided chiefly by what
Qing authorities termed a "letter" *(shuxin)* from Moorcroft, but which may
have been his Persian *sanad,* enjoining him to study Tibet's commerce and
geography. Although one of his supporters later claimed that Ahmed Ali was
resolved to aid the Company "regardless both of the Anger of the Rulers of
Bhoot [Tibet], and of risking the loss of his property and houses," it seems unlikely that he believed his activities to be risky (IOR: Khajah Fukheeroolla to
Sec. to G.G., Dec. 20, 1830). Indeed, Ahmed Ali later claimed to the British
that no less an official than one of the *ambans* knew of his voluminous cache
of information and would even occasionally visit him to be regaled with its
contents (IOR: Hodgson to Prinsep, June 5, 1831). Only an acrimonious
commercial dispute turned these anodyne jottings explosive.

It was his plan to appeal the judgment against him, Ahmed Ali believed,
that led his panicked cabal of enemies preemptively to denounce him as "a
spy on the part of the English" (IOR: Petition of A.A. to G.G., Aug. 21,
1830). Ashraf Ali seems to have been closer to the truth, however, when
he later told Brian Hodgson that the root of the problem was his brother's
decision to replace Abdullah with Fazl-ullah, who "fomented quarrels between
me and my brother, ruined his affairs, and got him committed to prison"
(IOR: Petition of Ashraf Ali, Feb. 10, 1832). Certainly it was Fazl-ullah
who turned Ahmed Ali in to Qing authorities. In Tibet, those authorities
consisted of a garrison composed principally of Han Chinese soldiers (the
Green Standard army) and a small number of civilian commissariat officials
(liangtai or *liangyuan),* the latter acting as deputies for the *ambans* in a variety
of capacities, including investigations involving Qing, as opposed to purely
Tibetan, justice (Xiao 1996, 85–98). Evidently, or so the Daoguang emperor
was informed, the heads of both services, commissariat official Zheng Jinbang
and his military counterpart Brigade Commander Sun Ruzao, had reported
to the *ambans* ominous rumors of a Kashmiri asking about "circumstances in
the core territories *(fudi)*" of the empire. Orders to investigate passed down
the chain of command to Company Commander Li Guo'an (LFZZ: 592:7).

Li sought a contact within the Kashmiri community to aid his investigation, and approached a man called in Chinese Ga-ma-er-zu. Like Fazl-ullah, Ga-ma-er-zu was born in Further Tibet but now lived in Lhasa. His father, Ma Fulong, had been granted insignia of the fifth rank during the Gorkha wars. This profile resembles what we know of A-qi-mu-ju-e-er, and it is possible that Ma Fulong was a Chinese name held in conjunction with a transliterated foreign name. However this may be, Li told Ga-ma-er-zu of his mission to find the rumored spy. Reminding him of his father's debt to the emperor, Li asked him, as a Kashmiri, to make secret inquiries in his own language. This he agreed to do. Setting out to find the culprit, Ga-ma-er-zu—putatively by a happy coincidence—ran into Fazl-ullah, who by then had broken with Ahmed Ali and earned his erstwhile employer's ire by (for reasons unclear) packing up Ahmed Ali's notes and letters and sending them to Further Tibet.[11] Upon learning of Ga-ma-er-zu's mission, Fazl-ullah recalled suspicious questions that Ahmed Ali had kept posing to him about Tibet and China *(neidi)*, and his curiously vehement demands to have his jottings returned. Accompanying Ga-ma-er-zu to the Qing military garrison he lodged his report, and Ahmed Ali was picked up for interrogation (LFZZ: 592: 1007, 1009; depositions of Ga-ma-er-zu and Pa-lu-zu [Fazl-ullah]). Even if this memorial accords Qing officials in Tibet an exaggeratedly proactive role in Ahmed Ali's capture, it is clear that he was turned in by his former agent Fazl-ullah.

Because Ahmed Ali spoke neither Chinese nor Tibetan, and had papers in Persian and English, a team of translators and interpreters was assembled. Worried that a total reliance on Qing Muslim subjects *(neidi Huimin)* would make it difficult to "win [Ahmed Ali's] confidence" *(zhefu qi xin)*, but that Kashmiris might collude to shield the prisoner, Qing officials formed a composite working group. Commissariat officials found two Qing subjects to interpret, one a Chinese Muslim from Sichuan named Jin Huailiang, and the other a Muslim subject named Ma-ma-ke-sha who had come from Qinghai and once been employed by Ahmed Ali's firm. Assisting them were the *ambans'* official Tibetan translator, the leaders of the Kashmiri trading community in Tibet, and the two men who had denounced Ahmed Ali, Ga-ma-er-zu and Fazl-ullah. Kashmiris who understood Persian explained the documents to others conversant in Tibetan (including the prisoner's brother Ashraf Ali), and the official Tibetan translator then rendered the material into Chinese. Processing three notebooks required Lhasa's Kashmiri community to work "day and night" for two months (IOR: A.A. reply to Hodgson, undated). They were discovered to contain information about the boundaries, passes, and topography of Tibet, the numbers and disposition of Chinese and Tibetan troops, the procedures of the Finance Department, itineraries for Tibet and Qinghai, general information about Sichuan and Gansu (the Chinese provinces lying athwart major trade routes into Tibet), and comments about roads from India to Tibet via Bhutan and Nepal. Only the letters in English could not be deciphered (LFZZ:592:7–8, 24–25).

Ahmed Ali's interrogation by the commissariat officials and *ambans* was laborious, as each question and answer had to be reiterated multiple times to get the meaning across. Ahmed Ali admitted gathering information about China and Tibet, but argued that his aims were innocent. In India his aptitude in managing tax and opium revenues brought him to the attention of the now-deceased leader *(touren)* William Moorcroft *(Eliyamu Mo'ergere),* who had sixteen years earlier proposed to grant him an investment and have him travel to Tibet, giving him a notebook to be sent back to India "in order to facilitate the dispatch of goods to Tibet as necessary." Ahmed Ali had neither agreed to this, nor taken the money, nor gone immediately to Tibet. Only his own affairs had brought him to Lhasa, and not a scrap of information has been sent back across the Himalayas. What notes he had taken were made "according to the customs of my homeland," and intended only to be compiled into a book *(zuanji chengshu)* (LFZZ: 8–10, 25).

Ahmed Ali's story struck his interrogators as implausible: Having been offered capital and notebooks from a British official, was he really planning only to write a book? If he were not honoring his earlier agreement, why then had he taken that old notebook on the long trip to Lhasa? Why had he copied a questionnaire given by a British official to another Kashmiri merchant entering Tibet via Nepal? Even if Ahmed Ali's motives were mainly commercial, it seemed almost certain that he was gathering political information about Tibet and China for a foreign power, and strictly speaking deserved punishment.

Diplomatically, however, there were reasons to handle the case with finesse. The state he served lay beyond Nepal, Bhutan, and Sikkim, and normally had no contact with Tibet. During its war with Nepal over a decade earlier, it had seemingly obeyed Qing orders to make peace. Extrapolating from the date of Ahmed Ali's first dealings with Moorcroft, the *ambans* correctly linked his commission to that war. If blame lay with the deceased Moorcroft and not any current leader, it seemed expedient to let the matter drop. Still, Qing prestige demanded some action, and they won the emperor's agreement for the following plan. Ahmed Ali would be allowed to wind up his affairs and then be permanently deported from Tibet, as would Ashraf and Abdullah.

Their lawsuit could be settled in their homeland. An official letter would be sent by the *ambans* to the state employing Ahmed Ali, outlining his confession and the evidence against him, and explaining that Qing law mandated a harsh punishment. However, since "you would not dare in this foolish and reckless fashion to send someone secretly to Tibet to make inquiries about its circumstances," the *ambans* had sought imperial mercy. Since news of this episode would doubtless inspire doubt and fear, this letter would detail the facts of the case and convey that it was proper that its recipients henceforth conduct themselves peacefully in gratitude for the emperor's clemency. From the Qing perspective the case was closed (LFZZ: 10–12).

As John Bray has elsewhere described the British response to the case in detail, it will only be summarized here (2011, 330–334). Ahmed Ali's petition led the governor-general to order Hodgson to solicit the intervention of Nepal's most powerful minister, Bhim Sen Thapa. By the time he was approached, in the spring of 1831, the Nepali statesman had already learned of Ahmed Ali's release from both Kashmiri merchants (whom Hodgson described as "a small junto . . . probably inimical to each other") and the correspondence network of a former Nepali ambassador to Beijing. Newari merchants in Lhasa also corroborated this, and soon a letter arrived from the *ambans* ordering Nepal to conduct Ahmed Ali onward to India (IOR: Hodgson to Prinsep, Apr. 20, 1831; Apr. 29, 1831). Ahmed Ali himself reached Kathmandu at the beginning of June, and after initial claims to have "fulfilled the instructions of the Council Board, in the time of Lord Hastings," he admitted that his inquiries had no official authorization, which British Indian archives soon confirmed.[12] Later that summer, the *ambans'* Chinese letter, accompanied by a Persian translation already prepared in Lhasa, was received via Sikkim. The British reply denied that Ahmed Ali was an agent or employee of the government, adding that it was not seeking information about "Chinese Tartary." Qing officials were chided for "foolish anxieties" about foreign merchants making notes.[13] I have found no record that this response, sent to Lhasa via Nepal, was forwarded to Beijing.

Qing Policy and the Question of Origins

Where then, was Ahmed Ali from, and what power was he supposed to have served? His arrest brought Tibet's Kashmiri community under particular Qing scrutiny for the first time. One consequence was new rules, devised by the *ambans* and approved by the emperor. Every Kashmiri entering Tibet was now to be diligently searched. Documents in the English script were forbidden. Tough surveillance regulations already in place for Newaris now extended to Kashmiris: any correspondence entering Tibet had to be submitted to Qing soldiers at the frontier posts, sent by them to the *ambans'* office in Lhasa, transmitted to the Kashmiri headmen for translation, and resubmitted for inspection. Outgoing correspondence had to be submitted for similar scrutiny via a Tibetan minister in Lhasa. Kashmiri headmen would be required to submit to the *ambans,* through a Tibetan minister, monthly written undertakings that no private correspondence had occurred outside of these channels (LFZZ:: 592:12). In theory, the Qing state now scrutinized all correspondence between Tibet and India.

In stark contrast to this vigorous counter-espionage, neither the *amban* nor the Qing court were inclined to gather detailed intelligence about the homeland of the expelled Kashmiris, its relationship to the regime that had recruited Ahmed Ali, and why that regime might be interested in Tibet. Basic geographic questions raised in the depositions were not pursued. Ahmed Ali, his brother Ashraf, and Abdullah all identified themselves in their depositions as "people of *Jiaga'er,*" that is, of *Rgya-gar,* a Tibetan word for India. A leader of the Kashmiri community named Jia-ma-po-da and Tibet-born Fazl-ul-lah were also identified as people of *Rgya-gar,* as was Ga-ma-er-zu's father. In short, these "Kashmiris" or their immediate ancestors were recorded as coming from India. Yet memorials giving the *amban*'s official interpretation of the case ignored *Rgya-gar:* In the memorials Ahmed Ali was termed a Kashmiri (*Keshimi'er fanmin*) and Abdullah as going to Kashmir (not *Rgya-gar,* as stated in the deposition) when he first sought to retire. This was not deception—the depositions were attached for the emperor's reference—but rather a gloss on that raw data. Since only Newaris and Kashmiris were noted in official regulations as trading in Lhasa, the *amban* presumably wanted to clarify to the emperor that these men were part of a known group. Only those born outside the Qing Empire were called "Kashmiris" in these memorials; those of Kashmiri ancestry born within it were referred to simply as Qing "Muslim subjects" *(Huimin).* This presumably signaled to the emperor that Fazl-ullah and Ga-ma-er-zu were *bona fide* residents of the empire, despite being of *Rgya-gar* descent, unlike the foreign Kashmiris Ahmed Ali, Ashraf Ali, and Abdullah, who were to be deported.

Jiaga'er was not the only term ignored. Qing documents on the case invariably referred to the polity whose headman Moorcroft had solicited Ahmed

Ali's help as *Pileng,* a Chinese term derived from the Tibetan *Phe-reng,* itself from the Persian *Farangi* ("Frank" or European) (Petech, 334). Written English was referred to as the "*Pileng* script" *(Pileng ziji)*. This land below Tibet had first come to the notice of Qing officials in 1792, and since then Nepal had repeatedly accused it of being an aggressive power with designs on Tibet and even China (Mosca 2013,139–147). In 1830 the *ambans* did not undertake even the most cursory investigation of the identity of the *Pileng,* their connections to Kashmir or *Rgya-gar,* or their economic and political activities. Daoguang was told simply that they were "puny foreigners on the periphery" *(zui'er bianyi)* who had "always been respectful and submissive" and normally had no interaction with Tibet (LFZZ: 592:10–11).

It is possible that neither the Daoguang emperor nor his officials felt any curiosity about the *Pileng,* or were persuaded that they posed no threat to Tibet. This was certainly the impression official correspondence was designed to convey. There is some evidence, however, that the Qing state deliberately avoided studying this issue. First, both the *ambans* and the emperor wished to end the case quickly and without conflict. Repeatedly invoking imperial benevolence, the *ambans* secured special treatment for Ahmed Ali. As a foreigner, it was "inexpedient to put him in prison, which might give rise to doubts and fears *(yiwei),*" so he was confined to a remote temple guarded by soldiers. Avoiding "doubts and fears" was also cited as a reason to excuse him from the full rigor of the law. Ahmed Ali himself claimed that the "authorities in Khetta from fear of the British Government have refrained from killing me, and also diminished the severities of my confinement."[14] As early as 1811, Manning claimed that the incumbent Qing *amban* had connected Calcutta to the English, whom he hated and feared (Markham 1971, 275–276). *Pileng* leaders were assured that there would be no Qing reprisals, albeit in terms that made clear Qing claims to political supremacy. Moreover, Qing officials ignored the opium issue. Patna, Ahmed Ali's base, was in the heartland of British opium cultivation. His testimony recounted that the *Pileng* grew opium, and an earlier Qing commentator's description of that polity had noted that it traded by sea with Canton. By 1830 the maritime opium trade was a major problem for the Qing state, but no attempt made to determine how the *Pileng* might be linked to coastal problems.

Placing the Ahmed Ali case in the context of developments between 1820 and 1840 offers further support for the hypothesis that the Qing state studiously ignored evidence implicating Kashmiris in trends inimical to Qing security. In the early 1820s, less than a decade before the Ahmed Ali case broke, the Daoguang emperor was told that Hindustan was under English *(Yingjili)* control, that Kashmir "obeyed" *(tingcong)* the English, and that an Englishman in Ladakh had Kashmiris among his retinue *(QSL-DG* 33:463 [26.20b] 1/11/14; *Shiliao xunkan* 1963, 114). After 1840, due to events in the Opium War, it was acknowledged that the *Pileng* who had recruited Ahmed Ali were the same English *(Yingjili)* fighting on the coast (Mosca 2013, 260). Kashmiris were among those captured in China during that conflict *(QSL-DG:* 38:636 [369.9a]; 22/3/6). Around the same time, it was learned that Kashmiris were bringing opium to Yarkand *(QSL-DG:* 37:1182–1183 [329.31b-32a]; 19/12/23). When Dogra forces invaded western Tibet in 1841, Kashmiri leaders were found among their ranks during the ensuing conflict (Meng-bao 1992, 30 [1:52a]).

Officially, the Qing state only acknowledged that Kashmiri traders were connected to British India when the British themselves forced the issue, formally notifying the emperor that Kashmir had come into their possession during the first Anglo-Sikh War (1845–46). Daoguang's own inquiries confirmed this. Qing fears that Britons might now appear in Tibet wishing to trade provoked a very telling comment about the preference for a commercial *status quo:*

> If [the British] desire only trade, then Kulu belongs to them, and Ladakh has rendered them allegiance [*guifu*], so that hiding their traces among these groups they can trade as much as they like. Moreover, in Nearer and Further Tibet there are no fewer than one thousand Kashmiri Muslim [*Keshimi'er Huimin*] households, newly become their subjects, who have brought along their families and act as merchants. They come and go transporting merchandise, so [the British] have even less need to fear shortages [of goods]. Why is it necessary for [the British] to fix their wishes on making things manifest and conspicuous, and trade with Tibet directly [*dimian,* lit. "face to face"]? *(CBYWSM:416)*

In short, by 1847 the Qing state was explicitly willing to overlook the fact that Kashmiris were now subjects of the British, because the alternative seemed to be direct trade with Englishmen. It is at least possible that behind the minimal and relatively conciliatory response to the Ahmed Ali crisis in 1830 lay this sense that the *status quo* was preferable to any new order that might emerge.

Ahmed Ali's case reveals the chain of contact allowing information to flow across the Himalayas in the early nineteenth century. One end was anchored in India, where the Patna-based Ahmed Ali came into contact with Moorcroft and, through him, indirectly with the highest levels of the British Indian government. Even if Ahmed Ali's engagement with the British was exceptional, other Kashmiris aided Hodgson and Gardner in their researches. As an intelligence asset, Ahmed Ali's value lay in his network of contacts with long-term Kashmiri sojourners in Tibet, Ashraf and Abdullah. Given that his premises housed Fazl-ullah's brother, we can surmise that Ahmed Ali's firm also had ties to Tibet-born Kashmiris. Fazl-ullah was the human watershed in the flow of information between India and Qing Tibet, supplying information equally to Ahmed Ali's notebooks, and to the Qing agents tracking him down. Next in the chain was Ga-ma-er-zu, another Tibet-born Kashmiri, but one whose family enjoyed a closer relationship to the Qing state dating back almost four decades. Ga-ma-er-zu in turn was sought out for assistance by the mid-ranking Green Standard officer Li Guo'an. Although Thomas Manning had found during his 1811–12 stay in Tibet that many of its Han Chinese residents, including Green Standard troops, were Sichuanese Muslims, this was apparently not the case with Li Guo'an (Markham 1971, 242n2).[15] Rather, Li's tie to Ga-ma-er-zu was that of shared political allegiance. From Li Guo'an, intelligence passed up the chain of command to the *ambans,* and then to emperor.

In other words, between the pinnacles of power in Calcutta and Lhasa lay a chain of men linked variously by ties of kinship, community solidarity, and commerce—but also divided by nuanced calculations of their self-interest vis-à-vis two imperial structures. In this sense, they reflect the fine shadings of identity that emerge, as Charles Wheeler has shown in the case of the Minh Huong, when mutable group identities encounter the complex political and commercial terrain between competing polities. The Qing state was just as capable as British India of finding Kashmiri informants along this chain. Its counter-espionage was thorough: Ahmed Ali was discovered and arrested, his Persian notes and correspondence recovered and translated, and the frontier tightened. However rigidly these rules were enforced thereafter, it seems that heightened Qing surveillance of the Kashmiri community was effective. In 1846, Huc and Gabet found the community's leader gravely concerned that their presence would inflame Qing suspicions about espionage in Tibet. Although in later decades British India did succeed in sending agents to Lhasa in the guise of merchants, this proved remarkably difficult.

Kashmiri merchants gave the Qing state a grip on a powerful intelligence mechanism, but one it employed only for internal and frontier security, without turning it back toward India to investigate the *Pileng* or the political circumstances of *Rgya-gar* and Kashmir. This returns us to the ambiguous issue of how Qing rulers and officials scrutinized the origin of foreign merchants in the context of frontier politics. In regard to Kashmiris we can draw a spectrum extending from 1721, when the Qing state acknowledged their presence without attributing it any political significance, to 1847, when it was decided to quietly accept that Kashmiris had entered the British Indian orbit. This chapter has argued for placing the Ahmed Ali case of 1830 closer to the latter end of the spectrum, with the Qing emperor and his officials probably suspecting Kashmiri ties to a hostile Western power but not wishing to undermine established frontier trade. If they did indeed opt for calculated ignorance, the reasons are not hard to find. Khoqand's invasion of 1830 made clear the dangers and futility of trying to embargo trade to exert pressure on a troublesome foreign country. Militarily, the Qing was weaker in Tibet than in Xinjiang, and the terrain was more challenging. If vigorous measures seemed inexpedient, it was politically easier to bury the issue than excavate it. Whether the Qing state cared where foreign merchants came from varied across time and space, depending on its strategic calculations of regional political circumstances.

Notes

1. At present the only published Qing document on this case is an extract from an imperial edict, dated DG10/11/12 (Dec. 26, 1830), copied into the dynastic Veritable Records (*QSG-DG, juan* 179). The First Historical Archives holds a full report memorialized by the *amban* Hui-xian, dated DG10/10/7 (Nov. 21, 1830), together with depositions (by Ahmed Ali, his brother Ashraf Ali, his agent Abdullah, his subsequent agent Fazl-ullah, a Kashmiri community leader named Jia-ma-po-da, and a witness named Ga-ma-er-zu) and a Chinese draft of the letter sent to British India. A second memorial of November 21 and a further report by Hui-xian and his colleague Xing-ke of DG11/2/16 (Mar. 29, 1831) are also held in that archive. In addition, the Grand Secretariat archive of the Institute of History and Philology, Academia Sinica, Taiwan, holds related correspondence from the Board of Personnel (DG/10/11/16, Dec. 30, 1830). Unless otherwise noted, "IOR" in parenthetical notes refers to India Office Record F/4/1384/55154. In citations, Ahmed Ali will be abbreviated A.A., the governor-general as G.G.

2. According to the Jesuit Antoine Gaubil, in June 1729, men from Kashmir had given news of Persian affairs to the emperor's brother Yin-xiang (1970, 237). Just under half a century later, George Bogle met in Tibet a Kashmiri who claimed to have traveled to Beijing via Khams, Yunnan, and Canton (and even to have met the emperor!) (Lamb 2002, 294).

3. Here *baibu,* "white cloth," is probably a corruption of *Balebu,* the term for Nepal and Newari merchants.

4. According to Fletcher (1978), however, in Xinjiang "Kashmiri" was a generic term for traders arriving from the south and southwest (84).

5. In Qing sources, Nearer Tibet [Ch. *Qian-Zang*] refers to the *Dbus* region centered on Lhasa, while Further Tibet [Ch. *Hou-Zang*] refers to *Gtsang,* centered on Shigatse and Tashilhunpo.

6. Qing reports state that Ahmed Ali was forty *sui* (approximately thirty-nine Western years of age) in 1830, thus twenty-three years old in 1814 (LFZZ 592:8).

7. In 1812 Moorcroft sent Mir Izzet-ullah, confidential Persian secretary at the British Residency in Delhi, to Bukhara (Alder, 287–288); in 1815 he found a "Fugeer" willing to enter Tibet and obtain samples of its script (BL:APAC:F/4/552/13386); later he facilitated the Tibetan studies of the Hungarian scholar Sándor Kőrösi Csoma (Alder).

8. Although in his first petition to the governor-general Ahmed Ali described both Ashraf Ali and Abdullah as his "brothers," Qing documents refer only to Ashraf as his younger brother, and Abdullah as an elderly agent hired by his father, Khwaja Muhammad Ali (Ch., Hua-zha Mo-ha-mai-de A-li).

9. This account synthesizes material from LFZZ: 592:7–9 with the depositions of Ahmed Ali, Ashraf Ali, and Abdullah.

10. Hodgson himself communicated to the Asiatic Society in Calcutta data from "Amír, a Cashmíro-Bhotiah [Tibetan] by birth" and interpreter to traders (*Asiatic Researches,* Vol. 17, 1832).

11. Ahmed Ali claimed that Ashraf, Abdullah, and Fazl-ullah "stole" his papers and gave them to Qing authorities. First sending them to Further Tibet might indicate an attempt to blackmail him.

12. IOR: Note by Swinton, July 22, 1831; Summary of the Correspondence in the Secret Department in 1816/17 Relative to Khajeh Ahmed Alli.

13. IOR: Smith to Swinton, July 25, 1831; Translation of a letter from the Chinese Authorities on the Frontier of Lepcha, through the medium of a Persian Translation which accompanied the original (dated DG11/3/30 = May 11, 1831; July 25, 1831 in English version), Prinsep to Ko Tarin (i.e. Hui-xian) and Shin Tarin (i.e. Xing-ke).

14. BL:APAC:F/4/1384/55154:Urzee of Khaja Ahmed Alli, Aug. 21 1830. "Khetta" is elsewhere called the "Durbar of the Tarun at Khetta," Tarun indicating *daren,* Qing *ambans.*

15. Li Guo'an, as Ly-Kouo-Ngan "Le Pacificateur des royaumes," was the officer charged with escorting the French missionaries Huc and Gabet from Tibet in 1846. They explained that he believed "ni aux Bonzes, ni aux Lamas . . . toute sa religion consistait en une fervente dévotion pour la Grand-Ourse" (Huc 1927, 239–240).

References

Alder, G. 1985. *Beyond Bokhara: The Life of William Moorcroft, Asian Explorer and Veterinary Surgeon, 1767–1825*. London: Century Publishing.

Boulnois, L. 2003. "Gold, Wool and Musk: Trade in Lhasa in the Seventeenth Century," in *Lhasa in the Seventeenth Century: The Capital of the Dalai Lama*, ed. Françoise Pommaret, 133–156. Leiden: Brill.

Bray, J. 2011. "Trader, Middleman or Spy? The Dilemmas of a Kashmiri Muslim in Early Nineteenth-Century Tibet. " In *Islam and Tibet: Interactions along the Musk Routes*. Farnham: Ashgate.

Chen Kesheng 陳克繩. 1969. *Xiyu yiwen* 西域遺聞. Taibei: Huawen shuju.

CSX (*Chongxiu Suzhou xinzhi*). 1967. 重修肅州新志. Taibei: Taiwan xuesheng shuju.

Das, S. C. 2000. *A Tibetan-English Dictionary*. New Delhi: Adarsh Books.

FDYZ (*Fuyuan dajiangjun Yun-ti zougao*). 1991. 撫遠大將軍允禵奏稿. Beijing: Quanguo tushuguan wenxian suowei fuzhi zhongxin.

Fletcher, Joseph. 1978. "Ch'ing Inner Asia *c.* 1800," in *The Cambridge History of China*, vol. 10, Late Ch'ing, 1800- 1911, Part I (Cambridge: Cambridge University Press, 1978): 35–106.

Gaborieau, M. 1970. *Récit d'un voyageur Musulman au Tibet*. Paris: Librairie C. Klincksieck.

Gaubil, A. 1970. *Correspondance de Pékin, 1722–1759*. Geneva: Droz.

He-ning 和寧. 2002. *Xizang fu* 西藏賦. In *Zhongguo shaoshu minzu guji jicheng (Hanwen ban)* 中國少數民族古籍集成 (漢文版). Chengdu: Sichuan minzu chubanshe.

Huc, R. P. 1927. *Souvenirs d'un Voyage dans la Tartarie, le Thibet et la Chine*. Paris: Librairie Plon.

IOR (British Library, India Office Records). Board of Control F/4/1384/55154.

Jäschke, H. 1998. *A Tibetan-English Dictionary*. Delhi: Motilal Banarsidass.

Jiao Yingqi. 1968. 焦應旂, *Xizang zhi* 西藏誌. Taibei: Chengwen chubanshe.

Lamb, A., ed. 2002. *Bhutan and Tibet: The Travels of George Bogle and Alexander Hamilton, 1774–1777*. Hertingfordbury: Roxford Books.

LFZZ (Junjichu Lufu zouzhe). 軍機處錄副奏摺, First Historical Archives. Beijing.

Markham, C. R., ed. 1971. *Narratives of the Mission of George Bogle to Tibet and of the Journey of Thomas Manning to Lhasa*. New Delhi: Manjusri Publishing House.

Meng-bao 孟保. 1992. *Xizang zoushu* 西藏奏疏. Beijing: Quanguo tushuguan wenxian suowei fuzhi zhongxin.

Moorcroft, W. 2005. *Travels in the Himalayan Provinces of Hindustan and the Panjab; in Ladakh and Kashmir; in Peshawar, Kabul, Kunduz, and Bokhara; from 1819 to 1825*. New Delhi: Munshiram Manoharlal.

Mosca, M. W. 2013. *From Frontier Policy to Foreign Policy: The Question of India and the Transformation of Geopolitics in Qing China*. Stanford, CA: Stanford University Press.

Na-yan-cheng 那彥成. 1995. *Na Wenyi gong zouyi* 那文毅公奏議 , in *Xuxiu Siku quanshu*, vol. 495. Shanghai: Shanghai guji chubanshe.

Newby, L. J. 2005. *The Empire and the Khanate: A Political History of Qing Relations with Khoqand c. 1760–1860*. Leiden: Brill.

Pemble, J. 1971. *The Invasion of Nepal: John Company at War*. Oxford: Clarendon.

QBJ (*Qinding Balebu jilue*). 1992. 欽定巴勒布紀略. Beijing: Quanguo tushuguan wenxian suowei fuzhi zhongxin.

Qi-shi-yi 七十一. 2001. *Xiyu wenjian lu* 西域聞見錄, in *Qing chaoben Lin Zexu deng xibu jixing sanzhong* 清抄本林則徐等西部紀行三種. Beijing: Quanguo tushuguan wenxian suowei fuzhi zhongxin.

QKJ (*Qinding Kuo'erka jilue*). 1992. 欽定廓爾喀紀略. Beijing: Quanguo tushuguan wenxian suowei fuzhi zhongxin.

QSL-DG (*Qing shilu*). 1985. 清實錄 Daoguang reign. Beijing: Zhonghua shuju.

Shiliao xunkan. 1963. 史料旬刊. Taibei: Guofeng chubanshe.

Song-yun 松筠. 1992. *Xizhao tulue* 西招圖略. Beijing: Quanguo tushuguan wenxian suowei fuzhi zhongxin.

WZTZ (*Wei-Zang tongzhi*). 1995. 衛藏通志. In *Xuxiu Siku quanshu*, vol. 683. Shanghai: Shanghai guji chubanshe.

XFX (*Xining fu xinzhi*). 1998.西寧府新志. Xining: Qinghai renmin chubanshe.

Xiao Jinsong 蕭金松. 1996. *Qingdai zhu-Zang dachen* 清代駐藏大臣. Taibei: Meng Zang weiyuanhui.

Zhang Hai 張海. 1968. *Xizang jishu* 西藏紀述. Taibei: Chengwen chubanshe.

Zhou, Ailian 周藹聯. 2006. *Xizang jiyou* 西藏紀游. Beijing: Zhongguo Zangxue chubanshe.

8

Circulations via Tangyan, a Town in the Northern Shan State of Burma

WEN-CHIN CHANG

Tangyang (當陽)[1] is located in a valley. The place was very poisonous, full of miasma in the past. The word "yan" means gunpowder in Burmese. There used to be a saying among the Chinese in nearby places: "Before going down to Tangyang, you should marry off your wife to another man."[2] (Ma Zineng,[3] September 9, 2011)

This chapter investigates the politico-economic history of Tangyan,[4] a valley town in the northern Shan State of Burma (or now Myanmar), from the 1950s to 1980s, the Cold War era. This place, formerly regarded as a poisonous location, was originally composed of a few Shan villages. In contrast to capitals, port cities, or border entrepots, which have easy access to the central state or the outside world beyond national boundaries, Tangyan is situated in a mountainous region, still distant from the border to its east and north. Although the Salween River flows by to the east of the town, its course is flanked by high mountains on both sides and renders very few sites suitable for ferries. Moreover, the currents are too rapid to be navigable. Despite these negative factors, since the early 1950s Tangyan's population rapidly increased following influxes of Yunnanese refugees, composed of Han and Muslims.[5] Soon it became a lively, animated town and an important node for circulations of people, commodities, capital, and information within a vast area covering southwestern China, Shan State of Burma, northern Thailand and even reaching nations beyond mainland Southeast Asia. More distinctively, from the mid 1960s to 1973, during the period of the Burmese socialist regime (1962–1988) when the government strictly implemented a controlled economy and carried out a series of economic

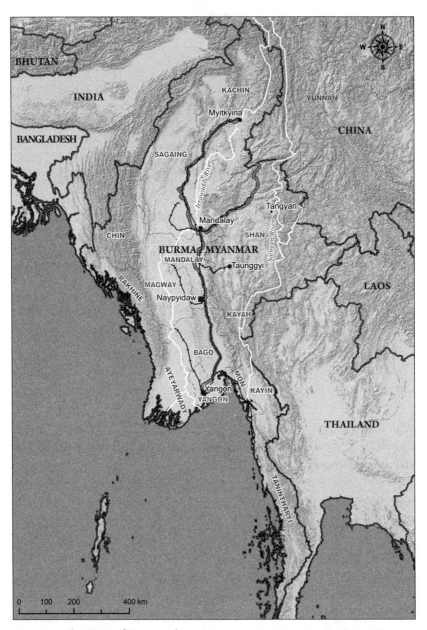

Tangyan in Shan State of Burma and its terrain. (Courtesy of the Center for Geographic Information Science, RCHSS, Academia Sinica)

measures to nationalize trade and industry, Tangyan evolved to be the hub of the black market *(hmaung-kho)* economy in upper Burma. Enormous amounts of opium and silver were transported illegally from Tangyan to Thailand by mule trains in exchange for huge quantities of consumer goods and gold bars, which were smuggled back to Tangyan and further transported to other places. How did this development take place? What is its significance to our understanding of "place" or "geography" in connection with human mobility, economic life, and political activities?

In a paper reflecting on grassroots globalization, Appadurai advocates that academics "make a decisive shift away from what we call 'trait' geographies to what we could call 'process' geographies" (2000, 6–7). The former type coincides with the conventional perception of seeing "areas" as fixed geographies that possess enduring properties. In contrast, the latter type denotes areas with shifting boundaries tied to various forms of human activities, including "trade, travel, pilgrimage, warfare, proselytisation, colonization, exile, and the like" (ibid., 7). Under this new perspective, "places" or "geographies" are no longer immobile or sedentary, but have social lives that can be extended over time and space following the course of human interactions and movements. In close relation with this thinking, Markovits, Pouchepadass, and Subrahmanyam (2003) use the concept of circulation for analysis of the itinerant cultures in South Asia under colonial rule. According to them, "Circulation is different from simple mobility, inasmuch as it implies a double movement of going forth and coming back, which can be repeated indefinitely" (2–3); moreover, circulation refers to "more than the movement to and fro of men and goods. . . . Apart from men and goods, many other items circulate in a society (and between a given society and other societies): information, knowledge, ideas, techniques, skills, cultural productions (texts, songs), religious practices, even gods" (2). In practice, this reciprocal circulation goes beyond two fixed destinations to encompass other potential trading hubs that may also transform and expand.

Drawing on the interpretations of "process geography" and "circulation," this chapter attempts to explore a dynamic social history of Tangyan by looking into its ethno-political and economic landscapes.[6] The bulk of data is derived from interviews with informants of Tangyan who are now located in Burma (Tangyan and other places), Thailand and Taiwan, in addition to limited written materials. While unfolding their peripatetic travels and affiliation

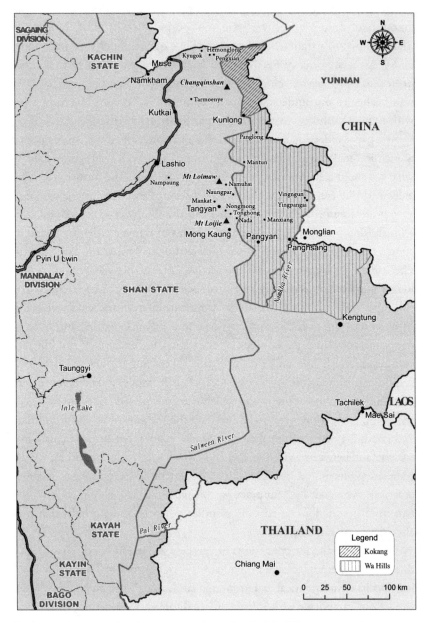

Tangyan and connected trading posts nearby and in the Wa Hills. (Courtesy of the Center
for Geographic Information Science, RCHSS, Academia Sinica)

with multiple armed groups, informants' stories reconstructed Tangyan as a place replete with endless tensions and competition, characterized by continuous circulations of a wide range of objects. Through these circulations, Tangyan was tied in with different tiers of markets extending from its environs to the Wa Hills[7] in northeastern Shan State, as well as to northern Thailand and other far-flung places and nations.

Tangyan's Ethno-Political Landscape

There are very few written materials on Tangyan. The earliest one I have been able to locate is from J. G. Scott's *Gazetteer of Upper Burma and the Shan State* (1901) (the *Gazetteer* hereafter) which gives brief information about its demography, politics, trade and agriculture. According to the *Gazetteer* (215–216), the whole administrative circle of Tangyan covered a central headquarters and an outlying terrain, with an area of six hundred square miles, inhabited by a population of 7,962, primarily Shan and secondarily Palaung (Benglong). Rice was the main agricultural produce for export. In addition, Tangyan traded opium from the Wa Hills and English goods from Mandalay. It also says the region was frequently ravaged by wars, but no further information was given. With regard to the headquarters of Tangyan (the center for economic activities and migration flows in later days), the *Gazetteer* gives the following details:

> [Central] Tang Yan is really composed of three villages, namely: (1) *Wying*[8] Tang Yan (the *Myoza's* [Chief's] village); (2) Tang Yan, Man Kyawng (or monastery village); (3) Tang Yan, Man Kat (or bazaar village), containing in 1897 thirty-one, ten, and twenty-four houses respectively, or a total of sixty-five houses with a gross population of one hundred and fifteen males, one hundred and forty-seven females, seventy-eight boys, and one hundred and twenty-two girls. It possessed one hundred and sixty-four buffaloes, three hundred and seven cows, fifty-three bullocks and forty-seven ponies, and worked eighty-two acres of lowying [sic] paddy-land and one hundred and eighty acres of hill paddy.[9]
>
> *Wying* Tang Yan was built by the present *myoza,* the old town being one-and-a half miles due north on the site now occupied by the village of *Wying* Lao, where the ruins of an old pagoda and signs of the old monastery are still to be seen. The old town is said to have been of great antiquity and to

have contained two hundred houses. It was deserted owing to the outbreak of an epidemic.

[Central] Tang Yan is situated in the middle of a long stretch of rolling downs and is watered by the Nam Hawng and other tributaries of the Nam Pang. The monastery is a large rambling building with a group of pagodas and a *wat* [temple].

The present incumbent has been *myoza* since 1224 B.E. (1862). The office is hereditary.

Hare are plentiful and wild ducks are to be seen in large numbers in the cold weather. (216)

Accordingly, central Tangyan (or Tangyan town) was still fairly rural and small at the end of the nineteenth century. Although it was a fortified site with a political structure sustained by a hereditary chieftainship,[10] the place was plagued by repeated battles and epidemics that obstructed its development. The town did not gain its fame until the influxes of Yunnanese refugees from the 1950s onward that spurred an economic boom as well as political struggles. Today the whole administrative circle of Tangyan is a township of Lashio District in Shan State. Its area is 1,818.84 acres, with a population of 230,000, composed of Shan, Wa, ethnic Chinese, Palaung, Burmese, and Indians. The Shan are the majority. The ethnic Chinese are concentrated in the central town; the Han account for around 700 households or 6,000 people and the Hui around 160 households or 800 people. The Indians constitute about 200 households or 1,000 people.[11]

Yunnanese Traders in Tangyan

Historically, Yunnanese undertook the long-distance trade via mule caravans back and forth between Yunnan, Burma and other upland Southeast Asian countries. Their role as economic intermediaries in this wide stretch of area has long been recognized (Chen 1992; Chiranan 1990; Fletcher 1927; Forbes 1987; Giersch 2006; Hill 1998; Sun 2000; Wang and Zhang 1993; Yang 2008). Drawn from the Ming (1368–1644) sources, Sun points out three main trading routes leading from Tengchong (a border town in southwestern Yunnan) to Burma's Mogaung, Ava and Pegu respectively (2000, 188). Forbes (1987, 45) and Hill (1998, 39) refer to another important economic route in history, which connected Yunnan's Simao to northern Thailand via Burma's Kengtung. These trading channels did not include one that passed through

Tangyan. In other words, Tangyan was not an economic node frequented by long-distance traders from Yunnan, possibly because of its uninhabitable condition as reflected in a Chinese saying quoted at the beginning of this essay, or because of both wars and epidemics referred to in the *Gazetteer*. However, this area was not completely devoid of Yunnanese trading activities. A few elderly informants pointed out that before 1950 some Yunnanese traders had already lived in nearby places, such as Tonghong, Namuhsi and Mong Kaung. (See the map of Tangyan and the connected trading posts on page 246.) These places were on a higher elevation and more suitable for living than Tangyan, which was located in a miasma-filled valley. Moreover, some informants stressed that their fathers or grandfathers had ventured to the Wa Hills during the 1940s. These traders acted as economic middlemen by selling consumer goods from the lowland (such as salt, sugar, salted fish, needles and clothes) to the indigenous people and purchased highland products (including opium, herbs and animal hides) to take back to Yunnan.

Despite its unsuitable living conditions, a small number of Yunnanese merchants arrived in central Tangyan to conduct business prior to the Second World War, according to another written source by Zhao Xian (1976), a Yunnanese resident of Tangyan for several decades. Zhao refers to the return of more than ten Yunnanese households from Yunnan to central Tangyan to reconstruct their businesses after the Second World War. (During the war, a large number of ethnic Chinese in Burma were compelled to flee the country because of the Japanese occupation. Most Yunnanese immigrants in upper Burma went back to Yunnan.) Zhao Xian calls these people the vanguards of Tangyan's development. They founded the first Chinese association and Chinese school, and also built a Guanyin temple, which conducted five major religious ceremonies each year. The establishment of these cultural facilities helped them transfer their original lifestyle to this place of immigration. In addition, a few hundred fellow traders plied between Yunnan and Burma via Tangyan in the wake of the war (ibid., 61-62).

After 1949 Tangyan's population expeditiously expanded, as waves of Yunnanese refugees, primarily from Tengchong (騰衝), Longling (龍陵) and Mangshi (芒市), flowed in due to the communist takeover of China and a series of subsequent political movements (from the 1950s to the early 1970s). As a result, the demography of Tangyan township quickly increased to over 4,000 households in the early 1950s (ibid., 62),[12] and the Yunnanese Han became the primary ethnic group in central Tangyan. Many original

Shan residents sold their land to the Yunnanese and moved to the outlying areas. While some of the refugees managed to establish an economic niche here, others continued to move onward to other places in Shan State or to Thailand.

Zhao Jiatong escaped from Tengchong to Namkham in 1957 at the age of fifteen, moved to Tangyan town the following year, and stayed there until 1963.[13] He said that while he was in Tangyan town the ethnic Chinese accounted for around 80 percent of the total population; among them the Han constituted three-fourths and the Hui (also known as Panthay in Burma) one-fourth. In addition, the Shan accounted for about 15 percent, Indians 3 percent, and the Burman and Wa about 2 percent. The Indians were businessmen like the Chinese. Most of the indigenous Shan were farmers and a small portion of them were petty traders in local markets. The Wa were from chiefs' families, moving from the Wa Hills. The Burmans were civil servants, soldiers, and their dependents. Except for the Shan, the other groups moved to Tangyan largely after 1950.

Without legal status, most Yunnanese refugees hid themselves in rural Shan or Kachin States when they first arrived in Burma. Although an underdeveloped place in a remote area, Tangyan was connected with several border villages, towns and cities to its north, such as Namkham, Muse, Kutkai, Lashio, Kyugok, Hemonglong, Pengxian, Tarmoenye, Kunlong and Panglong, and also with Mong Kaung to its south, and Pangyan and Panghsang (or Pansam, now Pangkang) to its east. (See the map of Tangyan and the connected trading posts on page 246. Mong Kaung and Panghsang linked further southward to Thailand.) These characteristics combined fortuitously to bring waves of Yunnanese refugees to Tangyan. In Zhao Jiatong's case, his maternal uncle arrived in Tangyan in the early 1950s. On receiving a letter from Zhao Jiatong in 1958 about his escape to Namkham, this uncle went to Namkham to take him to Tangyan via Tarmoenye and Mt. Loimaw (Chang 2014). About half a year later, Zhao Jiatong's mother and a brother also fled to Namkham. Zhao Jiatong then went to Namkham to take them to Tangyan. Several other informants narrated similar experiences. They said that it was difficult for all family members to flee together. Many of those who ran away first helped other members who came out later. They described such continuous relocations of different members as *yige la yige* (one pulling another—一個拉一個). As a result, Tangyan turned into a primary haven for receiving Yunnanese refugees.

Drawing on their economic penchant, many of them engaged in trade and quickly developed central Tangyan into a vibrant town.

While as outstanding as the Han in economic engagement, the Hui were distinctive from the Han in their Islamic practice. According to informants, over 60 percent of the Yunnanese Muslims in Tangyan have a Panglong background. Panglong is a village located in the northern Wa Hills which formerly played an important role in the immigration history of Yunnanese Muslims in Burma.[14] Many Yunnanese Hui escaped from Yunnan in the wake of the failure of the Muslim Rebellion (1856–1873) (Atwill 2006; Huang 1976; Yang Zhaojun et al. 1994) and arrived in Panglong. The earliest arrivals sought permission for resettlement from a local Wa chief and made the place a sanctuary for fellow Muslims. Consequently, more and more Yunnanese Hui arrived in Panglong. They were later known as Panglong Muslims or Panglong Hui.[15] Unfortunately, the Panglong Hui were pushed out of the area because of a series of wars from the 1920s to 1940s. A majority came to Tangyan in the early 1950s and built the first mosque there in 1954, which was also used by the Indian Muslims. After the communist takeover, the Panglong Hui were joined by fellow Muslims from Yunnan. The later arrivals built two other smaller mosques. Together, the Hui community organized classes that taught Arabic and Islamic studies, which provided young Yunnanese Muslims a chance to pursue further Islamic education in other places inside Burma (such as Mogok, Meiktila, and Yangon) or abroad (including Egypt, Turkey, Saudi Arabia, and Syria). Some of these graduates went to Taiwan and Singapore to train as religious specialists.

The KMT Guerrillas

Among the Yunnanese refugees to Shan State, there were stragglers from the Chinese Nationalist (Kuomintang or KMT) army and local self-defense guards. Some of these warrior refugees rallied together and organized themselves into guerrilla forces in 1950. Renewing their connection with the Nationalist government in Taiwan, they procured official recognition, material supplies, and training from military professionals who came from Taiwan to set up instructional programs. They also sought assistance from the United States, as it led anti-communist efforts during the Cold War and considered these KMT troops useful for prevention of the Chinese communist penetration to Burma and Thailand.

The convergence of Yunnanese refugees in Tangyan and their economic undertakings were closely connected with the establishment of the KMT guerrillas, entrenched in posts widespread throughout Shan State (Chang 1999; Chao Tzang Yawnghwe 1990; Qin 2009; Republic of China 1964; Union of Burma 1953; Young 1970). While receiving supplies from Taiwan and the US, the KMT were also involved in the opium trade, a lucrative business that enhanced the army's financial resources as well as leaders' personal wealth. Areas neighboring Tangyan, especially Kokang (to Tangyan's north) and the Wa Hills, produced a high quantity and quality of opium. With its location, Tangyan turned out to be a major center for opium transaction and its shipment to Thailand by means of mule caravans. A large number of Yunnanese traders sought protection from the KMT troops for the trafficking of opium. According to Zhao Xian, the amount of opium traded in Tangyan reached more than 200 tons prior to the mid-1970s (1976, 62).[16]

However, under international pressure, these KMT guerrillas disbanded twice—in 1953–1954 and 1961.[17] Although after the second disbandment the KMT guerrillas officially ended, two remnant armies, the Third and the Fifth Armies, under the leadership of Li Wenhuan and Duan Xiwen, totaling about 4,600 troops, survived (Qin 2009, 276). The main portion of these two armies entered northern Thailand in the early 1960s with the tacit approval of the Thai government and continued drug trafficking between Burma and Thailand. The KMT armies controlled several trading routes from Tangyan to Thailand from 1961 to 1973 and were considered the largest drug traffickers in the area during this period. According to informants, both armies had a military post in Mt. Loijie, southeast of Tangyan (about half an hour by jeep from the town, or three hours on foot). Each was stationed with a few hundred troops and served as the starting node for its army's guarded caravans to set off to Thailand, and the last node for the caravans coming from Thailand. Prior to 1973 the KMT were the strongest political entities in Tangyan's surrounding area, but in 1973, the troops were compelled to retreat southward in Shan State, following intensifying confrontation among the Burmese army, the Communist Party of Burma (CPB) and numerous ethnic insurgent groups. With their troops aging, by the end of the 1970s both the KMT Third and Fifth Armies started to lose their power. They finally disbanded by the end of the 1980s.

Taiwanese Intelligence

In connection with the KMT forces, the Intelligence Department (under the Ministry of National Defense) in Taiwan began its espionage networks in Burma in the early 1950s. It created Division 1920, headquartered in Chiang Mai Province in the early 1960s, which supervised several posts in upper Burma, especially Shan and Kachin States. These posts had their own troops, in addition to intelligence members who were mostly recruited from Yunnanese refugees in Burma and a few who were dispatched from Taiwan. An informant in Taunggyi who worked for the Taiwanese intelligence in northern Shan State from the 1960s to 1970s said that the Taiwanese espionage network was composed of more than 3,000 people. However, in 1975 Thailand shifted its diplomacy from Taiwan to mainland China. The Taiwanese intelligence was compelled to disband its military wing in Burma in 1975, as the latter's required arms were shipped from northern Thailand (Qin 2009, 338). Yet, Taiwanese espionage in Burma continued and was concentrated in towns.

Teacher Yang, who worked for the Intelligence Department from 1984 to 1988 and now lives in a border town in northern Thailand, confided that he had a network of about 30 informers in Yunnan and Burma who provided useful materials, such as military documents and training programs. These informers also helped spread propaganda leaflets and instigated defections in Yunnan. Teacher Yang's salary from the Intelligence Department was about 200 US dollars a month, plus monetary rewards for collected materials. He said a military training manual which was printed within the previous three months was worth 3,000 US dollars, at half a year old it was worth 1,500 US dollars, and when a year had passed it had no monetary value. Intelligence materials were, therefore, treated as commodities and priced according to their production date. After collection, intelligence members delivered them to the headquarters in Chiang Mai, and they were sent back to Taiwan. While the Taiwan espionage networks of spies and informers may have looked impressive, conflicts among intelligence members and the KMT forces frequently occurred. Informants belonging to both groups in the past pointed out the intertwinement of intelligence, counter-intelligence, mutual surveillance, and false accusations. Notwithstanding these entanglements, the flow of personnel, information/commodities, and capital from one place to another and from one nation to another persisted. Connecting to Tangyan, there were

several intelligence bases including one in Mt. Loijie, one in Nampaung (one
hour by car from Tangyan) and one in Yingpan (or Yingpangai營盤街) (in
the Wa Hills, about six or seven days on foot from Tangyan).

Indigenous Ethnic Forces

Apart from the KMT troops and the intelligence unit from Taiwan, there were
several indigenous armed groups around Tangyan. Burma was (and still is) a
land with a long history of contesting external rule; it did not resolve its internal division and violence in the wake of its independence in 1948 (Callahan
2004; Charney 2009; Thant Myint-U 2006). Continued resistance against the
central state from different ethnic communities succeeded in creating confrontation between a series of local powers and the British colonial government and later Japanese rule. In 1962, General Ne Win ended the short-lived
parliamentary government (1948–1962) through a military coup. During
his reign (1962–1988), he implemented a socialist economy and employed a
ruthless military control, causing further deterioration in ethnic rifts (Lintner
1994; Smith 1993; Callahan 2004). The country was mired in an ongoing war
between the state army and ethnic insurgents.

Among the indigenous ethnic forces, Khun Sa's army was a major group in
northern Shan State. Khun Sa claimed to be a Shan from a *myoza* family in
Mt. Loimaw,[18] north of Tangyan, four hours by jeep or one and a half days on
foot. He established his army with a few hundred followers in 1960. According to informants, Li Wenhuan of the KMT Third Army supported him with
some weapons at the beginning. Most of Khun Sa's important cadres were
Yunnanese from the KMT armies. However, the relationship between Khun
Sa and the KMT tarnished later because of economic conflicts. They fought
many times over gaining control of trading routes, including the one in 1967
in Ban Khwan, a Laotian village across the Mekong River (Lintner 1994, 245;
McCoy 1991, 333–334) and a series of battles from 1984 to 1987 along the
northern Thai-Burmese border (Chang 2002, 143–144). Claiming to fight
for the independence of the Shan people in Burma, Khun Sa's troops lived on
the opium trade and by taxing traders who passed the territory he controlled,
which stretched from northern Shan State to the northern Thai border.[19]

Khun Sa had an office in Tangyan and also ran a Chinese school there for
a brief period. In 1962, he converted his army into a unit of the *Ka Kwe Ye*
(KKY) forces (Chen 1996, 136), which were auxiliary local defense troops

officially recognized by the Burmese government. According to informants, by collaborating with the Burmese army in fighting against ethnic insurgents and the communists, the KKY were rewarded by being allowed to purchase supplies cheaply from the Burmese government and also to conduct underground trade. However, like many other KKY units, Khun Sa's collaboration with the Burmese government was not stable. Anxious about Khun Sa's growing power in the region, the Burmese government caught him in 1969 and put him in a Yangon prison until 1974. During this period, Khun Sa's main cadre moved the army's stronghold to Ban Hin Taek, a border village in northern Thailand, but kept a base near Namuhsi (about one day's walk north of Tangyan) with about 1,000 soldiers stationed there in order to continue the opium trade. After Khun Sa's release, the army expanded quickly (ibid., 211). Khun Sa became the largest drug trafficker in Southeast Asia from the mid-1970s to the 1980s. Tangyan and its surrounding areas were under his influence despite the presence of Burmese troops there. While the latter from time to time took men from Tangyan (especially from the outlying areas) by force to be porters, the former recruited the people of Tangyan to be soldiers. The recruiting principle was that a family with two sons had to contribute one son to the army, and a family with three sons had to contribute two.[20]

According to Zhao Jiatong and other informants, from 1962 to 1973, aside from the KMT and Khun Sa's army, there were a few small KKY units around Tangyan, respectively led by Wu Chunfeng (based in Mt. Loijie), Chen Shaowu (based in Nongmong), Bo Lai Oo (based in Manxiang), Khun Wo (based in Mantun) and Maha Khong (based in Vingngun). (See the map of Tangyan and the connected trading posts on page 246.) The first two leaders were Yunnanese Han, the last three Wa. Some of these groups were in collaboration with the KMT during the 1950s (and later with the KMT Third and Fifth Armies); their leaders even went to Taiwan for military training (Lintner 1994, 208). In 1973, the Burmese government disbanded the KKY, on the one hand because of pressure from the US government who accused these ethnic militias of engaging in drug trafficking, and on the other because of their inability to fight the Communist Party of Burma. There were 23 KKY units in Burma, and only 19 of them accepted disarmament (Chen 1996, 193–194). Some of the KKY groups around Tangyan joined bigger ethnic forces, such as Khun Sa's or the CPB. In that area, Ma Zineng pointed out, all groups were sometimes friends and at other times enemies. They knew their own position and competence. When small conflicts occurred, such as disputes of toll payments, they normally settled them through negotiation. This was good for communal survival. However, when more serious contests erupted and negotiation failed, there would be wars.

The Communist Party of Burma

In the second half of the 1960s, the Communist Party of Burma (CPB) began to penetrate northern Shan State, giving rise to a series of wars among the CPB, the Burmese army, the KMT and local armed ethnic groups. In 1969, the CPB took control over Kokang, and in 1973, it entrenched its rule in the Wa Hills and established its headquarters in Panghsang, which is six to seven days on foot from Tangyan. The KMT armies were compelled to retreat from their posts in Mt. Loijie and other places in northern Shan State southward, thus losing its influence in the area. Khun Sa and the leader of another armed group, Luo Xianhan, became the strongest warlords in the drug trade in northern Shan State. (Luo was originally based in Kokang, but retreated to Lashio after the CPB penetrated Kokang.) Although the Burmese government was able to maintain Tangyan as a garrison town,[21] from the 1970s through 1980s many Tangyan people moved away to more stable places to avoid the chaotic political situation as well as coercive recruitment by various armed units. A large number of Yunnanese traders left for Lashio, Pyin U Lwin (Maymyo), Mandalay, Taunggyi, Kengtung and northern Thailand. But meanwhile, many Yunnanese traders in the Wa Hills crossed the Salween River and moved to Tangyan. Ma Zineng related the flight with his father in 1972 from Manxiang, a Wa village, located east of the Salween River (two and a half days on foot from Tangyan):

> I was trading in Manxiang when the communists were approaching. I had three mules and one horse, all loaded with opium. We left at night. My father was old and couldn't carry things. He walked with a stick. The horse was panting and couldn't catch up; in a few hours, it died. I had to remove most of its load to the other three mules. I myself carried two bags of opium, each weighing about six kilos. After crossing the Salween River, we had to climb up the mountain. We then encountered a group of Burmese soldiers who were also retreating. A Burmese officer was sitting in a vehicle. I went to plead with him to take us back to Tangyang. He asked how old I was. I told him 18. He asked again how many people were in our group. I said four. He then turned his head and told his subordinates at the back to make space for us. We put our loads on the truck. The officer asked me what

the loads contained. I said 'agricultural produce.' He didn't inquire further and ordered the driver to set off.

While there was no absolute line to distinguish friends from enemies among various political entities, the same situation existed between these entities and civilians. On the one hand, both the Burmese army and armed ethnic groups bullied the civilians, but on the other hand, civilians sometimes depended on them for protection or help, as Ma Zineng described here. This ambiguity mobilized people to move from one group to another, and also from one place to another or, even from one nation to another (e.g., Thailand or Taiwan). Moreover, the flow created circulation of other objects, including money, information, and goods as shown earlier. The next section on the economic landscape of Tangyan examines the role of economic activities that further contributed to these circulations.

Tangyan's Economic Landscape

> Apart from the trade of consumer goods in Tangyan's markets, the town was the hub for transactions of opium and gold bars. Traders converged here for these ventures. (Yang Kaizhi 2009, 253)

From the 1950s onward, the town of Tangyan turned out to be an economic center connecting to the northern frontier (adjacent to Yunnan), the Wa Hills to its east (joining Yunnan and also leading southward to Kengtung and then Thailand), Lashio to its northwest (linking southward to Mandalay), and Mong Kaung to the south (going further southward to Thailand). There were two major types of trade connecting to Tangyan town: the short-distance trade to its surrounding minority villages and the Wa Hills across the Salween River, and the long-distance trade back and forth between Burma and Thailand. Northern Shan State is a mountainous region. The land was barren. Local people grew opium during the dry season and corn and hill rice during the rainy season. Most consumer goods had to be imported from outside through mountain tracks by oxen carts, horses or mules, and Yunnanese traders were the primary middlemen engaging in this job. The needed commodities were brought in from Mandalay and Yunnan before 1949, but when the Sino-Burmese border trade came to a halt after the communist takeover in China, Tangyan became a transit node for the circulation of goods in demand

that were transported primarily from Mandalay. This supply line lasted until
the mid-1960s. In 1962 the Ne Win government implemented a socialist
economy that quickly brought down the nation's economy and resulted in a
shortage of consumer goods. Subsequently, supplies from Mandalay dwindled
and the black market economy in connection with the underground trade from
Burma's neighboring countries thrived to make up the shortage. According to
some estimations (Lintner 1988, 23; Mya Than 1996, 3), over 80 percent of
Burma's total consumption consisted of smuggled products, with Thailand
providing most of it. My informants estimate that before 1980 around 70
percent of these black market Thai goods were brought in through Shan State.
Well into the 1980s this was primarily carried out by long-distance mule
trains, until vehicle transportation gradually replaced them by mid-decade.

The Long-Distance Trade

The long-distance caravan trade between Thailand and Burma was dominated
by Yunnanese traders, which accounted for 70 to 80 percent of it.[22] Many big
merchants, primarily Yunnanese based in Kengtung and Chiang Mai, hired
agents to collect opium from indigenous farmers or shop owners in northern
Shan State. Apart from opium, silver coins were another type of commodity
sought by merchants. Zhao Jiatong, whose uncle ran a small shop in Yingpangai (in the Wa Hills) since the 1950s, described the purchase of opium and
silver coins by traders in the region:

> Many traders in the Wa region purchased opium for big traders from lo-
> cal farmers. The big traders paid some down payment to the smaller trad-
> ers in advance. And the smaller traders in turn also provided some ad-
> vance credit to the farmers. This is called *maiqiuyan* (買秋煙purchasing
> autumn-opium). After the harvest, the farmers had to sell their produce to
> these smaller traders at a lower price than the market price. . . . In addition,
> traders also bought silver coins from the Kawa [Wa]. At that time, the Kawa
> people still used old silver coins from China[23] and Indian rupees in trade.
> Four Yunnanese silver coins were exchanged for one Indian rupee, and one
> Indian rupee for three Burmese kyat. The Burmese kyat, issued by the U
> Nu government, had good value, but it was not widely circulated in the
> mountainous regions. Some places used Burmese kyat; other places still
> used silver coins. The silver coins brought to Thailand were melted for the
> reproduction of silverware.

After collection, merchants entrusted their commodities to ethnic forces for escort to Thailand. Many people in Tangyan and its vicinity raised mules and let them for conveyance. Mule trains set off from Mt. Loijie southward to northern Thailand or eastward through the Wa Hills and then southward to Thailand. An escorted convoy could be composed of a few hundred to over a thousand mules. Traders paid "taxes" to the armed groups for escort. The collection of taxes from traders was the major income for most armed forces, while the latter also engaged in the opium business. Traders hired porters to carry gold bars from Thailand for purchase of opium and/or for sale in Tangyan and nearby areas. Porters wore special jackets with many pockets that contained gold bars—one pocket for each bar. An elderly informant whom I met in the mid-1990s had participated in this practice. He said that one porter carried 32 gold bars; each weighed five *liang*.[24] Other informants said that the gold bought in Thailand or Laos was imported from France or Switzerland, and its purity was higher than Burmese gold, and thus had higher value. Merchants made good profits when selling smuggled gold brought from Thailand in Burma as it was not officially taxed. Part of the gold sold in Burma was further smuggled to India for sale. Ma Zineng said his father was a well-known middleman in gold transaction in Tangyan. Many traders entrusted their gold bars to Ma's father for sale. Local people even used Ma's father's name as a nickname for the gold bars he sold.

Thanks to the implementation of a socialist economy, central Tangyan thrived and became the hub of the black market economy in upper Burma from the mid-1960s to 1973. While opium was sold to Thailand, Thai consumer goods flowed into Burma.[25] The return mule caravans were loaded with Thai commodities, including textiles, medicine, yarn, monosodium glutamate (MSG), cigarettes, washing powders, radios, flip-flops and construction materials. They stopped at posts in Mt. Loijie. The goods were unloaded and transported in separate cargoes to central Tangyan secretly. After arriving in Tangyan, these commodities were further delivered to other redistribution nodes, such as Lashio, Mandalay, and Taunggyi. From these latter nodes, the merchandise went to different parts of the country. According to informants, informal taxes were paid to the Burmese authorities at check points for the circulation of this contraband.

After 1973, the hub of the black market economy shifted to Taunggyi because of socio-political intensification in northern Shan State. Many traders took other trading routes from northern Thailand that led to Taunggyi, the capital of Shan State. However, trading activities in Tangyan and other parts of northern Shan State were not terminated. Opium, silver, and gold remained the major commodities traded in Tangyan, and ethnic forces still lived on taxation from merchants. The following section on the short-distance trade will cover this topic.

Short-Distance Trade

Besides the long-distance trade, many Yunnanese traders from Tangyan took up trade in rotating markets (*zhuan gai/jie* 轉街).[26] The system of rotating markets may have started very early in southwestern China and upper mainland Southeast Asia.[27] Five markets in five clustered villages constituted a full rotating cycle. Each village took turns holding a market once every five days. For example, village A held a market on day 1, village B on day 2, and so on. This five-day cycle also became the local people's calendrical unit. Traders normally traded in two to three markets, depending on the distance from one market to another. (This system of rotating markets still exits in rural Shan State.)

A rotating market was always an animated venue that attracted different groups of people. While the Yunnanese traders predominated at rotating markets in terms of the quantity and value of traded commodities, the Shan and Wa traders were the majority. In addition, there were small numbers of Lisus, Luoheis, Palaungs and Kachins. Shan was the markets' lingua franca. About 80 percent of the traders were from indigenous ethnic groups. They primarily sold a few kinds of vegetables and pickled and/or cooked food in their resident markets. The Yunnanese, in contrast, traveled from one market to another and sold large amounts of rice, salt, oil, peanut candy and clothes. Most Indians conducted business in Tangyan, but a small number also took part in trading to other villages, mostly selling hardware.

The villages near central Tangyan which organized a rotating market included Naungpar (six hours northeast of Tangyan on foot), Nongmong (two hours east of Tangyan on foot), Tonghong (one hour east of Nongmong on foot), Loijie (three hours southeast of Tangyan on foot, or half an hour by car), Mankat (half an hour northwest of Tangyan by car), and Namuhsi (one day's walk north of Tangyan). (See the map of Tangyan and the connected trading posts on page 246.) Yunnanese traders from Tangyan transported their commodities by oxen carts in groups to nearby villages. Mrs. Ma, in her mid-sixties, used to travel with her husband to several places for trade:

We loaded traded commodities onto two oxen carts, each one pulled by two oxen. The traded goods included clothes, salt, rice and oil. We traveled with other traders; in total more than ten households' carts set off together. Today we went to Naungpar, tomorrow to Tonghong, and the day after tomorrow to Nongmong. Business was good. The clothes were made in Tangyang. A male jacket which we purchased for 100 kyat was sold for 110 kyat. The Shan and the hill people had to work on farms and had no time to make clothes. On the market day, they carried their bamboo baskets on their backs to buy needed goods: a bit of oil and a bit of rice, some popped rice and some peanut candy, etc. If their clothes were tattered, they bought clothes.

Among traded goods, informants repeatedly referred to popped rice (*chao-mihua* 炒米花) and peanut candy (*huashengtang* 花生糖). They said hill people ate much of both. According to Ma Zineng:

The choices of food were very limited in the mountains. The land was barren and couldn't grow much produce. Hill people ate a lot of peanut candy and popped rice, especially when they were traveling or working on farms. The peanut candy was made with sticky rice, red sugar from sugar-cane and peanuts. We first steamed the sticky rice, and then dried it under the sun. . . . Later we fried the dried sticky rice with sugar and rolled it out into a fine layer. Afterwards, we fried peanuts and mixed them with syrup made from red sugar. Finally, we poured the sugared peanuts onto the layer of sticky rice and cut the whole slab into smaller pieces. Traders kept peanut candies in zinc containers. A full container of peanut candies weighed 20 kilos; we call it *yi bong* [one bong]. Many Chinese traders made peanut candies; each one transported 20 to 30 *bong* for sale. The hill people bought a lot of peanut candies. When hungry, they ate a few pieces or mixed some popped rice with water in a bowl, which served as a simple meal.

Apart from trading in nearby markets, some Yunnanese traders went across the Salween River to the Wa Hills. The trails in the Wa Hills were narrower than the ones around Tangyan and could only be accessed by horses and mules and not by oxen carts. Some traders conducted business only in one fixed place by opening a small shop; others traveled to a few villages following a rotating-market schedule. Zhao Jiatong worked for his uncle who traded in Yingpangai during the dry season. Zhao and a couple of friends moved back and forth between Tangyan and Yingpangai for replenishment a few times a month (from 1958 to 1960):

My uncle only opened this shop during the dry season. Each year prior to the advent of the rainy season by the fourth month [of the lunar calendar], he returned to Tangyang, for it was too difficult to move around the mountain areas when it rained. His shop sold oil, salt, rice, clothes, textiles, shoes, needles, threads and other types of consumer goods. He had eight mules for conveyance. [I and the other two chaps] used to transport our goods with another trader's caravan, in total composed of about twenty mules. On the way, all the muleteers ate from the same pot of rice and shared tasks by division of labor. I was younger and assigned to wash dishes and help tend the mules with a few other muleteers.

Trade to the Wa Hills was interrupted for a few years after the CPB took control of the region, but by the mid-1970s, traders resumed their ventures. Both the Burmese army and the CPB acknowledged traders' activities despite the antagonistic relations of the two sides. Many Yunnanese traders from Tangyan traded to more than one place in the Wa Hills. Zhang Shiqing[28] conducted trade in the Wa Hills between 1976 and 1979; he gave detailed information about the trading routes and traded commodities:

I started to go to Panghsang to trade at the age of thirteen. There were no roads for vehicles in the Wa Hills; the trails only allowed humans, horses, and mules. We set off from Tangyang at eight or nine o'clock in the morning. We had to obtain a permit in advance for traveling to the Wa Hills from the Burmese army in Tangyang. The permit indicated the commodities we carried with us. Our group consisted of about twenty horses and mules, sometimes fourteen or fifteen, and seven or eight people. My father and I had three horses.[29] We walked eastward for four hours to Nada and stayed there for a night. The next day we walked downhill an hour and a half to the riverside. There was a checkpoint guarded by the Burmese army at the ferry. All the goods had to be unloaded and checked. It could take a long time. Afterwards, we put our goods on rafts and also took our mules onboard to cross the river. After reaching the other side, we climbed uphill for an hour and arrived at another Burmese checkpoint. All the carried stuff had to be cleared again. They were afraid that traders smuggled arms and ammunition to the CPB, but traded goods were allowed. We then walked for about one hour to a CPB base. A Wa village was next to the base. It took another three hours to walk from that Wa village to Manxiang. If the two Burmese checkpoints took too long, we had to stay the night in the Wa village and go to Manxiang the next day. There was only one route from Nada to Manxiang; you had to pass all these checkpoints. This route was for civilians and traders. The Burmese army and the CPB seldom fought on this route while I was in the caravan trade. You might call it a kind of mutual understanding. Normally it took about two and a half days to go from Tangyan to Manxiang on foot. There was a Buddhist temple in Manxiang where we could stay for a night. The monks were mostly Wa. The temple welcomed traders because they would make donations. From Manxiang we walked south-eastward . . . to Panghsang, a border town. From Tangyang to Panghsang, it took six to seven days on foot in total. Panghsang was a transit node for caravans from Thailand via Kengtung [south of Panghsang]. It took four or five days on foot from Panghsang to Kengtung. We sold our goods in Panghsang and three or four other villages [following the local rotating-market schedule]. Our commodities comprised MSG, cheroots, the red lime to put in betel nuts, salted fish, clothes, etc.

From Panghsang, we crossed the Namkha River to Monglian in Yunnan. There was a Chinese checkpoint which required our registration. We told them we were from the CPB area and the guards would let us pass. The shops in Monglian were all run by the government. We mostly bought thermos bottles and bicycles [in component parts]. We used Chinese money there, which was exchanged in Panghsang. People in Panghsang used silver coins from the colonial period, Burmese money and Chinese money. Back in Panghsang, we could buy goods from Thailand, such as western medicine, textiles and flip-flops. For those who had much capital, they could buy Swiss watches, such as Roamers and Juvenias. The Roamers were very good watches. They didn't get damaged even if you accidentally dropped them. After the purchases were made, we returned to Tangyang and sold our merchandise wholesale to shops there. We didn't have much capital and needed to sell the articles quickly in order to buy new stuff for our next trip. The Burmese guards didn't care what goods you brought in from the CPB area. We didn't need to pay tax to them but gave them one or two traded items. Round-trip to Panghsang took about one month.

Zhang Shiqing's narration illuminates the politico-economic situation in the region after the CPB took control of the Wa Hills. Despite the confrontation between the Burmese army and the CPB, economic activities continued, as both sides needed the flow of goods from Thailand and China. Lintner's description below complements Zhang Shiqing's information on the entry of Chinese goods:

> A bridge had been built from Panghsang, across the Nam Hka border river to the Chinese side, and supplies were transported daily into the CPB's

area: arms and ammunition, uniforms, radio transmitters, army jeeps, pet-
rol, military maps, and even rice, other foodstuffs, cooking oil and kitchen
utensils. (1994, 230)

The bulk of the goods brought from Tangyan to the Wa Hills were domestic
products, especially foodstuffs, but the return loads comprised Thai and Chinese
articles, as well as local produce, such as opium from the Wa Hills. In effect,
the Yunnanese traders' itinerant movement ensured the exchange and circulation
of these commodities from various sources. But while the Yunnanese acted as
the main economic force back and forth between Tangyan and the Wa Hills,
the Shan and Wa also exerted significant economic and political influence. Each
group's supplies and demands were connected with other groups' through nexuses of itinerant trade dominated by Yunnanese traders, which in effect composed
what Bhattacharya in his study on the peddlers and itinerants in northwestern
India (2003, 210) calls "complex structures of mutual dependence." This reciprocal interaction sustained the region's economic operation even under intensified
circumstances. When certain trading routes were closed off, alternative routes
would be opened up. For example, Zhang Shiqing pointed out that the route
from Nada to Manxiang was closed off for some time after 1985; traders then
took the route from Tangyan to Namuhsi that led eastward to the Wa Hills.

Northern Shan State was crisscrossed by numerous political entities during
the Cold War period. The KMT were active from the 1950s to the early 1970s.
The CPB was entrenched in the Wa Hills (and Kokang) until its disintegration
in 1989, and Khun Sa's army was in force until 1996. Intermittently, many
smaller armed groups rose and fell. Multiple alliances (even with the Burmese
army) and shifting of affiliations were common. Simply put, the geo-politics
and economics of Tangyan and its surrounding region were characterized by
mobilization of different ethnic groups and armed forces, both in the lowland and highland, intersecting with symbiotic as well as conflicting relations.
Meanwhile, circulations of people, information/ideas, capital and commodities persisted and in effect turned the area into a mobile politico-economic
zone or what Markovits et al. calls a "circulatory regime" (2003). Vis-à-vis
the political domination by multifarious powers, the organization of civilian movement in the form of oxen and horse/mule caravans for economic
engagement demonstrated resilience and dynamism. The itinerant travels of
the Yunnanese traders that highlighted their traditional function as economic

middlemen were especially distinctive. The complex interactions among different ethnic communities and political entities attested to the interplay of politics and trade in the region, a persistent phenomenon pointed out by several scholars studying Yunnan and upland Southeast Asia (e.g. Giersch 2006; Hill 1998; Sun 2000). Accordingly, the geopolitics and livelihood in this region cannot be simplified in dichotomy division of the lowland versus the highlands, or reduced to Scott's "Zomia" argument, which pictures the formation of highland societies as basically generated from avoidance of the lowland state governance (2009).

Seen from Appadurai's "process geography" and Markovits's "circulation," the political and economic interactions among heterogeneous groups in Tangyan and its neighboring areas have constantly crisscrossed ethnic and topographic boundaries.[30] Tangyan is definitely not a fixed geographical place, but more a living being subjected to ongoing transformations because of continuous flows of people and many kinds of objects. Its dynamics are tied to the area's topography, geo-politics and economic development that links other parts of northern Shan State as a whole to far-flung markets and political entities. In the course of circulation, human mobility is the most fundamental factor that mobilizes the flow of other objects. The itinerant travelling of Tangyan Yunnanese traders attests to this fact. In addition to economic trips, many Tangyan Yunnanese chose to leave Tangyan in order to escape repeated fighting. However, their outflow did not sever them from the place, but further stretched their Tangyan connections. There have been Tangyan Yunnanese enclaves in several places, including Lashio, Pyin U Lwin and Mandalay in Burma, Mae Sai and Chiang Mai in northern Thailand, and Xiandian and Zhongli in northern Taiwan. It is not uncommon that family members and relatives are dispersed in a range of places and even countries. Their interconnections are reinforced by means of remittances, mutual visits, electronic communication, and further migration or traveling for education, jobs, marriages or medical treatment.[31] As a result, the dispersal of Tangyan people, their webs of connections and access to resources have expanded the circulatory regime of Tangyan.

Notes

In writing this chapter I am particularly indebted to three major informants: Ma Zineng (馬自能), Zhang Shiqing (張世清) and Zhao Jiatong (趙家統). I would also like to thank Jacque Leider for interpretation of a few messages in the *Gazetteer of*

Upper Burma and the Shan State (1901), especially on the data of the populations in the headquarters of Tangyan and the administrative circle of Tangyan. I am also grateful to the Center for Geographic Information Science, Academia Sinica, for their help with producing the maps.

1. Ethnic Chinese commonly pronounce the place name as "Tangyang."

2. The saying in Chinese is: 要下當陽壩，先把老婆嫁 (*yaoxia dangyangba xian ba laopojia*).

3. Ma Zineng is Yunnanese Muslim, born in 1954 in Tangyan. He left Tangyan and moved to Pyin U Lwin in 1976, and then went to Japan in 1988 via Taiwan for eight years as an illegal guest worker. Since 1996, he and his family have been settled in Taiwan.

4. Tangyan is located on 22°29'N 98°24'E (Chinese Wikipedia, accessed September 19, 2011).

5. Yunnan is a multi-ethnic province in southwestern China. The Yunnanese traders referred to in this chapter are Yunnanese Han and Yunnanese Muslims (also known as Hui), commonly classified as Yunnanese Chinese.

6. Relevant to this chapter, Wheeler's chapter in this volume explores the human ecology of the Sino-Vietnamese littoral at the end of the eighteenth century that illuminates the shifting of social status/identities and political affiliation among merchants, expatriates and pirates along the course of human migrations between the coast of southern China, Taiwan and Vietnam.

7. The Wa Hills stretch from east of the Salween River to the border, south of Kokang and north of Kengtung (see the map of Tangyan and the connected trading posts on page 246), often referred to as the Kala mountains (*kala san* 卡拉山) by the Yunnanese. The height of the great hills reaches nearly 8,000 feet (Harvey 1957,126)

8. *Wying* (or *vieng* or *wiang*) is a Tai word, meaning a fortified place. Thanks to Jacques P. Leider for clarifying its meaning.

9. On page 215, the *Gazetteer* gives information on the population of the whole Tangyan administrative area—nearly 8,000 in 1897.

10. Chieftainship was a common political practice in Shan and other States in Burma before and during the British colonial period. It was, however, removed in 1959, as General Ne Win compelled all hereditary chiefs (*sawbwas* and *myozas*) of Burma to hand over their governing power and replaced them with appointed officers (Sai Kham Mong 2007).

11. The total spatial and demographic figures of Tangyan were provided by Hua-Wen Chinese School in Tangyan in November 2011. The principal obtained the information from the local Burmese government earlier that year. The population information of the Han was given by the Ethnic Chinese Association of Tangyan (*Tangyan huaqiao huzhuhui* 當陽華僑互助會), and that of the Hui and the Indians by Hui informants, also in November 2011. Among the ethnic Chinese, the Yunnanese Chinese are the overwhelming majority, accounting for about 99 percent; the remaining

1 percent are Guangdong and Fujian Chinese, whose predecessors came from southeastern China by sea and settled in lower Burma. This latter group, often referred to as maritime Chinese, moved to Tangyan for trading opportunities during the 1950s and 1960s; mostly opening shops or gambling houses. The Han population covers the Yunnanese Han and the Guangdong and Fujian Chinese. The focus subjects of this chapter are the Yunnanese, both Hans and Muslims.

12. Zhao's demographic figure does not specify whether it referred to Tangyan township or Tangyan town. But According to elderly informants, the town itself had a population of about a thousand households in the 1950s. Therefore, Zhao's figure should refer to the population of Tangyan township.

13. After leaving Tangyan, Zhao Jiatong was engaged in the trans-border trade between Burma and Thailand until the mid-1990s, but in 1980 he moved his family to Taiwan.

14. A Yunnanese Muslim scholar in Mandalay estimated that about 30 percent of Yunnanese Muslims in Burma today are descendants from Panglong.

15. For more information about the Panglong Hui, see Forbes (1986; 1988), Scott (1901, 740) and Yegar (1966).

16. Zhao possibly refers to the total amount of one seasonal transaction.

17. The initial number of KMT stragglers in early 1950 was around 2,900 (Republic of China Ministry of Defense 1964, 10, 11, 18). The forces quickly expanded to 16,068 soldiers in 1953 (ibid., illustration 6). However, compelled by a resolution from the United Nations in 1953 to drive out these foreign troops, the KMT government disbanded the KMT forces in Burma in 1953–1954 and evacuated 6,568 people back to Taiwan (Qin 2009, 168). The reorganization of KMT guerrillas soon took place in Shan State. In June 1960, the number of troops increased to 9,718 (Republic of China Ministry of Defense 1964, 91, 97, 229). After being defeated by the Burma army (in collaboration with troops from the People's Republic of China), the KMT forces had to conduct a second disbandment in 1961 when 4,409 people were evacuated to Taiwan (Qin 2009, 269). A portion of the evacuated in 1953–1954 and 1961 were civilians.

18. According to informants, Khun Sa's mother was Shan, but his patrilineal line was Han Chinese.

19. An informant who served in Khun Sa's taxing department from 1981 to 1989 pointed out that traders passing his sphere of power had to pay 25 percent of the transported commodities' value in cash or in-kind for tolls.

20. When the situation was more relaxed, the principle changed to a family with three sons having to contribute one son and those with five sons having to contribute two sons.

21. The Burmese military post was located near the entrant of central Tangyan to the west. An informant estimated its number of troops at 300 to 400 during the 1970s; another estimated them at around 1,000.

22. Elsewhere I have explored the organization of the long-distance caravan trade between Burma and Thailand during the socialist period: the trading routes, traded commodities and the socio-cultural meanings underlying this practice (Chang 2009).

23. The silver coins from China were Yuan Shikai dollars (*Yuan-da-tou* 袁大頭), issued by Yuan Shikai from 1914 to 1921.

24. One *liang* is about 37.5 grams.

25. Informants said that from the 1950s through the early 1960s traders took very small amounts of Thai merchandise back to Burma, as Burma was not short of consumer goods at that time. Many return mules to Burma thus carried an empty load.

26. Yunnanese pronounce it *zhuan gai* instead of *zhuan jie,* which is the Mandarin pronunciation.

27. There are records of it in the late-Ming *Xinanyi fengtuji* (You 1994, 366–367). Giersch suggests that it was originally a practice among the Tai (2006, 167).

28. He was born in Tangyan in1963, left for Thailand in 1979, and then moved to Taiwan in 1989.

29. Mules can carry more goods and walk longer distance than horses. The price for a mule is about three times of that for a horse.

30. I have not been able to research the aspect of socio-cultural interaction in Tangyan, but I have observed the spread of Chinese education to children of non-Chinese ethnic groups and frequent ritual ceremonies *(pwe)* which attracts onlookers of different ethnic communities. Whether there is systematic organization of ritual ceremonies based on Buddhism and local beliefs across ethnic boundaries requires further studies.

31. I have recorded cases of Tangyan Yunnanese going to Yangon, Chiang Mai or Taipei for medical care via the assistance of their family members, relatives or countrymen who have settled in these places. I have also met several Tangyan Yunnanese couples who got married in places of settlement via introduction or arrangement by family members or countrymen.

References

Appadurai, Arjun. 2000. "Grassroots Globalization and the Research Imagination." *Public Culture* 12 (1): 1–19.

Atwill, David G. 2006. *The Chinese Sultanate: Islam, Ethnicity, and the Panthay Rebellion in Southwest China, 1856–1873.* Stanford, CA: Stanford University Press.

Bhattacharya, Neeladri. 2003. "Predicaments of Mobility: Peddlers and Itinerants in Nineteenth-century Northwestern India." In *Society and Circulation: Mobile People and Itinerant Cultures in South Asia 1750–1950,* ed. Claude Markovits, Jacques Pouchepadass, and Sanjay Subrahmanyam, 163–215. Delhi: Permanent Black.

Callahan, Mary P. 2004. *Making Enemies: War and State Building in Burma.* Ithaca, NY: Cornell University Press.

Chang, Wen-Chin. 1999. "Beyond the Military: The Complex Migration and Reset-
    tlement of the KMT Yunnanese Chinese in Northern Thailand." Ph.D. disserta-
    tion, K. U. Leuven, Belgium.

———. 2002. "Identification of Leadership among the KMT Yunnanese Chinese in
    Northern Thailand." *Journal of Southeast Asian Studies*, 33(1): 123–146.

———. 2014. "By Sea and by Land: Stories of Two Chinese Traders." In *Burmese
    Lives: Ordinary Life Stories Under the Burmese Regime*, ed. Chang Wen-Chin and
    Eric Tagliacozzo. New York: Oxford University Press.

Chao Tzang Yawnghwe. 1990. *The Shan of Burma: Memories of a Shan Exile*. Singa-
    pore: Institute of Southeast Asian Studies.

Charney, Michael W. 2009. *A History of Modern Burma*. Cambridge: Cambridge Uni-
    versity Press.

Chen Ruxing. 1992. "Han Tang zhi Song Yuan shiji zai Miandian de Huaren" (Chi-
    nese in Burma during the Han, Tang, Song and Yuan periods). *Haiwai huaren
    yanjiu* 2: 41–57.

Chen Wen. 1996. *Kunsa jinsanjaio chuanqi* [Khun Sa: Stories of the Golden Triangle].
    Taipei: Yunchen wenhua.

Chiranan Prasertkul. 1990. "Yunnan Trade in the Nineteenth Century: Southwest
    China's Cross-Boundaries Functional System." Institute of Asian Studies, Chu-
    lalongkorn University, Asian Studies Monograph no. 044.

Fletcher, H. G., comp. 1927. *Tengyueh: Route Book of Travels in Neighbourhood, Hints
    for Travellers, Market Day Dates, and Notes on Yunnan Pronunciation, etc.* Shanghai:
    Statistical Department of the Inspectorate General of Customs.

Forbes, Andrew D. W. 1987. "The 'Cin-ho' (Yunnanese Chinese) Caravan Trade with
    North Thailand during the Late Nineteenth and Early Twentieth Centuries." *Jour-
    nal of Asian History* 21 (1): 1–47.

Giersch, C. Patterson. 2006. *Asian Borderlands: The Transformation of Qing China's
    Yunnan Frontier*. Cambridge, MA: Harvard University Press.

Hill, Ann Maxell. 1998. *Merchants and Migrants: Ethnicity and Trade among Yunnanese
    Chinese in Southeast Asia*. New Haven: Yale Southeast Asia Studies.

Huang Chia-Mu. 1976. *Dianxi huimin zhengquan de lianyin waijiao* [British Relations
    with the Panthay Regime of Western Yunnan 1868–1874].

Institute of Modern History, Monograph Series no. 37. Academia Sinica, Taipei.

Lintner, Bertil. 1994. *Burma in Revolt: Opium and Insurgency since 1948*. Bangkok:
    White Lotus.

Markovits, Claude, Jacques Pouchepadass, and Sanjay Subrahmanyam. 2003. "Intro-
    duction: Circulation and Society under Colonial Rule." In *Society and Circulation:
    Mobile People and Itinerant Cultures in South Asia 1750–1950*, ed. Claude Marko-
    vits, Jacques Pouchepadass, and Sanjay Subrahmanyam, 1–22. Delhi: Permanent
    Black.

Ma Zishang, et al. 2009. *Chamagudaoshang de chuanqi jiazu* (History of a family in the long-distance mule caravan trade). Li Xu, comp. Beijing: Zhonghua shuju.

McCoy, Alfred W. 1991. *The Politics of Heroin: CIA Complicity in the Global Drug Trade.* Brooklyn: Lawrence Hill Books.

Mya Than. 1996. *Myanmar's External Trade: An Overview in the Southeast Asian Context.* Singapore: ASEAN Economic Research Unit, Institute of Southeast Asian Studies.

Qin Yihui. 2009. *Jinsanjiao guojun xieleishi* (The Tragic History of the KMT Troops in the Golden Triangle, 1950–1981). Taipei: Zhongyang yanjiuyuan and Lianjing chubanshe.

Republic of China Ministry of Defense. 1964. *Dianmian bianqu youji zhanshi* (History of Guerrilla Wars in the Sino-Burmese Border Areas). 2 Vols. Taipei: Guofangbu shizheng bianyinju.

Sai Kham Mong. 2007. "The Shan in Myanmar." In *Myanmar: State, Society and Ethnicity,* ed. N. Ganesan and Kyaw Yin Hlaing, 256–277. Singapore: Institute of Southeast Asian Studies.

Scott, J. G. 1901. *Gazetteer of Upper Burma and the Shan States. Part II. Vol. III.* Assisted by J. P. Hardiman. Rangoon: Government Printing.

Scott, James C. 2009. *The Art of Not Being Governed: An Anarchist History of Upland Southeast Asia.* New Haven: Yale University Press.

Smith, Martin J. 1993 [1991]. *Burma: Insurgency and the Politics of Ethnicity.* London: Zed Books.

Sun, Laichen. 2000. "Ming-Southeast Asian Overland Interactions, 1368–1644." Ph. D. dissertation, The University of Michigan.

Thant Myint-U. 2006. *The River of Lost Footsteps: A Personal History of Burma.* New York: Farrar, Straus and Giroux.

Union of Burma, Ministry of Information. 1953. *The Kuomintang Aggression Against Burma.* Rangoon: Ministry of Information.

Wang Minda, and Zhang Xilu. 1993. *Mabang wenhua* (Culture of Caravan Trade). Kunming: Yunnan renmin chubanshe.

Yang Kaizhi. 2009. *Yang Kaizhi bashisui huiyilu* (Memoir of Yang Kaizhi's Life over 80 Years). Unpublished manuscript.

Yang Zhaojun et al., eds. 1994. *Yunnan huizushi* (History of the Yunnanese Muslims). Kunming: Yunnan renmin chubanshe.

Yang, Bin. 2008. *Between Winds and Clouds: The Making of Yunnan (Second Century BCE–Twentieth Century CE).* New York: Columbia University Press.

Young, Kenneth Ray. 1970. "Nationalist Chinese Troops in Burma: Obstacle in Burma's Foreign Relations, 1949–1961." Ph.D. dissertation, New York University.

Zhao Xian. 1976. "Mabang kaifa de Tangyan." (Mule Caravans Contribution to Tangyan's Development). *Yunnan wenxian* 6: 61–65.

9

Turning Space into Place

British India and the Invention of Iraq

PRIYA SATIA

This chapter is about the British invention of Iraq in the early twentieth century—or, more specifically, the trans-local, British and Indian invention of a place called Iraq, in the course of which the British articulated a new kind of developmentalist colonialism. Like Willem van Schendel's chapter in this volume, this is a story about how colonialism shaped space and place, how Asia was partly produced in Europe, although my focus is on the objective, colonial efforts to shape place rather than the lived experience of the region's inhabitants.[1] This version of the colonial story unfolds through four pivotal moments: first, the British understanding of southwest Asia as a mere thoroughfare to the Indian jewel in the crown was replaced by a new view of it as a region unto itself in the shifting geopolitical context of the early twentieth century. Second, military failure at Kut al-Amara in the midst of World War One inspired an intensive effort to draw on Indian resources to remake the region, to transform it from an endless frontier zone into a recognizable, self-contained place. Third, this development effort radically reshaped India's place in the imperial structure. Fourth, as Iraqis rebelled against the remaking of their terrain, the British invention of disciplinary aerial control ultimately stripped the colony of all sense of place.

The Arabian Utopia

To begin with, we need to understand the no-place that was first in the British mind. At the turn of the twentieth century, the Arabic-speaking parts of the Ottoman Empire began to engage the attention of British imperial planners with a new intensity. The Ottoman Empire, an old British ally astride the land route to India, had begun to rumble from within as provincial movements for autonomy gathered strength. More troubling, Germany had begun to rival British influence inside the empire. So, the British government began to plan for the possible demise of their long sick friend at the edge of Europe by trying to learn something about the vast stretch they knew quaintly as "Arabia," and which acquired the name "Middle East" in the course of the scholarly and diplomatic conversation they launched (Satia 2008, 13–16). The neologism referred to "those regions of Asia . . . bound up with the problems of Indian . . . defence" (Chirol 1903, viii, 5). In other words, the Middle East was conceptually a geographical and political extension of the North West Frontier of India, both imagined as essentially barren and tribal spaces, a land for which "no definite boundaries exist," vaguely the "land of Holy Writ." Defining it more precisely was deemed a somewhat "academic question" since topographic and ethnographic continuities with adjacent geographies made it impossible to draw lines in the sand. It was, according to the geographer David Hogarth, "a Debatable Land," a mere "thoroughfare . . . between the West and the West-in-East" (1902, 280–281).

Despite these new efforts to understand it, "Arabia" remained largely unknown—a dreamlike place of mystery, romance, and, most especially, espionage—an antidote to the bourgeois modernity that some Edwardians were becoming disillusioned with at home. This entire swathe of Asia was thought to be controlled by "vast and mysterious agencies . . . incomprehensible to rational minds"—the arcane political universe that Rudyard Kipling immortalized at the start of the century in *Kim* (Churchill 1898, 38–39). (Matthew Mosca reveals some of the making of that world in his essay for this volume.) Long enchantment with childhood tales from the Arabian Nights and the Bible radically shaped British efforts to understand the region. To the agents, officers, and scholars charged with the task, Arabia inspired imaginative pleasure above all else; once they gained entry to the notoriously forbidden region, they could scarcely perceive a real place in real time (Satia 2008, chs. 2, 3).

It was not only figuratively but geographically a mystery, to the great relief of those nostalgic for the days of pioneer-style Victorian exploration. The Royal Geographical Society termed it officially "Still Unknown" (Hogarth 1908, 549–550). And, most important, essentially unknowable: its apparent featurelessness and natural phenomena like mirage, duststorms, and shifting rivers and dunes made it so protean and deceptive to the British eye that Britons deemed it a cartographic impossibility (Satia 2008, ch. 3)—something like Lu's Chaolian, as documented by Helen Siu in this volume, but exacerbated by a colonial outlook. Even to the determined spy, Arabia was "infinite and immeasurable," "interminable, featureless"—unmappable (Sykes 1915, 436; Bell 1911, 167). Indeed, explorers often had great difficulty determining where they were. A prominent geographer concluded it was "a land which as a whole is so vaguely known that it is better fitted for the half light of literary description than for the hard and inevitably definite expressions of cartography" ([Halford John Mackinder], "Unknown Arabia," review of *Penetration of Arabia,* by Hogarth, *TLS,* 10 June 1904, 178). Theorists of space ascribe the death of place to the "expropriatory" impulse behind mapping, which strips all places of their particular meaning and history, converting them to mere sites on a grid (Casey 1998, 201). Arabia was unique in that its defiance of existing mapping techniques allowed it to remain a place defined paradoxically by its emptiness. Whatever its actual topographical reality, it remained for the British a desert idyll, "very much the same everywhere," a "void," space itself (Hogarth on Butler, 1909, 533). Edwardian cultural needs had inspired a shift from the old fascination with exotic and erotic bazaars of the Orient to the Desert Sublime—a heterotopia of compensation for modern European life (Satia 2008, ch. 3).

Arabia offered a very particular experience of space to Britons at a time in which Newtonian notions of space as uniform and homogeneous were being challenged in numerous ways, by biologists, sociologists, artists, novelists, anthropologists, physicists, mathematicians, and philosophers grappling with the heterogeneity of space (Kern 1983, 132). Although Britons who ventured to the Middle East were rarely members of this cultural avant-garde, it was in part their openness to the notion that "Arabia" offered the experience of a different sort of space that drew them there. To this generation, Arabia was extraterrestrial, "uncanny," in the words of the naturalist and agent Douglas Carruthers, who felt "suddenly transplanted to the . . . moon" (1935, 68).

Just when occultists were making astral journeys to barren planets, travelers in Arabia found themselves beyond the pale of the planet they called home (Owen 2004). It was a space out of time as much as off the map where they could "step straight from this modern age of bustle and chicanery into an era of elemental conditions . . . back into the pages of history to mediaeval times" (Bury 1911, xxi).[2]

However pragmatic and worldly the ways of the people who lived there, the British understood their ability to navigate in a void as the result of a special, intuitive ability rather than well-honed empirical skill. Jack Philby insisted, "The ordinary Arab . . . [was] equipped with an almost instinctive power to read the signs of the desert." They "sensed" direction through featureless terrain. To the British, the Bedouin worked not with data—whether astronomical or topographical—but with signs in a cosmologically ordered space (Satia 2008, 118–122). John Buchan was intimate with this community, and his story "Space" (1912) usefully highlights this early twentieth century fascination. The protagonist, an enigmatic genius with intellectual tastes on the "borderlands of sciences, where mathematics fades into metaphysics," asks, "How if Space is really full of things we cannot see and as yet do now know? How if all animals and some savages have a cell in their brain or a nerve which responds to the invisible world?" He panics about "civilized man": "*Don't you see it is a perception of another kind of reality that we are leaving behind us?*" His effort to recover that reality takes him into the occult world until at last he perceives it and, scribbling on a postcard, "I know at last—God's mercy," plunges to his death in the Alps (1912, 101–109, 116).

Through the writings of British Arabists, these notions have been absorbed into our theories of space, giving us the distinction between "smooth" and "striated" space found in the work of Deleuze and Guattari, the former being tactile rather than visual, where directions are heard and felt as much as they are seen and natives simply know how to get around, even when no directional markers are discernable. Thus, smooth space "provides room for *vagabondage*, for wandering and drifting between regions instead of moving straight ahead between fixed points." Such "nomad space" "always occurs *as a place*" (Casey 1998, 304; Satia 2008, 336).

It was this sort of lost "native" knowledge that our Edwardian Arabists sought to recover with their travels in Arabia—including an apocalyptic knowledge of God. Nomadism, they felt, was the key to the Arabian experience. Moving without immediate objective allowed the mind to "wander into the past and pry . . . into the future," explained Mark Sykes, honorary attaché at the Constantinople embassy and informal spy (Sykes 1904, 219). The desert's minimalism brought spiritual and aesthetic redemption. There, wrote Gertrude Bell, "the mind ranged out unhindered . . . and thought flowed as smoothly as the flowing stream." Its vastness and changelessness "filled the eyes, and satisfied, for the moment, the most restless mind" (Bell 1911, vii; Bell, 28 Jan. 1914, quoted in Burgoyne, *Gertrude Bell*, 1: 292). The very experience of space in Arabia was therapeutic; it restored one to an innate spiritual understanding that the bustle of industrial life at home obscured. God's unseen power was expressed physically "in these barren regions of the earth," appealing "through our eyes and ears to the regions in us beyond the senses" (Jebb 1909, 185, 203, 160–163). This was a knowledge beyond empiricism. Aimless drift in such a place was critical to the metaphysical insights these travelers were after as they searched for escape from Western science, which had begun to produce an unsettling sense of human insignificance and inexorable cosmic entropy (Hynes 1968, 134–138; Kern 1983, 38; Owen 2004). At a time of intense fascination with the ancient sites of occultism, Arabia seemed a kind of palimpsest of human spiritual experiment, a place for miraculous conviction, visionary prophets, and extremes of experience (Sykes 1915, 57).

In this, it was the quintessential place for art, an embodiment of the minimalist aesthetic that fascinated the likes of T. E. Lawrence, Sykes, and others who found its "very emptiness . . . full of secret possibilities and hidden wonder" (Jebb 1909, 63, 260). They saw in Arabs a poetic quality derived from their surroundings; hence their fanciful place-names for places that barely merited the distinction of "place" (Candler 1919, 1: 120; Bell 1907, 50, 60–61). This was an artistic sensibility British travelers sought to emulate.

On the whole, then, as a place, Arabia was not, to British observers, empirically knowable or fully real. It was beyond "the longest arm of the law" (Carruthers 1935, 42), a place so "infinitely mysterious . . . misty and unreal, incomprehensible . . . unfathomable" (Bell 1928, quoted in O'Brien 2000, 9–10), it could not yield facts but might restore faith. Travel there numbed the senses but it also allowed one to "'see, hear, feel, outside the senses'" (Jebb 1909, 264–265). This was not, to this generation of Britons, the kind of place you could *discipline* in the way that European environments were increasingly being disciplined. And this was a good thing in the eyes of many Edwardians anxious about European decadence. Sykes praised Arabs for having no place in "civilised community"—defined disdainfully as "a community living in towns and in houses, suffering from infectious and contagious diseases, travelling in railway trains, able to read and write, possessing drinking shops, reading newspapers, surrounded by a hundred unnecessary luxuries, possessing rich and poor, slums and palaces, and convinced that their state is the most edifying in the world" (1904, 12n). Arabia had escaped the affective and aesthetic sacrifices demanded by "progress." The journalist Meredith Townsend mused in his best seller,

> Imagine a clan which prefers sand to mould, poverty to labour, solitary reflection to the busy hubbub of the mart, which will not earn enough to clothe itself, never invented so much as a lucifer match, and would consider newspaper-reading a disgraceful waste of time. Is it not horrible, that such a race should be? more horrible, that it should survive all others? most horrible of all, that it should produce, among other trifles, the Psalms and the Gospels, the Koran and the epic of Antar? (1904, 307)

Arabia not only did not need development but proved the bankruptcy of the very concept. Such notions, so dramatically shaped by the cultural anxieties of the Edwardian moment, were severely tested when Britain went to war against the Ottoman Empire in 1914.

Making a Place Named Iraq

The war revealed the practical pitfalls of otherworldliness, inspiring a new effort to make the region into something that Britons might recognize as a real, material place. This was not merely a discursive shift. The British occupation of the Middle East during the First World War heralded a practical, material effort to turn its constituent parts into places that could be empirically grasped and disciplined. In particular, colonial development in the name of military logistics attempted to convert the muddy no-place of Mesopotamia into the nation-state of Iraq.

The Mesopotamia campaign began as a small, Government-of-India operation for the defense of Indian frontiers and British interests in the Persian Gulf (Cohen 1976; Davis 1994; Busch 1977, ch. 1). However, once at the Gulf, Indian Army Force D began to rapidly advance north along the Tigris and Euphrates rivers in a characteristic effort to shore up what it already held. Baghdad quickly became its object, not least because its fabled past ensured that everyone at home had heard of it: "It was the Arabian nights" (Lynden-Bell

1977).[3] For Britons, the campaign might have remained a picturesque subplot of the war's grand narrative but for a monumental failure in the midst of its surge up-river: A reverse at Ctesiphon forced the troops under General Charles Townshend to retreat to Kut, where they were besieged through the winter of 1915–16. After more than twenty thousand troops were lost in botched rescue attempts, nine thousand soldiers and thousands of noncombatants surrendered to the Turks in April 1916—"the British Army's greatest humiliation in the First World War" (Popplewell 1990, 139). The London War Office took control of the campaign, and Parliament launched an inquiry. In its report of June 1917, the Mesopotamia Commission censured the Indian army and government for their rash decision to advance on Baghdad and their inadequate provisioning of the force.

The Indian government's central role in this drama was the product of the official perception of the land of two rivers as an extension of the North West Frontier—and the practical political arrangements dating from the nineteenth century also stemming from that perception.[4] The influential war correspondent Edmund Candler insisted, "The physical features of the country are familiar to our Indian troops," adding, "The villages resemble those of the Punjab or the North-West Frontier" (1919, 1: 34). Hence that government's initially dilatory attitude towards transport and other provisions; frontier wars were by definition exercises in resourcefulness and economy. The Mesopotamia Commission belatedly enlightened the Indian authorities that the "climatic and military" conditions of the frontier and Mesopotamia were in fact "very different" (*MCR,* 1917–18, 13, 105).

Before Kut, as the tragedy of the Western front unfolded, the Mesopotamia campaign promised the adventure and heroism of old-fashioned imperial adventure. There they could fight "war as we used to imagine it"; Mesopotamia proved that "in the right place war even to-day can be a romance" (Clark 1918, 2, 47–49; Swayne 1917, 102; Nunn 1932, 153). It promised "release" from the killing fields of France into fabled locales (Candler 1919, 2: 198; Barnett 1917; Army YMCA of India 1915). In letters and memoirs, soldiers described being "immensely moved by the close contact" with the Garden of Eden, Ezra's tomb, the Tower of Babel, Ur of the Chaldees, and other Old Testament sites (Kinch n.d., 27).[5] They felt transported to a divine land where miraculous natural phenomena were daily occurrences. There, a war correspondent wrote, "you live the story of the Bible, and you do not wonder in the least if it is true; you know it is" (Egan 1918, 76).

But the narrative of imperial adventure also triggered a shift in the image of an Arabian escape from technology. In the script of imperial conquest, Mesopotamia was cast in the role of a colonial heart of darkness, a "treeless waste of swamp and desert," "bleak emptiness to conquer,"—in Candler's un-minced words (1919, 1: 33, 176). A soldier put it pertly: "Adam and Eve might well have been excused in such a country." "Mesopotamia welcomes no man," he concluded (Swayne 1717, 17, 51). Its freedom from the technolog-ical burdens of modern life, which had made it a refuge for Edwardians, now made it a No Man's Land in its very essence, a place incapable of belonging to anyone, its peculiar spatial qualities now acquiring a sinister edge. Its mi-rages, sandstorms, and limitless horizons seemed to overwhelm technology's meager purchase on the country: Camels resembled "huge dissipated com-passes" and floating ships, infantry became sheep, a car became a "few filmy lines," and wagons merely black dots (Candler 1919, 1: 47, 111–120). Visual signaling was useless in "a fairyland that danced and glimmered" (Bird 1923, 58). Soldiers struggled to observe their fire and discern its results. The country remained unmapped for much of the war. Official intelligence summaries and private reports described rivers that shifted course daily, unnavigable marshes, and homes and villages whose locations were fleeting at best (Satia 2008, ch. 3). Mesopotamia was fundamentally remote, "far away from home, civiliza-tion, and comfort," in the rueful words of one naval captain (Nunn 1932, 10). Technology could only improve a land so far from England, so close to God, especially after the disaster at Kut, when "the conditions of France were re-peated in Mesopotamia" (Candler 1919, 1: 164). As the campaign went badly wrong, the more treacherous aspects of its biblical ecology gained ground in British representations. "[W]e were in a country of excess, where the elements are never moderate or in humour," wrote Candler, "and there was something almost Biblical in the way the deities of this ancient land conspired to punish us . . . malice in the sky and soil . . . heat and drought; hunger and thirst and flies; damp and cold, fever and ague, flood, hurricane and rain . . ." At the actual site of the Great Flood, these punishments seemed like a "Biblical visi-tation" (1919, 1: 72; 1916).

Unlike in France, where "No Man's Land" represented technology's deso-lation of nature (Fussell 1975; Leed 1979), technology maintained a positive image in a region depicted as a vast, autarkic wasteland, a fallen Eden discon-nected from the world and its economy that the British had come to rescue from Ottoman tyranny. This spatial imaginary excused military failure. The difficulty of using modern boats was blamed on the strange rivers and under-developed port of Basra rather than design errors (Satia 2007, 221). Basra Intelligence explained, "in Iraq all military problems . . . are affected by climate and physical conditions to an extent rarely met with in any theatre of war" ("Physical and Climatic Difficulties of the Mesopotamian Theatre of War"). The Mesopotamia Commission Report likewise opened with a section on the challenges posed by "Physical and Climatic Peculiarities" (*MCR*, 9). Military failure in Mesopotamia was the fault of Mesopotamia. Rather than lament that technology had paralyzed military activity, those involved in the campaign lamented that military technology was either in too short supply or too sophisticated for their backward theatre.[6] The Indian government had failed to provide wire-cutters, water-carts, rockets, mosquito nets, periscopes—the stuff of "war carried on under modern conditions" (*MCR*, 37–38). In France, Candler noted, the wounded were whisked away in "smooth motor ambulance wagons" and provided "every saving device that Science can lend," while in Mesopotamia, "all was chaos." The campaign's mobility was a mark of backwardness, frustrating both efficient medical service as well as "the business of range-finding and registering, so easy in the stationary conditions on the Western front," however fruitless the ability in those conditions (1919, 1: 47, 56). Modern warfare had come to mean the *mobile* supply of an army *immobilized* in a clearly demarcated battlefield.

After a reformed Indian government began to supply the force (on which more below), it succeeded in taking Baghdad in October 1917, continuing north through the end of the war. These successes strengthened faith in technology as enabling rather than paralyzing. Armed with all the paraphernalia of modern warfare, they now waged "war as it should be waged, with the spirit of movement in it" (Candler 1919, 2: 223–224). At Ctesiphon, a naval officer mused on the great armies and historic figures that "had passed this way before the coming of men in khaki, with their aeroplanes and wireless" (Nunn 1932, 168). If technology's dark side was exposed in France, a new aspect of it was unveiled in Iraq: in the hands of "experts," it could resurrect a military campaign and a devastated civilization (Candler 1919, 1: 51, 132). British imaginings about Mesopotamia as a romantic, otherworldly, autarkic land underwrote a progressive image of technology at a moment when its image was cracking elsewhere.

With this constructive vision of technology, the campaign soon claimed redemption of the cradle of civilization—turning space into place—its true calling.

The abject failure at Kut had raised the stakes of the campaign. Mesopotamia was represented less as a "side-show" and more as the place where war could find meaning, less an escape from industrialism than the proving ground for industry and empire. By "reclaim[ing] a wilderness" and "rebuild[ing] a civilization after many years of anarchy and desolation" for "a new country and a new people," the force determined to give meaning to the sacrifices of British soldiers (Reynardson 1919, 272; Cato 1917, 106, 117). Revitalizing a civilization of "mysterious and divine" origins, Bell, then a powerful force in the British civil administration, felt "rather like the Creator" (Bell 1918, qtd. in Burgoyne 1958–61, 2: 101).

This new idealism heralded a rethinking of Mesopotamia's spatial orientation. Rather than an extension of the Indian frontier, it became the fallen frontier of the West. Rather than "unchanging," wartime representations stressed that this bit of the East had metamorphosed from a locus of secular power and worldly riches tightly bound to Hellenistic-Christian culture to a "sordid relic." "When European Christendom looks to-day at the desolation of these lands," wrote the historian Edwyn Bevan, "it is looking at a lost piece of itself." Technology promised to precipitously reconnect Mesopotamia with the rest of the modern world after Kut revealed how dangerous its utopic autarky was. Restoring Mesopotamia's position along the great artery of commercial traffic was a development goal borne of military failure. The object of the campaign was nothing less than a "regenerated Babylonia, in which the ancient streams reflect once more mighty structures of men and gardens like Paradise, and in the streets of whose cities traffickers from all the earth once more meet." Man would once again be "master of the great waters," prophesied Bevan. The wanton destruction wrought by feckless and savage imperial tyrants since the Mongol invasion would end as they resurrected an older imperial tradition of *improvement,* recalling the Persians, Seleucids, Parthians, Sassanids, and the Saracen caliphs (1918, 10–11, 112, 124–126).[7]

Developing Mesopotamia was hailed as a refitting of the ancient land with modern technology that would enable it to resume its traditional role in a modern world. Technologies like dams, aircraft, and roads would not only produce battlefields from Mesopotamia's disordered landscape but also produce Mesopotamia itself as a geographical and political place, tied to the West. They would both improve the fabulous and terrible country and bring it within the realm of the knowable, within the pale of the economy that development sought to make.

For some, remaking Mesopotamia for a prosperous postwar West invested the entire war with meaning. In an essay much circulated amongst the troops, Bell described how, once again, the ancient markets of Iraq would thrive and "add immeasurably to the wealth of a universe wasted by war" (1916, 201–202). "Nowhere, in the war-shattered universe," she held, "can we begin more speedily to make good the immense losses sustained by humanity" (Bell to Florence Bell, 15 Nov. 1917, in Bell 1927, 2: 431–432). Candler too was comforted "that the war which had let loose destruction in Europe was bringing new life to Mesopotamia" (1919, 2: 183). And in this global salvation lay the salvation of the empire. An officer wrote, "All this show of ours out here is . . . a beginning of something that will materialise a hundred or two hundred or a thousand years hence. We are the great irrigating nation and that's why we're here now . . . We'll fix this land up . . . and move the wheels of a new humanity. Pray God, yes—a new humanity!" (qtd. in Swayne 1917, 166). Mesopotamia proved that the British could still *civilize,* if they had lost civilization itself. "British seed" would make the desert "bloom as the rose," an officer announced to those who called empire "a thing of pitiless blood and iron" (Reynardson 1919, 172). As always, explained Sykes, the British imperial ideal was "not . . . conquest but . . . redemption" ("Political Note on our Advance in Irak," 17 Sept. 1917). Theirs was a queerly selfless imperialism: Bell mused, "We save from destruction remnants of oppressed nations, laboriously and expensively giving them sanitary accommodation, teaching their children, respecting their faiths," yet remained cursed by subjects, who, nevertheless, "when left to themselves . . . flock to our standards" (to Hugh Bell, 10 Nov. 1922, in Bell 1927, 2: 657). The prodigious Indian effort for Mesopotamia proved that even Indians knew Britain ruled them for their good, not for exploitation, exulted a parliamentary paper (*East India [Military],* PP, 1914–16 [Cd. 7624], 49: 15). The "development" packaging convinced: an American remarked the "blue-eyed tribe" now ruling Baghdad:

Angles they call these men, and they are not like the other conquerors who flowed into Iraq with sword and torch in the days whose record may be read in the ash piles along the Tigris. They are children—fussy children—eternally worried over the removal of rubbish, the "improvement" of roads and bridges that for hundreds of years served our ancestors . . . the disciplining of the police force and what not. (Casey 1928, vii–viii)

These fussy "Angles" had come to remake the Middle East and redeem empire. James Mann, an aspiring political officer, reasoned, "if one takes the Civil Service, or the Bar, or Literature, or Politics, or even the Labour movement, what can one do that is constructive? Here on the other hand I am constructing the whole time" (to his mother, 25 Jan. 1920, in Mann 1921, 206).

Thus, British officials, journalists, and politicians claimed a special status for the new colony—it was *the* site for imperial expiation through technocratic development. In India, by contrast, signs of wartime modernization were most often viewed as a violation of the colony's romantic aura, betokening social, cultural, and political chaos (Sinha 2006). The idea of developing Iraq did not raise the preservationist fears of rapid economic change upsetting indigenous social and political order that otherwise tended to undermine the fulfillment of visionary wartime plans for colonial development (Constantine 1984; Cooper 1997, 65–70). It also differed from earlier antecedents—and from, say, state management of poverty in Britain—in the totality of its spatial ambition, its positing of an entire proto-nation-state as its object.[8] Although in practice development focused on activities that would make Iraq a supplier of raw materials rather than an industrial nation in its own right, for Iraq, even this humble role implied the country's glorious resurgence as an imperial entrepot.

In 1919, Britain asked the League of Nations to award it the mandate to rule Iraq as compensation for British sacrifices for the country's development (Busch 1977, 158, 190, 275), reconfiguring a war of conquest as an international development effort. To most Iraqis, the mandate scheme was a flimsy semantic disguise for colonial rule, which they rebelled against until Iraq finally joined the League as an ostensibly independent country in 1932. Meanwhile, many of the developmental projects the British undertook (mainly, after all, to serve the needs of the army) were abandoned, partly because of financial stringency and partly because, as we shall see, postwar air control hijacked the development discourse.

How Making Iraq Remade India

Britons may have begun to see Iraq as a long-lost part of the West, but many in India remained committed to the notion that Iraq was essentially bound to its geography, a notion only strengthened by the knowledge that Iraq's increasingly apparent modernity was the product of Indian generosity: It was

India that sent most of the equipment and personnel for the job.[9] This section examines the Indian contribution to Iraq's development and what it meant for India. Iraq's new shape produced a re-evaluation, in Britain and India, of the kind of place India might be in the overarching structure of the British Empire. As India's industrialism in the name of Iraqi uplift earned the colony a promotion of sorts, it too took on the dimensions of a modern nation-state, tempering the old vision of a subcontinent of political chaos.

So what did India do for Iraq? First came the boats, which were not only plucked from Indian rivers but were specially constructed in Indian ship-yards—until then used only for repair and re-assembly of British craft. The impact on Indian shipbuilding—in both its capacity and technological so-phistication—was transformative, as contemporary assessments noted. Mes-opotamia's topographical "peculiarities," by defying the use of allegedly uni-versally adaptable modern technology, created an opportunity and need for Indian shipbuilding. Construction of small, wooden craft suitable for "eccen-tric" rivers became something of an Indian specialty—not least because of the pressure to protect British shipbuilding interests and an immense shortage of steel. But those committed to Indian self-rule thought Indian shipyards might do even more, given cheap labor and abundant teak. Shipbuilding came to be seen as *the* mark of self-sufficiency and was, to many Indian nationalists, the industry most important to reclaiming India's precolonial glory (Satia 2007, 237–239).[10]

Besides boats, India supplied all the iron and steel for the railway and water transport systems built in Iraq, besides telegraphic and telephonic equipment, hundreds of engines, thousands of vehicles—all of which Montagu listed in Parliament in August 1917, days before his famous declaration that the Brit-ish government was in favor of responsible government in India. Indian la-bor came in the train of this equipment, most numerous among the diverse peoples employed on the docks at Abadan and Basra. By the end of the war, there were upwards of seventy-one thousand men, mostly Indian, in the Labor Corps, besides forty-two thousand in the IWTD. Indian technical expertise in developing ports, rivers, and boats also proved critical. The IWTD drew heavily on engineering firms at Calcutta, Bombay, Karachi, and Rangoon (Sa-tia 2007, 241). George Buchanan, the engineer plucked from India to advise much of the construction, brought a survey party of fifty-three Anglo-Indians and Indians. He recalled from France two of his "best Rangoon engineers" and a staff of engineers and surveyors from the Indian Public Works Department.

From Bombay he brought a Chinese contractor and his gang of a thousand carpenters to build the Basra wharves. His own staff consisted of three men with experience in Indian ports. In February 1918, a Mesopotamian Irrigation Directorate was formed with experts from India. Land and river surveyors arrived. Basra was to be reorganized "along the lines of an Indian commercial port" and the entire country run like an Indian province, a move Buchanan enthusiastically supported, since "Indian Provincial Administration was . . . the most efficient in the world" (1938, 36–37, 73, 89, 99–101, 110, 127, 250, 267). Now, more than a mere training ground and laboratory for engineering expertise, India had become the imperial fount of state-led, technocratic development dispensed as a total system for a newly configured proto-nation-state.

All this activity spelled major change in India. In Simla, everyone was in khaki, there was a new quartermaster-general, new bureaux for army recruitment, and a new Indian Munitions Board under Sir Thomas Holland, which hired Buchanan on his return from Basra. Holland had earlier headed the 1916 Indian Industrial Commission, whose objective had been the transformation of India into a "worthy partner in Empire" to avoid "the dangers to which industrial unpreparedness exposes a nation" (commission report, qtd. in "India's Great Need," Times, 10 Dec. 1918, 7). India's performance in Mesopotamia was heralded as proof of its own progress and of the need for a permanent technocratic policy of "energetic intervention" in Indian industry. The new Viceroy Lord Chelmsford visited the Tata steel works in the new industrial town of Jamshedpur and praised the company's enterprise in producing the steel that had saved the Mesopotamian campaign. The Tatas had obtained American assistance, and they, too, made reform of their own government's indifference to Indian industry their goal. Dorabji Tata served on the Industrial Commission, which proposed a "large administrative and technical Government organization" to support Indian entrepreneurship, billed by the Times as an "epoch-making," "complete change in Government policy." Indian reform had long been on the table,[11] but the expansion of the reform agenda from administrative matters to a more entrepreneurial attitude towards industry can be traced largely to Kut.[12]

Indeed, administrative reform also owed something to Kut. In explaining the early bungling of the campaign, Montagu described the India Office regime as "an apotheosis . . . of red-tape . . . beyond the dream of any critic." Even Lord Sydenham, the former governor of Bombay who would staunchly oppose the Montagu declaration of August 1917, insisted the Indian government "must be overhauled." The Industrial Commission closely agreed with the changes recommended by the Montagu-Chelmsford Act of 1919; that totemic piece of postwar legislation responded to moderate nationalist demands for political and administrative reform but also to the Mesopotamia Commission Report's revelation of the need to better prepare India for total war by making its government less autocratic and bureaucratic. To many Britons this implied reducing the Indian government's subordination to Whitehall in order to *decentralize* the empire *and,* in the words of a *Times* editorial of July 1917, giving *"Indians a further share in the control of their own affairs"* (Montagu, speech in the Commons, *Times,* 13 July 1917, 10; Sydenham in Lords debate, 12 July 1917, *Times,* 13 July 1917, 8; "Defects of the Indian System," *Times,* 2 July 1917, 9).[13] Montagu himself used the Commons debate on the Mesopotamia Commission Report (MCR) as a platform for urging a commitment to giving Indians a "bigger opportunity of controlling their own destinies . . . by control . . . of the Executive itself." Within a week, he was appointed secretary of state for India, the Mesopotamia scandal having forced Austen Chamberlain to resign. His declaration of August 1917 prompted the Montagu-Chelmsford Report on constitutional reform the next year. In debate on this report, which laid the groundwork for the 1919 Act, the Indian government's success in turning itself around in Mesopotamia was critical: Montagu made the case for constitutional reform by enthusing about India's contributions of materials, experts, and labor. Likewise, in a speech on constitutional reform in Simla, Chelmsford catalogued Indian contributions to the campaign—boats, railroads, personnel (Montagu, Commons debate, July 1917, quoted in Mehrotra 1965, 101 and 6 Aug. 1918, *Times,* 7 Aug. 1918, 8; Chelmsford, speech in Simla, 5 Sept. 1917, qtd. in "India's Work in the War," *Times,* 17 Oct. 1917).

Nationalists' goal of greater Indian independence was thus guaranteed at least partly by a demonstration of India's own paternalistic powers;[14] it was tinged with the glamour of empire, which continued to color the assertion of Indian independence. Indian officials' early view of the campaign as a mere frontier skirmish morphed into a notably more extravagant vision of a Mesopotamian colony for India that would make up for India's earnest sacrifice, at London's bidding, of the men, money, and materials needed to make Mesopotamia fit for modern warfare. The Indian government had long seen itself, in significant ways, as entirely separate from the Home government to which it was legally subordinate (Galbraith 1984, 375). While Britons saw Mesopotamia as the frontier of a renewed West, the Indian government and nationalists stoked imperial dreams of their own. If Mesopotamia was an extension of the Indian frontier, it should logically be annexed to the Indian empire. In early discussions about the postwar fate of Iraq, India's strategic, commercial, political, and religious interests, besides the fact that the campaign was being fought by Indian troops, seemed, to many, to justify incorporation of the country into the Indian empire and even Indians' colonization of the country as settlers. Officers of the Indian Army and Indian Political Service quickly imported Indian administrative methods. Indian police, currency, legal code—all followed within a week of the occupation of Basra. London's warnings against prematurely annexing Basra as an Indian province did nothing to curb its overnight Indianization (Busch 1977, 41–42, 50–54). It was "taken for granted that at the end of the campaign Mesopotamia would become a British possession," Buchanan explained after the war, "probably controlled from India" (1938, 261).

This was far from uncontroversial, given other officials' anxiousness to rejoin Mesopotamia to the West. Many Cairo- and London-based Arabists, who had long romanticized Arabs as a naturally free and democratic people akin to the "freeborn Englishman" (Satia, 2008, ch. 2), fought bitterly against Indianization of the nascent colony. India's customs and laws were radically different from Arabs', argued Sykes; Arabs, unlike Indians, could not be run "on black and white lines" (minute, Dec. 1916, qtd. in Busch 1977, 121–122). Through mid-1916, Cairo's attempts to overwhelm Indian influence in Iraq failed, but, previous scholars have argued, after the campaign's transfer to the War Office, India's influence diminished: hence the new Indian commander-in-chief Charles Monro was now directly responsible to the Chief of General Staff and Army Council in London rather than through the Indian bureaucracy (Busch 1977, 100–109). The 1917 MCR's revelations profoundly shook any residual British confidence in Indian administration of Iraq. The Mesopotamia Administration Committee insisted on the creation of a government service for Iraq drawn from the Levant and Sudan, not from India; the India-derived legal code would not be extended to the Baghdad vilayet; and Indians would not be employed in administration (Busch 1977, 37, 112, 141–147, 207). It was thus that Britain rather than India received the Iraqi mandate after the war. (As an independent member of the League of Nations, India certainly could have, as South Africa had in the case of German Southwest Africa.) The Indian government's new irrelevance to Iraqi affairs was most symbolically evident in its total exclusion from the Cairo Conference of 1921 where the form of Iraq's government was finally settled.[15]

Still, it is worth pointing out the Indian government's lingering influence on Iraq through the India Office and the India-derived political establishment as long as it continued to supply the campaign in Iraq and those launched from Iraq into the Caspian and Persia. But I want to argue that even more ambitious hopes for wider Indian influence did not dissipate entirely after 1916. Despite metropolitan determination to retain control of Iraq in London, some Britons continued to expect the expansion of Indian power and influence within the empire, based on the colony's new industrial strength. In the midst of the fury over the publication of the MCR in June 1917, the *Times* commended the colony for "doing more than people credit her for. The Government have taken up with vigour the development of Indian resources for the production of war material . . . India may be able to expand her powers considerably, and to take at least a portion of the burden from England in many particulars" ("Mesopotamia: Past and Present," 29 June 1917, 7). The idea that India was pulling its weight effectively enough to expect an enlarged role in the Empire was still being articulated in 1917. In the wake of the postwar decision in favor of an Arab government for Iraq, Indian supporters in Britain continued to insist on the preservation of Indian "rights" there, particularly of settlement and commercial influence, in recognition of India's new status as a "partner in the British Empire," a rank purchased during the war in blood and money (J. A. S., letter to the *Times,* 20 June 1921, 6).

These British calls were amplified by those of Indians themselves for whom the post-1916 effort to transform Iraq continued to herald the beginning of an Indian empire. The Aga Khan, whose opinion British officials and the British press took seriously, examined "Indian expansion westwards" in his 1918 book, foreseeing "a vast agglomeration of states, principalities and countries" from Aden and Mesopotamia to "India proper" to the Malay Peninsula, Ceylon, and Tibet, making up a "South Asiatic Federation . . . of which India must be the centre and the pivot" (11, 13, 24, 29). Whatever became of British-Mesopotamian relations, "[Mesopotamia's] relations with India must so grow as to give us in practice a trans-Gulf frontier to defend." This was an imperial ambition founded not on administrative Indianization (as in, say, Burma or Aden) but on *development,* as an Indian area of expertise to be performed in a place India had a history of improving—nineteenth-century donations from the Shia kingdom of Awadh had mostly been spent on public projects such as the construction of the Hindiyya canal to bring water to the holy cities (Cole 1986).[16] That Indian public opinion on the matter was strong

is evident from the fact that British officials worried that an absolute end to
Indian influence in Mesopotamia after 1916 would excite "bitter and legitimate resentment" in *India,* that it was highly *impolitic* to order Indian laborers
and personnel to return home. Besides the thousands of laborers, so many
private Indian citizens had begun to arrive that in April 1920 the Viceroy was
forced to issue an Order in Council restricting recruitment of Indians in Mesopotamia to government service only, and that too as a concession to public
opinion. By 1921 Gandhi had taken up the fate of would-be Indian settlers in
Iraq (Viceroy to Secretary for India, 27 Apr. 1917, qtd. in Busch 1977, 143;
Gandhi "A Wail from Mesopotamia" in *Young India* (May 1921), qtd. according to Busch 391n37, in Chelmsford's Order in Council, 30 Apr. 1920).

The impression that India had been in some sense promoted within the
empire inspired a revaluation of India's qualities as a place, in the sense of
a distinct, developed site of civilization. Buchanan pronounced its climate
much less cruel than Mesopotamia's, given the relief afforded by "all the ame-
nities and safeguards that go with civilisation." His Indian surveyors "had
never worked under such trying conditions" (1938, 106, 109, 111). Candler
contrasted the successful taming of Indian terrain with the utterly degenerate
state of Mesopotamian nature. "Convalescent Tommies" longed for transfer
there, and ailing Indian troops were evacuated to Bombay for food, drink,
and "cheerful society," allegedly declaring even Punjab "a health resort," while
holding "both [Mesopotamia] and its inhabitants in equal contempt." Ad-
mirably "set off by the rabble on the bank," the sepoys questioned "'why the
Sirkar should desire this Satanlike land'," Candler enlightening them that "a
wise Sirkar might find the means of rendering it fertile" (1919, 1: 34–35, 237).
A British soldier affirmed, "There is no love lost between the Indians and the
Arabs," the latter having long feared "the incursion of India into their country, for they know that the Indian farmer under the British engineers would
make Mesopotamia blossom like a rose" (Swayne, 1917, 78, 161). In British
portrayals, Indians saw Mesopotamia with the orientalist eyes of the agent of
development. And India gained greater definition as an incipient nation-state.

India may have been promoted within the imperial system, but the empire
had a glass ceiling; wooden river-craft were not steel steamers. Like the Tongking Gulf described by Charles Wheeler, the Arabian Sea was an old arena
of connection, but here we find how the politics of colonialism shaped those
connections at a particular historical juncture. This is not the space to fully
flesh out the postwar implications of the Indian discourse about developing

Iraq, but I will venture to say that the wartime effort to develop Mesopotamia played an important role in the shaping of Indian national and imperial ambitions—specifically, the imperial nature of Indian national ambitions.[17] Combatting those ambitions remained crucial to Iraq: hence was exclusion of Indians such a priority for the new Iraqi government as it attempted to assert its independence after 1932 (Bose 2006, 93–94).

A New Place Called Iraq

How did Iraqis respond to all this imperial beneficence? They rebelled, with particular force in 1920 (Haldane 1922),[18] inspiring Buchanan's lament, *The Tragedy of Mesopotamia* which sadly affirmed that the British had become "more hated than the Turks themselves had ever been." Iraq was a monument to the White Man's Burden, "a tragedy of heroism, suffering, wasted lives, and wasted effort" (1938, 182, 261, 276–278, 284–285). As development projects were abandoned in the face of postwar austerity, rebellion inspired another use of technology: aerial surveillance as a means of pacification. The "enormous political possibilities" of aircraft had also been discovered during the war; they were the other side of the coin of technological development of the Middle East (Salmond, commanding Middle East Brigade, RFC to CGS, GHQ EEF, 12 Nov. 1916: PRO, WO 158/626; Satia 2006).[19]

Air control radically shifted understandings of the kind of place Iraq was, transforming the rolling dunes and featurelessness of the Edwardian imagination into a (theoretically) striated space, empirically graspable at last. It not only annihilated the distances of the desert sublime; it transformed the desert into a series of "sites"—places made calculable at last for mapping and thus stripped of their particular aura and history (Casey 1998, 201).

Aircraft were ubiquitous in Mesopotamia after Kut. Official postwar assessments recognized that airpower proved its potential as an independent military arm in the Middle East rather than Europe. Aerial photography likewise reached its highest development in Mesopotamia, as did air signaling. This intense use of aerial power was intimately tied to British imaginings of Arabia as a particular kind of space. As a new technology with their own mystique, aircraft became intimately associated with a Mesopotamian site of exception. British Arabists, attracted to the region as a medieval utopia, saw in the airplane a means of restoring chivalry and vitality to modern warfare. Over the austere terrain of Biblical deserts flight seemed to reach new heights of sublimity and even divinity (Satia 2008, chs. 4, 5, 7). Arabists perceived a congruence between the aircraft and the desert warrior, both operating in empty, unmapped, magical spaces. Lawrence prophesied, "What the Arabs [as guerrillas] did yesterday the Air Forces may do to-morrow. And in the same way—yet more swiftly" (qtd. in Hart 1934, 438). He joined the RAF in 1922, in search of the same literary inspiration that he had found in the desert. His views were echoed by other Arabists and in the RAF (Satia 2008, ch. 7). "There appears to be a sort of natural fellow-feeling between these nomad arabs and the Air Force," remarked the RAF's Director of Research, "both feel that they are at times in conflict with the vast elemental forces of nature" (Brooke-Popham 1922).[20] Its wondrousness apart, airpower seemed to offer a means of overcoming the information problems posed by an unmapped desert; a bird's-eye view promised vision beyond the mirages, sandstorms, and horizonlessness that bedeviled two-dimensional observation. Political officers had long pined, "Oh for some aeroplanes. If there was a country in the whole world eminently suited to these machines this one is: Flat flat as your hand" (Dickson to Gwenlian Greene, Feb. 7, 1915, 1st booklet, Dickson Papers). Aircraft were essential in a land where "little can be trusted that is seen," one general put it bluntly (One of Its Officers, 1918, 70–71). Air control promised to transform the shifting sands of the Edwardian imagination into an empirically knowable space.

In 1919, aircraft and bombs were employed against unrest all over the Eastern empire (Omissi 1990, 11). But notions of Iraq's peculiar suitability made it the only colony where airpower became a permanent instrument of imperial administration and policing. It was there that the British first practiced the technology of bombardment and attempted to theorize the value of airpower as an independent arm of the military. Reasons of cost and topography mattered, certainly, but it was cultural imaginings about the kind of place Iraq was that made it the first site of air control. Arabists at the new Middle East Department of the Colonial Office considered Iraq *peculiarly* suitable for air operations, for aesthetic as much as topographical reasons: its presumed flatness promised many landing grounds, little cover to insurgents, and the possibility of "radiating" British power from a handful of fittingly spartan bases, while the reality of Iraq's varied and protean topography, when acknowledged, was held to offer an ideal training ground, exposing the RAF to mountains, marshes, deserts, and so on. Air action was deemed *in*appropriate for police action in the densely populated urban environments of Britain, Ireland, and even Palestine (Satia 2008, 10, ch. 7).

The RAF officially took over in Iraq in October 1922. Its squadrons patrolled the country from a network of bases, bombarding villages and tribes as needed to put down unrest and subversive activities. Air action was used against Turkish and Najdi raiders into Iraq—at a time when frontiers were a work in progress, part of the making of the place of Iraq—as well as Kurdish and Arab rebellions within Iraq proper.[21] Despite the promise of omniscience, the regime was plagued by error—bombardment of wrong towns and tribes and failures to sight targets (Satia 2008, ch. 7). Even assessing the effect of bombing operations was "largely a matter of guesswork" (E.A.S., Mar. 30, 1922, CO 730/20, PRO). But in an infamously deceptive land, all this inaccuracy, indeed information itself, was of little consequence: The head of civil administration Arnold Wilson explained that news of mistakes was exaggerated, as all information in the country, not least because mirage prevented anyone from judging pilot accuracy. Moreover, accuracy itself was moot, since aircraft were meant to be everywhere at once, "conveying a silent warning." This *"moral effect"* of patrolling aircraft "which can drop Bombs whenever necessary would effectually check disturbances" (Wilson, Note on Use of Air Force in Mesopotamia, Feb. 26, 1921, AIR 5/476, PRO). Even destruction of property did not matter as it might elsewhere, given the austerity of tribal existence, a condition imagined to extend to all Iraqis (Satia 2008, ch. 7). Just as spatial conceptions inspired the scheme's invention, so they excused its failures.

Such misperceptions proved costly in Iraqi lives. Entire villages and tribes were bombed for "general recalcitrance" (refusal to submit to government), harboring wanted rebel leaders, and evading the high rates of British taxation (Satia 2008, ch. 7; Sluglett 1976, 262–270).[22] But old notions of the region's existence somewhere off the map of the real world were again mobilized to justify even such excesses. Experts assured that Iraqis expected harsh existence; they could tolerate random acts of violence in a way that others could not (e.g. Glubb, Note on the Southern Desert Force, [c. 1930s], Glubb Papers). British officials assured one another that unlike the outrages inevitably committed by ground troops, "bombing from the air is regarded almost as an act of God" (F. H. Humphreys to Sir John Simon, Dec. 15, 1932, AIR 8/94). "It is not punishment, but a misfortune from heaven striking the community," explained Lawrence ([June 1930], qtd. in Hart, 1933, 159). The perception of environmental excesses that had inspired an effort to join this biblical land to the modern world in the name of civilization simultaneously underwrote the notion that it could tolerate a level of brutality no other place could, also in the name of civilization. In its Iraqi cocoon, the RAF was safe from criticism of inaccuracy, protected by the British imaginary of a place so otherworldly it was beyond empirical verification. From Iraq, air control spread to Palestine, Transjordan, and elsewhere, albeit in modified version (Satia 2008, ch. 7). Mandana Limbert's essay in this volume reveals the centrality of RAF bombardment to the making of place in 1950s Oman.

Particular understandings of the Middle East as a place were thus crucial to the history of bombardment as a military strategy and to the making of the Middle East as a political region. The vindication of air control grew out of long-circulating imaginings of a land miraculously exempt from the this-worldliness that constrained human activity in other parts of the world. Arabia's legendary otherworldliness made it fit to bear the unearthly destruction wreaked by bombers; its moral world was distinct from their own. The romantic world of the RAF in Iraq, with its miraculous wireless infrastructure, compounded the sense of being in a place apart, only tenuously linked to civilization (Satia 2008, 7). British officials may have found Arabia extraterrestrial, but it was their technological innovations that ultimately produced the surreal world of random bombardment in which Iraqis were condemned to live, actually removing Iraq beyond the reach of secular and humanitarian law.

This regime was understood in the same developmental vein as the wartime infrastructure projects. Air control, its defenders argued, facilitated greater understanding between administrators and Iraqis by enabling British personnel to roam without fear (and, incidentally, gather the intelligence that would guide future bombardments) (Satia 2008, ch. 7). Moreover, it had made Baghdad the "Clapham Junction of the air," fulfilling that noble dream of remaking an ancient cosmopolitan crossroads ("Britain and Mesopotamia," *Daily Telegraph*, 10 May 1921; Coke 1929, 11–12). Far from disruptive, aircraft recalled the region's fabled past: "The inhabitants take these things as a matter of course," assured the *Times*, "The age of miracles has happily returned, and we may see strange Arabian nights in the coming years" ("A Traveller in Mesopotamia," review of E. S. Stevens, *By Tigris and Euphrates*, 14 Dec. 1923, 8). The furrow ploughed across the desert to guide pilots to Baghdad was lauded as a feat of British ingenuity. The "romance" of desert flight derived from the "demonstration of the power of modern inventions which are able to conquer vast open spaces of the world, as yet little known to civilised man"—technology remained the handmaiden of progress (Ilay Ferrier, "The Trans-Desert

Route—Baghdad—Jerusalem," 1926, Papers by Ilay Ferrier, IOR: Eur Mss C874, BL). The air afforded a lofty view from which to observe the effects of the new loftier imperialism, to witness "'adoring Asia kindle and hugely bloom'" (*Illustrated London News*, 1 Feb. 1919, 149).[23] Aerial policing fit neatly into this vision of liberal empire in the sky. Flying over the desert, Hubert Young of the Foreign Office "felt that a new era had dawned, and that with the goodwill of His Majesty's Government and the powerful help of the Royal Air Force the Arabs of Iraq would undoubtedly win their independence at last" (1933, 338).

If these arguments did not convince, others claimed a dose of repression would pave the way to gentler improvements. A wing commander argued, "The cheaper the form of control the more money for roads and development and the sooner it will be no longer necessary to use armed forces to do with explosives what should be done by policemen and sticks" (Peck 1928, 541). While Buchanan mourned the abandonment of wartime infrastructure projects, others saw in air control the salvation of the wartime hopes for a global payoff from the Mesopotamian adventure. The development of the geographical center of the world's most ancient and most modern traffic routes would "safeguard humanity from famines, wars, and social revolution" (Wilkinson 1922, 665). The press and politicians continued to urge development of Iraq on the premise that "a country once so rich may surely be made rich again by modern methods," stubbornly anticipating "some recompense for the great sacrifices we made in the Great War" (*Times*, 17 Mar. 1923, 11; Amery, qtd. in *Times*, 9 Feb. 1926, 11). The notion that they might develop Iraq so that it would be able to "stand on its own feet" sustained each government's commitment to holding Iraq, whatever its political complexion.

Iraq's pivotal position in imperial air networks made it even more difficult for the British to contemplate withdrawal from the country; hence the only nominal independence of 1932: The RAF kept key elements of Iraqi defense—aircraft, wireless, armored cars, intelligence sources—out of the hands of the nascent Iraqi Army (Satia 2008, chs. 7, 8). For them, the change in 1932 was to be "more apparent than real" (Air Policy with Regard to Iraq, n.d. [Oct.-Nov. 1929], AIR 2/830). The Middle East had become as essential to British preeminence in airpower as airpower was to Britain's ability to control the Middle East. In the British imagination, it was "the Land of the RAF," a region devoid of place, uniform and contained, a collection of sites in the range of bombsights. The British effort to stake out Iraq as a political-economic space depended in the end on defining it as part of an imperial air route, ever a thoroughfare to more fabled locales further on. Indeed, Asia itself remained a thoroughfare to South Asia and the South Pacific. RAF squadrons were gradually reduced, but the country was fully reoccupied during the Second World War, and the RAF only departed in 1958; the rest of Asia was always at stake in control of Iraq. It had become, again, a no-place, and this time, stripped of its aura of wonder.

Development and policing were two sides of the same technocratic coin that endeavored to create places from the mysterious no-place of Arabia, at least in British understandings. In trying to create Iraq, the British ultimately obliterated all sense of place, turning the region into a site of exception in official minds. As Timothy Mitchell has noted, the supposed abject aridity, mineral wealth, and lack of natural national cohesion of the Middle East has become the canonical developmental problem (2002, 44, 210–211, 223). Certainly, our imagination about Iraq has evolved. We have, for instance, broken the old habit of blurring it into India—although George W. Bush nearly resurrected it with his certainty that Afghanistan's Al Qaeda was in Iraq—and oil figures more prominently than grain in images of Iraq's share of global wealth. But the image of an autarkic, hermetic desert that forbids modern ideas and goods continues to tempt those dreaming of a regenerated Babylonia, and the years of sanctions and occupation in pursuit of that imperial folly have helped make the image of autarky something of a reality. With drones overhead, Iraq is once again the site of a first in the history of aerial technology, as we continue to speak a development language constituting itself as a neutral form of knowledge despite its role in producing the country's current devastation.

Notes

1. On the history of the concept of place, see Casey 1998.

2. The Romantics had also looked to Eastern philosophy and culture for alternatives to Occidental materialism, but Edwardians were more interested in escape than imitation and combined escape with intelligence work. Nor did they recoil from the "real" Orient as the Romantics had. See for instance Fraser, 1909, 234. On the Romantics, see Said, 1978, 100–115.

3. For further discussion see Satia 2008, ch. 5.

4. Administratively, the London and Indian Governments overlapped in Mesopotamia. Satia 2008, ch. 1. The Persian Gulf was the "maritime frontier of the Indian Empire on the west," in Curzon's formulation. Quoted in Rothwell 1970, 277. There

were also older regional ties between India and Mesopotamia, including trade, Shia pilgrimage, and the Oudh Bequest (which channeled millions of rupees from India to the holy cities through British mediation). Bose 2006; Cole 1988; Litvak 2001, 2000. During the war, the Raj reached into all aspects of military life in Mesopotamia, extending the fiction of contiguity. Satia 2007, 246–247.

5. For countless other examples of the perceptions described in this and the following paragraph, see Satia 2007, 218n23, 220n30.

6. On the view on the Western front that technology was paralysing, see Leed 1979, 122–123.

7. See also Reynardson 1919, 50; Robert Cecil, House of Commons debate, 23 July 1918, quoted in Wilson, 1931, 99. For further examples, see Satia 2007, 226n51.

8. On the imperial reach of Indian engineering, see Gilmartin 2006. On the nineteenth-century roots of development, see Cowen and Shenton, 1995, 29; Watts, 1995, 48, 51. On the centrality of colonialism to development, see Mitchell 2002, esp. 4–6, 15, 82–83, 210; Hamlin 1998, 264–266.

9. See also Ulrichsen, 2011, on this new logistics-inspired imperialism.

10. Before the war, India had built crude river-craft for inland trade and transportation, as British ships could not negotiate the bends of eastern Indian rivers.

11. Busch, 1977, 133–134 (which adds that it came soon after the war thanks partly to the "considerable role" of the Mesopotamian scandal). Davis argues that the postwar reform of the Indian government and army were the "only real actions taken after . . . the Report," but concludes the MCR was a waste of time, since Indian reform was already on the table (1994, 220, 226).

12. Gandhi may have seen industrialism as the source of the world's ills, but other nationalists denounced the colonial state for stunting India's industrialization. See Bose 1997, 47, 50.

13. My italics. See also Shah 1918, 30; Commander Josiah Wedgwood, minority report, *MCR,* 132; Montagu in a House debate, quoted in Busch 1977, 133.

14. The "dyarchical" scheme instituted by the 1919 act transferred the nation-building departments of provincial government—agriculture, industries, education, public works, public health, and so on—to ministers responsible to elected legislatures (reserving departments critical to the maintenance of imperial rule, such as finance and revenue, for the governor).

15. This conference determined to establish a constitutional monarchy under Feisal, garrison the country with the Royal Air Force, create an indigenous army, and formulate a new treaty specifying in particular the functions of and financial arrangements for the British advisory officials in the Iraqi government.

16. That the Aga Khan had development rather than formal empire in mind was made explicit in his two-part article in the *Times* protesting the indefinite garrisoning of Mesopotamia by Indian troops and asking that the country be left alone to work out its destiny ("British Policy in the East," *Times,* 5 Nov. 1920, 13, and "Our Mistakes in

Mesopotamia," 6 Nov. 1920, 11; emphasized further in "India and the Middle East," editorial, *Times,* 5 Nov. 1920, 13). When Sydenham pointed out that the Aga Khan had urged a much more forward policy in his 1918 book (letter to the editor, *Times,* 10 Nov. 1920, 13), one of the latter's defenders used that text to show that His Highness had always argued for the influence of Indian *civilization* in the region, regardless of which flag flew there (Malabar Hill, letter to the editor, *Times,* 13 Nov. 1920, 12).

17. For more on this, see Bose 1997, 53; Ludden 1992, 278. Besides the Indian state's imperialism at home, Indian technological transfers and military aid to Iraq also shed light on its continuing role as a global source of technical expertise and a regional superpower. Evidently, former BJP Home Minister and fervid Hindu nationalist L. K. Advani continues to dream of "happy days when India, Pakistan, Sri Lanka, Bangladesh, and Myanmar (formerly Burma) would be reunited in a single South Asian "confederation".' Talbott 2004, 101.

18. This fairly large conventional war lasted several months and involved much of the country. Roughly a thousand British and Indian troops were killed, and another thousand were wounded. Roughly ten thousand Iraqis were killed.

19. For a postwar account of wartime achievement, see, for instance, Coke 1927.

20. He reiterated this thought after serving as Air Officer Commanding Iraq from 1928–30 and as High Commissioner and Commander-in-Chief in 1929. See Notes for a lecture at Downside on Feb. 7, 1932, Brooke-Popham Papers, File 2/3. See also Wing-Commander R. M. Hill, lecture at Royal Aeronautical Society, quoted in Monk and Winter, 1938, 47.

21. In a single two-day operation, a squadron might drop several dozen tons of bombs and thousands of incendiaries and fire thousands of rounds of small arms ammunition. The last British battalion left in 1927; the last Indian, in 1928.

22. It is difficult to say how many Iraqis were killed in these operations, from the bombs themselves as well as through starvation and the burning and machine-gunning of villages, but a hundred or more casualties was certainly not unusual in a single operation.

23. The quotation alludes to Stephen Phillips's poem *Marpessa,* first published in 1897.

References

Air Ministry papers, PRO.
Army YMCA of India, "The Land of Two Rivers," found in various editions among the papers of many soldiers in Mesopotamia in the Liddle archive, Leeds University (30,000 copies had been printed in the first edition alone).
Barnett, F. S. G. to his mother, 10 Mar. 1917: Liddle, GS 0089 (Barnett Papers), file 2
Bell, Gertrude. 1907. *The Desert and the Sown.* London: Heinemann.

————. 1911. *Amurath to Amurath.* New York: Dutton.

————. 1917. *The Arab of Mesopotamia.* Basrah: Government Press.

Bell, Lady Florence, ed. 1927. *The Letters of Gertrude Bell,* 2 vols. London, E. Benn.

Bevan, Edwyn. 1918. *The Land of the Two Rivers.* London: E. Arnold.

Bird, W. D. 1923. *A Chapter of Misfortunes: The Battles of Ctesiphon and of the Du-jailah in Mesopotamia, with a Summary of the Events which Preceded Them.* London: Forster Groom.

Bose, Sugata. 1997. "Instruments and Idioms of Colonial and National Development: India's Historial Experience in Comparative Perspective." In Frederick Cooper and Randall Packard, eds., *International Development and the Social Sciences: Essays on the History and Politics of Knowledge.* Berkeley: University of California Press.

————. 2006. *A Hundred Horizons: The Indian Ocean in the Age of Global Empire.* Cambridge, MA: Harvard University Press.

Brooke-Popham, Robert. 1921. "Aeroplanes in Tropical Countries," Proceedings of meeting of the Royal Aeronautical Society on Oct. 6, 1921, *Aeronautical Journal* 25 (Mar. 1, 1922), Brooke-Popham Papers, Liddell Hart Center for Military Archives, King's College, London.

Buchan, John. 1912. "Space," in *The Moon Endureth: Tales and Fancies.* London: Hodder & Stoughton.

Buchanan, George. 1938. *The Tragedy of Mesopotamia.* London: W. Blackwood.

Burgoyne, Elizabeth. 1958–61. *Gertrude Bell: From her Personal Papers,* 2 vols. London: E. Benn.

Bury, G. Wyman [Abdullah Mansur, pseud.]. 1911. *The Land of Uz.* London: Macmillan.

Busch, Briton Cooper. 1977. *Britain, India, and the Arabs, 1914–1921.* Berkeley: University of California Press.

Butler, Capt. S. S. 1909. Lecture, "Baghdad to Damascus via El Jauf, Northern Arabia," 22 Feb. 1909, *Geographical Journal* 33, 533

Candler, Edmund. 1919. *The Long Road to Baghdad,* 2 vols. New York: Houghton Mifflin.

Carruthers, Douglas. 1935. *Arabian Adventure: To the Great Nafud in Quest of the Oryx.* London: H. F. & G. Witherby.

Casey, Edward S. 1998. *The Fate of Place: A Philosophical History.* Berkeley: University of California.

Casey, Robert J. 1928. *Baghdad and Points East.* London: Hutchinson.

Cato, Conrad. 1917. *The Navy in Mesopotamia: 1914 to 1917.* London: Constable.

Chirol, Valentine. 1903. *The Middle Eastern Question, Or Some Political Problems of Indian Defence.* New York: Dutton.

Churchill, Winston. 1898, *The Story of the Malakand Field Force, an Episode of Frontier War.* New York: Longmans.

Clark, Arthur Tillotson. 1918. *To Bagdad with the British*. New York: D. Appleton.

Cohen, S. A. 1976. "The Genesis of the British Campaign in Mesopotamia, 1914," *Middle Eastern Studies* xii.

Coke, Richard. 1927. *Baghdad: The City of Peace*. London: Thornton Butterworth.

———. 1929. *The Arab's Place in the Sun*. London: Thornton Butterworth.

Cole, Juan. 1986. "'Indian Money' and the Shi'i Shrine Cities of Iraq, 1786–1850," *Middle Eastern Studies* xxii.

———. 1988. *Roots of North Indian Shī'ism in Iran and Iraq: Religion and State in Awadh, 1722–1859*. Berkeley: University of California Press.

Constantine, Stephen. 1984. *The Making of British Colonial Development Policy, 1914–1940*. London: F. Cass.

Cooper, Frederick. 1997. "Modernizing Bureaucrats, Backward Africans, and the Development Concept." In *International Development and the Social Sciences: Essays on the History and Politics of Knowledge*, ed. Frederick Cooper and Randall Packard, . 64–92. Berkeley: University of California Press.

Cowen, Michael, and Robert Shenton. 1995. "The Invention of Development," and Michael Watts, "'A New Deal in Emotions': Theory and Practice and the Crisis of Development," in Jonathan Crush, ed., *Power of Development*. London: Routledge.

Cox, Jafna. 1985. "A Splendid Training Ground: The Importance to the Royal Air Force of its Role in Iraq, 1919–32." *Journal of Imperial and Commonwealth History* 13: 157–184.

Davis, Paul K. 1994. *Ends and Means: The British Mesopotamian Campaign and Commission*. London: Associated University Presses.

Dickson, H. R. P. Papers of H. R. P. Dickson. MEC Archive, GB165–0085. The Middle East Centre, St Antony's College, Oxford.

Egan, Eleanor Franklin. 1918. *The War in the Cradle of the World: Mesopotamia*. New York: Harper.

Fraser, David. 1909. *The Short Cut to India: The Record of a Journey along the Route of the Baghdad Railway*. Edinburgh: W. Blackwood.

Fraser, Lovat. 1918. "Problems of Indian Administration." *Edinburgh Review* llvii: 166–187.

Fussell, Paul. 1975. *The Great War and Modern Memory*. London: Oxford University Press.

Galbraith, John S. 1984. "No Man's Child: The Campaign in Mesopotamia, 1914–1916." *International History* Review: vi (6): 358–385.

Gilmartin, David. 2006. "Imperial Rivers: Irrigation and British Visions of Empire." In *Decentring Empire: Britain, India and the Transcolonial World*, ed. Durba Ghosh and Dane Kennedy. New Delhi: Orient Longman.

Glubb Papers, Box I, File: Iraq S. Desert (1), 1927–1928, MEC.

Haldane, Aylmer. 1922. *The Insurrection in Mesopotamia, 1920*. Edinburgh: W. Blackwood.

Hamlin, Christopher. 1998. *Public Health and Social Justice in the Age of Chadwick: Britain, 1800–1854*. Cambridge: Cambridge University Press.

Hart, Basil Henry Liddell. 1933. *The British Way in Warfare*. New York: Macmillan.

———. 1934. *"T. E. Lawrence": In Arabia and After*. London: Jonathan Cape.

Hogarth, D. G. 1902. *The Nearer East*. London: Heinemann.

———. 1908. "Problems in Exploration I. Western Asia," *Geographical Journal* 32, 549–50.

Hynes, Samuel. 1968. *The Edwardian Turn of Mind*. Princeton: Princeton University Press.

Jebb, Louisa. 1909. *By Desert Ways to Baghdad*. Boston: Dana, Estes.

Keith, C. H. 1937. *Flying Years*. London: J. Hamilton for the Aviation Book Club.

Kern, Stephen. 1983. *The Culture of Time and Space: 1880–1918*. Cambridge, MA: Harvard University Press.

Kinch, Edward. n.d. Autobiographical notes covering early life in England and career in Iraq, 1896–1959, MS, n.d., 27: Middle East Centre Archive, St Antony's College, Oxford (hereafter MEC) (Kinch Papers), file 1/2.

Leed, Eric J. 1979. *No Man's Land: Combat and Identity in World War I*. Cambridge: Cambridge University Press.

Leith-Ross Papers, National Army Museum. (This includes the document Leith-Ross, "The Physical and Climatic Difficulties of the Mesopotamian Theatre of War," 14 Aug. 1916.)

Litvak, Meir. 2000. "A Failed Manipulation: The British, the Oudh Bequest and the Shi Ulama of Najaf and Karbala." *British Journal of Middle Eastern Studies* xxvii: 69–89.

———. 2001. "Money, Religion, and Politics: The Oudh Bequest in Najaf and Karbala, 1850–1903." *International Journal of Middle Eastern Studies* xxxiii: 1–21.

Ludden, David. 1992. "India's Development Regime." In *Colonialism and Culture*, ed. Nicholas Dirks, 247–287. Ann Arbor: University of Michigan Press.

Lynden-Bell, L. A. Interview with Peter Liddle, TS, Oct. 1977: Liddle Collection, Leeds University Library, GS 0993 (Lynden-Bell Papers).

Mann, James Saumarez, Sr., ed. 1921. *An Administrator in the Making: James Saumarez Mann, 1893–1920*. London: Longmans, Green.

Mehrotra. S. R. 1965. *India and the Commonwealth, 1885–1929*. New York: Frederick A. Praeger.

Mesopotamia Commission Report (MCR), Parliamentary Papers, 1917–18 (Cd. 8610), xvi.

Mitchell, Timothy. 2002. *Rule of Experts: Egypt, Techno-Politics, Modernity*. Berkeley: University of California Press.

Monk, F. V., and H. T. Winter. 1936. *The Royal Air Force*. London: Blackie and Son.

Nunn, Wilfrid. 1932. *Tigris Gunboats: A Narrative of the Royal Navy's Co-operation with the Military Forces in Mesopotamia from the Beginning of the War to the Capture of Baghdad (1914–17)*. London: A. Melrose.

O'Brien, Rosemary, ed. 2000. *Gertrude Bell: The Arabian Diaries, 1913–1914*. Syracuse, NY: Syracuse University Press.

Omissi, David. 1990. *Air Power and Colonial Control: The Royal Air Force 1919–1939*. Manchester: Manchester University Press.

One of Its Officers. 1918. *With a Highland Regiment in Mesopotamia: 1916–1917*, 70–71 (in ch. 7, whose author is identified as A. G. Wauchope) (repr. from *Blackwood's Mag.*, 1917. Bombay: Times Press.

Owen, Alex. 2004. *The Place of Enchantment: British Occultism and the Culture of the Modern*. Chicago: University of Chicago Press.

Parliamentary Papers. *East India (Military)*, P.P., 1914–16 (Cd. 7624), xlix.

Peck, R. H. 1928. "Aircraft in Small Wars." *Journal of the Royal United Services Institute* 1 Feb.:: 73.

Popplewell, Richard. 1990. "British Intelligence in Mesopotamia: 1914–1916," *Intelligence and National Security* v, 139–172.

Reynardson, H, Birch. 1919. *Mesopotamia, 1914–15: Extracts from a Regimental Officer's Diary*. London: Andrew Melrose.

Rothwell, V. H. 1970. "Mesopotamia in British War Aims, 1914–1918." *Historical Journal* xiii: 273–294.

Said, Edward. 1978. *Orientalism*. New York: Vintage.

Satia, Priya. 2006. "The Defense of Inhumanity: Air Control and the British Idea of Arabia," *American Historical Review* 111: 16–51.

———. 2007. "Developing Iraq: Britain, India, and the Redemption of Empire and Technology in World War I," *Past and Present* 197: 211–255.

———. 2008. *Spies in Arabia: The Great War and the Cultural Foundations of Britain's Covert Empire in the Middle East*. New York: Oxford University Press.

Shah, Sultan Muhammad [Aga Khan III]. 1918. *India in Transition: A Study in Political Evolution*. London: P. L. Warner.

Sinha, Meeta. 2006. "'Where Electricity Dispels the Illusion [of the *Arabian Nights*]': The British and the Modern in Interwar India." Paper presented at the Pacific Coast Conference of British Studies, Irvine, CA, March 24–26. Sluglett, Peter. 1976. *The British in Iraq: 1914–1932*. London: Ithaca.

Swayne, Martin. 1917. *In Mesopotamia*. London: Hodder & Stoughton.

Sykes, Mark. 1904. *Dar-ul-Islam; A Record of a Journey through Ten of the Asiatic Provinces of Turkey*. London: Bickers & Son.

———. 1915. *The Caliph's Last Heritage: A Short History of the Turkish Empire*. London: Macmillan.

Mark Sykes papers, MEC.

Talbott, Strobe. 2004. *Engaging India: Diplomacy, Democracy, and the Bomb*. Washington, DC: Brookings Institute.

Townsend, Meredith. 1904. *Asia and Europe: Studies Presenting the Conclusions Formed by the Author in a Long Life Devoted to the Subject of the Relations between Asia and Europe,* 2nd ed. New York: G. P. Putnam's Sons.

Townshend, Charles Vere Ferrers. 1920. *My Campaign,* 2 vols. New York: J. A. McCann.

Ulrichsen, Kristian. 2011. *The Logistics and Politics of the British Campaigns in the Middle East, 1914–22.* Houndsmills, Basingstoke, Hampshire: Palgrave Macmillan.

Wilkinson, Capt. R. J. 1922. "The Geographical Importance of Iraq," *Journal of the Royal United Services Institute* 61: 660–665.

Young, Hubert. 1933. *The Independent Arab.* London: J. Murray.

10

Marriage and the Management of Place in Southern Arabia

MANDANA E. LIMBERT

In April 2005, soon after the declaration of a new marriage law in the Sultanate of Oman, an editorial appeared in the United Arab Emirates-based English language daily, *The Gulf News*. In the editorial, a Pakistani-Omani expressed his continued frustration with current marriage laws saying that he had to wait five years for approval to marry a cousin from Pakistan.[1] Though the 2005 law in the Sultanate had eased restrictions on marriage between Omanis and citizens of the states of the Gulf Cooperation Council, it had not changed the restrictions on marriage between Omanis and citizens of other states, including citizens of Asian countries. Marriage between Omanis and non-GCC foreigners continued to be permitted only under particular circumstances, such as if the Omani man wishing to marry were disabled or elderly. These laws had been in force since 1986 when marriage between Omanis and most foreigners was essentially banned in a seemingly sudden decree that drew the attention of news agencies from China to the US, from the Xinhua Overseas News Service to *The Christian Science Monitor*. This small statement of frustration that appeared in *The Gulf News* nearly twenty years later underscores broad and continuing tensions around the processes of citizenship, statehood, marriage, and place-making in Oman at the end of the twentieth and beginning of the twenty-first centuries. In the Arabian

Peninsula, where territorial and citizenship boundaries have been so recently drawn to exclude (or include) people who trace or are called upon to trace origins in Africa or Asia, laws of marriage have been regularly reformulated to help determine who is a "national." Debates about marriage and descent thus concern not only issues of equality and rights, as feminist scholars have long pointed out, but stand at the center of debates about political sovereignty and national statehood as well as the processes of affective place-making and of reinforcing territorial boundaries.

The production of place in Oman (and other Persian Gulf states) in relation to Asia in particular, could, undoubtedly, be explored in a number of ways. Primarily, one could examine the ways that migrant laborers from Asia shape Omani distinctiveness as well as its connections with different polities and communities throughout Asia: from Korea and Nepal to Bangladesh and India.[2] Indeed, much excellent work has been written about the ways that a number of states in the Arabian Peninsula manage their Asian populations and the ways that those Asian populations reshape both life in the peninsula as well as politics and social life in Asia (Ahmad 2009, Gamburd 2000; Gardner 2010; Longva 1999; Mahdavi 2011; Nagy 1998, 2004, 2008; C. and F. Osella 2012; Vora 2013). When a substantial minority or even a majority of those residing in a state are citizens of other states, the dynamics of how "place" is constituted is clearly a rich field of investigation. How do migrants and non-migrants reshape, reconfigure, and understand their experiences of movement and belonging in the late twentieth and early twenty-first centuries? How do older forms of migration intersect with these experiences? And, of course, how do the ephemerality and socio-economic hierarchies of migratory labor in the Gulf shape senses of place? This chapter takes a different approach and explores instead how marriage legislation in Oman, and debates about it, attempt to reinforce boundaries, both national and intimate, while at the same time reveal the tensions and motion of people-in-place. The physical space and territorial exclusivity of Oman takes shape not only through map making and the control of migratory labor, but also through the legalities and experiences of marriage, as well as their limits, and the determination of children's citizenship. This chapter, therefore, focuses on the ways that "Oman," as a place, comes to be produced through the intersection of territory, citizenship, and personal status laws as well as debates about and opposition to those laws.

As a series of states that either gained independence from Britain or became formally established "modern" states (with determined boundaries and state bureaucratic structures and institutions) in the second half of the twentieth century, the states of the Arabian Peninsula instituted policies and laws that aimed at demarcating rather quickly the boundaries of citizenship and belonging. The states of the Arabian Peninsula established, at various times, their "Nationality Laws" *(Qānūn al-Jinsīyya)* that detail regulations on citizenship and marriage. For example, Kuwaiti nationality law was first established in 1959 (though an official definition of "original Kuwaiti" was provided earlier, in 1948), the United Arab Emirates first established its law in 1972, Qatar's law was first established in 1961, and Bahrain's in 1963.[3] Oman's first official nationality law was decreed in 1972 and was reformed in 1983 as Royal Decree 3/83, and again in 2014 as Royal Decree 38/14.[4] Certainly, the establishment of these laws does not mean that controls and debates about belonging or subjecthood had not occurred prior to these laws, as will be explored below, but the declaration of these laws undoubtedly helped institutionalize the processes of modern state-formation in the region.

Citizenship in these states has been primarily based on *jus sanguinis* (right of blood) rather than *jus soli* (right of soil), as determined patrilineally (though some states allow for matrilineal genealogical nationality under particular circumstances) through a historic, and not contemporary, connection to the place or territory of the new state. Thus, while the primacy of the right of blood over the right of soil in citizenship highlights the significance of population over land, the ensuing tensions and uncertainties of this preference in the making of Oman also reveal that neither is mutually exclusive. Still, the primacy of blood over soil, and the power to determine what constitutes historic connection to a place, has enabled these states to limit quite severely who qualifies for citizenship. However, while other Persian Gulf states specify historic connection to a territory, Oman's Nationality Law does not explicate what constitutes The Sultanate of Oman historically. It is unclear, for example, whether or how this polity includes descendants of Omanis who lived in East Africa, not to mention how to contend with territories within the boundaries of contemporary Oman that—over the course of the twentieth century—had been considered autonomous or semi-autonomous regions or polities.[5] The 2005 marriage law did, however, ease marriage restrictions for those living in border areas, perhaps suggesting recognition of the relative arbitrariness of national boundaries, the fluidity of those living on the borders, as well as the familial and tribal connections of those living in these regions. The 2014 nationality law outlines the conditions for foreign men and women to gain

Omani nationality, including marriage to an Omani national that has been approved and solemnized by the Ministry of the Interior and continuous residency in Oman. Men may gain Omani nationality without marriage, while women must also be proficient in Arabic and have borne a son.

Empire and Territory, "Indians" in Oman

Though the establishment of nationality laws and marriage regulations became significantly more urgent in the middle and late twentieth centuries when the states of the Persian Gulf gained independence from Britain or came to be established as "modern" states, the question of political belonging—especially of Asians in Arabia and Omani East Africa—was also important in the Indian Ocean in the nineteenth century. From the late nineteenth through the middle of the twentieth centuries, people residing in the territory of contemporary Oman were, as elsewhere, described in official British correspondence as subjects of the Sultan of Muscat or the Sultan of Muscat and Oman. This was, undoubtedly, a vague characterization of people residing in this territory, not least of all because this territory now includes what was, in periods over the course of the nineteenth and twentieth centuries, a quasi-autonomous polity of the Imamate of Oman and, certainly, many people living in this territory saw themselves loyal and responsible to or belonging with tribal leaders, regional and town elders, or representatives of the Imam rather than a distant Sultan. For their part, Sultans did not expect to have much authority over people living in Imamate territory (much less in their own territory). Indeed, local Omani histories of the early twentieth century are very clear that political loyalty and authority varied significantly and that this variation ranged from local governors and tribal leaders to the Imamate administration with its own appointed governors. The Sultans in Muscat were seen to rule the coast, if that, and had very little authority in the interior regions. Thus, though in general, British officials referred to populations residing throughout the territory of contemporary Oman as subjects of the Sultan of Muscat (or Sultan of Muscat and Oman), even British officials recognized that such an appellation was tenuous and did not reflect the actual loyalty of people in these territories, nor did it reflect the authority of the Sultan over people. Such questions did not have much significance for the British in particular, however, until slave-trade restrictions began to dominate Indian Ocean diplomatic and military relationships and policies. Indeed, who was subject to changing slave-trade restrictions (as well as what kinds of ship-flagging practices were legal) in the Indian Ocean became a central concern of British policy.

Thus, though much has been made of the increasingly racialized distinctions between "Africans" and "Arabs" over the course of the nineteenth and early twentieth centuries in the Western Indian Ocean, the first extended debates about political subjecthood and nationality focused not on "Arabs" or "Africans," but on "Indians" who resided in the Indian Ocean and who, because of their potential status as British subjects, would be banned from partaking in the Indian Ocean slave trade.

The famous British consul Colonel Atkins Hamerton, who was stationed in Zanzibar from 1840 to 1857, attempted to identify "Indians" in the Indian Ocean, and in particular Zanzibar and Arabia, to make them subject to anti-slave trade treaties.[6] As Reda Bhacker (1992) has noted, in the attempt to pressure the Omani Sultan, Sayyid Sa'id bin Sultan (r. 1804–1856), who ruled both Zanzibar and Oman, to forbid his subjects (ra'iya) from selling slaves to British Indians, the question of who exactly British Indians were, never mind who the Sultan's subjects were, arose. For his part, Sayyid Sa'id bin Sultan, unsure himself, turned to the British for clarification on whether Indians born in Omani dominions (including Zanzibar) or long-time residents, who had also taken local wives, were Omani or British. He also seemed quite clear that he did not care whether Banyans were subjects of Zanzibar (and thus Oman) or Britain. In other words, the Sultan himself seemed to feel that little was at stake in deciding whether some people were *his* subjects, and thus Omani or Indian, Arab, Asian, or African.

Colonel Hamerton, who seems to have considered or found it pragmatically convenient to consider all Indians to be British subjects at first, eventually argued that although Sindis were not Omani (as Britain gained control of Sind in 1840), Kutchis residing in Oman or Zanzibar could be Omani, and thus were not British subjects. Therefore, while Sindis would be subject to slave-trade restrictions, Kutchis could continue to trade in slaves.[7] Such "Indians" were thus also Omani. As Bhacker also notes, Hamerton's successor, Christopher Rigby (1858–1860), did not distinguish between Kutchis and other Indians for these purposes, including Baluch and Zadgalis from Makran. For Rigby, if someone was not Arab or African, then he must be Indian and therefore a British subject and potentially punishable by the British for slave-trading. Rigby's own successors, however, denounced Rigby's approach, returning to the policy laid out by Hamerton.

Sultan Thuwayni bin Saʿid al-Bu Saʿid, who was Sayyid Saʿid's third son and who became Sultan of Oman when Zanzibar and Oman were divided into separate polities in 1861 was, in 1858, able to obtain a guarantee from the British that Lawatiyas and Khojas who had settled in Oman prior to 1840 were *his* subjects, and were thus not to be regarded as British subjects. It seems that between the era of Sayyid Saʿid bin Sultan and Sultan Thuwayni bin Saʿid something significant had changed. While the former ruler seemed to care little whether people from the sub-continent were his subjects or not, the latter argued that some communities were certainly his subjects, whether from Asia or not. By the same token, such debates expose the tensions between the significance of ethnic groups, regional (princely) territories, and a broader colonial mapping of India.

In the subsequent decade more questions about who was British or British-Indian arose in Oman and Zanzibar. In 1865, Sayyid Majid bin Saʿid, who was the sixth son of Sayyid Saʿid bin Sultan and who became Sultan of Zanzibar after Oman and Zanzibar were divided, issued a decree that any "local" woman who married a British subject would herself become a British subject. In other words, the decree determined that the union of a British male subject and local woman in Zanzibar would not only produce British children, but that the woman herself would become British.[8] "British" seems to have meant British-Indian and local meant subjects of the Omani Sultan in Zanzibar, including Omani-Zanzibaris. The declaration of losing one's subjecthood or citizenship because of marriage to a foreigner (as would be the case in late-20th century Oman) was clearly a practice of the nineteenth century as well. In 1869, the Rao of Kutch also issued a decree pertaining to subjecthood, reversing Hamerton's position and declaring instead that people from Kutch who permanently resided or frequented Africa, Arabia, and the Persian Gulf because of trade were to be considered Indian and therefore British subjects.

It should be noted that the question of who was considered a subject of the Sultan and how such a status could be determined also became a central matter of the Muscat Dhows Arbitration case, decided at the Permanent Court of Arbitration at the Hague in 1905. The case between the British and French governments, which was one of the first cases heard at the Hague, revolved in part around the question of whether subjects of a sovereign (the Sultan of Muscat) could fly French flags on their ships if those subjects and the French government considered them to be protected persons, or *protégé*. In the ensuing debate, some of the signatories to a letter declaring loyalty to the Sultan also wrote letters requesting continued French protected status based on residency or property ownership in French colonies and declaring that they had been coerced to sign the letter of loyalty. This is to say that at the turn of the twentieth century, though the Sultan of Muscat (with support from British officials) declared that residents of the coastal town of Sur, 90 miles Southeast of Muscat, were his subjects, the conditions and limits of that subjecthood was hardly firmly established locally or internationally.

Though Oman's centuries-old connections to East Africa constituted (until the 1964 revolution in Zanzibar in which its "Arab" population either fled or was killed) its primary trans-oceanic tie and it is the complex relationship of Oman and Zanzibar that has elicited most scholarly attention, historic trans-oceanic trade with the Indian subcontinent was obviously also integral to all Omani Indian Ocean relationships, movement, and to the debates about who exactly could be considered an Omani. In fact, it was specifically in relation to discerning whether "Indians" in Oman were Omani or not that the limits of Omaniness were first debated.

However, not only were South Asians traveling to the Arabian Peninsula and East Africa (as traders or mercenaries) affecting and raising doubts about who was a subject of what polity or which sovereign, Omanis were also moving to South Asia. Most famously was movement to the territory of Gwadar in the province of Baluchistan in contemporary Pakistan. In 1784, this port city had fallen under the control of or given as a gift to, depending on the source, Sultan bin Ahmad al-Bu Saʿid, who had fled Muscat as a rivalry within the emerging ruling family of the al-Bu Saʿid heightened.[9] When Sultan bin Ahmad returned to Muscat to rule, he retained control of the city. It remained under Omani rule until 1958 when the recently formed Pakistani state purchased it from Oman for $US300,000. Though the territory was relatively tangential to Omani foreign policy and a large number of Omanis did not migrate there in the nineteenth century, its long history—as well as the long history of Baluch presence in Oman more generally (often serving as soldiers for the Sultans, and more recently in the police force)—forms part of the fabric of Omani citizenship. This long relationship with the sub-continent, and contemporary Pakistan, is not confined, of course, to Baluchistan as the previous discussion indicates. However, the role of Oman in Gwadar for over 150 years underscores the long history of the difficulty of discerning the limits of what constitutes the territory of Oman, much less Omanis.

Indeed, Oman and Omanis have continued to be invested in Gwadar. In 2010, the Omani government pledged $US45 million to the Baluchistan government for development there, including for the renovations of the central fort as well as for the building of a hospital, asphalt roads, and piped water.[10] The following year, in 2011, the Omani government bestowed a further grant of $US17 million for a new international airport in Gwadar.[11] And, also in 2011, discussions began on the possibility of establishing ferry service between Muscat and Gwadar, though this plan seems to have stalled as there seemed to be little support either from Omani-Pakistanis or Pakistanis working in Oman.[12] Despite this obvious historic (and on-going) connection with Baluchistan as well as with the rest of the sub-continent, marriage policies within the Sultanate have made it exceptionally difficult to enable the ties to be embodied or manifest through marital relations.

Beyond the complications of discerning whether "Asians" from the subcontinent were Omani or not (much less whether and which "Zanzibaris" were "Omani" because of where they lived), a series of other political tensions within and on the borders of contemporary Oman confounds further the links between territory, genealogy, political loyalty, and authority that have served as the presumed basis of historic connection to place. Attention to the history of the contemporary territory of Oman could raise questions about the status of Dhofar (in the South, bordering Yemen), the region bordering the Emirate of Abu Dhabi (under dispute in the 1950s), the lands bordering Saudi Arabia, and the internal conflicts and autonomous regions of the Imamate. In the nineteenth century, a member of the al-Bu Said family declared himself Imam (1868–1871), ruling over Muscat and Oman. This was, however, both short-lived and his authority was even more circumscribed than the al-Bu Sa'id Sultans of the nineteenth century. The twentieth century Imamate was different. Its establishment in 1913 marked more forcefully a separation from the coast and the authority of the al-Bu Sa'id Sultans. A series of Imams, based in the town of Nizwa, ruled the territory now known as Interior Oman from 1913 to 1959 through appointed governors after Imamate forces had taken control of the region. The relationship with the coastal Sultan changed over the years, but in general Imam and Sultan saw their territories as rather distinct. Indeed, as late as World War II, when British official attempted to institute travel restrictions on Omanis traveling to East Africa, the aim of requiring travelers from Arabia to carry a travel or identity document proved futile, which not only suggested that people were not obeying edicts of the Sultan of Muscat on the coast, but also perhaps that they may have felt very little loyalty to him if they were from the interior territories of the Imamate theocracy. With the collapse of the Imamate administration in 1959 (after British military supported the Sultan in bombing and controlling interior towns), Sultan Sa'id bin Taimur al-Bu Sa'id instituted a new era of political power whereby his coastal-based Sultanate would rule the interior territories of the former Imamate. Sa'id bin Taimur thus declared himself Sultan of Muscat *and* Oman.

On the one hand, the emphasis on *jus sanguinis* over *jus soli* in citizenship law helps circumvent these complicated histories. On the other hand, *jus sanguinis* raises multiple questions about how citizenship, and the boundaries of what constitutes Oman, can be determined. If a family from Gwadar were traveling back and forth over the course of the nineteenth century, would their descendants be able to obtain Omani citizenship? More to the point, would an Omani citizen of Baluch descent be able to marry a cousin from Gwadar, who has Pakistani citizenship? Or would that Omani lose his citizenship because he married a "foreigner?" Might he have to wait five years for permission?

Personal Status Law

While a history of Indian Ocean arrangements about political subjecthood confounds neat distinctions between Asia, Arabia, and Africa (evident through the attempts of various officials to clarify these distinctions) and contemporary nationality laws are silent about Oman's historic borders as well as about the history of empire (British or Omani), Omani royal decrees of 1986 through 2012 pertaining to marriage, on the other hand, are very clear about the role of nationality in marriage. With the initial ban on marriage between Omanis and all foreigners in 1986, a series of amendments and royal decrees were passed that both created sanctions (in the form of losing one's nationality) and enabled exemptions from the ban. In 1986, it was declared that while anyone found to have married a foreigner could lose his or her nationality, anyone over 60, anyone interested in marrying someone from a GCC state, or anyone who was disabled could marry a foreigner with prior approval from the Ministry of Interior.[13] In 1993, Royal Decree (59/93) was promulgated making it possible for Omanis to obtain permission to marry non-GCC citizens after approval from a committee comprised of officials from the Ministry of the Interior, the Ministry of Social Affairs and Labor, and The Royal Oman Police.

Conditions for approval included "valid social and health reasons to justify the marriage."[14] In 1993, one of the other exceptions to marriages with foreigners was for those people who lived on Oman's border regions and were interested in marrying citizens of other states also living at the borders.[15] In 1996, the law was amended again to include extended residence in a foreign country as a satisfactory reason for marriage with a foreigner.[16] This amendment was becoming increasingly important as Oman's economy expanded and more Omanis (primarily men, but also some women) were traveling to other countries in the Arab world, to Europe, and to the US to study and work.

At the same time, however, in 1996, The Ministry of Social Affairs and Labor conducted a much-publicized study on marriage between Omanis and foreigners. It found that "80 per cent of the Omanis married to foreigners confront marital problems related to the upbringing of the children, relationship with the in-laws and the strong urge in the wife to return to her roots and her inability to adapt to Omani habits and traditions."[17] Given that the ban and then restrictions on marriage to foreigners came into effect from 1986, and obviously did not succeed in preventing such marriages, this study was, in some ways, not only an admission of the limits of the sanctions, but also another way of attempting to hinder such unions. Indeed, in the end, the report suggested that public and private funds should be made available to facilitate marriages in Oman of Omanis to Omanis. Thus, on the one hand, individuals were theoretically allowed to apply for permission to marry foreigners, but those permissions were granted sparingly (and with some suggestions of personal connections, *wasta,* with officials in these ministries required to obtain permission) and other public policies and discourses forcefully worked to limit such unions. At the same time, social-scientific studies publicized the hazards and difficulties of "cross-cultural" marriages.

One year after this study, Oman passed its Personal Status Law (32/97), a comprehensive law outlining the state's legal position on personal affairs, and in particular, marriage, divorce, guardianship, and the care of children.[18] It is a highly detailed legislation outlining the intimate limits and relations between men and women in marriage. This legislation also outlined marriage and divorce of Omanis of different statuses as well as the marriage of Muslim men and women to Christian and Jewish men and women, which was of particular (and generally theoretical) interest to Omanis that I knew. In particular, in the new law, Article 35 outlines that a Muslim man may only marry women who are "of the book" *(kitābiyya),* while a Muslim woman may not marry a non-Muslim man. And, Article 109(b) notes that "divorce shall not be granted if the wife knew about the poor condition of the husband prior to the marriage and accepted [it]" and Article 109(c) notes "the rich wife shall not be divorced from her poor husband."

That most people I knew were as interested in what the law said about marriage between religious groups, rather than nationalities, ethnicities, or wealth, was striking. Indeed, echoing comments I heard from friends in Bahla in the 1990s when the Personal Status Law was proclaimed, internet blogs in 2012 and 2013 discussing marriage law have contained consistent complaints that the laws that prohibit marriage between Omanis and Muslims of non-GCC countries are "against Islam." According to this logic, women, and men, should be allowed to marry Muslims in Asia, Africa, or wherever as long as guardians approve and as long as the relevant status differences are understood and acceptable. This opposition to the limitations on marriage between Muslims is not universal, of course, and numerous people in person and in blogs have also expressed their views that it makes sense to limit marriage based on nationality.

And, finally, in April, 2005, as mentioned above, another twist in the legislation on marriage took place. On April 13, it was announced that Omanis no longer needed prior approval to marry GCC citizens. Though marriage between GCC citizens had not been banned, people had still required permission, which was cumbersome and easy fodder for complaints about the uneven processes involved in dealing with state bureaucracies. This relaxation of the legislation was very welcome, though marriage between Omanis and other foreigners, including other Arabs Egyptians, Jordanians and Tunisians and other Asians with whom one may be related continued to be banned and to be the potential cause for citizenship cancellation. Of course, these various limits and restrictions do not, as mentioned above, necessarily reflect what people do, how people understand the restrictions placed on them, even how other state and religious authorities issue opinions about personal matters. Nevertheless, they help structure what is seen to constitute Oman.

Strikingly (and in line with hypergynous assumptions that few Omani women would be marrying foreigners in any case), the focus of the 1997 study and most of the legislation in Oman since 1986 has focused on Omani men marrying foreign women (though nationality law does also address Omani women marrying foreign men). Indeed, the vast majority of discussions about cross-border or "cross-cultural" marriages are of Omani men with foreign women, though some discussions of Omani women marrying non-Omani (including Asian) men do appear in the 2014 nationality law and on the internet, though the discussions are often prompted by a non-Omani man who declares his love for an Omani woman. For example, on the Omanforum blog, a Pakistani man in 2008 declares his love for an Omani "girl" and asks whether it is possible for them to marry. The responses and advice in the blog differ significantly, though they tend to be sarcastic and dismissive. Responses include: "Take her to Pakistan, and get married there. She can easily get a Pakistani citizenship . . . ," and "If I was the girl I wouldn't marry to end up living in Pakistan!!! No matter how much I love you dude!! Good luck though," as well as the more helpful "obtain a booklet available at the ministry [of interior] detailing all the legal requirements and associated legal clauses and study it before applying for a permit."[19]

In another English language blog called "How to Live Like an Omani Princess" that purportedly aims at "European" women looking to formalize their marriages with Omani men (and also gain Omani citizenship), a discussion in 2010 about Omani marriage limitations focused primarily on how these laws were not Islamic (and were unnecessarily nationalistic).[20] One commentator even argued that the law that bans Muslims from marrying each other because of differences in nationality is *shirk* (apostasy). Another commentator, however, wrote "I agree with the ban as I see it as protection to people from themselves and for the sake of their kids," while yet another suggested how, as a mother of a woman who married an Omani man, she appreciated how difficult it was for her daughter to marry because it proved that the two of them truly loved each other and could overcome inevitable difficulties in their future.

On the same blog, founded by three "European" women with different experiences of trying to marry Omani men, one woman describes her failed attempts at marrying the Omani man with whom she fell in love as a teenager. According to the woman's account, when the two meet again years later as adults and facing little hope of marrying her love, she provides a list of ten actions she could imagine taking in order to try to marry. This list ranges from protesting to the Sultan and hoping to marry as a "Bedouin wife" where no one would know who she was to wishing to become the man's "slave." The woman declares that she even wrote to a Saudi Sheikh for a *fatwa* (legal opinion) asking him whether this was legal (there is no clarification whether the Sheikh responded).[21] The notion that this woman would "choose" to become this man's slave (or "maid," as another commentator wrote about her proposed ideas) in order to marry him, not only opens the discussion of the pressures of cross-border marriages to "Europe," but also raises multiple questions about notions of romance, servitude, agency, and law that are also at stake in the marriage legislation and politics.

In the summer of 2012, foreign-marriage legislation was amended again, making explicit the place-based difficulties of Oman's marriage legislation. According to *The Times of Oman*, the Ministry of Information announced that: "the marriages of thousands of Omanis with foreign nationals may be legalized."[22] This decision to legalize marriages suggests that despite all the sanctions against marriage with foreigners, including loss of citizenship, such marriages were occurring regularly enough to require recognition. It should be noted that this would be possible not only outside Oman (as the response to the Pakistani man who wanted to marry an Omani woman suggested), but also within Oman as marriages—to be recognized "locally"—do not require state approval. A recitation by a local Sheikh in the presence of witnesses would suffice.

However, this policy shift was declared not simply in order to legalize what was already occurring, but more significantly because the sanction of citizenship loss to Omanis and the refusal to grant citizenship to foreign spouses (and children) created a situation whereby numerous "stateless families" resided within Omani territory. Indeed, immediately following and connected to the declaration of marriage legalization, the Ministry of Information clarified its citizenship application requirements for foreign spouses (a ten-year residency requirement and very limited travel outside Oman) and, according to *The Times of Oman*, "initiated a rigorous screening process to study the cases of stateless families in the Sultanate."[23] In 2014, yet another nationality law was decreed. Royal Decree 38/14 requires 20-year residency for foreign men, unless married to an Omani woman, in which case the man must have 15-years of continuous residency. Ultimately, by attempting to define and possibly defend "Oman," as a unique, bounded, and increasingly homogeneous place through restricting its population from marrying "foreigners," including Asians, it created "stateless families"—families without official political "place."

"They Will Do Anything to Stay"

On a trip in December 2012 to Bahla, a town in the interior of Oman where I have been visiting and conducting research since 1996, I asked an old friend about an "Indian" woman who had, when a housemaid in Bahla fifteen years earlier, married a lower-status Omani man in her neighborhood. At the time, the marriage was a topic of local talk that vacillated between dismissiveness and admiration. In its dismissive moments, the talk was accompanied by suggestions of the failure of the man to be able to afford the dowry that a Bahlawi girl or woman might require. Though many people complained about the excessively high dowry prices and recognized that as a descendant of a slave the man was less likely to be wealthy (though this was not at all universal), his "inability" to afford the dowry was still often considered an individual failure. Alternatively, local talk suggested the bravery of the couple in breaching standard practice, arguing that as both the man and the maid were Muslim and poor, it made perfect sense that they would marry. In fact, as numerous women pointed out, dowries *were* inexcusably high.

As we drove by the man's house more than fifteen years after the original marriage, I asked my friend what had happened to the couple. I had partly expected to hear an account of struggle and "cultural" conflict or, at least, homesickness. Instead, my friend explained that the man had tragically died in a car accident several years earlier. I then asked if the woman had returned to India or had stayed in Bahla. At this point, my friend's mother, who was driving in the car with us, spoke up, saying—with confidence—that, of course, the Indian wife stayed in Oman. After all, she had several children with him and they are Omani, she pointed out. Her adamant response suggested my possibly naïve presumption that the woman's homesickness, or being-out-of-place, would over-ride the practical benefits she believed would necessarily lead to the woman remaining in Oman. As Nicole Constable (2005) has pointed out, however, presumptions of abuse and passivity as well as presumptions of upward mobility miss the (often) contradictory transnational desires and imaginings of marriage.

Our conversation about this tragedy and, especially, the expressed understanding of the "obvious" desire by the woman to remain in Oman continued. When I then asked my friend if there were other marriages between Omanis and housekeepers, my friend assured me that there were many—especially with Indians. "They will do *anything* to stay," he added. Though my friend did not say explicitly or exactly what this "anything" was, whether sexual or otherwise, the supposedly obvious draw for foreigners to marry Omanis (and presumably foreign women to marry Omani men) was clear. Indeed, though based on different grounds, the "European" woman who declared that she would welcome being the Omani man's "slave" in order to marry him had expressed a similar sentiment. Therefore, though far from the norm, as the vast majority of laborers and domestic workers from Asia (from my conversations with laborers and domestic workers suggest) do not *want* to *stay* in Oman indefinitely, the impression that female workers in particular (and possibly other foreign women) "will do anything to stay," is pervasive within Oman.

This impression is further supported by the seemingly growing institution of foreign-marriage brokerage in towns like Bahla. Indeed, as the conversation with my friend continued, he told me of a local marriage broker, who worked in the Bahla *suq* and who regularly arranged for travel for Bahlawi men to India to select wives. As the complications of foreign-marriage are quite well known within Oman, a marriage broker would also be expected to navigate (or circumvent) the shifting and intricate bureaucracies and laws.

As opposed to this image within Oman of female housekeepers from Asia doing "anything" to stay, not only do most laborers not hope to stay indefinitely, the vast majority of accounts in newspapers of such marriages portray the women as manipulated by families and brokers (both Indian and Omani), powerless, and abused. Certainly, there is a wide range of experiences among female domestic workers as well as brides from South Asia. Tensions between a desire or ability to be in Oman and a desire or ability to be "home" are hardly easily resolved or disconnected from fear of abuse and loneliness. In conversations with Omanis in Zanzibar who had married their daughters to men in Oman, tales of sadness, abuse and loneliness were similarly rampant.

This suggestion of extreme actions, including legal marriage, as well as an account of an active local marriage broker raises doubts, of course, about the limits to territorial and hereditary citizenship that the state's nationality and personal status laws attempt to enforce. This also suggests the pervasiveness of the image of a presumed desire to stay, while the practice of male travel to India in search of brides simultaneously increases. Similarly, the fact that active marriage brokerage exists, not to mention—undoubtedly—sexual relations and abuse between Omanis and non-Omanis, also suggests that the affective boundaries of what constitutes Oman's territory, and its citizenry, is hardly as stable as the state's laws project.

If one of the ways that place is constituted is through the composition of its citizenry and there are significant pressures to maintain an image of that citizenry as homogeneous, then the policing of borders must include the man-agement of marriage, sexual relations, and children. Similarly, if one of the "choke-points" of the management of place is immigration control, then so too is the management of marriage. Given the various attempts to control what comes to constitute Oman through its marriage policies and the various ways that people understand, maneuver, and experience these controls, what form and sense of place emerges?

On the one hand, Oman—and the Arabian Peninsula—comes to be ex-clusionary, where homogeneity and a presumed Arabness dominate its com-position. Oman's laws come to be seen as restrictive and defensive, as well as a privilege, especially with regard to Asia. Oman, thus, becomes a site to desire, supposedly for women. This is, of course, in contrast to the image of Oman prior to the emergence of the modern state in the early 1970s. Though Oman also had highly restrictive laws, famously focusing on the banning of sunglass-es and radios, for example, marriage and sexual relations were not the apparent focus of the state per se (though certainly examples of this in the nineteenth century are evident). This image is also in contrast to those circulating in the popular press outside of the Arabian Peninsula where the abuse of Asian women dominate.

At the same time, the place of Oman comes to be—partly through its laws—one in which statelessness is rather pervasive, or appears rather perva-sive. Indeed, marriages of Omanis with non-Omanis have not only created a situation in which nationality laws and personal status laws must legalize what was previously made illegal in order to legitimize existing practices. Marriage laws have also created a nation with stateless individuals, including children of marriages of Omanis and Asians, unable to leave or prove political belonging as well as former Omanis who have lost citizenship. In Oman, as in many countries, that simultaneously draws on labor from beyond its borders and attempts to limit intimate relations between people, Oman as a place can only be understood through the processes that aim to manage, circumvent, and ultimately interpret its intimate choke-points.

Notes

1. *The Gulf News,* April 14, 2005. Last accessed April 25, 2005. Similar stories appear in Oman-based blogs such as www.omanforum.com and www.englishsabla. com.

2. The official Omani census of 2010 indicates that of the total population of 2,773,479, 29 percent is expatriate. The census does not indicate what percentage of this expatriate population is Asian.

3. Gianluca P. Parolin, *Citizenship in the Arab World: Kin, Religion and Nation-State* (Amsterdam: Amsterdam University Press, 2009).

4. http://www.rop.gov.om/english/rophistoryevents.asp provides the date for the first citizenship law, last accessed January 9, 2013. Oman's current nationality law is also available, in Arabic, at: http://www.rop.gov.om. References to the original Royal Decree 3/83 appear in numerous publications (including of the UNHCR), though I have not been able to acquire an official copy of it or its amendments in either English or Arabic.

5. See the Royal Omani Police's publication of the citizenship law (in Arabic). http://www.rop.gov.om/pdfs/roplaws/arabic/ROPRULE-7.pdf. Or see, for example, www.realityinoman.com/2010/02/08/obtaining-the-omani-citizenship/. Last accessed January 9, 2013.

6. For an account of anti-slavery laws in the 1840s-1870s in the Indian Ocean, see Limbert (2013).

7. M. Reda Bhacker, *Trade and Empire in Muscat and Zanzibar: Roots of British Domination* (New York: Routledge, 1992), 166.

8. For a comparison of French and Dutch laws and concerns about "mixed" marriages and the legal identities of children in the late nineteenth century, see, for example, Ann L. Stoler (1992).

9. John C. Wilkinson, *The Imamate Tradition of Oman* (Cambridge: Cambridge University Press, 1987), 53.

10. *The Express Tribune* (with the *International Herald Tribune*), June 19, 2010.

11. *Dawn.com* (a Pakistani news source available in Urdu and English), November 21, 2011.

12. *The Muscat Daily,* January 9, 2011.

13. The *Xinhua General Overseas News Service,* February 3, 1986.

14. *Times of Oman,* November 15, 1993.

15. Ibid.

16. Ibid., January 21, 1996.

17. Ibid., May 20, 1996.

18. Described as either *Qānūn al-Aḥwāl al-Shakhshsīyya* or as *Qānūn al-Aḥwāl al-Madanīyya,* see: http://www.rop.gov.om/pdfs/roplaws/arabic/ROPRULE-3.pdf (in Arabic). Last accessed January 18, 2013.

19. www.omanforum.com/forums/archive/index.php/t-21181.html. Last accessed, January 9, 2013.

20. www.howtolivelikeanomaniprincess.blogspot.com/2010/06/this-is-for-omani-readers-ban-on.html. Last accessed, January 9, 2013.

21. www.howtolivelikeanomanipricess.blogspot.com/2010/07/one-opnos-list-of-how-to-marry-omani.html. Last accessed, January 9, 2013.

22. *Times of Oman,* August 6, 2012.
23. Ibid.

References

Ahmad, Attiya. 2009. *Limits of Conversion: Islamic Dawa, Domestic Work and South Asian Migrant Women in Kuwait.* Ph.D dissertation, Duke University.

Bhacker, M. Reda. 1992. *Trade and Empire in Muscat and Zanzibar: Roots of British Domination.* New York: Routledge.

Constable, Nicole. 1999. "At Home but Not At Home: Filipina Narratives of Ambivalent Returns." *Cultural Anthropology,* 14 (2): 203–228.

———, ed. 2005. *Cross-Border Marriages: Gender and Mobility in Transnational Asia.* Philadelphia: University of Pennsylvania Press.

Gamburd, Michele. 2000. *The Kitchen Spoon's Handle: Transnationalism and Sri Lanka's Migrant Housemaids.* Ithaca, NY: Cornell University Press.

Gardner, Andrew. 2010. *City of Strangers: Gulf Migration and the Indian Community in Bahrain.* Ithaca. NY: Cornell University Press.

Limbert, Mandana E. 2013. "If You Catch Me Again At It, Put Me to Death: Slave-trading, Paper Trails, and British Bureaucracy in the Indian Ocean." In *Slavery and the Slave Trade in the Indian Ocean,* ed. Robert Harms and Bernard Freamon. New Haven: Yale University Press.

Longva, Anh Nga. 1999. *Walls Built on Sand: Migration, Exclusion, and Society in Kuwait.* Boulder, CO: Westview Press.

Mahdavi, Pardis. 2011. *Gridlock: Labor, Migration, and Human Trafficking in Dubai.* Palo Alto: Stanford University Press.

Nagy, Sharon. 1998. "This Time I Think I'll Try a Filipina: Global and Local Influences on Relations between Foreign Household Workers and Their Employers in Doha, Qatar." *City and Society,* 10 (1): 83–103.

———. 2004. "Keeping Families Together: Housing Policy, Social Strategies, and Family in Qatar." *MIT Electronic Journal of Middle East Studies* 4: 42–58.

———. 2008. "The Search for Miss Philippines Bahrain—Possibilities for Representation in Expatriate Communities." *City and Society* 20 (1): 79–104.

Osella, Caroline, and Fillipo Osella. 2012. "Migration, Networks, and Connectedness across the Indian Ocean." In *Migrant Labor in the Persian Gulf,* ed. Mehran Kamrava and Zahra Babar. New York: Columbia University Press.

Parolin, Gianluca P. 2009. *Citizenship in the Arab World: Kin, Religion and Nation-State.* Amsterdam: Amsterdam University Press.

Stoler, Ann L. 1992. "Sexual Affronts and Racial Frontiers: European Identities and the Cultural Politics of Exclusion in Colonial Southeast Asia." *Comparative Studies in Society and History* 34 (3): 514–551.

Sultanate of Oman. 2010. *General Census of Population, Housing and Establishments 2010.* Muscat: Ministry of Information.

Vora, Neha. 2013. *Impossible Citizens: Dubai's Indian Diaspora.* Durham: Duke University Press.
Wilkinson, John C. 1987. *The Imamate Tradition of Oman.* Cambridge: Cambridge University Press, 53.

Newspapers

The Times of Oman
The Muscat Daily
The Gulf News
Dawn.com
The Express Tribune (with the *International Herald Tribune*),
Xinhua General Overseas News Service

Internet Blogs

www.howtolivelikeanomanipricess.blogspot.com/
www.realityinoman.com/
www.omanforum.com/
www.englishsabla.com.

Legal Decrees and Laws

Sultanate of Oman. *Qānūn al-Aḥwāl al-Shakhshsīyya* or as *Qānūn al-Aḥwāl al-Madanīyya* [Laws of Personal Status].
Sultanate of Oman. *Qānūn al-Jinsīyya* [Laws of Nationality].
Sultanate of Oman. Royal Decree 3/83
Sultanate of Oman. Royal Decree 59/93

Romanization without Rome

China's Latin New Script
and Soviet Central Asia

JING TSU

In recent years, there has been a burgeoning interest in how things tie to-gether rather than stay apart. The growing awareness of historically fluid, moveable boundaries has sparked new interpretations of Asia. Some of these connections are currently colliding in innovative ways. In search of a nar-rative that builds less on the indictment of any single state or past colonial power, humanists and social scientists turn their gaze to the inner and global dynamics of Asia—and even of multiple Asias. Still coming to light, the overlay of old and new linkages across its tight and vast regions has led crit-ics to choose different bars of comparison. Some argue for Asia as a method (Takeuchi 2005; Frank 1988; Chen 2010), i.e., articulating its historical formation as not a resistance to the outside but an unfulfilled path. Others turn to the borderlands and divided continents as a window into proprietary histories (Perdue 2005; Struve 2004; Lewis and Wigen 1997). Meanwhile, there are still those who prefer the analysis of national entities writ large. In this last instance, China is garnering special attention as a possible new breed of global power that differs in kind from the European and American variety of recent centuries.

The Place of Language and the Language of Place

Amidst this vibrant conversation, drawing from disciplines as varied as geography, history, anthropology, and philosophy, language as a unit of analysis, however, is notably missing. Space and place have been the primary categories for analyzing the different scales of social and political expressivity across national and regional terrains. How language operates as a place-determinant, or index for spatialization, however, often trails behind these categories, where it functions largely as an example. Language is seen to reinforce, but not steer, the terms for thinking about places. In this way, many take language as a mode of representation or aspect of phenomenology that fits into an existing landscape. In the formative period of linguistic anthropology, for example, the adaptation of a people to their environment is reflected in, but not determined by, the particular development of their lexicon (Boas 1911). For the human geographer commenting on that tradition, words represent, "contain and intensify [a] feeling" that is already there, in contrast to demarcated spaces that can "hold emotions" as the physical threshold of their emergence (Tuan 1977, 107; cf. Massey 2009). Philosophers, distinct from both perspectives, are drawn more to the general conditions of linguistic being, or coming into being in language, than the specific histories that transform them into extended social processes (Tuan 1977, 1991; Casey 1993, 1997). Serving larger claims about the gains and perils of where one's subjectivity is always already lodged, then, the significance of language has been made accessory to other assumptions about one's subordination to, or affective investment in, a given place or setting. Taking either place or language as where the other happens, their material and institutional imbrication is often left out of purview.

Departing from these approaches, I suggest that learning how to use a language—spoken or written—entails a great many more social obstacles that only begin with the recognition of language as a given mode of perception or a common tool. To be born into a language, and to use it, are two different things. Knowing how a language is or should be written—and spoken—does not always coincide with the place where one belongs or disbelongs. When not met, such material or epistemological thresholds can disrupt or set the limits of geographical experiences and imagination, as is evident in how language has been—and is—at the heart of most inter-Asian connections. This is true whether one considers the eighth-century translation of Buddhist texts from Sanskrit into Tibetan, the rendering of the Qur'an from Arabic into Javanese or Urdu in periods of religious and cultural expansion, the call to use old Chaghatai classics and heroic epics to reinvent a Turkic lingua franca for Central Asia in the nineteenth century, the lasting impact of British and Dutch colonial language policies on post-colonial India and Indonesia, the long-standing informal use of Malay as the language of trade, travel, and Islamization, written Chinese as the former lingua franca of East Asia and Vietnam, or the Japanese imperialization project in Korea and Taiwan—whereby the colonial subject is required not only to speak and write but also to "think" in the Japanese language. In all cases, it is not just the circumstance of translation that guides these processes. The degree and type of language access provides a pivotal lens through which to see anew the histories, textures, voluntary, and forced linkages that throw distant places into new relief.

Taking this as a point of departure, the following discussion has two objectives. First, it introduces an important layer of resolution to the picture of sounds and scripts against the generally accepted place-dominant narratives in current Sinophone studies. In recent years, references have been made to China's historically complex landscape of languages and tongues in conversations about ethnic and cultural diversity within, or against, a professed Han-dominant—or pure Chinese—tradition. I have argued that this ecology is organized around various dissents and complicities among native speakers and languages, even though these dynamics are often misread as the exclusion of local tongues from national languages (Tsu 2010). Drawing attention to the fact that the simple polarization of the haves and the have-nots no longer serves our understanding of the evolving, contemporary terms of language, I introduced "literary governance" as a differentiating conceptual tool that accounts for, but is not limited to, the stakes of Sinocentrism versus anti-Sinocentrism (Tsu 2010). This move shifts away from the familiar postcolonial explanations and related critiques of centrism. It focuses on the underlying global reality that neither place nor language can be taken for granted as a reliable measure for engaging the other, as though one can be fixed while the other is put into motion.

This recognition poses a new set of questions about language and place and, implicitly, how language corresponds to geographical areas at all in what has been known as "Area Studies." In particular, I construct an interconnected view of two script movements. One is Dunganese, a Sinitic language that has been written exclusively in non-Sinitic scripts. Insulated from the turmoil of mainland China's language reforms in the twentieth century, but not from that of the former Soviet Union, Dunganese is a Northern Sinitic dialect that is spoken by the descendants of the Chinese Muslims who fled the border into Russian Central Asia in the 1870s. As a Sino-Tibetan minority language in present day Kyrgyzstan, it had existed, like many Turkic dialects in the former Soviet Central Asia, largely as an oral tradition. It did not acquire a script system—in fact, several—until after the 1920s under the Soviet pursuit of a multinational and -lingual empire. The development of a writing system for Dunganese, and its subsequent literary output, charted a course of linguistic survival that persisted between the cracks of standardization and nationaliza-tion, on the one hand, and speech and writing, on the other. It has engendered literary themes and sensibilities that do not align with the prevailing pathos in reading diasporic writers. As a case in point, the poetry of the Dunganese poet Iasyr Shivaza (1906–1988) that I examine is expressive of the geopolitics of socialist brotherhood, rather than a perennial stake in Chineseness.[1] To date, the centrality of Chineseness has been widely assumed in discussions of displaced Sinitic writers.

The unique development of Dunganese, moreover, was far from mar-ginal in impact. Little discussed by scholars of China or Sinophone studies, Dunganese forged a crucial link, across the Soviet border, to one of the most contentious alphabetization experiments in twentieth century China—the Romanization of the Chinese language in the movement known as Latinxua Sin Wenz (Mair 1990; DeFrancis 1952). It raises new questions about the measure of the Sinophone—i.e., Chinese-language or -speaking—and its sig-nificance when generated out of the place, unbound to the Chinese-speaking world. Though the Dunganese' exemplarity is rare, its message is not singular. Amidst the plethora of bilingual and multiscriptive paths that are now coming into light and reshaping our criteria for understanding the scope of Chinese diaspora, language has emerged from these processes as a most crucial com-mon denominator. It compels us to grasp the relationship between place and language in a more intertwined, precise way than ever before, urging us to consider it as a mutually invested process of the *language-becoming of place,* and *the place-becoming of language.* Language does not just fit into a place, as if the latter is a physical container, given in advance. Place grows from language too as a new origin, insofar as speakers of a language can reshape any sense of place through their linguistic presence and practice.

This consideration forms the second objective of my analysis. While the Sino-Islamic example carries an intrinsic value from both linguistic and

historical perspectives, its empirical specificity draws attention to a core interpretive issue. Linguistic survival is often assumed to be an instance of social
precarity, a minoritarian act after the fact of nationalism, colonialism, or other
occasions for redress. Reinforcing this view, conversations about language and
diasporic culture often build on highly emotionally charged notions of depri-
vation like nostalgia and homelessness, with no further questions asked about
the material constitution of those affective determinants. One consequence of
this propensity is that the gain and privation of a rightful place like an ancestral home is writ large as a most visible token of loss. Meanwhile, the increasingly common circumstance of secondary and tertiary language acquisitions
remains more or less unseen, even as they make and break places as people
move from one host environment to the next for various reasons. Instead of
accounting for this new reality, strategies for linguistic survival are interpreted
almost exclusively in light of disempowerment or standardization, rather than
their ongoing constructivist evolution. As language changes hands and place,
it becomes something one has to repeatedly earn and create, rather than own.
The following analysis of sounds and scripts, then, shifts the focus from an
identity-driven pathos to the structuring power of linguistic materiality, in the
very writing systems that embody both fixity and change.

The Latinization of Chinese

> The fact that during the great Muslim rebellion of the 1870s thousands of
> Dungan refugees fled from the Gansu Corridor into Russian Central Asia
> was filed away in my mind as a minor bit of information when I first learned
> about it long ago . . . Chinese and Western scholars have long been battling
> the nonsense that Chinese characters are pictographic or ideographic and that
> the language can only be written with the traditional script and not with an
> alphabetic one . . . one of the things that cinched the claim that Chinese *can*
> be written alphabetically was my discovery that descendants of those Dungan
> refugees were actually writing that way. For over half a century the seventy
> thousand Chinese speakers in Russian Central Asia have been publishing
> newspapers, scholarly works, and all sorts of literature in a simple script based
> first on the Latin and later on the Russian script. (DeFrancis 1993)[2]

John DeFrancis was the one of the first Sinologists in the English-speaking world
to take note of the minority language that is practiced in the Central Asian republics of Kyrgyzstan, Kazakhstan, and Uzbekistan. Before him, and since the

late nineteenth century, the Dungans have been well documented by Soviet
linguists and ethnographers as a unique ethnic community that observes Sinitic
customs and speaks dialects from northwestern China (Rimsky-Korsakoff Dyer
1992, 1967).[3] In the 1920s and 1930s, this knowledge played a pivotal role in
state language planning and the nationalization of minority languages under
the indigenization language policy of the former U.S.S.R. The development of
the first systematized writing system for Dunganese followed the post-imperial
and centralization imperatives of in the Bolshevik and Stalinist eras. During this
de- and re-Russification process that pursued a strategy of divide and conquer,
Dunganese was brought into the turmoil of nationalizing the various Turkic minority languages in Central Asia. Its linguistic evolution bears testimony to these
historical vicissitudes. While the Soviet Union's main concern was to thwart the
processes of pan-Turkism and Islamization, few ethnic groups—including those
that are not Turkic in origin—were left unaffected. By 1934, the new alphabet
was used by seventy nationalities, forty of which had no writing proper writing
systems before 1917 (Shprintsin 330). By 1936, all of the Soviet nationalities in
Central Asia as well as the small peoples of northern and northeastern Siberia
had received an alphabetic script (Allès 2005).[4]

Dunganese is an element (Riedlinger 1989, 167) in this larger picture.
Comprised of 15,000 speakers, it has since grown to the current-day number
of around 120,000.[5] Between 1927 and 1954, Dunganese, despite its oral Sinitic form, was converted from the Arabic script to Latin letters, then from Latin to Cyrillic. Since the collapse of the Soviet Union, its linguistic, literary, and
cultural vitality came to be fostered under state-sponsored initiatives (Huskey
1995).[6] Historically speaking, one cannot talk about the Dungans without
referring to the vast and diverse world that is Islamic Chinese. From Southeast
Asia to Central Asia, the influences reflect the proximity of Malay and Arabic
cultures. The most direct source of the Dungans in the former Soviet territory
are the Chinese Muslims in China, loosely encompassed by the ethnic desig-
nation, Hui. During the course of 130 years of Hui exodus from northwestern China into different parts of present-day Central Europe, the movement
outwards included the Chinese Muslims from provinces and regions such as
Shaanxi, Gansu, Ningxia, Qinghai, and Xinjiang. A greater number of dialects
existed among them, which can be further identified according to prefectural
and local clusters. Their dispersion covers a large geographical area, though
they have generally held themselves apart from one another and settled in
small communities.

A distinction exists between Muslims within the Chinese territory, who are called "Hui," and those who are called "Dungan" and reside in the three Central Asian Republics. The distinction was an official classification under the Soviet state. The Dungans informally refer to themselves as "Hui Hui" "Old Huis" ("lao Hui ren"), or "Central Plains people" ("Zhongyuan ren," i.e., Chinese) (Hu 2006). A further distinction, and even mutual dislike, persists between the Dungans who speak the Gansu dialect and those who speak the Shaanxi dialect. The Dungans are the descendants of the Muslim rebels who revolted in northwestern China in the last quarter of the nineteenth century. In 1877–78 and 1881–1884, the Chinese Muslims fled across the border via Xinjiang to Russia after their failed uprisings in Shaanxi and Gansu. Having made the decision of, according to one Russian traveller to their settlement, "either stay[ing] under the oppressive, much-hated Manchu rule or move to Russia," they migrated in two waves, further subdivided into four groups (Rimsky-Korsakoff et al. 1992). The history of their exile constitutes a core part of their identity. Descendants of the group led by the Muslim leader Bai Yanhu from Shaanxi continue to commemorate his heroism in folklore and the oral songs, while the Chinese statesman Zuo Zongtang, who was responsible for crushing the Muslim rebels and their subsequent genocide, is still ominously evoked in popular nursery rhymes.

The Dungan population grew quickly under the Soviet policies of birth planning. In 1907, there were about 18,000 Chinese Muslims in the Republics. In 1979, the number reached over 50,000. Currently, the population is estimated to be 120,000 (Lin 2008). By the time Russia officially surveyed its ethnic minorities in the 1920s, the group was officially recorded as Dungan, though some speculations still exist as to where the term originated. Benefitting from the Soviet policy of unity in diversity, they were given their own classification in the 1926 census (DeFrancis 1952).

Before the mid-1980s, Dunganese was a subject of Russian studies rather than Chinese studies in mainland Chinese scholarship. When the Chinese scholars began to study the Dungans in the 1990s, they relied mostly on the earlier Soviet ethnography. How to classify the scholarship entailed some thought. Originally part of Soviet Sinology, the Dungans were studied as one of the ethnic minorities of the former Soviet Union. Its confinement to the niche of national language history is similar to that of the Latinxua Sin Wenz movement in China in the 1930s, which is still narrated mainly as an internalist account of the modern Chinese language reform. As was the policy under

Stalin, the Dungans were permitted to have their own writing system, though it took a few tries. Current-day Dungan writing system comprises 33 Cyrillic letters and 5 supplementary letters to accommodate phonemes that are found only in the speech of the Chinese Muslims. The development of the Dungan alphabet, significantly, was the first Soviet attempt to alphabetize a northwestern Chinese language—or any Chinese language or dialect, for that matter (Shprintsin 1974).[7] The renowned Soviet sinologist A. A. Dragunov defined Dunganese as a different language from Chinese in 1938 (though he included examples from it in his 1952 grammar of modern Chinese), then called it a "colonial dialect" of Shaanxi and Gansu Mandarin in 1952 (Dragunov 1952, Wexler 2011).

Despite its physical appearance, Dunganese is written almost entirely with the dialectal properties and lexicon of Shaanxi and Gansu speech. It is important to note, however, that Latinized Dunganese was set to the standard of the Gansu topolect, even though its speakers are from both the Gansu and Shaanxi provinces, each with their numerous dialectal varieties. A few words of Russian, Arabic, and Persian entered its vocabulary over time, but overall the language remains heavily rooted in the oral speech of the countryside of northwestern China. In some cases, colloquial usage from the late Qing period, some of which are no longer extant in China today, is still vividly evident in Dunganese. Some references are from a 13th-century colloquial Chinese language teaching text, Lao Qida, which was written for Korean traders during the time of the Mongol conquest. Other notable characteristics like reversed binomes, such as "caishu" for "shucai" (vegetable), can be found in popularly performed and read vernacular fiction like Shuihuzhuan (Chang 2010).

As most of the early migrants had little literacy to begin with, written Chinese was and remains difficult to master, leaving the oral tradition as the primary means to keep the folk customs alive. The early Dungans, like in many rural parts of China, were largely illiterate peasants. Illiteracy, in fact, was almost 100% in 1926. The Dungans would have been part of the targeted audience for the many linguistic reforms and mass mobilization movements in China. But their exile insulated them from the vicissitudes and experimentation of China's language standardization reforms. In the absence of centralized Chinese cultural influence, the oral forms that were transmitted in Dungan culture took on a stronger Islamicist color, especially with regard to customs and moral conduct. One example is the figure Han Xin, a general in the second century B.C.E. at the founding of the Han dynasty who was portrayed sympathetically in the *Shiji* as a would-be hero with a few fatal flaws (Li 2011). The forgiving tone did not carry over into the Dungan universe. Han Xin's loss of Liu Ban's trust was sternly interpreted as the result of his lack of moral integrity. Details in the narratives about Han Xin were accordingly altered, as an otherwise passing episode was highlighted. Instead of his culpability in political intrigues, Han's greater moral crime, in one version, was to have violated the teachings of the Koran by intruding upon a naked woman in her bath (Chang 2010).

Many folk tales such as the one adapted from the *Shiji* circulated widely among the Dungans. They helped to pass on a tradition that otherwise had no written ties to the place of origin. At the same time, the circumstance of being outside of China means, importantly, that they also missed the vernacular revolution that changed the course of modern China. With little literacy to tie them to a classical tradition, the Dungan language survived without the constraints of Chinese nationalism. While they were hardly literate in elite classical Chinese, the Dungans also did not have to unburden themselves of a tradition to which they had little access. They were, in fact, the quintessential peasant speakers who became highly valorized during the heated debates of mass literature and arts throughout the Communist period, much controversy of which centered on materializing the spoken style in the written medium. Their language is, as one critic recently points out, more peasant than the peasant writer par excellence of the 1940s and 1950, Zhao Shuli.

This comparison, however, does not reveal the wide gulf between the two linguistic worlds. Modern Dungan writers acknowledge their relationship to written Chinese with distant passion rather than persistent nostalgia, an issue we will consider later in the case of Iasyr Shivaza. When the process of movement has taken them so far away from even the usual diasporic frontiers, neither old notions of nostalgia nor ready-made definitions of exile can capture their experience, let alone integrate it into a coherent cartography of Sinophone writings. This makes them quite distinct from the well-studied diasporic writers in Southeast Asia (Li Yongping, Zhang Guixing), Taiwan (Kim Chu Ng), Europe (Gao Xingjian, François Cheng), and North America (Ha Jin, Lin Yutang), to name a few representatives. In contrast to the Dungans, these writers' decision to use, or not use, the Chinese linguistic written medium is often interpreted as expressed gestures of cultural belonging or disbelonging. In all instances, however, their mastery of a literary language—Chinese, French, or English—is not in question. Literacy is generally a distant issue in literary studies. That literary studies, by definition, pay attention to mainly accomplished usages of language, however, actually obfuscates an issue that is most unique and central to the study of extra-national literatures and cultures: what happens when the basic access to writing and literacy is neither given nor native?

The disjuncture between speech sounds and written script, then, not only problematizes language itself. It also forces a drift in the accepted practice of attaching language to a place. Around the same time that the Latinization of Dunganese got underway, topolects from southern China were being transcribed en masse in the Latinxua Sin Wenz movement in China. The language problem was not merely a question of the high and the low. A unified solution was not feasible and split, instead, into separate tracks of reform for the oral and the written. Nationalism charted a linguistic course that was materializing against the full concretization of space, territories, nations, and places, even as it was recruited in their making.

The Latinization of Dunganese and Latinxua Sin Wenz, though separately propagated, shared their roots in the Soviet literacy campaigns. It was the Latinization campaign for the Chinese laborers in Vladivostok and Khabarovsk that sparked the subsequent movement in China. From 1930 to 1932, in fact, the literacy campaign in the Soviet East explicitly observed directives to target not only the small peoples of the north and the Finns and the Chuvash, but also the Chinese and Korean languages (King 1997). The idea was that the Soviet Latinization campaign would continue beyond its borders. It was imagined to be an instrument of proletariat internationalism, for sure, and the hope was to start a new cultural revolution: "Not the twenty million strong population of Korea, but the 170 thousand strong population of the Soviet Union should become the advance-guard of the cultural revolution of the Korean people" (Martin 2001, 199). Of the five Chinese topolects that were originally slated for their own alphabets—Guandong, Fujian, Shandong, Jiangsu, Jiangxi—however, only the Shandong scheme was approved and implemented.

Irrespective of the intended audience, Sin Wenz and Dunganese partook in a transnational and -regional language movement that overwrote the native constraints of language and place. Indigenous sounds married foreign systems of transcription as a matter of expediency. No strings were attached, at least not the kind that one cannot sever. Concurrent alphabetization movements were sweeping through non-alphabetic parts of the world. Not only China, but also Japan, Turkey, Russia, Southeast Asia, Persia, and parts of the Middle East were embroiled in debates about the future of their writing systems. Alphabetization was distinct from other types of technological assimilations of the West. It was a practical matter, to be separated from the stakes of culturalist debates. The project was pursued, in effect, as a process of westernization without the West, Romanization without Rome. This important distinction is uniquely demonstrated in the modern history of language script standardization, and can be better understood with a closer look at the Chinese Latinization project.

As is well known, in 1929–1930, Qu Qiubai (Strakhov), an important figure in the Chinese Communist Party, collaborated with Soviet linguists A. A. Dragunov and V. S. Kolokolov to devise a system to aid quick literacy. Other Chinese collaborators, also members of the CCP, included Wu Yuzhang (Burenin), Xiao San (Emi Siao), Lin Boju (Komissarov), and Wang Xiangbao (Martynov). Sin Wenz had six goals: (1) to offer a purely phonetic script; (2) to be fully in sync with any spoken language; (3) to be simple and accessible; (4) to facilitate internationalization; (5) to accommodate media and communication technology such as printing, typewriting, telegraphy, cataloguing, and Chinese character retrieval systems; (6) to minimize the amount of time, expense, and mental effort that is needed in reading, writing, and printing (Xin wenzi rumen 1936, 14).

Admittedly, Qu was less trained as a linguist than his Soviet and Chinese colleagues (Peng 1982).[8] But his ideological perspective offered a trenchant critique of the "national language" that captured the general tenor of the debate in China. How Chinese was to be romanized was not merely a question of convenience. Whether China was better off going with the Communist or the Nationalist vision also divided the conversation on how best to modernize the Chinese script. When the Nationalists proposed a return to the use of literary Chinese during the neoconservative swing to the New Life Movement in 1934, language politics was catapulted to the forefront of cultural wars. The battle over language standardization was not a Chinese problem, Qu underscores, but emblematic of the fate of all national languages. The national interest to extend and consolidate its sphere of influence at home as well as abroad inevitably steered the debate.

While a language system tends to evolve toward simplicity the longer it is in use, Qu laments, this was not the case in China. In an early draft of the Latinxua Sin Wenz proposal that was published in Moscow in 1930, he points out that the Chinese language had been resistant to such a change.[9] Despite the long-standing problem of widespread illiteracy among peasants in the countryside, the written Chinese script has been beyond their reach. It was enshrined as a symbol of cultural elitism. Meanwhile, divergences between regional dialects and topolects grew by the day, and people from the north can barely understand those from the south. The written language has not evolved to mend these gaps, even less to give regional speech its due recognition.

In a 1931 essay, explaining why China should turn to full-scale vernacularization, Qu invites his Chinese readers to consider an analogous situation: "Imagine you're in London. You come across its largest newspaper publishing house only to find that everything they publish is in Latin, Old English, Middle English, and so on. But no modern English—the one language you hear on the streets. How would you feel about that?" (Qu 1985a) At Qu's injunction, the reader would have been struck by the strangeness of the scene. It would not be, though, because the city was in a foreign country where people spoke a foreign language. Place was not the issue. Instead, the problem would be that, despite the fact that they spoke a vastly different language and observed different customs half a world away, the English had the same problem as the Chinese: the palpable disconnect between the spoken and the printed word. This lapse is meant to strike one as absurd. Falling behind speech, Qu shows by way of the English example, writing systems lapse in everyday utility, becoming calcified and inert to the passage of time. The problem, importantly, was not place bound or unique to any part of the world. Neither was the solution.

At the time of Qu's writing, the point was already well made. A contentious project to revise the elitist, classical written medium according to the needs of everyday speech had begun in the late nineteenth century. Inspired partly by Japan's advancement and partly by China's hard won lessons in dealing with the modern world, the Chinese language reform was a key issue in the debates on regional fragmentation, westernization, and modernization. That what people spoke did not match what they wrote, however, was only one facet of the problem. The widening gulf between what people speak on the ground and what the literati wish to salvage as a written literary language threatened to hold off a true linguistic revolution. Added to the problem is the tremendous difficulty of mastering the Chinese script itself. Even if one could rely on a common written language to bridge the regional gaps, the complex and unsystematic nature of the Chinese character construction made written mastery a privilege reserved for only the few.

Qu's recount of the problem plaguing the Chinese language was not new. But he pushed the problem of China's vast regional differences to center stage. Seeing it through a Marxist lens, Qu held that before national unity is accomplished in the economic sense, one cannot ignore the different speeds of advancement and the reality of local roots in China's hinterland. Against the prevailing sentiment of romanizing only Mandarin, the national language (*guoyu*), Qu proposed a digraphic system as a transitional measure. In short, Sin Wenz would provide the phonetic means for any dialect to easily transcribe into a writing system, alongside the standard language. Regional writings would be marked for local place use only, as "auxiliary scripts" (*fuzhu wenzi*). National language, also romanized in Sin Wenz, would meanwhile maintain its national and international stature as China's "primary script system" (*zhuyao de wenzi*) (Qu 1953).[10] Thus there would be the New Shanghai Script, New Beiping Script, New Fujian Script, or the New Guangzhou Script, but only one New China Script.

In a series of articles published after completing the blueprint for Sin Wenz, Qu pressed further on the script question. This time he took it beyond the frontlines of linguistic reform and used it to attack the residual cultural conservatism that had held China back from making true progress. He targeted the state of New Literature, by then twelve years old since the May Fourth Movement's early declaration to vernacularize modern literature for the people. The linguistic imperative, formally expressed by Hu Shi in 1918, of a new vernacular alongside a new literature was a core platform. Looking back on this recent history, Qu's diagnosis was unforgiving. He pointed out the egregious failure in bringing about a true vernacular revolution that was sworn to the masses. Recalling the initial goals stated by the leaders of New Literature, like Cai Yuanpei, Hu Shi, and Chen Duxiu, Qu saw only a trail of broken promises (Qu 1953).[11] Despite these intellectuals' call for using the "language of the soil," or native speech, at the end of the day they found it hard to imagine everyday language penetrating the walls of elite institutions of learning like Beijing University, where all three critics held posts. When it came down to it, Qu charged, they were unwilling to abandon the classics. Not only were these revered texts written in the literary Chinese that no average person could understand (Qian Quantong 1918).[12] The feudalistic social and political doctrines they conveyed also remained untouched. Conceding half-heartedly to the use of the vernacular, the intellectual reformers saw only yet another venue for reinforcing the learned tradition of the canon. Qu took on all the important figures at the time for their complicity in this process. For him, New Literature was thus bred from a half-realized vernacular and a still revered classical language. It was nothing less than a caricature, a monstrous half-breed "somewhere between a horse and a donkey."[13] It could neither commit itself to a living or human speech (*renhua*) nor return to embrace a language of the dead (*guihua*).

Apart from making a familiar indictment of the May Fourth's incomplete project, Qu articulates important insights. The appropriate approach to a national language, for him, is not to homogenize all tongues irrespective of their origins. Language standardization cannot afford to overlook how languages vary spatially, or are place-dependent, in the first place. The negative impact on the development of local literatures is only half of the problem. More importantly, it would not serve the interest of the nationalization project itself for two main reasons: (1) a unifying script system does not spell one standard to reign over the rest, but entails a communicable system. By communicability, however, Qu does not refer to an unconditional, universal access. He clearly recognizes that two speakers in Guangzhou or Fujian would prefer the New Script that is local and place-appropriate to those provinces over the New China Script; (2) what matters is to devise a script system in which any single place identity can be represented, but not to the exclusion of other place-specific languages. Without the material inscription to give durability to their spoken languages, there is no room for places in the question of unification. Linguistic nationalization itself would ring hollow when it will have no differences to recruit, no places with which to connect. This distinction and co-implication is key to managing the tension between difference and unity. To render Qu's argument into a simple formulation: language becomes place at the same time that place emerges through language. Any prospect of China's linguistic modernization has to account for these two coterminous imperatives. Nationalism is not all or nothing. In order to have a mandate, it has to maintain its own incompletion, in which the possibility of dissent is also its greatest source of legitimacy.

Only a few, in Qu's opinion, grasped the importance of the language question in this light. Zhao Yuanren, for instance, inventor of the Gwoyeu Romatzyh—the rival system to Sin Wenz that was officially promulgated in 1928—was a worthy foe in this regard. But even he, Qu pointed out, failed to prioritize the needs of local realities and, instead, put the cart before the horse (Qu 1953, 662–672).[14] First, Zhao decided to keep rather than to abolish the four tones that were particular to the pronunciation of Mandarin. While the dialects that were spoken in Jiangsu or Zhejiang provinces can have seven or eight tones, and Guangdong nine, Gwoyeu Romatzyh can only accommodate four. Second, one of Gwoyeu Romatzyh's distinguishing features is to provide a physical indicator of the tonal marks (Wu and Zhong 2006, 61).[15] Given that the system requires this physical feature, it favors speakers from the north who are already familiar with Mandarin, and excludes those from the south, where the greatest dialectal variations and most urgent need for representation are. Examples include consonants that are prevalent in the southern dialects, which resembles the tonal features of ancient Chinese: "z," "c," "s," and "j." In Mandarin, the same sounds are made in retroflex with a curling or concave position of the tongue: "zh," "ch," "sh," and "jh." Qu points out the undue influence of western phonology in Zhao's use of "j" to represent the Chinese phoneme "出. "

For his part, Zhao saw things differently. Romanization was a task for linguistic science, not an instigator of class revolution. That Mandarin was chosen as the national standard was a pragmatic choice, not the elitist sleight of hand that it was made out to be. During the imperial days, the use of Mandarin in official correspondence at court was "regarded as a convenience rather than a matter of prestige" (Zhao 1980, 103–121).[16] Similarly, there was no shame in speaking in a dialect that is not from the north. It was more of an inconvenience than stigma (Zhao 1961, 712).[17] Furthermore, Zhao explains, the idea of a dialect, or "speech of a locality" (*fangyan*), is an unfortunate misnomer. Suggesting an etymological relation to locality and place, it assumes that language must be attached to a certain place (*difang*), and that any difference between the languages is primarily due to the difference in place. A dialect, Zhao suggests to the contrary, should be more broadly conceived. In the more dramatic cases, a Shandong dialect and a Wenzhou dialect can be as different as Spanish and French. Just as often, though, dialects reflect more the styles of speaking. When seen as a style rather than topolectal divergence, dialects are no longer geographically bound. It can be an idiom that is particular to a social or economic class; i.e., the latest urban slang or immigrant idiolect. According to Zhao's more expansive notion, then, a dialect needs more than one axis of differentiation. A taxonomy that separates topolects and dialects according to fixed places of nativity fails to grasp the relation between language and place on this fundamental level. It acknowledges the fact of distance, but not the process of distanciation that aligns places with languages, and connects languages to places.

In light of Zhao's observations, the radicalism of Qu's ideological position now seems limited. His espousal of the given fact of linguistic variety and local distinction, in fact, does not go far enough. Regional Latinization is promoted as a parallel, but ultimately restricted, track next to the national script. There may be many local standards, in other words, but only in the service of one national standardization. What he fails to seize on, then, is the very geographic-dominant assumption that underlies both the national standard and the related possibility of regional standards. While he recognized the good of the alphabet as the linguistic medium that can facilitate both national and regional romanizations, he did not see how linguistic diversity fundamentally changes how a dialect is brought into relief as a concept and practice. Zhao's notion of dialect can be more minimally understood as a portable style of self-representation that is intrinsic to any speaker or user of language. He cites as an example the Cockney dialect, which is based on class rather than place. Throughout his various essays on the topic, in fact, one discerns an important thread. What Zhao suggests, and what Qu was unable to see, was that the real problem lies in how the historical coexistence of Mandarin and regional speech came to be seen as a matter of elitism versus massification, intellectual versus the people, oppressive standard versus place-based dialects. By overidentifying dialects with place, Zhao notes, one overlooks how dialectal distinctions are recruited from a greater spectrum of social distinctions, where a particular style of speech can just well express class or cultural markers. A place-based notion of dialects conceals the social and economic factors that animate linguistic differences and raise their stakes. In an unwitting move, Qu did more to put Mandarin on an elitist pedestal than anyone he could have blamed.

Indeed, the technical difference between Gwoyeu Romatzhy and Latinxua Sin Wenz is much smaller than the ideological differences behind them. Zhao and Qu were not the only voices in the debate. Other linguists and political reformers defended the strengths and weaknesses of the two systems. They impassioned opinions came in the forms of readers' comments, pamphlets, manuals, scholarly journals, and other venues that foretold the coming script revolution. People commented on the comments of the commentators, and the opinions filled the pages of widely circulated newspapers and journals. It was a revolution in the real sense, as there was also the greater fear of what widespread literacy would unleash in the masses during the volatile and divided Warlord Era (1916–1928). For instance, Zhang Zuolin, military warlord of Manchuria, banned even the teaching of the auxiliary system National Phonetic Alphabet, promulgated in 1918, and ordered the return to literary Chinese in the publication of school textbooks. The pull between conservatism and reformism, not to mention between divided regional and political loyalties, personal and institutional squabbles, thwarted any successful and lasting implementation. Emotions ran high, but the enormity of the challenge only strengthened the resolve of the committed. A special August issue of *National Language Monthly* (*Guoyu yuekan*) came out in 1922 in strong support of Romanization. Its cover design captures the revolutionary fervor with a provocative image. At the center, soldiers, clad in the uniform of the Republican army, wield weapons that are modeled on the symbols of the National Phonetic Alphabet (*zhuyin fuhao*). They are slaughtering their way through a horde of bloodied traditional Chinese characters, which are written in the ancient seal-script style. On the other side, the masses watch from a cool distance, as they stand united behind a row of Latin letters that spell out "Roman script" in Gwoyeu Romatzyh.

The Alphabetic Revolution of the East

Despite the setbacks and fallouts, the will to overhaul the Chinese writing system persisted. To understand this commitment, one has to appreciate how far the conversation has come. The alphabetization of the Chinese script has been, strictly speaking, more than 400 years in the making. It was at first a foreign affair. From the Jesuit missionaries in the sixteenth century to Russian Sinologists in the nineteenth century, non-native learners of Chinese played a pioneering role in tackling the complex system. While Chinese philologists since the second century have been organizing and reorganizing this body of scripts through the identification of more basic, commonly shared character components and phonetic rhymes, it was not until the late nineteenth century that the Chinese themselves began to seriously contemplate writing Chinese in an altogether different notation system. The advent of nationalism in the early twentieth century selectively shaped these initial stirrings with the powerful impetus of modernity. Together with nationalism, the two currents inspired ideas to overhaul the 5,000 year-old writing system. The ambition was to promote literacy on an unprecedented scale and—what was perhaps most urgently felt—to participate and influence the international informational network in the areas of printing, telegraphy, postal system, and typewriting.

The Chinese script revolution was the longest revolution of the twentieth century. The late Qing script reformers made the first indigenous proposals, the Nationalists made it an explicit agenda soon after the founding of the Republic, and the Communists returned to the issue mere months after the founding of the People's Republic of China (Mills 1956).[18] Latinxua Sin Wenz was introduced into China in 1933–1934. In a declaration signed by 688 progressive intellectual and cultural figures, Sin Wenz was embraced as the best vehicle for national salvation: "Script is like a means of transportation. The Chinese script is like a monocycle, Gwoyeu Romatzyh a steamship, and Sin Wenz the airplane. Once you take a seat on the plane to spread the message of national salvation, you will realize that not only does Sin Wenz not stand in the way of China's unification. It has the real power to mobilize the masses to save our dying country" (Cai 1989). Despite the turmoil of the War of Resistance against Japan, the development of Sin Wenz continued between 1937 and 1942 under battle fire in key cities like Hong Kong, Shanghai, Chongqing, Yan'an, Hankou, and Guangzhou. It joined the cause of national salvation and became one of its main platforms for mass mobilization. The movement reached as far as San Francisco, Lyon, and Xinjiang, and spilled over into Southeast Asia in places like Bangkok, Singapore, Penang, Kuala Lumpur, Jakarta, and the Philippines (Ni Haishu 1948).[19] As modern China contemplated the future and shape of its writing system in the 1920s and 1930s, the twin prospects of nationalization and internationalization hung in the balance. Unlike previous centuries, the Chinese script came closer than ever before to embrace alphabetization. For people like Qu and Zhao, the question was not if but how.

The historical forces that made Latinxua Sin Wenz possible in the 1930s, however, were not drawn from the internal impulse of China's state-building alone. Nor was it entirely accurate to attribute it, as Qu did, to the May Fourth ideals of enlightenment. Just as alphabetization began with outsiders' interest in making religious and economic inroads into China, it remained an internationalist project bound up with larger geopolitical trends. This transnational context bears reminding, as over the course of the twentieth century, Chinese language reform came to be narrated, narrower and narrower, as a state project of literacy, as though it were an internalist history.

The fact was that a globalist vision of language was converging from different corners of Asia and nearby regions. Despite how it has been argued, alphabetization did not confirm the triumph or superiority of western civilization

over the rest of the world. Those who engaged in that rhetoric may have utilized the discourse to get people to consider the proposal. Yet it is clear that
Latinization drew from primarily pragmatic motives. It confirmed the utility
of a linguistic medium, one that Europe wisely developed but did not own.
This point was at times suggested by the Chinese language reformers themselves, and Zhao's instrumentalist view represented this perspective. At the
time, however, the material medium of language was yet to be disentangled
from the sensitive questions of ownership and origin, whether it was western
or indigenous, and the superiority or inferiority of the alphabetic versus Chinese writing systems. Zhao was one of the few who approached the issue separately as a linguistic science, as did Lin Yutang, who took language reform into
the realm of typewriting technology and invented a pathbreaking typewriter
in the 1940s that intercepted a crucial stage of global information technology
(Tsu 2010).[20] Apart from the few linguists who could maintain an objective,
technical interest, the alphabetization of Chinese was highly embroiled in culturally and emotionally weighted debates.

It is worth bearing in mind that other comparable contexts of alphabetization witnessed parallel debates and reactions. On the one hand, there were
those in Central Asia, during Soviet Union's wide sweeping Latinization campaigns, who believed that the script they had, generally Arabic, was simply
more backward and ill-suited to the needs of the Turkic dialects, which required certain vowels that Arabic cannot convey. In this sense, the alphabet
was seen as the script of modernity, progress, and western science. As the
beginning of a poem by a Soviet Tajik poet conveys: "When the Latin letters
adorned the new alphabet/Soon the demand became slow for the Arab alphabet./In the scientific era the new alphabet is like a plane/The Arabic alphabet
is like a weak donkey in pain. . . ."[21] On the other hand, there were also pro-
ponents who saw in the alphabet a concrete, universal instrumentality that is
greater than any of its originating contexts. They could care less about where it
came from, and were much more concerned about where it could take them.
In an argument for why the alphabet is perfectly compatible with the Muslim
context of Azerbaijian in 1922, the first Soviet Central Asia Republic to be introduced to the alphabet in 1926, an advocate states that "The Latin alphabet
is not only international; it is pananthropic" (Winner 1952).[22] By the same
distinction, importantly, for Chinese language reformers like Zhao, there was
no conflict or contradiction in using the alphabet for China's own purposes.
Admittedly, opponents to the project often played on, and perhaps bought

into, the hierarchical order. The obsession with comparing China to the West according to a western bar, in other words, limited the interpretation of what was in fact a broader transnational history of alphabetization—even today.

Indeed, it is no exaggeration to say that the scope of Latinization was beyond what one might find feasible now. For the language reformers, the fate of the world was inextricably bound with the failure and success of the alphabet. Samed Agamali-Ogly, an Azerbaijani revolutionary, recounts his 1923 visit to the dying Lenin, who reputedly left him with these immortal words: "Latinization is the great revolution in the east" (Martin 2001, 187).[23] By "the east," Lenin meant the Soviet East, where the Russian leader had been dismayed by the linguistic and religious gulf. Azerbaijian later became the first Soviet republic in the east to adopt the Latin script as its official medium. That shining example, however, was in no way representative of the degree of division and dissent that plagued the campaign from beginning to end (Smith 1998, 133).[24] Throughout the last Czarist regime, the Russians did not overlook the importance of recognizing the diverse cultures and peoples of the east. Missionaries had devised Russian alphabets for the small peoples of the north, but always with an eye on local forms. After the Bolshevik revolution, the diversity issue served a new agenda, one that distanced itself as much as possible from the old regime. As scholars of Russian studies have amply shown, the newly-formed Soviet Union was confronted by the scores of languages and sub-languages that had been little studied or systematized.[25] In official documents of the state, for instance, confusion about what ethnicities resided in which republic abounded. Azerbaijianis were called Tartars, Uzbeks as Sarts, Tajiks as Uzbeks, and so on. The Bolsheviks had their work cut out before them, and cast their eyes over the Soviet East as a culturally untamed land, "extremely savage and backward" (Smith 1998, 43).[26]

When Qu made his first trip to Moscow as a journalist in 1920–1921, he saw a Russia recovering from the ravages of a revolution. At the time, Qu had not yet been converted to Marxism (Qu 1935).[27] In the new Soviet Union, he came to believe in the way of socialism as the true bearer of democracy. He remarked on the common sight of equality among the cadres and was swept up in the revolutionary euphoria of the workers and peasants who were dancing in the Red Square in celebration of May Day (Qu 1985b, 145). The watershed moment came when he met and spoke with Lenin at the Third Congress of the Communist International in June 1921 (Lu 1995: 151).[28] The encounter changed the course of his thinking. As he later recalled to a friend, it was not only the political commitments of the Bolsheviks that inspired him. What deeply moved him was their dedication to stamping out illiteracy when they were greatly stricken by material scarcity (Peng 1982, 108). He began during this period to study the question of Latinization, and joined the Communist Party the following year.

Returning to Moscow in 1928 on the occasion of the Sixth National Congress of the Chinese Communist Party, Qu began to work out a concrete Latinization scheme at the end of the year (Xiao 1959; Shprintsin 1974).[29] Earlier in February 1928, a group at the Communist University of the Toilers of the East began to study whether Chinese could be latinized. By then, attempts to help the Chinese laborers in the Soviet Union to acquire literacy in the Chinese language had failed. As A. G. Shprintsin later recalls, "the teaching of hieroglyphs did not carry the crusade against illiteracy too far," as the Soviet government ensured its failure (Shprintsin 1974, 330). At the Institute for Scientific Research on China of the Communist Academy in Moscow, Qu worked with V. S. Kolokolov and Shprintsin, along with Wu Yuzhang, Xiao San, and other members of the CCP. Kolokolov helped Qu devise the Chinese Latin alphabet and transcription system. Qu made an internal report on a draft of the Chinese Latinization scheme in early 1929 to a small audience of specialists and Chinese students. The draft, *Zhongguo ladingshi zimu cao'an,* appeared under Qu's adopted Russian name. Up until May of that year, the study was primarily conducted among the Chinese students, which numbered in the hundreds. A larger conference was then held towards the end of May. Mainly Sinologists were invited to participate in the broader discussion about the draft proposal. The project acquired additional reinforcement when, in April 1930, contact was made with the Commissariat of Education, the Council of Nationalities of the U.S.S.R. Central Executive Committee, and the Down-with-Illiteracy Society. The new alliance led to further collaboration with A. A. Dragunov of the Institute of Oriental Studies of the U.S.S.R. Academy of Sciences in Leningrad. Dragunov had also been conducting research on Chinese Latinization sometime before and made a presentation in Moscow in May 1930, where many of the Latinization campaigners for the New Turkic Alphabet in the Soviet East were in attendance. In principle, they supported Qu and Kolokolov's scheme, and it was decided that Qu, Kolokolov, and Dragunov would work together on the final draft of the proposal. *Zhongguo ladinghua zimu* was published in 1930. The title on the cover appeared in three scripts: Latinized Chinese, Chinese characters, and Russian.

While Romanization reached a new landmark with the introduction of Sin Wenz into China in the following year, that revolution neither began nor ended with Latinization. Before the Latinization campaign for Dunganese started, a young Dunganese writer, Iasyr Shivaza, together with his classmates Yu. Yanshansin and Kh. Makeev at the Tartar Institute in Tashkent, worked on creating the first Dungan alphabet (Rimsky-Korsakoff Dyer 1991: 27–30, 240–245). Initially based on the Arabic script that they learned from reading the Koran in Muslim classroom instruction, they drafted a Latin scheme in 1927 (Riedlinger 1989, 75–79). When the different Turkic nationalities in Soviet Central Asia began to adopt the New Turkic Alphabet, the Dungans followed their example. But it soon became clear that it would not suit the linguistic requirements of spoken Dunganese. Though the Latinized alphabet was adopted by the Dungans in 1928–1929, by spring 1930 the process was halted until further official review. Meanwhile, the research for Latinxua Sin Wenz gathered momentum in Moscow. When Qu's first draft was submitted, the two movements inched ever closer together. Dragunov became the nodal point, along with sinologist B. A. Vasiliev, who published on Dungans and their literature in the early 1930s. After working with Qu on Latinxua Sin Wenz, Dragunov began to publish on Dunganese as well and later presided as the chairman of the Committee of Experts for the Creation of a New Dungan Alphabet in 1952, when Dunganese made its belated transition to the Cyrillic script. Shivaza continued to be involved in the subsequent proposals for Dunganese and served on this committee. The research on Dunganese dovetailed with the implementation of Latin Sin Wenz. The Latinization of Dunganese and China's New Script did not only share an origin in the Soviet language campaigns. Their paths crisscrossed, though never explicitly acknowledged as a concurrent history. Despite the impact of Soviet sinology on the modern research into the Chinese script reform, the extent of this collaborative history has been little known. Added to that is the unique role that Dunganese played in the history of modern China's governance of sounds and script. In the same way that Shivaza's role in devising the first Dunganese alphabet has only quietly intersected China's linguistic history, his literary encounter with modern Chinese literature also made a memorable crossing.

Meeting Places

In 1956, Iasyr Shivaza joined a group of Kyrgyz writers in welcoming a delegation of 16 writers from China. It was the first Sino-Soviet friendship group in Frunze (Rimsky-Korsakoff Dyer 1991). The only person he was able to converse with was writer Ge Baoquan. The language they had in common was not Chinese but Russian, as Ge spoke Shanghainese, which was far from the range of familiar northern dialects. After the conference, Shivaza was left with the reminder that "the Chinese, though friends, are aliens and quite different from Dungans." This feeling of familiarity and unfamiliarity persisted in his writing in different forms.

The event in Frunze led to a reciprocal invitation. The following year, in 1957, Shivaza visited China for the first—and only—time. The itinerary itself allegorized the journey from a place between worlds, an interplace, to the heart of Beijing. His visit began with attending a meeting of writers of the Xinjiang-Uigher Autonomous Region, where he, then the national poet of Kirghiz S.S.R., was one of the seven representatives from the Soviet Union. His cohort included writers from Uzbekistan, Kazakhstan, Turkmenistan, and Tajikistan. During the 15-day meeting, Shivaza read a poem before the audience, entitled "For the Poet Qu Yuan" (Gei Qu Yuan shiren), an ode to the third century B.C.E. poet and political exile whose loyalty to his ruler is enshrined in *The Songs of Chu* (Shivaza 2011). Though it was delivered in Dunganese, no translation was necessary. Shivaza's Chinese listeners understood the unmistakable northwestern inflections in his speech (Rimsky-Korsakoff Dyer 1977–78).

Shivaza's recitation was poignant, and the poet persona was familiar enough to draw his Chinese audience close to him. But it carried layers of address that they would not have intuited entirely. In the poem, Qu Yuan is addressed as the second person. As the speaker makes his speech in the present, he recognizes all the while the difficulty of the attempted contact across time and space:

My grandfather and great-grandfather were born on the Miluo River,
They lived there, they died there, they never forgot you.
They sang your song, they remembered you,
Because you never finished your song but jumped into the big river.
They say you liked to eat *zongzi,* they never forgot that,
Each spring they wrapped the *zongzi* to remember you.
They threw the *zongzi* into the big sea, into the ocean,
Because you were hungry when you threw yourself into the big river.
I was born far away, have never seen the Miluo River,
On the Volga I did not forget you.
I, too, sang your song, to remember you,
I, too, threw *zongzi* into the Volga River.[30]

The eulogistic mode of the poem shows that it is intended to be sung, just as the speaker's paternal predecessors had done before him. The repetition, to be sure, harks back to the speaker's own line of descent over three generations. But it is by no means continuous. While the allusion to Qu Yuan as a trope of homelessness and political exile is commonplace in Chinese literature, it is precisely the place of its invocation, in this case, that is not common. The speaker's grandfather—and his father before him—sang this ode to Qu Yuan from the place of Qu's suicide at the Miluo River. They took it upon themselves to carry on Qu Yuan's song at the place where it was left incomplete. They performed this successive lineage on site for the duration of their lives, until they themselves ceased to exist.

The speaker's present invocation, however, breaks this attachment to place sameness and the temporal lineage it sanctions. "On the Volga, I did not forget you" (line 10), the speaker said, echoing the act of non-forgetting that his predecessors had performed before him at the Miluo River (line 2). It is true that Qu Yuan's mythical exile is invoked, but only in juxtaposition with the speaker's own sense of being elsewhere, a place "far away." The perception of the speaker's place of birth, strikingly, is not articulated as the place on hand—i.e., where he is right here and now—but assumes instead the perspective of Qu Yuan. The speaker chooses not to privilege his own place-based point of view, according to which Miluo, not the Volga, would be more logically the place that is "far away." Instead of treating distance as an interval governed by two fixed points, then, he asserts the elasticity of distanciation, and its elusive quality—and power—of making a place feel closer or farther away relative to one's desired vantage point. Yet one would be too hasty to conclude that the speaker does not see his own place of speaking as desirable because he is emotionally oriented toward Miluo as the place of his origin, and all the more so because he never experienced it firsthand. A crucial interception disrupts this nostalgic reading: the analogy that the Volga is to the speaker as the Miluo was to Qu Yuan and the speaker's forebears. The analogy preempts an exclusive reading of lineage that aligns his allegiance with that of his forebears.

The evaluative content of Qu Yuan's place, the origin from which the speaker's own patrilineal lineage flows, has in fact fundamentally altered through the analogy. Miluo, a place of birth, life, and death, ceases to retain its value as an absolute origin, as though it were an inert setting that is merely there as a fixture, where time comes to pass, people live and die. The Miluo where his predecessors performed their mourning rituals is not the Miluo he now invokes and animates. Nor does it have to be. And this is the important move: space is cast into relief not so much against the passage of time as against the possibility of other spaces. Instead of reaffirming the primacy of Miluo as the origin and place that his grandfather and great grandfather honored, it is now commemorated once more only insofar as it can be honored in relation to the speaker's present place of speaking. As a place, Miluo can ultimately claim no more value in being associated with the historical persona of Qu, in other words, than the Volga can in the speaker's utterance. This important analogy puts two things into play: First, it opens up the temporal succession of a single line of lineage to the simultaneous juxtaposition of places. Miluo still exists, but it is experienced only relationally with reference to another place that cannot and must not coincide with it. Second, this spatialization has an impact, in turn, on the modality of the temporal basis of memory. Whereas the speaker's predecessors took Qu Yuan as the object of their mourning and commemorative rituals, in whose name they performed the act of remembrance and continuity, the speaker does not have to—and is not at liberty to decide to—bind his loyalty to the same Qu Yuan or Miluo River. He had never been to Miluo, whereas his grandfather, and his grandfather's father, underwent birth, life, and death there. The circle of nativity will thus never close for him the way it did for them. He can only insert himself as a link into a chain of recall and commemoration, an interception that he uses to forge an ongoing process so that the obligation of the mourning was still being fulfilled as it passes from Qu to his predecessors, and his predecessors to him in an active incompletion. Importantly, what the speaker loses with the fixity of origin, he also gains in simultaneous, juxtaposed spatialization. The spatial relief here is all the more significant, given that Miluo is here understood as a metonymic reference to China, just as the Volga would be to Russia.

Thus far, the juxtaposition of different places would seem to trump the importance of singular origins. Still, if the main contribution of juxtaposed places were simply to prove the impossible exclusivity of origins, it would be a rather small point for quite a lot of analytical labor. It would also still bind us to the same logic of privileging one axis (spatial) against another (temporal), just according to the opposite valuation. In fact, something else expresses time more compellingly, and immediately, than the idea of successive lineage. Just as place is a historical and lived instantiation of space, so too must our concept of time and succession be tested against an embodied unit of measure. For this, one needs only to step outside of the poem's diegetic frame. One immediately recognizes, then, that place was being carved out, and specifically claimed by the language of the voice that recited the poem. At the time Shivaza recited this poem before his Chinese audience, his voice did not blend in inconspicuously with its setting or occasion. The inflections of his unmistakably northwestern dialect created dissonance and likeness, familiarity and dissimulation, in the ears of its Chinese listeners. In this language, he summoned a concatenation of places that his listeners could only partially relate from the vantage of one. And that place is only identifiable to the extent that the speaking voice uses a language that has traveled and lived elsewhere. In this way, the language-becoming of place marks the process through which place comes to inhabit, grow into, forget, erase, lose, and reconnect with a particular language; while the place-becoming of language marks the process through which language can shape, morph, isolate, bury, connect, and rebuild a place. Such are the twin key dynamics in the politics and history of Chinese diaspora, which bears the deep mark of the incongruity between speech and writing, sound and script.

How the speaker in "For the Poet Qu Yuan" is structured at a specific temporal and spatial intersection facilitates an important understanding of Shivaza's encounter with China. By the time he reached Beijing, it was hardly the endpoint of a pilgrimage of nostalgia. He already had a distinguished career and strong intellectual roots in the Slavic world. In 1934, he was one of the first Dungan writers to be accepted into the Union of Soviet Writers. From 1939 to 1941 he was the chairman of the Union of the Kirghiz Writers. The first Russian translation of his poetry appeared in Moscow in 1937, followed by translations into Kirghiz, Kazakh, and other languages in just a few years. Shivaza was not only the leading voice of Dungan poetry and literature, but an active conduit in introducing Dungan literature to the Russian readers at large. A strong advocate of Dunganese literature and arts, during his eight years of tenure (1930–38) as an editor of Dungan works in the Kirghiz State Publishing House, Shivaza mentored young Dunganese writers and promoted Dungan-related cultural affairs.

In Beijing, Shivaza met mainland Chinese writers such as Lao She, Mao Dun, Guo Moruo, Xiao San, officials such as Zhou Enlai, and important scholars of Chinese Muslims like Bai Shouyi, Ma Jian, Ding Yimin, Liu Geping, and Da Pusheng. He had met Lao She and others already the year before at the Urumqi conference. A photograph of Shivaza with Lao She, and Yang Wenqian in Urumqi shows the excitement of a young minority writer,

standing next to the renowned Chinese writer of the May Fourth generation, who is himself not ethnically Han but Manchu (Rimsky-Korsakoff Dyer
1991: 61). For Lao She, though, who was at the time deeply involved in promoting local culture and speech in the writing of literature, especially for China's ethnic or "brother nationalities" (*xiongdi minzu*), the encounter did not
stand out (Lao She 1991a, 385–392). His trip to Xinjiang was one of a number of cultural delegations that were orchestrated in promotion of the socialist
brotherhood between China and the Third World from the early Communist
period up through the Cultural Revolution. The ceremonial aspect left him
exhausted and he could barely keep up with the number of writers he greeted
(Lao She 1991b).

While Lao She and Shivaza's encounter was a missed opportunity, Shivaza
did have an emotional reunion with Qu Qiubai's close collaborator in the
Latinxua Sin Wenz project, Xiao San. Shivaza had met Xiao San almost twenty years earlier in the summer of 1938, when Xiao San was welcomed by
the Union of the Kirghiz Writers in Frunze (Xiao 1952). Xiao San celebrated
Shivaza as a great Dunganese poet and dedicated a poem to him in the spirit
of socialist brotherhood: "You and I had known each other for thousands of
years,/ Together we once sang the same song./ But you were forced to leave
your home country./ It's your good fortune that you found a wholly new ancestral land./ But you and we are still singing that same song./ I believe that
the two households will merge as one,/ And many families will unite into a
large family./ Perhaps here, perhaps there, you and I will see each other again./
We will sit down around the same table,/ And together let our voices soar in
singing that song!"

By the time of his encounter with the Chinese writers, Shivaza was already
quite familiar with the works of Lu Xun, Xiao San, Ba Jin, Zhao Shuli. He
himself had also translated some of Ba Jin's short stories into Dunganese from
Russian. He read others, like Pearl Buck, who wrote about China from an
outside perspective. But the China he knew from all these vantage points was
through the lens of the Russian language. Ultimately, as much as he was influenced by the Chinese revolutionary writers, he was even more intimately im-
pacted by the works of Kyrgyz, Kazakh, Uzbek, and Uyghur writers and poets,
with whom he shared and breathed in the same milieu (Rimsky-Korsakoff
Dyer 1991).

It is an ironic reflection on modern Chinese literature why Dunganese
was not recognized as one of its dialogic counterparts. While Leftist Chinese

writers were heavily invested in developing the cultural arts and languages of the masses, no one seemed to recognize its extraordinary preservation of regional and ethnic speech against the odds of history. Dunganese' expressivity of the mother tongue in script, one might say, embodied the very form they sought. Lao She, in many ways, missed what was right in front of him. The historical possibility of Dunganese was unthinkable in the Chinese context. The kind of dialectal or local color that Lao She promoted took standard Chinese as the normative substrate on which ethnic identities can be inscribed. Ethnicities had their places in the Chinese nation, and were impossible—and indeed irrelevant—outside of it. Dunganese was the exception that proved the rule. It was a language that was out of place, but borne of a place that was only possible through the materialization of a spoken Chinese language. Both place-defying and place-dependent, Dunganese is thought provoking not only as the early example of writing Chinese in different scripts. It also poses a foundational challenge for rethinking the linguistic foundation of modern Chinese literature.

Rather than easily fitting into the framework of Chinese Nationalist, Chinese Muslim, Sinophone, or even Area Studies, Shivaza is one of the many examples of the decoupled experiences of language and place. How to analyze both language and place as specific modalities of temporal, spatial, and material intersection is the challenge that Dungan literature brings to bear. In a way that is crucial to analyses of space and place, it shows how language materializes space into a lived place, and vice versa. The point, however, is not that language has to be wrested from a naturalized place of nativity. That is only one part of the conceptual turn of the language-becoming of place, and the place-becoming of language. Instead, to understand that nativity is not given once and for all, in place or in language, means to rethink both units as they continue to emerge from a coterminous history. The mutually constitutive process here is not just how language makes places, and places make language. The entwined history between Latinxua Sin Wenz and Dunganese reminds one of the stakes that compel us to reconstitute our present sense of connected intimacies and estrangement.

Notes

1. The amorphous concept of "Chineseness" continues to constrain ongoing discussions, even as they seek to break away from its habits of criticism. A recent

collection of essays on Sinophone studies both embodies and raises one's awareness of the problem (Shu-mei Shih et al., eds. *Sinophone Studies: A Critical Reader*. New York: Columbia University Press, 2013.).

2. John DeFrancis, *In the Footsteps of Genghis Khan*, 228; original emphasis. For an account of the nineteenth-century Muslim revolt, see Bai Shouyi, *Huimin qiyi* (Shanghai: Shenzhou chubanshe, 1952), chs. 3 and 4; Jonathan N. Lipman, *Familiar Strangers: A History of Muslims in Northwest China* (Seattle: University of Washington Press, 1997).

3. While Dunganese studies is well established in Russian scholarship, it is only relatively recently, when Sino-Soviet relations were restored in the mid-1980s, that scholars in mainland China began research in this area. At the time of the writing of this essay, the full picture is still incomplete in the Chinese-language scholarship and restricted to largely ethnographic and linguistic studies. For an 1897 account, see Svetlana Rimsky-Korsakoff Dyer, V. Tsibuzgin, A. Shmakov, "Karakunuz: An Early Settlement of the Chinese Muslims in Russia," *Asian Folklore Studies*, 5.2 (1992): 243–278. For others, see Elizabeth Allès, "The Chinese-speaking Muslims (Dungans) of Central Asia: A Case of Multiple Identities in a Changing Context," *Asian Ethnicity* 6 (2) (June 2005): 121–134.

4. 134.

5. The figure of 15,000 (compared to 14,600 according to 1926 census) comes from a 1937 Russian document on orthography for Dunganese. It is translated into German and included in Heinz Riedlinger, *Likbez: Alphabetisierung bei den sowjetischen Dunganen seit 1927 und ihr Zusammenhang mit den Latinisierungsbestrebungen in China*, 167. See Allès 2005.

6. As late as the 1980s, the majority of Dungans were unable to communicate in their own language. Kyrgyzstan began reversing the situation by encouraging academic research and teaching of the language. A Department of Dungan studies was established at the Kyrgyz State University in 1988. See Eugene Huskey 1995, "The Politics of Language in Kyrgyzstan," *Nationalities Papers: The Journal of Nationalism and Ethnicity* 23 (3) (1995): 549–572.

7. This becomes a significant fact in the later latinization project for the 100,000 or so Chinese laborers in Vladivostock.

8. After returning from Russia in the early 1930s, however, he did continue to devote himself to working out the technical details of a viable latinization scheme for the Chinese language, despite his ill health. With the help of his friend Peng Ling, Qu probed the question of dialectology. See Peng Ling's reminiscence, "Nanwang de xingqi san: Huiyi Qiubao Zhihua fufu" (The Unforgettable Wednesdays: Remembering Qu Qiubai and His Wife Zhihua), *Xin wenxue shiliao* 4 (1982): 107–110.

9. Qu, "Xin Zhongguo wen cao'an" (A Draft Proposal for the Chinese New Script), *Qu Qiubai wenji* (Beijing: Renmin chuban she, 1953), vol. 3: 705–706.

10. Ibid., 706.

11. Qu, "Xuefa wansui!" (Long Live the Academic Warlords!), *Qu Qiubai wenji* (Beijing: Renmin chuban she, 1953), vol. 3: 596–597.

12. Here, Qu echoes the earlier assertion by Qian Xuantong in a March 1918 letter to Chen Duxiu, in which Qian emphatically wrote, "If you want to abolish Confucianism, you must first get rid of the Chinees script. If you want to eradicate the childish, barbaric, and obstinate habits of mind, you can't afford not to abolish the Chinese script first." This sentiment came to be known as the first open charge for Han scrip revolution, and resuscitated the discussion of Romanization despite the ascendancy of the National Phonetic Alphabet at the time. See Qian Quantong, "Tongxin: Zhongguo jinhou zhi wenzi wenti" (Correspondence: China's Script Problem in the Present and Future), *Xin Qingnian* 4 (4) (1918): 70–77.

13. Qu, "Xuefu wansui" 595–596.

14. For Qu's full critique of Gwoyeu Romatzyh, see Qu, "Luomazi de Zhongguo wen haishi roumazi de Zhongguo wen?" (Roman Script in Chinese or Nauseating Script in Chinese?), *Qu Qiubai wenji*, vols. 3/4 (Beijing: Renmin chuban she, 1953): 662–672.

15. Zhao, "Gwoyeu Romatzyh or the National Romanization." In *Linguistic Essays by Yuenren Chao*, ed. Wu Zongji and Zhao Xinna (Beijing: Commercial Press, 2006), 61.

16. See Zhao, "Hewei zhengyin?" [What is Standard Pronunciation], in *Yuyan wenti* [Problems of Language], ed. Zhao Yuanren (Beijing: Shangwu yinshuguan, 1980), 103–121

17. "What Is Correct Chinese?" In *Linguistic Essays by Yuenren Chao*, ed. Zong-ji Wu and Xin-na Zhao (Beijing: Commercial Press, 2006), 712.

18. Harriet C. Mills, "Language Reform in China: Some Recent Developments," *Far Eastern Quarterly* 15 (4) (August 1956): 521.

19. Ni Haishu, *Zhongguo pinyin wenzi yundong shi jian bian* (A Short History of the Phonetic Script Movement in China), (Shanghai: Xiandai shubao, 1948), 150–172.

20. See my *Sound and Script in Chinese Diaspora*, ch. 3.

21. M. Mobin Shorish, "Planning by Decree: The Soviet Language Policy in Central Asia," *Language Problems & Language* Planning 8 (1) (Spring 1984): 39.

22. Thomas G. Winner, "Problems of Alphabetic Reform among the Turkic Peoples of Soviet Central Asia," *Slavonic and East European Review* 31 (76) (December 1952), 136. Just as the Latin alphabet was purely instrumental, once it served its purpose, its erstwhile supporters were just as ready to abandon it, as they did when Latinization was replaced by the Cyrillic scheme in 1939. Ibid., 146.

23. Quoted in Terry Dean Martin, *The Affirmative Action Empire: Nations and Nationalism in the Soviet Union* (Ithaca: Cornell University Press, 2001), 187.

24. Because it acquired its own Latin script early on, ironically, Azerbaijian was among the oppositions to the standards of the New Turkic Alphabet, adopted in 1928. See Smith 1998, 133.

25. The following discussion draws on Michael G. Smith, *Language and Power in the Creation of the USSR*, especially 28–79.

26. Ibid., 43.

27. Qu, "Duoyu de hua."

28. Lu Yuan, trans. "Qu Qiubai yu tongdai ren" (Qu Qiubai and His Contemporaries), in *Qu Qiubai yanjiu* 7 (Qu Qiubai jinianguan ed.) (Shanghai: Xuelin chubanshe, 1995), 151.

29. The account of just how New Script was devised is subject to discrepancies between different accounts. I bridge here the differences between the two key members of the project, Xiao San and A. G. Shprintsin (Xiao San 1959; Shprintsin 1974).

30. This translation is minimally modified from that provided by Dyer.

References

Allès, Elizabeth. 2005. "The Chinese-speaking Muslims (Dungans) of Central Asia: A Case of Multiple Identities in a Changing Context." *Asian Ethnicity* 6 (2): 121–134.

Boas, Franz. 1911. "Kwakiutl," in *Handbook of American Indian Languages,* Bulletin 40, Part 1: 445.

Cai Yuanpei. 1989. "Women duiyu tuixing Sin Wenz de yijian" (Our Views on Carrying Out Latin New Script). In *Cai Yuanpei quanji.*Vol. 7. Beijing: Zhonghua shuju.

Casey, Edward. 1993. "Between Geography and Philosophy: What Does It Mean to Be in the Place-World." *Annals of the Association of American Geographers* 91 (4): 683–693.

———. 1997. *The Fate of Place: A Philosophical History.* Berkeley: University of California.

Chang Wenchang. 2010. *Shijie huayu wenxue de "Xin Dalu": Donggan wenxue lungang* (The "New World" of World Sinophone Literature: An Outline of Dungan literature). Beijing: Zhongguo shehui kexue chubanshe.

Chen, Kuan-hsing. 2010. *Asia as Method: Toward Deimperialization.* Durham, NC: Duke University Press.

DeFrancis, John. 1950. *Nationalism and Language Reform in China.* Princeton: Princeton University Press.

———. 1993. *In the Footsteps of Genghis Khan.* Honolulu: University of Hawai'i Press.

Dragunov, A., and K. Dragunov. 1952 (orig. 1936). "Über die dunganische Sprache," *Archív Orientální* 8 (1): 34–38.

Frank, Andre Gunder. 1988. *ReORIENT: Global Economy in the Global Age.* Berkeley: University of California Press.

Hashimoto, M. 1986. *The Altaicization of Northern Chinese. Contributions to Sino-Tibetan Studies* 5: 76–97.

Hu Zhenhua. 2006. *Minzu wenhua yanjiu wenji* (Collected Essays on the Studies of Ethnic Cultures). Beijing: Chongyang renmin daxue.

Huskey, Eugene. 1995. "The Politics of Language in Kyrgyzstan," *Nationalities Papers: The Journal of Nationalism and Ethnicity* 23 (3): 549–572.

King, Ross. 1997. "Experimentation with Han'gul in Russia and the USSR." In *The Korean Alphabet: History and Structure*. Ed. Young-Key Kim-Renaud, 296–339. Honolulu: University of Hawaii Press.

Lao She. 1991a. "Guanyu xiongdi minzu wenxue gongzuo de baogao" (On the Report on the Literary Construction of Our Ethnic Brothers). In *Lao She wenji*, Vol. 16: 385–392. Beijing: Renmin wenxue chubanshc.

———. 1991b. "Xinjiang banyue ji" (Notes from Two Weeks in Xinjiang). In *Lao She wenji*. Vol. 14. Beijing: Renmin wenxue chubanshe.

Lewis, Martin W., and Karen Wigen. 1997. *The Myth of Continents: A Critique of Metageography*. Berkeley: University of California Press.

Li Fuqing. 2011. *Donggan minjian gushi chuanshuo ji* (A Collection of Dungan Folklores and Legends). Shanghai: Shanghai wenyi chubanshe.

Lin Tai. 2008. *Zhongya huizu Shaanxi hua yanjiu* (A Study of Central Asian Muslim Shannxi Language). Yinchuan: Ningxia renmin chubanshe.

Lu Yuan, trans. 1995. "Qu Qiubai yu tongdai ren" (Qu Qiubai and His Contemporaries). In *Qu Qiubai yanjiu*, Vol. 7, 146–159. Ed. Qu Qiubai jinianguan. Shanghai: Xuelin chubanshe.

Mair, Victor. 1990. "Two Non-Tetragraphic Northern Sinitic Languages." *Sino-Platonic Papers* 18: A1–A19.

Martin, Terry. 2001. *The Affirmative Action Empire: Nations and Nationalism in the Soviet Union, 1923–1939*. Ithaca, NY: Cornell University Press.

Massey, Doreen. 2009. "The Possibilities of a Politics of Place Beyond Place? A Conversation with Doreen Massey," *Scottish Geographical Journal* 124 (3–4): 401–420.

Mills, Harriet C. 1956. "Language Reform in China: Some Recent Developments." *Far Eastern Quarterly* 15 (4): 517–540.

Ni Haishu. 1948. *Zhongguo pinyin wenzi yundong shi jian bian* (A Short History of the Phonetic Script Movement in China). Shanghai: Xiandai shubao.

Perdue, Peter C. 2005. *China Marches West: The Qing Conquest of Central Eurasia*. Cambridge, MA: Harvard University Press.

Qian Xuantong, 1918. "Tongxin: Zhongguo jinhou zhi wenzi wenti" (Correspondence: China's Script Problem in the Present and Future). *Xin Qingnian* 4 (4): 70–77.

Qu Qiubai. 1935. "Duoyu de hua" (Superfluous Words). In *Qu Qiubai wenji*. Vol. 7, 693–725. Beijing: Renmin wenxue chubanshe.

———. 1953. "Xin Zhongguo wen cao'an" (A Draft Proposal for the Chinese New Script). In *Qu Qiubai wenji*. Vol. 3, 705–706. Beijing: Renmin wenxue chubanshe.

———. 1985a. "Guimenguan yiwai de zhanzheng" (The War Outside of Hell's Gate) In *Qu Qiubai wenji*. Vol. 2, 620–621. Beijing: Renmin wenxue chubanshe.

———. 1985b. *Chidu xinshi* (A History of Moscow in the Mind). In *Qu Qiubai wenji*. Vol. 1. Beijing: Renmin wenxue chubanshe.

Riedlinger, Heinz. 1989. *Likbez: Alphabetisierung bei den sowjetischen Dunganen seit 1927 und ihr Zusammenhang mit den Latinisierungsbestrebungen in China*. Bochum: Studienverlag N. Brockmeyer.

Rimsky-Korsakoff, Dyer, S. 1967. "Soviet Dungan: The Chinese Language of Central Asia: Alphabet, Phonology, Morphology." *Monumenta serica* 26: 352–421.

———. 1977–78. "Soviet Dungan Nationalism: A Few Comments on Their Origin and Language." *Monumenta Serica* 33: 363–378.

———. 1991. *Iasyr Shivaza: The Life and Works of a Soviet Dungan Poet*. Frankfurt am Main: Peter Lang.

Rimsky-Korsakoff Dyer, S., V. Tsibuzgin, and A. Shmakov. 1992. "Karakunuz: An Early Settlement of the Chinese Muslims in Russia." *Asian Folklore Studies* 51(2): 243–278.

Shivaza, Iasyr. 2011. *Jiuxiang bailing'er wo chang ne* (Like a Lark I Sing). Trans. Ma Yongjun. 2 vols. Beijing: Zhongguo wenhua chubanshe.

Shprintsin, A. G. 1974. "From the History of the New Chinese Alphabet." In *The Countries and Peoples of the East: Selected Articles*, 329–338. Moscow: Nauka Publishing House.

Smith, Michael G. 1998. *Language and Power in the Creation of the U.S.S.R., 1917–1953*. Berlin: Mouton de Gruyter.

Struve, Lynn A., ed. 2004. *The Qing Formation in World-Historical Time*. Cambridge, MA: Harvard University Asia Center.

Tsu, Jing. 2010. *Sound and Script in Chinese Diaspora*. Cambridge, MA: Harvard University Press.

Tuan, Yi-Fu. 1977. *Space and Place: The Perspective of Experience*. Minneapolis: University of Minnesota Press.

Wexler, Paul. 2011. "Hieratic Elements in Soviet Dictionaries of Yiddish, Dungan, and Belorussian." In *The Politics of Language Purism*, ed. Björn H. Jernudd and Michael J. Shapiro, 141–168. Berlin: De Gruyter Mouton.

Winner, Thomas G. 1952. "Problems of Alphabetic Reform among the Turkic Peoples of Soviet Central Asia, 1920–41." *Slavonic and East European Review* 31 (76): 133–147.

Wu Zongji and Zhao Xinna, eds. 2006. *Linguistic Essays By Yuenren Chao*. Beijing: Commercial Press.

Xiao, San. 1952. *Heping zhi lu* [The Road to Peace]. Beijing: Renmin wenxue chubanshe.

———. 1959. "Zhu ZhongSu wenzi zhi jiao" (A Tribute to Sino-Russian Script Friendship), *Yuwen jianshe* 21: 2–3.

Xin wenzi yanjiu hui, ed. 1936. *Xin wenzi rumen*. Shanghai: Xin wenzi chubanshe.

Zhao, Yuanren. 1961. "What Is Correct Chinese?" *Journal of the American Oriental Society* 81 (3): 171–177.

———1980. *Yuyan wenyi*. Beijing: Shangwu yinshuguan.

12

Riding the Wave

Korea's Economic Growth and Asia in the Modern Development Era

PARK BUN-SOON

In 1960, South Korea (hereafter "Korea") was one of the poorest countries on earth, with per capita income comparable to the least developed countries in Africa. By the end of 2011, however, Korea had reached income levels higher than the average EU member state.[1] Korea's development trajectory thus makes it a unique case study of a nation rising from poverty and aid dependence to middle class status within a single generation. Not long ago, Korea was considered a near basket case by most Western observers.[2] As a small agrarian country in a region historically dominated by China with no natural resources of its own, Korea's status in the mid-twentieth century, on first examination, showed little promise of future growth. Korea, however, has a cultural background that played a significant part in its escape from poverty. Though it is a nation, Korea still retains some aspects of a rural village writ large. The country is small in land area (about equal to China's Guangdong Province), and largely homogeneous in language, ethnicity, and Confucian culture. These qualities were further bolstered after the Korean War, when Korea's government turned to anti-communist nationalism to bind the nation together. In this sense research on Korea's national cohesion can have significant implications, as with the small village research of Helen Siu and the cross-border area research of Peter C. Perdue.

In addition to its culture, Korea also maintained unique geographical circumstances after the Korean War. With its terrestrial borders closed for political reasons, Korea increasingly drifted apart from North Korea and its long-time diplomatic partner China, while increasing maritime ties to the outside world through trade. This in some sense marked a revival of earlier episodes in the nation's history, as Korea was a significant maritime power before the fourteenth century. One powerful maritime figure, Jang Bogo of the Silla dynasty, used Korea's maritime position to control both sides of the West Sea (Yellow Sea) between Korea and China for decades in the ninth century. At that time, the heavily trafficked Yellow Sea functioned as Asia's Mediterranean, as Charles Wheeler describes the Tongking Gulf in his book. Even the Goryeo Dynasty (918–1392) was a maritime kingdom until the midfourteenth century, before Japanese pirates disrupted conditions on the Korean coast. By the Chosŏn dynasty (1392–1910), however, Korea's sea trade had dwindled, as Chosŏn put priority on inland agriculture rather than commerce.

After surviving the Korean War in the 1950s, and with only a marginal supply of natural resources, Korea chose an outward oriented growth strategy that relied heavily on maritime trade. The most important factor in Korea's rapid growth was its export-led strategy (Amsden 1989; Koo 1986; Song 1990). The United States was the most important trade partner, providing both military security via the alliance and a large market for labor-intensive Korean goods. In the twenty-first century, however, Asia emerged as the new center of gravity for the world economy, and Korea's trade relations shifted accordingly. Over the past ten years, Asia has recorded massive current account surpluses while accumulating huge foreign exchange reserves. Asia (including the Middle East) now accounts for more than 60 percent of Korea's exports and more than 50 percent of its manufacturing investment. Korea imports most of its primary commodities (particularly crude oil) from Asia. Asia is now also the main market for Korea's exports of cultural products.

The purpose of this chapter is thus to evaluate Korea's interactions with Asia, in particular Southeast Asia and China, during its developmental era in terms of people, goods, and culture. It poses two key questions. The first question is "How did Korea utilize Asia for its outward oriented economic development?" The second question is "What factors affected Korea's utilization of Asia." To this end, I analyze economic cooperation between Korea and Asia in terms of trade and investment, as well as in the movement of personnel and cultural content.

Evolution of Korea's Economic Cooperation with Asia

In this section I will examine the most important areas of economic cooperation which are human resources exchanges, trade and investment cooperation, and pop culture between Korea and Asia. As labor was plentiful and employment opportunities were not sufficient in the era of economic development, Korea exported its workforce to Asia in order to obtain foreign currency necessary for economic development. Since the 1980s the center of economic cooperation has moved to trade and investment. As Southeast Asia and China started industrialization in an orderly manner, Korea developed earlier increased export and investment to those countries. In the 2000s, Korea's pop culture was widely accepted in Southeast Asia and China. Based on this, Korea emerged as a country which produced cultural products called Hallyu and exported it to the world.

Movement of People

Korean emigration first began in the late nineteenth century during the Chosŏn Dynasty as it entered its final period of stagnation and decline. At the time, most Korean emigrants moved to Northeast China and Eastern Russia. Japan and its newly acquired empire emerged as a new destination in the early twentieth century, after it annexed and colonized Korea. Some who emigrated at this time did so involuntarily, with men sent as forced laborers and conscripted soldiers to Southeast Asia, and with women sent as "comfort women" for the Japanese army. These were the first Koreans to visit Southeast Asia in the twentieth century. Most other emigrants left due to poverty, and the desire to find new opportunities. After the war, some of these emigrants who lived in China and Japan were unable to return.

The story of one comfort woman illuminates Korea's relations with Asia, and in particular, Southeast Asia from the 1940s to the 1970s. The late Noh Su Bok was taken to Singapore as a comfort woman. Soon after World War II, she was imprisoned in a concentration camp in Ipoh, Malaysia. She escaped from the camp and went to Hat Yai, a city in southern Thailand. She settled there but was unable to conceive a child due to her previous life as a comfort woman. When Korea regained independence it had little interest and few resources to devote to people like her. Just as Korea forgot her existence, Noh also forgot her homeland and mother tongue. When Noh was found by a

Japanese journalist in the mid-1980s, she could not speak any Korean other than a folk song which she remembered from childhood. The Japanese reporter wrote that the interview with Noh was the saddest she had ever conducted (Kim 2008, 259–260). After being discovered, Noh visited Korea a few times but continued to live in Thailand until she died in December 2011 at the age of 90. As she struggled to survive in Southeast Asia, Korea also struggled to emerge from poverty.

While the early emigrants were forgotten in Korea in the 1960s and 1970s, another wave of Korean emigration to Asia started from the 1960s, when Korea entered its economic development era. This time the Korean people encountered Asia by entering the Vietnam War. Korea sent a total of 325,517 soldiers to Vietnam under the banner of helping the free world against communist North Vietnam from 1964 to March 1973, when it withdrew its last troops (Defense Military Institute 1996: 152). In addition to troops, civilian laborers and non-combatant technicians engaged in construction work, supplying goods, and providing services for military procurement.

The main activity for construction companies operating in Vietnam was "dredging." Korean companies built up their technical skills from this work and leveraged them later in construction projects in the Middle East. From 1973, Saudi Arabia and other oil producing countries started building infrastructure using the flood of oil money that poured in after the first oil shock. Korean companies won a project for $US2.4 million for the first time in 1973, and orders increased to $US8.0 billion by 1980. From 1981 to 1982, average construction orders from Middle Eastern countries reached $US12 billion.

Participation in the Vietnam War and in Middle East construction contributed greatly to the early phase of Korea economic growth. The most important motivating factor was the effort to obtain foreign currency, which was urgently needed in the early stages of economic development. Income was not limited to payment of Korean soldiers working overseas. The US government provided soft loans, grants, and increased military aid, which had been reduced after the armistice suspending the Korean War. The Korean government forced soldiers to send 80 percent of their paycheck to their family, so the amount of money flowing into the country reached $US200 million (Institute of Military History Compilation 2004: 424). Indirect income was even more important. Income from the export of goods and the provision of construction services for military procurement, as well as income from worker remittances was greater than income directly related to troops. In 1968 alone, the actual amount of various Vietnam-related earnings was $US180million, accounting for 16 percent of Korea's total receipt of foreign funds and 2.8 percent of GNP in that year. Nearly 70 percent of earnings came from this "invisible trade," which had a substantial impact on Korea's holdings of international liquidity" (Kim 1970).

Construction proceeds from work in the Middle East became a major source of foreign exchange earnings. Korea's overseas construction orders amounted to $US421 billion from 1965 to 2010, of which $US258 billion (61.2 percent) came from the Middle East. From 1973, when expansion to the Middle East began, to 1979, total construction orders in the Middle East reached $US20.6 billion accounting for 94.9 percent of the $US21.7 billion in orders from abroad. Middle East contracts, other than the purchase of materials from third countries, were kept as company profits or paid as wages to Korean workers and remitted to Korea. Revenue from construction work in the Middle East became a major source of compensation for the trade deficit, which was sustained prior to 1986 because of high domestic investment.

The Vietnam War and the Middle East construction boom also paved the way for growth among Korean companies. Though only nine Korean firms were in Vietnam in 1966, that number grew to fifty-six by 1970. Likewise,

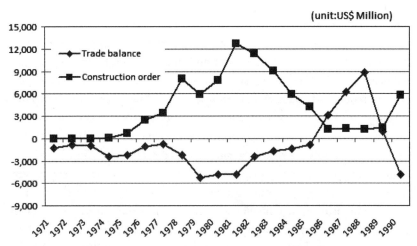

FIGURE 12.1. Trends in Korea's trade balance and construction orders, 1970–1990 (in $US millions). (*Data sources:* Korea International Trade Association and the Korea Overseas Construction Association database.)

the number of Korean firms in the Middle East was nine in 1974, engaged in a total of eleven construction projects, but grew to eighty-one companies involved in 558 different projects by 1981, when orders reached their peak.[3] Companies participating in the Vietnam War and the Middle East construction boom grew rapidly, and some of them evolved into today's "chaebols." Hanjin, for example, was involved in logistics in Vietnam and today is the Hanjin Group, a logistics conglomerate that includes Korean Air. Hyundai Engineering and Construction, whose remittances from Vietnam accounted for more than 50 percent of Korea's total revenue for civil works from 1966 to 1969, was the fastest-growing construction company during the Vietnam War (Choi 2001, 229). Hyundai Engineering and Construction established Hyundai Heavy Industries and Hyundai Motor Company, and led Korea's heavy industry based on the capital and knowledge it accumulated in Vietnam and the Middle East.

In addition, income from workers in Vietnam and the Middle East was a source of capital accumulation and social stability in 1970s Korea. A wave of urbanization beginning in the late 1960s in Korea, Vietnam, and the Middle East provided valuable jobs for young people moving in from the agricultural sector. The number of civilian laborers and technicians in Vietnam increased from ninety-three persons in 1965 to more than ten thousand by the following year. The total number of civilian workers in Vietnam (other than military personnel) reached 22,287 for the entire period.

In 1975 the number of workers in the Middle East was 6,466 persons, or 30.8 percent of all workers employed overseas, later increasing to 120,535 persons, or 82.3 percent of all workers abroad (Song and Seong 2009: 61). Most of these overseas Korean workers were employed at construction sites. Working in the Middle East became so popular for young men and so important for Korea's economic strategy that the government established an oversight organization, the Overseas Development Corporation, to select, train and manage overseas workers. Overseas construction workers declined through the 1980s, and by 1990, the number of workers in the Middle East fell to 8,000 due to reduction of investment in infrastructure by oil producing countries and expansion of job opportunities at home. Nonetheless, working in Vietnam and the Middle East from 1964 to 1985 contributed greatly to the achievement of social stability through the creation of jobs and the accumulation of wealth, despite the presence of authoritarian regimes under Park Chung Hee and Chun Doo Hwan.

Trade and Investment Relations with Asia

Korea's modern trade relationships with Asia began with Japan, where Korea exported its raw materials. When Korea began to implement its First Five-Year Plan for economic development in 1962, food, minerals, and raw materials accounted for 75.2 percent of total exports. Korea's main export markets were Japan and the US, whose shares were 42.8 percent and 21.8 percent respectively. As industrialization progressed, exports of manufactured products increased sharply to 42.2 percent of total exports by 1970, while raw materials like food and mineral products declined to 19.8 percent. It was at that time that the US market, which absorbed Korea's labor-intensive products, surpassed Japan with a share of 47.3 percent compared to Japan's 28.1 percent. From this time onward, the US would be the biggest market for Korea's exporters until it was itself surpassed by China in 2003.

Trade relations with Asia from the 1960s to 1980s were characterized by the import of natural resources, especially from the Middle East and Southeast Asia. Primary commodities have always been Korea's chief imported goods since the 1950s. Among commodities, crude oil was a lifeline, as Korea has no oil reserves. Korea imported its crude oil largely from the Middle East, including Saudi Arabia, Kuwait, the UAE, Qatar, Iran, and Iraq. Korea also imported crude oil, oil gas, and natural rubber from Southeast Asia, including Thailand, Indonesia, and Malaysia.

Until the mid 1980s, Korea utilized the US for export of manufactured goods, but relied on the Middle East and Southeast Asia for natural resources. It was thus natural for Korea to record huge trade deficits with those two regions. Among Asian countries, Japan was a market for Korea's raw materials as well as a partner for the import of capital and intermediate goods for industrialization. Korea maintained no diplomatic relations with Communist China at the time.

Korea's trade relations would be greatly transformed with the arrival of the 1985 Plaza Accord, which provided important new opportunities for Korea. Under the Plaza Accord, the five Western powers agreed to allow the Japanese yen and German mark to appreciate. Soon after, Korea's exports surged on improved price competitiveness vis-à-vis Japanese products. Exports to the US and Japan increased rapidly, and Korea's overall trade balance shifted to a surplus for the first time. The share of the US in Korea's total exports reached its peak of 40.0 percent in 1986.

At the outset, the share of exports to Southeast Asia (i.e. the Association of Southeast Asian Nations, or ASEAN) was small, but after the Plaza Accord, exports to ASEAN increased massively. Korea's exports to ASEAN increased by 47.3 percent in 1987, and soared 55 percent in 1988. In 1990 Korea's exports of $US5.2 billion to ASEAN exceeded Korea's imports of 5.1 billion dollars for the first time in history. ASEAN's share of Korea's total exports increased to around 15 percent in the mid 1990s, providing a market larger than that of Japan.

However, even as trade boomed, economic cooperation between Korea and Southeast Asia faltered in the late 1990s due to the East Asian financial crisis that began in Thailand in 1997. Import demand in Southeast Asia contracted sharply and the investment environment worsened. At the same time, China staged a rapid recovery from the Tiananmen crisis and once again commenced rapid economic growth. Before the establishment of diplomatic relations in 1992, Korea maintained some exports to China via Hong Kong. With the establishment of formal ties, however, exports to China exploded, surpassing exports to ASEAN by 2000. After China's ascension to the WTO in 2001, exports grew even more, from $US18.2 billion in 2001 to $US61.9 billion in 2005 to $US117 billion in 2010. China's share of Korea's total exports was 12.1 percent in 2001 and 21.8 percent in 2005, rising to 25.1 percent in 2010.

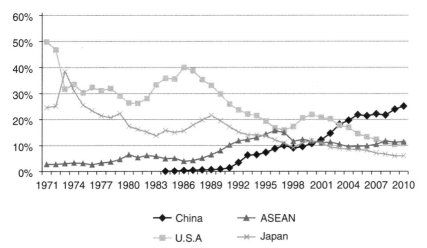

FIGURE 12.2. Shares for Korea's main export markets. (*Data sources:* Korea International Trade Association Trade database.)

One of the reasons for the fast growth in exports to ASEAN and China was Korea's heavy investment in both areas. During the first half of the 1980s, Korean manufacturers did not pursue "efficiency seeking investment," i.e., investment in countries with lower labor costs, because Korea's labor costs were already low due to government suppression of the labor movement. After the Plaza Accord, Korean companies experienced rising exports and profits due to the appreciation of the Japanese yen, a trend that dimmed when the Korean currency also appreciated.

At the same time Korea's once oppressed workers increasingly began to demand increased wages and improved working conditions, which increased labor costs at home. Like every other industrialized country, Korea had to face the fact that its export competitiveness in some industries was rapidly fading. Exports of garments decreased from $US6.9 billion in 1988 to $US5.2 billion in 1992, while exports of footwear decreased from $US3.6 billion to $US3.2 billion in 1992.[4] Labor-intensive light industries experienced the greatest loss of competitiveness, and these began migrating en masse to ASEAN countries like Indonesia, Thailand, and Malaysia. Korea's manufacturing investment in ASEAN accounted for 25.7 percent and 25.3 percent of its total overseas manufacturing investment in the late 1980s and early 1990s, respectively. As the share of ASEAN's GDP among world GDP was approximately 1 percent at this time, it is easy to understand why Korean investment was so concentrated in ASEAN.

Labor intensive and OEM based industries like clothing and footwear were the first comers to ASEAN, followed by labor-intensive light electronics manufacturing. When clothing and footwear manufacturers began to detect declining competitiveness around 1987 due to rising costs, they sought cheaper production bases for supply to the US and Europe. Indonesia was the preferred location due to its abundant cheap labor. By 1990 more than twenty footwear companies were in Indonesia. As a result, footwear exports by Korea's domestic producers decreased rapidly from $US3.2 billion in 1992 to $US1.8 billion in 1994. For electronics, Thailand and Malaysia were preferred over Indonesia, as they had better supporting industries and skilled workers for assembly of electronics.

Overseas investment can have a negative impact on export to host countries because direct production in host countries replaces exports from the home country. Korean investment to ASEAN was different because it produced goods for third countries rather than for ASEAN's domestic market. Korea's direct investment in ASEAN promoted the region's export of finished goods to third countries as well as the import of intermediate goods from Korea. Investment in ASEAN from the late 1980s to the mid-1990s increased export of Korean textile products, electronics parts and components, and steel, all of which were used in manufacturing for exports elsewhere.

When Korea and China normalized diplomatic relations in 1992, Korea's direct investment in Asia gradually migrated from ASEAN to China. In the early 1990s, 31.6 percent of manufacturing investment went to China and this share increased to 49.1 percent in the early 2000s. Initially, Korea's labor-intensive investment began in the Shandong Peninsula and Guangdong province to utilize their abundant labor and marine transportation networks. Products manufactured in the Shandong peninsula tended to be exported to Korea, while those made in Guangdong were exported to third countries like the US.

However, as industrial technology in China evolved and as the domestic market grew, Korea's investment moved gradually towards Shanghai, where parts and component procurement is easy and the domestic market is more accessible. In particular, the electronics industry tended to concentrate around Shanghai. Also unlike investment in ASEAN, investment in China has expanded to more capital intensive industries like automobiles, steel, and semiconductors, made for the domestic market rather than export abroad. Investment in China since the late 1990s played an even more crucial role in structural changes in Korea's trade with Asia. Korean subsidiaries in China imported parts and intermediate goods from their parent company and other suppliers in Korea.

TABLE 12.1 Share of manufacturing industry investment by region (percent)

	1986–1990	1991–1995	1996–2000	2001–2005	2006–2010
ASEAN	25.7	25.3	14.4	9.6	17.0
China	2.0	31.6	26.1	49.1	40.5
Japan	0.4	1.3	0.4	0.5	0.9
U.S.A	36.0	14.5	30.1	14.1	9.6
Others	35.9	27.3	29.0	26.7	32.0
Total	100	100	100	100	100

Data sources: Compiled from statistics of the Korea EXIM Bank database.

At the same time, the increase in exports to ASEAN and China contributed to stability in the trade balance in Korea. With exports growing faster than imports, Korea recorded a surplus with ASEAN for the first time in 1990. Even though the size of the surplus has recently become smaller, the surplus has been nevertheless maintained into the twenty-first century. The trade surplus with China is the same. Trade between the two countries was favorable for Korea from 1993 shortly after the normalization of diplomatic relations. As economic cooperation proceeds, Korea's surplus has continued to increase, reaching $US20.1 billion in 2004 and $US45.2 billion in 2010, greater than that of Korea's total trade surplus. Since Korea has to import natural resources, including agricultural products, securing sufficient foreign reserves is critical, and securing liquidity through trade surpluses with ASEAN and China has aided this process.

In addition to export creation, investments in Asia had a positive impact on the upgrading of Korea's industrial structure. When the competitiveness of Korea's labor-intensive light industries deteriorated rapidly, companies in the industry faced worsening profitability. However, even as they sent declining amounts to ASEAN and China, they sent greater amounts of parts and intermediate products. Parent companies in Korea were able to focus on sectors with high value-added.

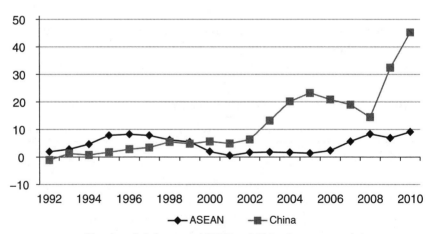

FIGURE 12.3. Korea's trade balances to ASEAN and China (1992 to 2010). (*Data sources:* Compiled from statistics from the Korea International Trade Association database.)

The Korean Wave in Asia

Since the late 1990s, Asia has become an important market for Korean cultural content, including dramas, movies, and pop music, a phenomenon called the "Korean Wave" (Hallyu).[5] Korean TV dramas were the first to succeed in Asia in the late 1990s. CCTV in China aired several Korean TV dramas and they proved very popular among the Chinese. After a strong reception in China, Korea's TV dramas were enthusiastically welcomed in Taiwan, Singapore, and Vietnam where Confucian family culture prevails. At that time the drama "Autumn Tale" was popular. In Singapore, "Autumn Tale" was screened in 2000 and proved so popular that the broadcaster was "inundated with 1,000 calls and emails requesting a rerun" when it ended" (Fu Su Yin 2009, 188). Hallyu likewise grew in Taiwan after the drama "Autumn Tale" aired in 2001.

However, it was in Japan that Hallyu made its most significant impact. Japan's NHK broadcast the Korean drama "Winter Sonata" twice in April 2003 (satellite) and in July 2004 (terrestrial) respectively. The audience rating for the broadcast in 2003 was 22 percent, and in 2004 reached 24 percent (Yasumoto 2006). For most of this period, Hallyu fans were women in their forties who were fond of actor Bae Young-joon, the leading character of "Winter Sonata". For some audiences "Winter Sonata" attained cult status in Japan and Bae Young-joon was referred to as Yon "Sama," a formal and respectful form of address. In many countries in Southeast Asia "Winter Sonata" was aired around this time further contributing to the establishment of Hallyu.[6] In 2004, the drama "Jewel in the Palace" (Dae Jang Geum) proved to be another success. "Jewel in the Palace" was popular throughout Asia, including Japan, Taiwan, Singapore, and Vietnam. "Many Vietnamese brides wanted to have their pictures taken in Korean traditional dress for their wedding photograph collection, and make-up and dressing in Korean style were not all that Vietnamese viewers demanded. Some wealthy Vietnamese viewers also wanted to be as beautiful as the actors on the show" (Ngo and Chuyen 2009, 101).

Hallyu in dramas and movies began to falter around 2005. The TV dramas at the center of Hallyu, and their dispersion by the mass media had reached a saturation point. Hallyu, then launched a new phase in the form of pop music. Popular entertainers performed to massive audiences across Asia, including the "Rain in Asia" tour, followed by TVXQ, Big Bang, and SNSD (Girls Generation). Consisting of groups of four to ten people singing and dancing, these boy and girl groups fanned out across Japan, China, and Southeast Asia. Currently the popularity of these groups has spread beyond Asia to the West through YouTube. This new music has come to be called "K-pop" in the West, and is building a growing fan base there.

The most dramatic acceptance of K-pop by the world is probably Psy's Gangnam Style. In July 2012, Psy released the song "Gangnam Style" and it ranked first on YouTube's "Most Viewed Videos" monthly chart on August 14. In late December 2012, Psy's Gangnam Style reached 1 billion views on YouTube. It became the first video to do so (Gruger 2012) at that time.[7] Psy's Gangnam Style ultimately reached 2 billion views on YouTube. It became the first video to do so. On the other hand, in this time the world had to witness the Gangnam Style fever in every corner of the village, town, and street. It was not difficult to see more than fifty people dancing together with the Gangnam Style on the street.

Even though Psy's music is part of the K-pop genre, chubby and little bit older, Psy doesn't have the stylized K-pop idol image of being young and good-looking. His dance is also somewhat different from other typical K-pop dance. In this sense, he was a post-modern artist who adds K-pop a diversified color.

Hallyu not only enhanced the pride of Koreans, it also contributed to the Korean economy. First, Hallyu become South Korea's major source of soft power. In a survey conducted by the Chicago Council in Global Affairs in 2008, respondents from China, Japan, and Vietnam viewed Korea's cultural soft power highly, and Chinese in particular view Korea's cultural soft power as more powerful than that of the US and Japan (The Chicago Council on Global Affairs 2009). According to a survey of KISEAS (Korean Institute of Southeast Asian Studies) (2011) more than 60 percent of people in Cambodia, Laos, Myanmar, the Philippines, Thailand, and Vietnam answered the question of "I like Korean popular culture" positively (strongly agree and agree). In addition, for the question of "I like Korean popular culture more than that of other Asian countries," the positive answers (strongly agree and agree) accounted for 60.3 percent in Myanmar, 54.3 percent in Cambodia, 53.6 percent in Laos, 41.6 percent in the Philippines, 41.4 percent in Thailand, 33.2 percent in Vietnam, and 30.6 percent in Singapore. As a result, when they were asked "which of the five countries do you like most?" more than 50 percent of the people in Myanmar, Cambodia, and Laos answered that Korea is their most favored country among the neighboring five countries (Australia, China, Japan, Korea, and India).

Okura Kijo who has researched Hallyu said that the "Hallyu boom in Japan was not a temporary trend, but has been changed into a national consciousness of knowing the Korean culture" (Maeil Economic Daily 2010, 128). The National University of Singapore started a complete Korean language course from beginner to advanced in 2008 (Fu Su Yin 2009). Young Thais wholeheartedly embraced Korean culture in the wake of Hallyu and the desire to learn about Korea, and the Korean language in particular, has become increasingly prevalent (Pavin 2010, 256).

Second, Hallyu has contributed economically to Korea. For a long time Korea was an importer of TV programs from the West, but due to Hallyu, Korea has become an exporter of cultural content. Export revenues from broadcast programs in 1998 grew from $US10 million to $US29 million in 2002 when exports exceeded imports, before reaching $US187 million in 2010 with more than $US10 million in surplus. The export of cultural content did not stop with broadcast programs, but expanded to K-pop related goods, and then to cosmetics, and mobile phones.

Korea has also experienced a surge in tourists from Asia. Since Winter Sonata came out in Japan, awareness of the Korean image has improved and Japanese tourists have come to Korea to visit the locations where dramas

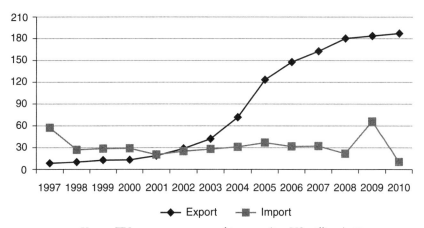

FIGURE 12.4. Korean TV program exports and imports (in $US millions). (*Data sources:* Ministry of Culture, Sports, and Tourism, 2011.)

were filmed. Visitors from Southeast Asia to Korea have also increased. The
number of foreigners who visited Korea in 2010 reached 8.8 million people, a significant increase compared to the 5.3 million in 2000. By region,
Asia including the Middle East accounted for 77.7 percent of the total. Of
course, the number of visitors from neighboring Japan and China account
for more than 50 percent, but visitors from Taiwan, Hong Kong, Thailand,
and Malaysia have also increased rapidly. For example, the number of visiting
Taiwanese increased from 127,120 in 2000 to 406,352 in 2010, which is a
3.2-fold increase. Thai visitors increased from 87,885 to 260,718 during this
period, while Malaysians increased 1.9 times from 59,933 to 113,675 people.
Korea's cultural status has thus changed from a peripheral country in Asia to
a central one.

Determining Factors for Korea's Economic Cooperation with Asia

This part explores the several factors that have created economic cooperation
between Korea and Asia. With regard to trade and investment, changes in the
Asian economic order since the mid-1980s' industrialization of South East
Asia and China have contributed to the development of Korea's economic
cooperation with Asia. Asian countries have adopted an outward-oriented
growth strategy, and this has provided an enormous opportunity for Korea.
Meanwhile, Korea continued to develop comparative advantages, including human resource development, encouragement of entrepreneurs, and
upgrading of industrial structure. Furthermore, in order to strengthen economic cooperation with Asian nations Korea has made efforts to integrate
its economy with Asia through signing FTAs and has expanded its ODA to
those countries.

Emergence of Asia

As noted earlier, the most important event shaping Korea's economic coop-
eration with Asia was the Plaza Accord of 1985. The exchange rate for the
Japanese yen after the Plaza Accord fell rapidly from 250 yen per dollar in late
June to 165 yen by June 30 of 1986. As appreciation of the yen could not be
reversed, Japanese companies started investment in Southeast Asia, including
Thailand, to maintain export competitiveness (Pasuk 1990). As a result some

Southeast Asian countries like Thailand, Malaysia, and Indonesia emerged as major production bases, and with exports surging, began to grow rapidly.

ASEAN's rapid export growth spurred the import of parts and components due to the comparative underdevelopment of local supporting industries. Southeast Asia's ethnic Chinese businessmen, who were active in retail, real estate, and finance, began to invest in capital and technology intensive industries like steel and petrochemicals. These investments further increased imports, giving Korea an opportunity to increase its exports.

Following ASEAN's rapid economic growth, China began to share in Asia's dynamism. After the onset of economic reforms in 1978, China achieved high economic growth on foreign direct investment. In the beginning FDI flowed from Hong Kong, which was interested in textile and other labor-intensive industries. This was followed by overseas Chinese investment from Southeast Asia and Taiwan. Overseas Chinese concentrated in the service sector while Taiwanese investors pursued light industry, including footwear and electronics. By the mid 1990s, low-cost manufactured goods from China were sweeping through world markets. Producers in Indonesia and Thailand came under increasing pressure.

Korea also began to take advantage of China's growth by shifting trade and investment from ASEAN to China. China played an important role in further intensifying the division of labor in Asia which had started between Northeast Asia and Southeast Asia. Northeast Asia's division of labor with China soon developed into a vertical division of production through fragmentation, with multiple nations participating in the production of goods. In this process, the production process for goods once made by a single firm was fragmented. This fragmentation allowed the exploitation of comparative advantage between nations arising from differences in technology or factor endowments, with companies carrying out foreign investment handling a particular part of the process, or with foreign companies participating in the process. China imports a number of parts and components from East Asia to assemble using its abundant labor, and then exports the final products to western countries. China's share in world trade, which was only 1 percent in 1980 compared to the 13.2 percent recorded by the United States, reached 2 percent in 1993 and then 4.1 percent in 2001. Since then China's trade has increased rapidly to 9.9 percent of total world trade in 2010, while the share for the U.S. fell to 10.6 percent. The United States remains the largest importing country, while China has become the world's largest exporter.

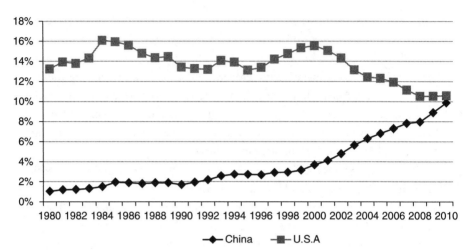

FIGURE 12.5. Share of U.S. and Chinese trade in world trade. (*Data source:* Compiled from statistics of the World Bank database.)

China's rapid growth provided a strong opportunity for the Korean economy. At the early stages of Korean investment in China, Korean investors made use of cheap production factors to produce exports for third country markets, using almost the same business model as it used in ASEAN. However, as China's domestic market expanded, incentives for investment gradually changed from efficiency seeking to market seeking. According to a survey from Korea EXIM bank on 369 companies investing in China (with assets of more than $US2 million who submitted annual business reports consecutively more than five years), 49.9 percent of their products were sold in the Chinese market in 2005. This share increased to 60.5 percent in 2009 (Korea Exim Bank 2010, 239). On the other hand, share for sales to third countries decreased from 40.4 percent to 15.4 percent in 2009. Those companies exported 9.6 percent to Korea in 2005 and 24.1 percent in 2009. The industrial division of Korea and China changed gradually from a vertical division of labor to an increasingly horizontal division of labor. Large companies tended to manufacture and sell in China. For example, a subsidiary of Hyundai Motor in China sells almost 100% of its products to the China market.

Creation of Comparative Advantage

Korea was able to make full use of the rise of Asia from the 1960s because it was able to create competitive advantage. First, Korea actively invested in human resource development. Before Korea started industrialization, Korea's arable land was comparatively small, a fact that disguised unemployment in rural areas. Korea's comparative advantage instead lay in abundant human resources. As a Confucian society, Korean families strongly emphasized children's education. In the 1980s, Korea's gross secondary school enrollment ratio was 82 percent among males and 74 percent among females, much higher than in other Asian countries. In contrast, the gross secondary school enrollment ratio of the Philippines, which has relatively high educational levels was 69 percent among females and only 60 percent among males. The cases of Indonesia and Thailand were much worse than Korea.

This means that a significant portion of workers at construction sites in the Middle East in 1980 had graduated from secondary school. The same applies when we consider female workers at major industrial complexes in Korea. Even in the 1970s the government encouraged large shoe and textile companies to found night high schools for employees. This emphasis on education contributed to workers' accumulation of skills and knowledge. In terms of utilization of human resources, Asia provided an important opportunity in the Vietnam War and the construction boom in the Middle East that Korea successfully exploited.

At the same time, Korea's entrepreneurship played a major factor in effectively leveraging the rise of Asia. One of Korea's greatest entrepreneurs, the founder of Hyundai Group declared at his 1963 New Year's address that "We will have great things this year." The "great thing" in mind was expanding

TABLE 12.2 Gross secondary enrollment ratio (percent)

	1980		1990	
	Female	Male	Female	Male
Korea	73.8	82.1	88.5	91.1
Indonesia	23.3	34.7	39.7	48.2
Malaysia	45.7	49.7	58.2	54.5
Philippines	68.8	59.7	72.9	73.5
Singapore	60.3	59.5	65.6	70.5
Thailand	27.9	29.6	29.6	30.6

Data sources: ADB (2000), Key Indicators of Developing Asian and Pacific Countries 2000.

Note: Refers to total enrollment, expressed as a percentage of the official school-age population in a given school year.

abroad. That same year Hyundai Engineering and Construction intentionally bid on the Saigon waterworks construction in Vietnam in order to fail,
but next year was awarded the Pattani-Narathiwat highway two-lane highway
construction project, a Thai government construction project, using IBRD
loans of $US5.2 million. Hyundai took thirty months to finish construction
and suffered significant losses, but was able to accumulate overseas construction experience.[8]

These experiences formed the basis for Hyundai's successful construction
in Vietnam and the Middle East. In these countries Korean companies' took
on comparatively low value added civil construction compared to their US
and European engineering counterparts. Considering Korea's economic development process and its technology level at the time, Korean companies
could not have taken on such work without bold entrepreneurship and a will-
ingness to take on daunting challenges. Korean companies maintained this
spirit of challenge when they entered ASEAN and China. In fact, most of Korea's present major industries, including steel, semiconductors, automobiles,
and shipbuilding, all began in the face of strong objections from Westerners,
who doubted their viability. Notwithstanding skepticism from mainstream
economists, who believed in comparative advantage, Korean entrepreneurs
embraced stiff challenges and succeeded.

In the 1980s Korean companies tried to extend the life of their competitive
advantage by investing in ASEAN. Companies facing rising production costs
in Korea responded by restructuring. They moved products and industries
with deteriorating competitiveness overseas, while developing technology and
expanding production of high value-added products at home.[9] Companies
investing abroad must have three advantages, namely an ownership-specific
advantage, an internalization incentive advantage, and a location-specific advantage (Dunning 1993). In this regard, firm-specific advantages for Korean
companies in ASEAN included having buyers overseas, maintaining production technology for light industrial products, and deploying well established
systems for procuring raw materials from parent companies. They did not,
however, maintain original technology, which is generally regarded as a company's core competency.[10] Nevertheless, this kind of ownership advantage,
which is not based on monopolistic technology, proved difficult to internalize
for a long time. Production technology for labor-intensive light industry was
easily transferred to host countries, so by the mid-1990s, Korean companies
in Southeast Asia were faced with rising competition in the world market. As

levels of per capita income in Southeast Asia increased and wages rose, Korean companies were forced to consider shifting their investment to durable goods and services rather than manufacturing.

At the same time, companies investing in China, where the domestic market was much larger than in Southeast Asia, were able to leverage a new competitive advantage by investing in technology and capital intensive industries. In contrast to Southeast Asia, in China the main targets of investment were automobiles, mobile phones, high-tech electronics, and steel. Korean firms entered China not because they faced weakening competitiveness at home, but because they wanted to create a market in China and increase competitiveness by producing there. Larger companies like Hyundai Motor, Samsung Electronics, and POSCO have been the most successful. Compared to Chinese companies, Korea's investors have higher technology and a well-known brand, while quality parts can be supplied from Korea. In this environment companies in China and Korea can take advantage of China's growth.

Korea's attainment of competitive advantage in investment and trade was based on its technological capabilities. Its attainment of cultural competence, however, was based on creativity. Few appreciated Korea's competitiveness in the content industry before the 1990s. Prior to 2000, Korea customarily imported Hollywood films and western popular music, while younger consumers seeking a more exotic culture enthusiastically circulated black market Japanese products, including Japanese comic books. President Kim Dae Jung opened Korea's cultural market to Japanese content over strong opposition from those who believed Japanese "low grade" culture would harm Korean's traditions and customs. Korea's cultural content industry then had to compete openly with Japan's, and had to turn to creativity to survive.

The purported causes for the success of Hallyu in Asia have typically been explained as "similar culture and traditions based on Confucianism" (Kim 2010). However, this alone does not explain why Korea's popular culture has been more appealing than that of other culturally Confucian countries. In this regard, it is more reasonable to claim that the comparative advantage of Hallyu is its creative story-telling based on democracy and freedom of expression. In fact, "(South) Korean popular culture rose from relative obscurity in the late 1990s, after decades of draconian internal censorship came to an end in the 1980s" (*The Economist* 2010). Korea's popular culture was thus based on democratization in the 1990s. One Thai observer argued that "Politically, the emergence of Korea's popular culture was perceived as an outcome of its

thriving democracy. Korean democratization began in the late 1980s and unleashed a series of domestic changes" (Pavin 2010, 252).

Korea's Policy toward Asia

After the 1948 founding of the Republic of Korea, Korea established diplomatic
relations with Taiwan (1948), the Philippines (1949), Vietnam (1956), Thailand
(1958), and Malaysia (1960), all nations within the sphere of influence of the
United States. As Korea faced continuous hostility from North Korea throughout
this time, it was natural that Korea formed relations with these countries based
on their shared anti-communist outlook. After Korea's 1965 establishment of
diplomatic relations with Japan and its participation in the Vietnam War, however, economic motives started to move to the forefront. Korea's mixed motives
were especially prominent in its relationship with Vietnam, which included both
anti-communism and economic gain.[11] When the Vietnam War ended in the
1970s, Korea's interests expanded into the rest of Southeast Asia. Korea and ASE-
AN initiated a sectoral dialogue relationship in November 1989 followed by full
Dialogue Partner status in July 1991. This was accompanied by deepening and
expanding economic cooperation in the late 1980s, when Korea's ASEAN investments increased rapidly.[12] Subsequently Korea normalized diplomatic relations
with China in 1992 at the expense of Taiwan, which had been its closest ally since
1948, to exploit the opportunities that were burgeoning in China.

However, even though Asia was important in terms of economic cooperation, and even though Asia continued to record high growth rates in the
1980s, the Korean government's policy towards the Asian region was noncom-
mittal with respect to deepening economic cooperation. The Korean government largely left cooperation with Asia to the market and the private sector.

The experience of the foreign currency crisis that Korea shared with Asia
in the late 1990s, however, spurred Korea to recognize itself as an East Asian
country. President Kim Dae Jung who came to power in 1998 emphasized
the importance of East Asia for the first time at the ASEAN +3 Summit in
October 1999. This summit established the East Asia Vision Group (EAVG),
a group of eminent persons from each country studying the future of East
Asia. After a two-year discussion, EAVG submitted to the ASEAN +3 Summit
a report titled "Towards an East Asian Community." This report became the
theoretical foundation for ASEAN+3's cooperation in East Asia.

The Kim Dae Jung government began a joint study with Japan from 1998 as the first Asian country for establishment of an FTA. First round negotiations started with the Roh Moo Hyun administrative in December 2003, however, negotiations ended unsuccessfully after the sixth round of negotiations in November 2004. Korea complained of Japan's strong insistence on agricultural protections, while Japan criticized Korea's protection of manufacturing, particularly in automobiles. Korea began a joint study on an FTA in 2003 with Singapore, and the Korea-Singapore FTA took in effect in 2006. When ASEAN grew more important in institutional economic integration, Korea and ASEAN signed the "Framework Agreement on Comprehensive Economic Cooperation" with ASEAN in 2005. In the same year both parties began FTA negotiations which took effect in 2007. In addition, a joint study with China commenced in 2005, but as of September 2011, an FTA with China was still awaiting official negotiations.

Korea began ODA in 1987 and the cumulative amount of bilateral ODA through 2009 reached $US4.5 billion based on gross disbursements. Grants account for 56.6 percent of ODA, while preferential loans account for 43.4 percent. Compared to the 83.9 percent share for grants among DAC members in 2009, Korea's ODA policy shows strong economic motivations. ODA to Asia stands at $US2.95 billion, and East Asia accounts for the largest share at $US1.61 billion. The share of loans in ODA to Asia still stands at 48.1 percent. ODA for Southeast Asia was only $US26 million in 2000, but jumped in 2009 to $US167 million. Although ODA is still small, it is growing fast. By country, Korea supplied the largest ODA to Vietnam, as Korea records huge trade surpluses with the still relatively poor country and Vietnam needs diverse infrastructure in its early stages of economic development. Korea thus considers Vietnam as a strategic partner.

It is hard to say whether Korea's FTAs and ODA to Asia has contributed to deepening Korea-Asia economic cooperation. What is clear is that Korea has never given much priority to Asia in terms of FTA Policy. Korea signed FTAs with the US and the EU before FTAs were actively considered with Japan and China, the two most important partners in economic cooperation. In particular, despite intense opposition in Korea, the government began FTA negotiations with the US in 2006 and finalized them in 2007. Regarding the Korea-US FTA, Korea may have to some extent favored the US, which needed an ally in East Asia in order to contain an emerging China.

Korea's ASEAN cooperation, which is considered the most institutionally mature, has come in the wake of Japanese and Chinese cooperation with ASEAN. For example, Korea signed the framework agreement with ASEAN in 2005 following the framework agreements of China-ASEAN (2002) and Japan-ASEAN (2003), using the same format and with similar content. Korea and ASEAN held a special summit meeting on Jeju Island in May 2009 which also followed the Japan-ASEAN summit in Tokyo in December 2003 and the China-ASEAN summit in Nanning in October 2006. The Korea-ASEAN FTA is also a response to the China-ASEAN FTA (2005) and Japan's FTA with ASEAN countries. Korea's ASEAN policy was thus largely a game of catch up with Japan and China, and lacked any leading initiatives. The only exception is the Korea-India FTA which came into effect prior to the Japan-India FTA. However, the Korea-India FTA was basic and excluded too many products on both sides to be considered a genuine FTA.

Korea's ODA to Southeast Asia is also not sufficient in quantity and quality. Almost 80 percent of Korea's ODA to Southeast Asia is tied, and overall grant levels are relatively low (Kwon 2010, 171). With respect to ODA, Sohn and Choi (2008) also found that Korea's ODA to ASEAN is based on economic cooperation rather than developmental cooperation. Korea's ODA is thus based on realism along the lines of Japanese "economic cooperation," and prioritizes political and economic self-interest. It is thus doubtful that Korea's ODA to ASEAN will ever bring about any positive effect.

Korea, as a small open economy, achieved high economic growth over the last 50 years by adopting an export-oriented economic growth strategy. Notwithstanding its poor endowment of natural resources and the influence of external powers, the past fifty years have validated Korea as a genuine success story. Culturally, Korea is like a small village with a homogeneous culture. Such characteristics, as well as an ability to put forth a unified effort have allowed Korea to skillfully navigate the waves of the global economy. In the process, Korea encountered Asia and utilized the opportunities that it has provided to grow over the last fifty years. Korea emerged as a world-class industrial country riding on the wave of Asia's development, eventually creating waves itself through economic structural change and the creation of competitive cultural content.

As previously discussed, Asia has had a positive impact on the Korean economy, which can be summarized as follows. First, Asia contributed greatly to capital formation in the early stages of Korea's economic development. Korea was able to greatly supplement its foreign currency holdings with earnings from the Vietnam War and the Middle East construction boom. Infrastructure investment in the 1960s and 1970s and import of primary products was also possible because of money from laborers working in Asia. Without participation in the Vietnam War and the Middle East construction boom, Korea would not have achieved industrialization.

Second, direct investment and derived exports from investment to Asia acted as the main cause for the advancement of Korea's industrial structure. As Korea's economy grew and production costs rose, falling competitiveness was inevitable. Korea thus invested in ASEAN and China, and consequently developed more value added industry in Korea. ASEAN, particularly in the late 1980s, provided strong locational advantages that Korean investors used to transfer sunset industries and to develop other emerging industries based on high technology.

Third, though Korea has historically been dependent on Confucian China and dependent on the US for security in modern times, Korea's economic development allowed it to find out who it is, and what it can offer through communication with Greater Asia. Asia, in turn, offered a stage on which Korea could show its own culture. Korean culture began to spread to Northeast and Southeast Asia in the form of Hallyu, and Asian people came to know of Korea as a dynamic and unique culture. The cultural content market provided by Asia functioned as an effective means for Korea to improve its image and project its soft power.

Fourth, Korea's policy and perceptions toward Asia have largely been in the form of pursuit of economic interest rather than as a cooperative partner who shares common values. Awareness of Asia as a partner has not spread to the population yet, while on the government level, FTA policy has largely been a rearguard action in the wake of leading attempts by Japan and China. Korea's ODA policies have also largely been for the purpose of Korea's economic benefit in the model previously established by Japan.

Korea's relations with Asia thus face many challenges. In particular, Korea must find ways to reduce its excessive economic reliance on China. In only a short period of time Korea's economy has become closely integrated with China's economy. If China succeeds in upgrading its parts and component industry to the level of Korea, Korea will lose competitiveness in both the Chinese and world markets. If Korea's dependence on China continues to deepen, moreover, any change in China will have a significant impact on Korea. To prevent this situation, trade and investment with other Asian countries must be expanded.

At the same time, Asia is transitioning to a new cooperative order with the rise of China. As a medium-sized open economy, Korea needs to maintain its dynamism and to play a role as a mediator in East Asia for economic cooperation and mutual prosperity. In order to do this, Korea has to respect values that are internationally accepted. More respect for Asia's culture, more understanding of Asian people, and more awareness of co-existence will be critical in this process.

Notes

1. "What do you do when you reach the top?" *The Economist.* November 12, 2011, 75.

2. To Westerners in the early postwar period, South Korea and Taiwan were unlikely development cases. Balassa once in his paper referred to South Korea and Taiwan as "hopeless countries."Balassa Bela, "The Lessons of East Asian Development: An Overview," *Economic Development and Cultural Change* 36 (3) (1988): 275.

3. Overseas Construction Association database (http://www.icak.or.kr/sta/sta_1001.php).

4. Clothing is HS Classification 61 (articles of apparel and clothing accessories, knitted or crocheted) and 62 (articles of apparel and clothing accessories, not knitted or crocheted), while footwear is 63.

5. The "Korean Wave," or "Hallyu," refers to the phenomenon in which Korea popular culture generates significant impact on the outside world. It started from neighboring countries in Asia and spread across Asia.

6. According to a survey "Signs of our Times" of The Strait Times (December 4, 2005), the third was the Dalai Lama, the fourth was Kim Jong Il of North Korea, the fifth was Bruce Lee, Hong Kong action star, the sixth was Lee Kuan Yew, and the seventh was Mahatma Gandi (Pavin 2010, 254, 276).

7. According to Gruger (2012), PSYs "Gangnam Style" is the first video in the history of the Internet to reach and surpass one billion views.

8. Hyundai Engineering and Construction, *The 35 years of Hyundai Engineering and Construction* (Seoul, 1982), 128–135.

9. In 1985 Korea's largest export good was clothing with an export share of 15.9 percent. Share for footwear was 5.2 percent, and textiles 3.2 percent. In 1995 the largest export good was semiconductors with a share of 14.1 percent, the second good was automobiles with 6.7 percent. In 2005 semiconductors, automobiles, and mobile phones were the top three with 10.5 percent, 10.4 percent, and 9.7 percent respectively.

10. Around this period, large companies' investment in developed countries did not succeed. Hyundai Motor's investment in Quebec, Canada in 1989 ended in major

failure. Samsung Electronics acquired US computer maker AST in 1995, and in the same year LG's acquisition of another US company Zenith resulted in failure. Both companies invested in the US companies for advanced technology. They did not succeed largely because Korean investors did not have firm specific advantage.

11. Choi Dong-ju argued that Korea's most important goal, even before dispatching troops, was economic benefits on the basis of the typical neo-mercantilism of the developmental state. Choi Dong-ju, "Revisiting Korea's Motivations in the Vietnam War." *Korean Political Science Review* 30 (2) (1996): 267–287.

12. Japan was already established as a dialogue partner with ASEAN from 1997, making Korea's overtures late by more than ten years.

References

ADB. 2000. *Key Indicators of Developing Asian and Pacific Countries 2000*. Manila, The Phillippines: Author.

Amsden, A. H. 1989. *Asia's Next Giant: Korea and Late Industrialization,* Oxford: Oxford University Press.

Bela, Balassa. 1988. "The Lessons of East Asian Development: An Overview." *Economic Development and Cultural Change* 36 (3): 274–290.

The Chicago Council on Global Affairs. 2009. *Soft Power in Asia: Results of a 2008 Multinational Survey of Public Opinion.*

Choi, Dong-Ju. 1996. "Revisiting Korea's Motivations in the Vietnam War." *Korean Political Science Review* 30 (2): 267–287.

———. 2001. "Impact of the Vietnam-Dispatch upon Korean Industrialization." *The Southeast Asian Review* 2 (Spring): 205~244.

Defense Military Institute. 1996. *Wŏlllam Pabyŏngkwa Kukka Baljŏn*. Seoul, Korea.

Dunning, John H. 1993. *Multinational Enterprises and the Global Economy.* Workingham: Addison-Wesley Publishing Company.

The Economist. January 25, 2010. http://www.economist.com/node/15385735/print (accessed August 12, 2011).

———. November 12, 2011, 75.

Fu Su Yin. 2009. "Mediascapes without Ideascapes: Hallyu in Singapore," Paper presented at the *Korea-ASEAN Academic Conference on Pop Culture Formations across East Asia in the 21st Century: Hybridization or Asianization,* 184–193. Burpha University, Thailand, February 1–4.

Gruger, William. 2012. "PSY's 'Gangnam Style' Video Hits 1 Billion Views, Unprecedented Milestone". *Billboard*. Retrieved December 21, 2012.

Hyundai Engineering and Construction. 1982. *The 35 years of Hyundai Engineering and Construction,* 128–135. Seoul, Korea.

Institute of Military History Compilation. 2004. *Hankwonŭro ingnŭn Vietnam jŏnchaengkwa Hankukkun.* Seoul, Korea.

Kim, Joong Keun. 2010. "The Korean Wave: Korea's Soft Power in Southeast Asia." In *Korea's Challenging Roles in Southeast Asia,* ed. David I. Steinberg et al., 283–303. Singapore :Institute of Southeast Asian Studies.

Kim, Se Jin. 1970. "South Korea's Involvement in Vietnam and its Economic and Political Impact." *Asian Survey* 10 (6): 519–532.

Kim, Young Aih. 2008. "Korean people in Thai Society in 1960–1970s." *The Past and Current Relationship between Korea and Thailand,* 251–296. In commemoration of the 50th anniversary of diplomatic relations, the Korean Association of Thai studies.

Koo, B. Y. 1986. "The Role of Government in Korea's Industrial Development." In *Industrial Development Policies and Issues,* ed. K. U. Lee. Seoul: Korea Development Institute.

Korea Exim Bank. 2010. *2009 Hoekyenyŏnto Haeoejikjŏp'uja Kyŏngyŏng punsŏk.* Seoul, Korea.

Kwon, Yul. 2010. "Korean Assistance to Southeast Asia." In *Korea's Challenging Roles in Southeast Asia,* ed. David I. Steinberg, 155–175. Singapore: Institute of Southeast Asian Studies.

Maeil Economic Daily. 2010. *One Asian Strategy Report.* Seoul: Mail Economic Daily.

Ngo, Thi Phuong Thien, and Truong Thi Kim Chuyen. 2009. "Effects of Korean Movies on Vietnamese Viewers." Paper presented at the Korea-ASEAN Academic Conference on Pop Culture Formations across East Asia in the 21st Century: Hybridization or Asianization, 97–104.Burpha University, Thailand, February 1–4.

Overseas Construction Association database. http://www.icak.or.kr/sta/sta_1001.php (accessed August 13, 2011).

Park, Bun Soon. 2011. "Review of Research on the Southeast Asian Economy in Korea." *Asia Review* 1 (1): 227–258.

Pasuk, Phongpaichit. 1990. *The New Wave of Japanese Investment in ASEAN: Determinants and Prospects.* Singapore : ISEAS.

Pavin, Chachavalpongpun. 2010. "A Fading Wave, Sinking Tide? A Southeast Asian Perspective on the Korean Wave." In *Korea's Challenging Roles in Southeast Asia,* ed. David I. Steinberg et al, 244–282. Singapore: Institute of Southeast Asian Studies.

Sohn, Hyuk-Sang, and Jeongho Choi. 2008. "Korea's ODA Policies toward ASEAN: A Duet of Economic and Development Cooperation." *The Southeast Asian Review* 18 (2): 137–174.

Song, B. N. 1990. *The Rise of the Korean Economy.* Hong Kong: Oxford University Press.

Song, Chang Yong, and Yang Kyong Seong. 2009. "Hoeoe Illyŏk Chinch'ul Hwalshŏnghwalŭl T'onghan Ilchari Ch'angch'ul." *The HRD REVIEW* summer: 55–79. Seoul, Korea.

Yasumoto, Seiko. 2006. "The Impact of the "Korean Wave" on Japan: A Case Study of the Influence of Trans-border Electronic Communication and the Trans-national Programming Industry." Paper presented at the 16th Biennial Conference of the Asian Studies Association of Australia in Woollongong, June 26–June 29.

13

The Circulation of Korean Pop

Soft Power and Inter-Asian Conviviality

WHANG SOON-HEE

Joseph S. Nye suggested the concept of "soft power" in the 1980s and developed the concept further in *Bound to Lead: The Changing Nature of American Power,* which was published in 1990. Since then, it has been recognized that culture, value, and policies can be influential powers that affect people. Soft power contrasts with coercive hard power, such as military and economic power. Soft power is obtained by attracting others through empathy, comprehension, and cooperation, and by influencing them to choose the preferred results, often by providing an attractive narrative. For example, a nation's soft power is demonstrated by attracting others to respect their culture, political value, and international policies. When soft and hard powers are used in conjunction, it becomes possible to exert extremely strong influence (Nye 2004).

Since the 2000s, with the advance of globalism and the information revolution, soft power has become increasingly influential on a global level. Furthermore, the circulation of soft power has become more rapid and new power items have been produced and consumed through the monopolization, dispersion, and fluctuation of power. This chapter analyzes "conviviality" and the soft power of Korean popular culture or "Hallyu [Korean style]," most popular with the younger generation throughout Asia. Its particular focus is the social phenomenon of Hallyu in Japan and South Korea. Here, the popular music of South Korea, referred to as K-pop, will form the center of my examination of popular culture.

Consumption Patterns of Hallyu in Japan and South Korea

In 2002, Japan and South Korea jointly hosted the World Cup. Beginning a year before the opening ceremony, the media of both countries attempted to arouse enthusiasm by introducing the culture of the other country. Since the success of the joint hosting in 2002, the mutual cultural interest in each nation has continued to increase.

The Hallyu boom started with the big hit, especially among middle-aged women, of the 2004 South Korean drama series, "Winter Sonata" (*Fuyu no Sonata;* Korean title *Gyeoul Yeonga*.) In 2008, the craze expanded to middle-aged men with the drama series "The Promise of Jang Geum, a Lady of the Court" (*Kyūtei Nyokan Changumu no Chikai;* Korean title *Dae Jang Geum* [Jewel in the Palace].) The 2011 trendy drama, "Brilliant Legacy" (*Karei Naru Isan;* Korean title *Chanranhan Yusan,*) further expanded the audience and attracted the younger generation in their teens and twenties.

At the same time, in 2005, a top South Korean pop-music group, *Tōhō Shinki* (TVXQ), debuted in Japan as a newcomer. They were the first South Korean idol group to participate in the Japanese national broadcast station NHK's end of the year programming "The NHK Red-White Singing Battle" *(NHK Kōhaku Uta Gassen.)* As a result of this occasion, from the latter half of the 2000s, South Korean music became extremely popular in Japan as K-pop. Korean fashion also became the focus of attention more frequently by women's fashion magazines and television programs as they became enthralled by the fashion, hairstyles, makeup, and dance moves of the K-pop idols. Furthermore, as the interest in health and beauty increased in Japan, an increasing number of Korean drama series stars and idol singers have appeared in commercials and caused a resulting fad in South Korean makeup and food as well. In this way, the scope of South Korean popular culture within Japan that started historically as Hallyu drama series has moved into the Neo-Hallyu phase, with an emphasis on K-pop. This has also changed the way Korean entertainment is enjoyed. Originally, in the Hallyu phase, the voices of the characters in the drama series were voiced over in Japanese.

However, in the Neo-Hallyu phase, the audience started to enjoy the original voices of the actors through the use of Japanese subtitles, even if some of the meaning was lost. In the case of K-pop music, they started to enjoy and gain satisfaction from listening to the musicians' voices. Therefore, we can see that the soft power of South Korean popular culture first expanded its audience and products, and secondly, changed the way it was enjoyed. Finally, as a result it enthralled its audiences and expanded cultural and economic consumption.

Why did Neo-Hallyu become a craze in Japan? Three social and cultural structures account for this craze. First, interest in international popular culture has increased greatly with the availability of the internet and globalism. Second, the younger generation with skills in exchanging and sharing information through the use of the internet, called the "internet generation," has become the central audience (Whang 2011). Third, this younger generation is fairly free from the symbolic hegemony of Western music.

Pierre Bourdieu placed people's music tastes on a cultural hierarchy of "orthodox taste," "middle-brow taste," and "popular taste." The criterion for placement on the cultural hierarchy is the "distance from necessity." "Orthodox taste" is far in terms of "distance from necessity" and as a result, is ranked high on the cultural hierarchy due to its taste of freedom. On the other hand, popular taste is close and considered vulgar, and since it is considered a taste of necessity, it is ranked low on the cultural hierarchy (Bourdieu 1984).[1]

However, although Bourdieu does not refer to it, there is a cultural hierarchy even within popular taste. Depending on the social realm and country, there is a cultural and symbolic structure connecting music and life, which creates cultural and symbolic status distinctions even within popular music. For example, within Japanese cultural consciousness, the status of western popular music was considered higher than that of Japanese popular music.

This younger generation of the 2010s differs from the generation that spent their youth between the restoration period after the end of WWII and the 1970s, who understood American and European popular culture to be high on the "cultural hierarchy" (Bourdieu 1984) and worshipped them (Nakajima 2011). This younger generation was born in the late 1980s during the bubble economy and within a mature Japanese society. They have gained freedom by maintaining a distance from the cultural envy of the West and were able to develop relativity of values. Furthermore, this generation grew up in an information-oriented society. As a result, they have not developed cultural rankings based on whether popular culture originates in the West or in Asia.

As long as it suits their preference, regardless of its origin, they consider these musical types as having an equal entertainment value. This generation can enjoy Hallyu and *Hualyu* (Chinese style), as equally as Western, without any consideration of superiority or inferiority.

Differences in the Consumption of Neo-Hallyu in Japan and South Korea

Korean popular culture is consumed in different ways in South Korea and Japan. For example, let us examine the case of K-pop. In South Korea, pop music singers are highly regarded when they prove that they can sing songs of various genres. This is because South Korean people have a "cultural consciousness" that demands that singers should be able to skillfully sing songs of various genres and images. A singer who becomes famous due to singing a ballad would try for her next song to do an upbeat dance number or even rap music. As a result, singers attempt to sing songs of different genres, and the audience also does not expect a singer to stick with one genre or a fixed image.

By contrast, in Japan, singers tend to be restricted to one genre or image established from their debut, and continue to sing similar songs within a designated framework. For a long period of time, they continue to sing songs of a similar kind. Therefore, even regarding K-pop singers who are operating in Japan, the Japanese audience desires to understand them within one category. As a result, Japanese media, such as music magazines and television programs, tend to introduce Korean singers by classifying them.

In Japan, Korean music has been established as a genre called K-pop (Sakai 2011). Therefore, in Japan, Japanese popular music is referred to as J-pop and is distinguished from K-pop. However, even K-pop singers are classified in the same ways as J-pop singers based on genres and images and are given particular images. As a result, in Japan, K-pop is consumed in the same style as J-pop. This is the Japanese consumption style of K-pop.

Let us then examine a specific example of how K-pop singers are categorized and consumed in Japan. Music magazines have separated K-pop singers popular in Japan into four groups based on two axes; one axis ranging from "dance style" to "listening style" at its endpoints and the other axis ranging from "sexy style" at one end to "familiar and healthy style" at the other (Sakai 2011). For example, the three groups that participated in the 2011 62nd NHK *Kōhaku Uta Gassen* (Red and White Music Battle), the female groups KARA and *Shōjo Jidai* (Girls' Generation), and the male group *Tōhō Shinki* (TVXQ) can all be separated into different types. KARA is classified as fitting into the group that falls into the quadrant named "lovable character style" covering the dance style and familiar and healthy style realms. *Shōjo Jidai* (Girls' Generation), on the other hand, is grouped in the dance style and wild and sexy style, characterized as the "hot style."

Furthermore, the male solo singer *Pi* (Rain) and the male group 2PM are also categorized along the same axes, with the former falling into the "charismatic style" quadrant and the latter referred to as the "beast style." *Tōhō Shinki* [TVXQ], however, even in Japan is famous for changing their image depending on each song, so they are categorized where the two axes intersect. As these examples show clearly, K-pop singers are categorized in this Japanese style, given a particular image, and labeled accordingly. The Japanese audience then expects the K-pop singers to continue to sing songs of a similar trend. In this way, the differences in the style of consumption of K-pop singers in Japan and Korea means that the singers are faced with different expectations.

The Community Development of Korean Town in Shin-Okubo, Tokyo

Since the screening of "Winter Sonata" in 2004, travel agencies started to lead Japanese tours to South Korean filming locations. However, an increasing number of individual travelers did not join such packaged tours, but rather carried out their own travels by researching and following their own interests. At the same time, the Hallyu and Neo-Hallyu boom have turned Korea Town in the Shin-Okubo area of Shinjuku in Tokyo into an area of interest. Travelers may go to Shin-Okubo prior to their trip to South Korea in order to experience the atmosphere, or visit it after their return in order to revive their memories of the journey.

For example, an imaginary filming site was even constructed in Shin-Okubo so that after watching a TV drama series, viewers could enjoy a "mini-tour to the film site." When the Korean drama "*Kōhī Purinsu Ichigōten* (Coffee Prince Store #1)" gained popularity in Japan, a café that was decorated following the image of the café in the drama series opened in Shin-Okubo. The name of the café was also "Coffee Prince" and as in the drama, young, handsome Korean men worked as waiters (Higa 2011). People visited this store in Shin-Okubo in the same way as they would visit filming locations in South Korea. They relaxed over coffee and dessert and chatted with friends, just as the characters did in the drama series. Many of the customers were women, who lived out a fantasy overlapping themselves and their friends with the story of the handsome men in the drama. By the time I visited the town for fieldwork, an additional café, "Coffee Prince #2" had appeared in response to public interest. Furthermore, television programs, and magazines discussed the stores in Korean Town, gaining publicity for the entire town.

Magazines and guide books refer to Shin-Okubo as "the Sacred Land for Hallyu, Shin-Okubo." They encourage visits by suggesting various ways of enjoying Korean Town, using such phrases and headings such as "Star Goods and Shin-Okubo Shop Guide," "Guide to the Favorite Shin-Okubo Stores of K-Stars," "How to Get *Purupuru* (Plump) Skin with Four Types of Korean Sauna," "The Hangouts of Korean Exchange Students. Finding the Hot Guys Visiting the Stores!!," and "50 Stores Where You Can Meet Hallyu Hot Salesmen" (Hashino 2011; Higa 2011). In addition, Shin-Okubo is occasionally written in Roman letters as SHIN-OHKUBO, such as in the case of

Guidebooks and calendars introducing Neo-Hallyu stars and Korean town. (Photo by Whang Soon-Hee)

the heading "Not Enough Time to Go to Seoul? But Would Like to Experience the Atmosphere and Obtain the Newest Information on K-pop? Then SHIN-OHKUBO is the Place for You" (Sakai 2011). Numerous photos of people enjoying Shin-Okubo as well as cute illustrations are used to illustrate the articles. Magazines and guide-books use many Roman letters and *katakana,* a syllabary used primarily for loan words, for the name of the town and for numerous other instances. From such tendencies, it is clear that they are trying to change and modernize the image of the town.

As a result, Korean Town has been able to transform its image into "Hallyu Town." The Neo-Hallyu boom has caused a major change in the Korean Town community. The image of the town has changed to (1) a safe town, (2) a happy, energetic town, (3) a town for fashion, (4) a town for

A female junior high school student searching for star-related items in a Hallyu shop in Korean Town. (Photo by Whang Soon-Hee)

trends, (5) a town for K-pop live music, and (6) a town for interaction. Especially since the Neo-Hallyu boom started in 2010, the speed of change has increased. The Neo-Hallyu boom triggered the revitalization of the Shin-Okubo community.

I have carried out ten years of fieldwork in Shin-Okubo from 2002, when Japan and South Korea jointly hosted the World Cup, until 2011. Every year, I recorded changes of the town with photographs, which show that because of the Neo-Hallyu boom, increasing number of young, often single, female junior and senior high school students walk about town or purchase Hallyu items without any concerns about their safety. Middle-aged and older women can now be observed visiting with their children or husbands in tow, as well as groups of young women. The preceding image is a photograph of a female junior high school student who was interviewed in a Neo-Hallyu item store in Shin-Okubo. On her bag, there are badges and name tags of K-pop idol stars written in Korean. She informed me that she was looking for items related to her favorite singers.

The Stage: Power, Conflict, and the Variability of Hallyu and Neo-Hallyu

If the fact that Korean popular culture arouses interest in Japan can be considered as soft power, to whom does this soft power belong? In the Hallyu phase, in the relationship of the Japanese media, Japanese fans, and Korean actors, which side had the strongest influence on consumption of K-pop in Japan? In fact, the Japanese media and fans had more power than the Korean actors who created these cultural products.

Let us consider the typical Hallyu period actor, Bae Yong-joon. During the intense popularity of the drama series "Winter Sonata," the icon of the Hallyu phase Bae Yong-joon, who played the main character, was so popular that he was referred to as "Yong *Sama* [Sir Yong]." The original Hallyu stars chose their work carefully, following the image expected by the Japanese media and fans. In the case of Bae Yong-joon, he continued to follow the direction that was produced for him in Japan by "Winter Sonata." Whenever he visited Japan, Japanese magazines and women's fashion magazines focused on him. For example, he was not even able to change his hairstyle by himself. If his hairstyle altered even slightly, so much as changing the division of his bangs from a 7:3 to 8:2 parting, it would reflect on the "Yon sama [Sir Yong] image. If it didn't suit his image of his character "Jun-san" of "Winter Sonata," Japanese magazines would publish complaints.

On August 23, 2005, Bae Yong-joon was presented at the promotion ceremony of his new film "April Snow"(*Sawalebom*). He had changed his hairstyle from a 7:3 to 8:2 parting of his hair. This alteration made him look like a "Japanese salaryman" ("A Shocking Hair Style!" 2005), which offended the readers of many Japanese women's weekly magazines. His Japanese fans strongly wanted to keep the same image for both "Bae Yong-joon" and "Jun-san" of his "Winter Sonata" character.

In this way, the image of Bae Yong-joon the person conflicted with the "Sir Yong" image of Bae Yong-joon which was established through his character in "Winter Sonata." As a result of this conflict, the symbolic power that reinforced the image of him as an actor put pressure on the actual person (Bourdieu and Passeron 1977). This symbolic power is an immobilizing arbitrary cultural power *(arbitraire culturel)* (Bourdieu and Passeron 1977). In this case, Japanese who are attracted to Korean popular culture demand their own forms and cultural patterns. It is the Japanese media and fans that have ownership of this arbitrary cultural power.

How was this structure formed, in which the actors producing the works have no ownership, but have to accept the power of Japanese media formats? The main reason is that the actors, Bae Yong-Joon included, were the first generation of the Hallyu boom. Even elements that would have been realized as individual characteristics in Japanese actors, were strictly restricted arbitrarily to prescribed behaviors, values, and images as a result of being newly notable Hallyu stars, considered as being representative of all Korean actors.

When Japanese actors are given a suitable character image in a production, they tend to study it and choose succeeding productions that fit that image and establish one's style. When within this structure of Japanese popular culture, not only actors, but also fans and media unconsciously follow this disposition as "habitus" (Bourdieu 1977).

The symbolic power of media and fans also puts pressure on the Korean stars that become famous in Japan. Such Hallyu stars start to feel psychological pressure even when choosing productions to participate in within South Korea or when acting as an individual.

The director of Bae Yong-Joon's former production company "imx," Seong Il-Hyun, stated the following in an interview he gave regarding the last ten years of Hallyu entertainment (Horinouchi 2011): "I have seen him suffer as a result of the established image from 'Winter Sonata.' I truly respect Bae Yong-Joon's temperament as an actor as he continues to nurture his given image for almost ten years." Bae Yong-Joon himself also discussed how he had debated whether he should choose his next production based on the "kind and sweet image of melodramas" given to him by "Winter Sonata" and whether he should participate in another melodramatic production, similar to it, following the boom of the drama series. Furthermore, he mentioned that this kind of uncertainty and debate was not restricted to just himself, but similar in the case of the director of "Winter Sonata," Yoon Seok-Ho.

The Variety in Entertainment Forms in the Neo-Hallyu Phase and the Joint Ownership of Soft Power

In the Neo-Hallyu phase, there has been a transformation in Japanese media and fans. First, there was a change in media. During the Hallyu phase, Japanese television media chose and imported productions from South Korea based on maintaining, strengthening, and further developing the image of popular actors. For example, for Bae Yong-Joon, they chose and showed one of his productions from his younger days, "*Hatsukoi* (First Love)." By doing so, they were able to strengthen his pure and innocent image developed by "Winter Sonata."

However, in the Neo-Hallyu phase, the Japanese media were no longer able to maintain their traditional method. First of all, there was an increase in the amount of dramas and movies available for import. Second, the genres of the imports became much more variable. The genres of the imports were expanded to include not only period pieces, romance, and comedies, but also fashionable dramas meant for audiences in their teens and twenties. Third, it became possible to broadcast simultaneously a production produced jointly by Japan and South Korea using both Japanese and Korean actors. Therefore, it became necessary in the Neo-Hallyu phase to show a variety of images of an actor. As a result, the traditional arbitrary power of Japanese media weakened as they stopped introducing productions that restricted the Korean actors to one image. In this way, the weakening of the soft power of the Japanese media resulted in power moving towards the producing and acting side, South Korea, and slowly shifted the power balance.

Second is the change in the consumers, such as the Japanese fans. They started to enjoy the variability and difference in the actors and singers, rather than expecting one established image. There were three reasons for this change. The first is that the Neo-Hallyu boom is supported mostly by a younger generation of consumers in addition to the original Hallyu fans. No longer do Japanese fans and consumers expect the Neo-Hallyu stars to fit only one cultural image. They began to accept actors who acted out different roles and images in different productions. Furthermore, they even began to enjoy the way that one actor could participate in a wide range of productions from melodramas to period pieces and act out various roles ranging from the innocent to the evil. As a result of their long-term exposure since the Hallyu phase started in 2003, fans have discovered a new way of enjoying Hallyu productions.

The second reason is that even within Japanese society, people have begun to accept the variability and multiplicity of an individual's self-images and identities. Within the postmodern society, self-image and identity no longer needed a singular central core. Through relationships with others, based on time, place, and occasion, an individual's image is differentially used and different selves are acted out. In this way by influencing how people think, others are controlled. At the same time, self-identities are reorganized and transformed. As a result, not only have people started to behave based on differentiated character images that stem from multiple structures of the images of themselves and others, but also have begun to perceive positively the gaps between the multiple images.

The third reason is that fans now access not only the traditional mass media outlets such as television and magazines, but also new media such as the internet and social networking service (SNS). They still use the traditional media, but actively obtain and share further information using new media. Using such information, they learn to enjoy Neo-Hallyu in a variety of forms and are constantly looking for even more novel ways to enjoy it.

For example, even in the case of music, the music of K-pop idols that was broadcast in Japan was restricted to types similar to the classifications of the Japanese media. Even CDs were produced by choosing music that would be preferred by the Japanese audience. However, fans can now go on the internet and listen directly to music programs that are broadcast by Korean broadcast stations. In addition, they can directly download music that their favorite K-pop idol groups have produced in South Korea by using the internet to access Korean sites directly. Furthermore, even middle-aged and older people are now able to use the internet.

As mentioned earlier, in South Korea, musicians are respected for their musicality only after they can show an ability to sing music of different genres. Therefore, singers in South Korea have a most-favored genre, but constantly attempt various music types and aim to continue changing like a chameleon. The young Japanese audience that enjoys Neo-Hallyu now uses the internet and relishes such multi-faceted, diverse, and heterogeneous elements. In this way, fan interests have mutated since the beginning stages of the Neo-Hallyu phase. As a result, the symbolic power of the Japanese fans over the K-pop singers has weakened. Japanese fans now enjoy both the Japanese culture of J-pop and the K-pop culture.

In this way, the soft power of Korean popular culture has shifted from the Japanese media and fan side during the Hallyu phase towards the broadcasting South Korean side in the Neo-Hallyu phase. Now, power relations are balanced between the broadcasters, the intermediary, and the consumers. In other words, the soft power is now owned jointly.

Space: The K-pop Concert Arena as a Meeting Place for Inter-Asian Fans

Just as the iconic person for the Hallyu phase was Bae Yong-Joon, Jang Keun-Suk is representative of the Neo-Hallyu phase. He has been in television drama programs since he was a child of five or six years old and is a multifaceted performer with talents as a movie actor and musician. He gained immense popularity in his role as a musician in a drama series called "Aren't You Handsome! (*Ikemen Desune* Korean title *Minam Isineyo*)" broadcast in South Korea in 2009, and gained his break when this was broadcast in Japan in 2010. In 2011, he debuted in Japan with his CD "Let Me Cry," which was ranked number one on the *Oricon* weekly single ranking and sold 21,000 units. In his following Japan Arena concert, 60,000 people gathered and in the succeeding concert at the Tokyo Dome, 45,000 people gathered (Hayashi 2012).

Japanese magazines provided Jang Keun-Suk with a manufactured fictional image that suited Japanese young women's preferences: a character who was tall and slender, kind, lovable, with beautiful skin and a charming smile. Many large photos emphasizing this image have been published (Sakai 2011). Japanese media refers to him as "Keun *Sama* [Sir Keun]" out of respect, but the magazines geared toward the younger generations refer to him as "Keun *Chan*" (an endearing term) to emphasize their affection towards him. As the alias of "Keun *Sama*" is high status and emphasizes social distance, for the younger generation, "Keun *Chan*" promotes familiarity. He was able to gain a lot of popularity using this "Keun *Chan*" image through Japanese television commercials and company advertisements.

Why are such images produced? It is strongly related to the characteristic "database consumption" of the Japanese postmodern society (Azuma 2001). Database consumption refers to the way that new characters for other productions are constructed by combining elements from a database that gathers elements of popular characters that had been attractive in the Japanese comics, animation, and games. Such attractive elements from comics and anime were added into the image of his character.

On July 7, 2012, a concert was held at Korea University in Seoul, South Korea as a start to Jang Keun-Suk's twentieth-year celebratory Asian Concert Tour. The stadium filled with fans who gathered not only from South Korea, but also from Japan, China, Singapore, Malaysia, and Thailand. I was present at the concert stadium for fieldwork, and was surprised to see that people from all over Asia came to Seoul to attend Jang Keun-Suk's concert. The images of

Decorations placed outside the K-pop concert stadium by Asian fan clubs. (Photo by Whang Soon-Hee)

Jang Keun-Suk each of them had were different from that of the casual entertainment level of Japan. In many countries all over Asia, fan clubs have been
established in their home regions. Each fan club decorated the outside of the
concert stadium with large flower decorations including their preferred image
of Jang Keun-Suk and messages directed to him written in their own languages, as seen in the following figure.

One Korean fan club emphasized his dependable, dutiful, and manly image by writing "the dutiful man" as their message to Jang Keun-Suk. This
is based on the extreme popularity of "Beethoven Virus—*Ai to Jyounetsu no
Symphony* (A Symphony of Love and Passion)," which even became a social
phenomenon that caused a craze in classical music. In this drama, he acted
the part of a young conductor with a keen sense of duty. Compared to this,
other fan clubs had chosen a photo of him with a sexy glance or one with him
with a princely attitude that recalled his character in "Aren't You Handsome."
One fan club from Thailand had even chosen a manga-style drawing of him
lecturing to a group of people looking happy and bright.

Members of the fan clubs enjoy taking photos of themselves in front of
their decorations or decorations of other groups and talk to other fans from
all over Asia, becoming friends instantaneously through their shared identity
as fans. Therefore, the concert stadium becomes a space for the members of
Asian fan clubs to make appeals for whichever image of Jang Keun-Suk they
find most attractive. Furthermore, these decorations are set up as a charity, in
which the members of the fan clubs donate rice so that it can be distributed to
unfortunate people. Underneath the decorations, there are bags of rice and the
weight is posted. Since many Asian countries consider rice as the main meal,
they happily participate in this campaign of sharing this "Rice of Love." Jang
Keun-Suk's office communicates through websites and fan clubs in notifying
the fans of its decisions about where to distribute this rice. In this way, fan
club members can personally feel that the rice that they donated was able to
help someone. In this way, the Asian fans can feel the gentle connection of
"us" as Asians in the space of the concert stadium.

"Convivial Consumption" and the
Individualization of Soft Power

I define "convivial consumption" as a form of cultural consumption where
fans, other consumers, producers, and mediators (performers such as actors
and idols) all participate in the generating process of the supply and demand

of cultural products and elicit a new consensus through the directed use of cultural influence. In the case of Bae Yong-Joon, "convivial consumption" was not intentionally deployed as a strategy, but rather it functioned as a result of his struggle in reestablishing his image. However, in the Neo-Hallyu phase, it is believed that Jang Keun-Suk intended to create "convivial consumption." The internet made it easier for fans and other consumers to have influence by participating in "convivial consumption." In addition, the producers and the actors also actively used the tool of "convivial consumption" in order to assure success in the production of an image that would minimize the risk of failure in a time of quickly changing fads.

Jang Keun-Suk, the icon of Neo-Hallyu stars, has conflicting images, comprising both a character with a beautiful, submissive, youth-like innocence and soothing smile and the opposite character, who is bass-voiced, manly, and dominating. Furthermore, in the love manual of the younger generation, he is given the sub-image of a "chihuahua type" dog. A "chihuahua type BOY" refers to "boys that have an endearing smile" (Shimizu and Ono 2012). In this way, by acting out characters with varying images, he is able to entertain his fans with the 'gap' between these characters. The Neo-Hallyu fans also do not demand a single established image from him either. In the above-mentioned concert in Seoul, he acted out characters with conflicting images through his talk, songs, and performance. His songs also ranged from romantic ballads to intense rock, ending with an explosive, energetic rap song. It becomes a pleasure for the participants to have their media-constructed images destroyed and reconstructed. Curious fans in Japan and South Korea start to look forward to the instability and discontinuity of his images, as he acts out diverse works. Fans become addicted to the appeal of the curiosity and interest in what new character he will produce and broadcast.

The Neo-Hallyu stars now need to consider not only the Japanese fans, but also the expectations and desires of fans and other consumers of different Asian countries, such as China, Malaysia, and Singapore, where the popularity of Neo-Hallyu stars is even greater than in Japan. Japanese fans have expectations for, or admire or criticize the Neo-Hallyu stars based on a Japan-centric perspective within the social and cultural structure of Japan. Therefore, considered in the framework of Asia, the expectations and demands to the Neo-Hallyu stars become diverse, and as a result a "twisted phenomenon" of incompatible demands is occurring on the consumer side of "convivial consumption." The fans respond by improving their ability to gain satisfaction from searching out their desired image themselves from the stars.

Furthermore, the production side, such as the South Korean agencies that the Neo-Hallyu stars belong to and various entertainment companies all over Asia that organize their international debuts or activities, experience cultural friction in the image creation and management strategies regarding distribution and profit of this cultural commodity. As a result, the production side of the "convivial consumption" also cannot avoid experiencing difficulties.

As discussed previously, in the time of the globalized era of the Neo-Hallyu, what kind of stance can the Neo-Hallyu stars take as actors faced with the difficulties of 'convivial consumption?' One strategy is for the Neo-Hallyu stars themselves to choose their own images and characters by understanding the expectations of both the consumers and producers of "convivial consumption." In the case of Jang Keun-Suk, he became a star at the center of attention not only in Japan and China, but throughout Asia, by virtue of his professionalism and personal appeal, reflected in his challenging spirit and unwillingness to resign himself to one character or image, his efforts when immersing himself in the creation of his roles, and his open and sociable manner towards the media. In this Neo-Hallyu phase, fans need to learn new methods of how to choose ways of enjoying not only the popular stars and works, but also the consumption of entertainment.

When Neo-Hallyu fans choose their entertainment, they have to depend not only on traditional media as was done in the original Hallyu period, but also on using new interactive media such as the internet. They imitate and transmit the dance and songs of the Neo-Hallyu stars. When they create a parody and make it available over the internet, people from all over the world can access and comment on it, and it becomes a popular topic. Popular culture of the global age transcends borders continuously and transforms itself through "convivial consumption" and "convivial creation" with participation from all over the world together with changes in social structure and active participation by individuals. In this way, soft power becomes dispersed to individuals and the power becomes individualized. As a result, individuals end up jointly owning the power.

The 2012 global craze of "Gangnam Style" by the K-pop star Psy is a representative example. People created new parodies based on their enjoyment of his work. This is a perfect example of how people all over the world were able to create and consume convivially a metaphor of K-pop. Both the original and parodies of "Gangnam Style" were accessed globally and rocketed to fame through the cycle of expanded reproduction and consumption. The circulation of K-pop dispersed its enticing power not only throughout inter-Asia, but also throughout the world via the space of the internet through individuals, all of whom owned soft power. As traditional media sources such as television and newspapers picked up the topic and as a result of the synergistic effect between the traditional and new media sources, people all over the world were able to enjoy "Gangnam Style" and its spin-offs. This became an opportunity for Asians living all over the world to become at least aware of not just a Korean diaspora, but rather an Asian diaspora.

In South Korea, as a sign of gratitude, Psy held a free concert for the younger generation who were delighted with his worldwide popularity. On October 4, 2012, an estimated 80,000–100,000 people gathered in the square in front of the Seoul City Hall (Jo and Song 2012). This is the same square where several hundred thousand people gathered patriotically to support the Japan-South Korea hosted FIFA World Cup soccer games in 2002. The result of that occasion was that South Korea placed fourth in the world. People shared a "collective memory" of this happy event (Halbwachs 1992). In this way, Psy's concert became associated with a culturally representative position and national pride in a similar way to the World Cup. The global circulation of K-pop, in this way, arouses past memories in the same space and causes happiness in South Korea. From this discussion it should be clear how soft power transcends political gain and as a "fun culture," becomes a "mediatory function" that connects people throughout inter-Asia.

Notes

This article is a revised version of Whang Soon-Hee 황 순희, "A Cultural Sociology of the New Korean Popular Culture Wave, Shin-Hanryu—the Structure and Practice of Shin-Hanryu Consumption in Japan," *Tsukuba Journal of Sociology* (2012): 1–20, translated from Japanese by Yukiko Tonoike, with revisions by Peter C. Perdue in consultation with the author.

1. "The true basis of the differences found in the area of consumption, and far beyond it, is the opposition between the tastes of luxury (or freedom) and the tastes of necessity" (Bourdieu, 1984, 177).

References

"A shocking hair style! 650 people glued to the 8:2 division of hair parting for 'Yong-sa-ma' [衝撃のヘアスタイル！ヨン様8：2分けに650人が釘付け]. 2005. http://www.cinematoday.jp/page/N00006987 (accessed December 12, 2014).

Azuma, Hiroki [東 浩紀]. 2001. *Turning into Beasts in the Post-Modern World: The Japanese Society from the Perspective of an Otaku Nerd* [動物化するポストモダンーオタクからみた日本社会]. Tokyo: Koudansha Gendai Shinsho [講談社現代新書].

Bourdieu, P. 1977. *Outline of a Theory of Practice*. Cambridge: Cambridge University Press.

———. 1984. *Distinction: A Social Critique of the Judgement of Taste*. Oxford: Routledge.

Bourdieu, P., and J. C. Passeron. 1977. *Reproduction in Education, Society, and Culture*. London: Sage.

Halbwachs, Maurice. 1992. *The Social Frameworks of Memory*. Translated and edited by L. A. Coser. Chicago: The University of Chicago Press.

Hashino, Hiroyuki [橋野宏之] (publisher). 2011. *K-pop: Going to Meet the K-pop Hallyū Stars! Seoul and Shin-Okubo Guide Book* [韓流スターに会いに行く！ソウル＆新大久保ガイド]. Tokyo: Nikkei BP [日経BP社].

Hayashi, Rumi [林るみ]. 2012. "A leap of the 'prince' Jang Keun-Suk ["プリンス"の飛躍 チャン・グンソク]". *Shukan (Weekly) Asahi [週刊朝日]*, January 27. Tokyo: Asahi Shimbun Publishing Inc. [朝日新聞出版], 5–8.

Higa, Nobuaki [比嘉信顕]. 2011. *The Hot Guys of Shin-Okubo Guide* [新大久保美男<イケメン>ガイド]. Tokyo: Million Publishing.

Horinouchi, Masakazu [堀ノ内雅一]. 2011. "Series: Humans [シリーズ人間]: Happiness of becoming a 'family' of Yong-sama and an 'eel' of Geun-chan: 10 years track of *Hallyu* entertainment [ヨン様の『家族』、グンちゃんの『ウナギ』となる幸せ—韓流エンタメ10年のキセキ—]". 2011. *Josei Jishin (Women Themselves) [女性自身]*, July 26. Tokyo: Koubunsha [光文社], 65.

Jo, Mung-gyu [조문규] and Chi-yong Song [송지영]. 2012. "How different are the methods for calculating crowds? [군중 숫자 계산법 어떻게 다를까?]. *New York Chungana Ilbo (Central Daily News)* [New York中央日報], October 12.

Nakajima, Kohtaro [中島耕太郎]. 2011. "Do you like the US? Changing perspectives" [米国がすきですか？変容するまなざし]. *Asahi Shimbum* [朝日新聞], October 29.

Nye, Joseph S., Jr. 2004. *Soft Power: The Means to Success In World Politics*. Cambridge, MA: Perseus Books.

Sakai, Mieko [酒井美絵子]. 2011. "Present ,past and future of Hallyu Boom"[『韓流ブーム』の現在と過去、そして未来]. *We Want to Meet Right Now! Hallyū Stars* [今会いたい！韓流スター] *AERAMook*. Tokyo: Asahi Publishing Company [朝日出版社], 68–71.

Shimizu, Yuko [清水祐子] and Ikuko Ono [小野郁子]. 2012. *The Hot Guys of K-STREET [K-STREET美男]*. Tokyo: Million Publishing House [ミリオン出版株式会社], 67–69.

Whang, Soon-Hee [黄 順姫]. 2011. "Tsukuba Jihyou (Tsukuba Current Events): The Development of the 'Neo- Hallyū' Fad by the Internet Generation [筑波時評—拡大する『新・韓流』ネット世代が流行形成—]" *University of Tsukuba Newspaper [筑波大学新聞]*, September 5, p.1.

———. 2012. "Neo-Hallyū, New Media, Young People [新韓流・ニューメディア・若者]" *Teaching Aid for Correspondence Course* [学習だより] 171: 12–16. Japan Center for Hairdressing and Beauty Education [日本理容美容教育センター]. Tokyo.

Contributors

Wen-Chin Chang is Associate Research Fellow in the Research Center for Humanities and Social Sciences, Academia Sinica. Her research interests include borderlands studies, migration, transnational trade, and ethnicity.

Mandana E. Limbert is Associate Professor of the Department of Anthropology, Queens College and the Graduate Center, City University of New York. Her research interests center on modernity, religion, gender, historical anthropology, the Middle East, and the Indian Ocean.

Liu Zhiwei is a Professor of the Department of History, Sun Yat-sen (Zhongshan) University. His areas of research include Chinese economic and social history of the Ming and Qing periods; he also studies popular religion and rural society.

Alan Mikhail is Professor of History at Yale University. He works on the early modern Muslim world, the Ottoman Empire, and Egypt. His research and teaching focus on the nature of early modern imperial rule, peasant histories, environmental resource management, and science and medicine. He is the author of *The Animal in Ottoman Egypt* and *Nature and Empire in Ottoman Egypt: An Environmental History* and is the editor of *Water on Sand: Environmental Histories of the Middle East and North Africa*.

Matthew W. Mosca is Assistant Professor of History at the College of William & Mary. His teaching and research interests center on Chinese and Inner Asian history, specifically the history of the Qing Empire (1644–1912), its foreign relations, and the intellectual history of Qing-era geography and historiography.

Park Bun-Soon is a Visiting Professor in the Department of Economics in Hongik University in Seoul. He retired from Samsung Economic Research Institute, which is a private think-tank. He teaches and researches on Southeast Asian economy and East Asian economic cooperation.

Peter C. Perdue is Professor of History at Yale University. His research interests lie in modern Chinese and Japanese social and economic history, history of frontiers, and world history.

Priya Satia is Associate Professor of Modern British History at Stanford University. She researches the statecraft and political economy of the British empire in the Middle East and South Asia, particularly the use and critiques of technologies of rule.

Willem van Schendel is Professor in the Department of Sociology and Anthropology and the International Institute of Social History, University of Amsterdam. He works in the fields of history, anthropology, and sociology of Asia.

Helen F. Siu is Professor of Anthropology at Yale University. Her teaching interests are political and historical anthropology, urban and global culture change. She has explored the nature of the socialist state and the refashioning of identities in South China. Lately, she examines China's rural-urban divide, cross-border dynamics in Hong Kong, and historical and contemporary Asian connections.

Eric Tagliacozzo is Professor of History at Cornell University. His research centers on the history of people, ideas, and material in motion in and around Southeast Asia, especially in the late colonial age.

Jing Tsu is Professor of Chinese & Comparative Literature and Chair of Council on East Asian Studies at Yale University. She specializes in modern Chinese literature and Sinophone studies from the nineteenth century to the present. Her writing and research focus on the historical, conceptual, and literary concerns of modern Chinese culture from an interdisciplinary and cross-regional perspective.

Whang Soon-Hee is Professor in the Department of Sociology, the Institute of Social Sciences, University of Tsukuba, Japan. Her research interests are the sociology of culture, education, sports, and popular media. She received the academic award of the Korean Association of Japanology for her book *Japanese Elite High School* (in Japanese) and the academic award of Korean Association of Japanese Education for *Sociology of Alumni* (in Japanese). She edited *Enthusiasm and Legacy of World Cup Soccer 2002: Korea-Japan* (in Japanese).

Charles Wheeler is an independent scholar with research interests in early modern Vietnam, maritime China, and the South China Sea. His publications address the role of the sea in Vietnamese history, Sino-Vietnamese merchant elites, littoral society, political ecology, piracy, and Buddhism in Chinese merchant diaspora.

Marcia Yonemoto is Associate Professor of History at the University of Colorado, Boulder. Her research interests are in the cultural history of Japan's early modern period (c. 1590–1868). She is the author of *Mapping Early Modern Japan: Space, Place, and Culture in the Tokugawa Period (1603–1868)*. Her scholarly articles have appeared in *Journal of Asian Studies, Japan Forum, Geographical Review, East Asian History, U.S.-Japan Women's Journal,* and other publications.

Acknowledgments

Asia Inside Out is a multi-year project put together by Eric Tagliacozzo, Helen F. Siu, and Peter C. Perdue. It has been supported by the Hong Kong Institute for the Humanities and Social Sciences (HKIHSS) of the University of Hong Kong, and the Inter-Asia Initiative of Yale University. The project began with the Yale Council on East Asian Studies and the Department of Anthropology hosting a brainstorming workshop in December 2009, where we sought intellectual synergy from colleagues in various disciplines.

This volume of essays, the second in our series that attempts to redefine Asia as a region, is the product of a workshop held in Qatar and Oman in December 2011. The Cornell University Medical Center in Doha kindly allowed us to use its facilities, and also provided much needed logistical support. We thank HKIHSS for generous funding, and for the remarkable administrative resources from its staff, particularly Emily Ip and Kwok-leung Yu. We must credit our meticulous "handler," Matthew Mosca, for herding the motley group through our field trip, although he could not prevent the Wahiba Sands in the Oman interior from destroying six of our cameras.

As before, we have enjoyed the intellectual companionship of a growing community of colleagues in sharpening the themes of the *Asia Inside Out* Project and in preparing the manuscript. Many share our enthusiasm in rethinking Asian connections and restructuring regional studies, and have offered critical comments. Among them are Deborah Davis, Eric Harms, William Kelly, Angela Leung, David Ludden, K. Sivaramakrishnan, and James Scott. Three of the authors in this volume—Alan Mikhail, Whang Soon-Hee, and Marcia Yonemoto—did not participate in the workshop and field trip, but have graciously produced chapters. Credit again goes to Isabelle Lewis for accommodating our ideas of mapping Asian connections a second time. We also thank Eric Chan, Yvonne Chan, Joan Cheng, Venus Lee, Gershom Tse, and Kwok Leung Yu of HKIHSS and Andrew Kinney of Harvard University Press for their editorial and technical attention. Yukiko Tonoike kindly helped with the translation of Whang Soon-Hee's essay, and Steven Moore generated the index in thoughtful ways. The publication of this volume has benefitted from substantial subsidies from HKIHSS. We are most grateful to our editor at Harvard University Press, Kathleen McDermott, for maintaining faith in the project. As always, she makes us sharpen our thoughts, tightens the organization of the chapters, and skillfully navigates us through the publishing process. We are very appreciative of her editorial insights and her tireless efforts to strike a balance between practical constraints in publication and our unpredictable bouts of imagination.

Index